Strategic Level

Paper F3

Financial Strategy

EXAM PRACTICE KIT

CIMA

PUBLISHING

KAPLAN

PUBLISHING

Published by: Kaplan Publishing UK

Unit 2 The Business Centre, Molly Millar's Lane, Wokingham, Berkshire RG41 2QZ

Acknowledgements

We are grateful to the Chartered Institute of Management Accountants for permission to reproduce past examination questions. The answers to CIMA Exams have been prepared by Kaplan Publishing, except in the case of the CIMA November 2010 and subsequent CIMA Exam answers where the official CIMA answers have been reproduced.

Notice

British Library Cataloguing in Publication Data

A catalogue record for this book is available from the British Library

ISBN: 978 0 85732 998 1

Printed and bound in Great Britain

CONTENTS

Key features in this edition

In addition to providing a wide ranging bank of real past exam questions, we have also included in this edition:

- Paper specific information and advice on exam technique.

- Guidance to make your revision for this particular subject as effective as possible.

- Enhanced tutorial answers packed with specific key answer tips, technical tutorial notes and exam technique tips from our experienced tutors.

You will find a wealth of other resources to help you with your studies on the following sites:

www.EN-gage.co.uk

www.cimaglobal.com

INDEX TO QUESTIONS AND ANSWERS

INTRODUCTION

For all strategic level papers (E3, F3 and P3), CIMA will release a "pre-seen" scenario approximately 6 weeks before the real exam. As part of section A of the exam you will then get further "un-seen" information relating to this case and question requirements. These will make up the whole of section A in the exam, worth 50%.

Section B questions will continue to be stand alone and hence the bulk of this exam practice kit consists of such questions. The majority of these are past CIMA exam questions. If changed in any way from the original version, this is indicated in the end column of the index below with the mark *(A)*.

KEY TO THE INDEX

PAPER ENHANCEMENTS

We have added the following enhancements to the answers in this exam practice kit:

Key answer tips

All answers include key answer tips, often taken from the examiner's official "Post Exam Guides", to help your understanding of each question.

Tutorial note

All answers include more tutorial notes, often taken from the examiner's official "Post Exam Guides", to explain some of the technical points in more detail.

Top tutor tips

For selected questions, we "walk through the answer" giving guidance on how to approach the questions with helpful 'tips from a top tutor', together with technical tutor notes.

These answers are indicated with the "footsteps" icon in the index.

SECTION A-TYPE QUESTIONS

SECTION B-TYPE QUESTIONS

INVESTMENT DECISIONS AND PROJECT CONTROL I – ACQUISITIONS AND MERGERS

ANALYSIS OF PAST EXAM PAPERS

The table below summarises the key topics that have been tested in the recent exam papers. The list of topics matches the chapter titles in the Study Text.

Note that the references (A or B) are to the section of the exam in which the topic was tested. Section A is the compulsory section whereas Section B contains a choice of questions.

TOPIC	May 11	Sept 11	Nov 11	Mar 12	May 12	Sept 12	Nov 12	Mar 13	May 13	Sept 13
Introduction to financial strategy	B	A	A, B	B	A	B	B	A, B	A	B
Performance measurement		A			A		B	B	A	B
Long term finance	B	A	B			B	A, B	A	B	B
Short term finance					B	A				B
Cost of capital	B			A, B				B		
Capital structure					B		B	B	B	
The role of treasury			B	B						
Investment appraisal – basic	A	B		B	A, B	B	B		A	B
Investment appraisal – further	A	B		B			B	B		A
International investment appraisal			B			A				
Business valuation	B	B	A	A			A	B	B	A, B
Mergers and acquisitions		B	A	A	A					A
Implementation and control procedures		B	B		B					

ix

EXAM TECHNIQUE

- Use the allocated **20 minutes reading and planning time** at the beginning of the exam to:
    - read the questions and examination requirements carefully, and
    - begin planning your answers.
- **Divide the time** you spend on questions in proportion to the marks on offer:
    - there are 1.8 minutes available per mark in the examination
    - within that, try to allow time at the end of each question to review your answer and address any obvious issues

    Whatever happens, always keep your eye on the clock and **do not over run on any part of any question!**

- Spend the last **five minutes** of the examination:
    - reading through your answers, and
    - **making any additions or corrections**.
- If you **get completely stuck** with a question:
    - leave space in your answer book, and
    - **return to it later.**
- Stick to the question and **tailor your answer** to what you are asked.
    - pay particular attention to the verbs in the question.
- If you do not understand what a question is asking, **state your assumptions**.

    Even if you do not answer in precisely the way the examiner hoped, you should be given some credit, if your assumptions are reasonable.

- You should do everything you can to make things easy for the marker.

    The marker will find it easier to identify the points you have made if your **answers are legible**.

- **Written questions**:

    Your answer should have:
    - a clear structure
    - a brief introduction, a main section and a conclusion.

    Be concise. It is better to write a little about a lot of different points than a great deal about one or two points.

- **Computations**:

    It is essential to include all your workings in your answers. Many computational questions require the use of a standard format e.g. net present value, adjusted present value.

    Be sure you know these formats thoroughly before the exam and use the layouts that you see in the answers given in this book and in model answers.

- **Reports, memos and other documents**:

    Some questions ask you to present your answer in the form of a report, a memo, a letter or other document.

    Make sure that you use the correct format – there could be easy marks to gain here.

PAPER SPECIFIC INFORMATION

THE EXAM

FORMAT OF THE EXAM

Number of marks

Section A:	A maximum of four compulsory questions, all relating to a pre-seen case study and some further new un-seen material provided within the examination. Note that the pre-seen material will be common to all three strategic level papers at each sitting.	50
Section B:	Two questions from a choice of three, each worth twenty five marks. Short scenarios will be given, to which some or all questions relate.	50
		——
		100
		——

Total time allowed: 3 hours plus 20 minutes reading time.

PASS MARK

The pass mark for all CIMA Qualification examination papers is 50%.

READING TIME

Remember that all three hour CIMA examinations have an additional 20 minutes reading time.

CIMA GUIDANCE

CIMA guidance on the use of this time is as follows:

> This additional time is allowed at the beginning of the examination to allow candidates to read the questions and to begin planning their answers before they start to write in their answer books.
>
> This time should be used to ensure that all the information and, in particular, the exam requirements are properly read and understood.
>
> During this time, candidates may only annotate their question paper. They may not write anything in their answer booklets until told to do so by the invigilator.

FURTHER GUIDANCE

Since there is a choice of questions in Section B, you must decide which questions to attempt, and in which order.

During the 20 minutes of reading time you should be able to review the questions in Section B and decide which ones are most appealing. All students have different strengths and preferred topics, so it is impossible to give general advice on which questions should be chosen. However, it is worth noting that numerical questions can often be more time consuming than written questions, so you are more likely to over run on numerical questions. Try to choose questions which give a balance between numerical and written elements.

In relation to paper F3, we recommend that you take the following approach with your reading time:

- **Skim through Section B**, assessing the level of difficulty of each question. Try to decide which question looks least appealing and ignore it.

- **Now focus on the other Section B questions** (which, by a process of elimination, you have now decided to attempt). Work out how much time you should spend on each part of the requirements (using the measure of 1.8 minutes per mark). Decide which techniques you will need to attack each of the questions.

- **Turn to Section A.** Skim through the requirement and decide what topics are being tested (e.g. business valuation, NPV). As you skim through the unseen case material, note any key issues from your pre-seen analysis which may be useful to link in to the given information.

- **Decide the order** in which you think you will attempt the questions:

  This is a personal choice and you have time on the revision phase to try out different approaches, for example, if you sit mock exams.

  A common approach is to tackle the question you think is the easiest and you are most comfortable with first.

  Others may prefer to tackle the longest question first, or conversely leave them to the last.

  It is usual however that students tackle their least favourite topic and/or the most difficult question in their opinion last. It is sensible to try to attack the preferred questions before attempting the difficult looking ones.

  Whatever you approach, you must make sure that you leave enough time to attempt all questions fully and be very strict with yourself in timing each question.

- **For each question** in turn, read the requirements and then the detail of the question carefully.

  Always read the requirement first as this enables you to **focus on the detail of the question with the specific task in mind.** Bear in mind the CIMA verb hierarchy. In paper F3, you are likely to have to face level 3, 4, and 5 verbs, so your answer will have to be quite detailed.

  For computational questions:

  Highlight key numbers/information and key words in the question, scribble notes to yourself on the question paper to remember key points in your answer.

For written questions:

Take notice of the format required (e.g. letter, memo, notes) and identify the recipient of the answer. You need to do this to judge the level of financial sophistication required in your answer and whether the use of a formal reply or informal bullet points would be satisfactory.

Plan your beginning, middle and end and the key areas to be addressed and your use of titles and sub-titles to enhance your answer.

For all questions:

Spot the easy marks to be gained in a question and parts which can be performed independently of the rest of the question.

Make sure that you do these parts first when you tackle the question.

Don't go overboard in terms of planning time on any one question – you need a good measure of the whole paper and a plan for all of the questions at the end of the 20 minutes.

By covering all questions you can often help yourself as you may find that facts in one question may remind you of things you should put into your answer relating to a different question.

- With your plan of attack in mind, **start answering your chosen question** with your plan to hand, as soon as you are allowed to start.

DETAILED SYLLABUS

The detailed syllabus and study guide written by CIMA can be found at:

www.cimaglobal.com

POST EXAM GUIDES (PEGs)

After each sitting, the examiners and lead markers produce a report for each paper outlining what they were looking for in the exam, how it related to the syllabus and highlights in detail what students did well and the areas that caused problems. This feedback is extremely useful to help you to focus on producing what the examiners want and thus increase your chances of passing the exams. The PEGs for F3 can be found here:

http://www.cimaglobal.com/Students/Exam-preparation/Strategic-level/F3-financial-strategy/Post-exam-guides/

APPROACH TO REVISION

QUESTION PRACTICE IS THE KEY TO SUCCESS

Success in professional examinations relies upon you acquiring a firm grasp of the required knowledge at the tuition phase. In order to be able to do the questions, knowledge is essential.

However, the difference between success and failure often hinges on your exam technique on the day and making the most of the revision phase of your studies.

The **study text** is the starting point, designed to provide the underpinning knowledge to tackle all questions. However, in the revision phase, pouring over text books is not the answer.

Revision cards are designed to help you quickly revise a topic area; however you then need to practise questions. There is a need to progress to full exam standard questions as soon as possible, and to tie your exam technique and technical knowledge together.

The importance of question practice cannot be over-emphasised.

The recommended approach below is designed by expert tutors in the field, in conjunction with their knowledge of the examiner and their recent real exams.

The approach taken for the lower level papers is to revise by topic area. However, with the strategic level papers, a multi topic approach is required to answer the scenario based questions.

You need to practise as many questions as possible in the time you have left.

OUR AIM

Our aim is to get you to the stage where you can attempt exam standard questions confidently, to time, in a closed book environment, with no supplementary help (i.e. to simulate the real examination experience).

Practising your exam technique on real past examination questions, in timed conditions, is also vitally important for you to assess your progress and identify areas of weakness that may need more attention in the final run up to the examination.

In order to achieve this we recognise that initially you may feel the need to practise some questions with open book help and exceed the required time.

The approach below shows you which questions you should use to build up to coping with exam standard question practice, and references to the sources of information available should you need to revisit a topic area in more detail.

Remember that in the real examination, all you have to do is:

- attempt all questions required by the exam
- only spend the allotted time on each question, and
- get them at least 50% right!

Try to practise this approach on every question you attempt from now to the real exam.

THE F3 REVISION PLAN

Stage 1: Assess areas of strengths and weaknesses

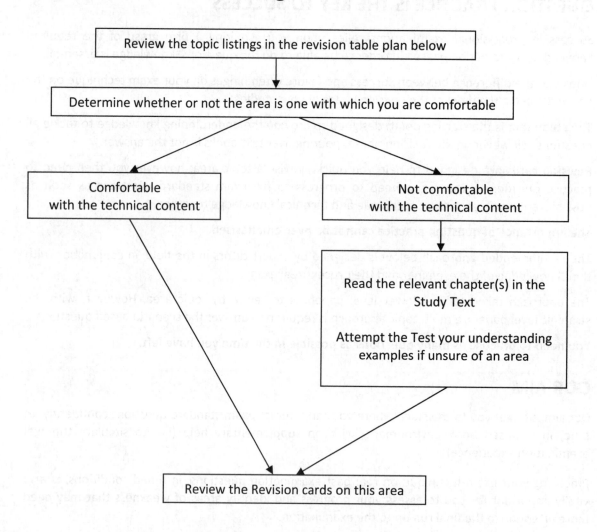

Stage 2: Practice questions

Follow the order of revision of topics as recommended in the revision table plan below and attempt the questions in the order suggested.

Try to avoid referring to text books and notes and the model answer until you have completed your attempt.

Try to answer the question in the allotted time.

Review your attempt with the model answer and assess how much of the answer you achieved in the allocated exam time.

Fill in the self-assessment box below and decide on your best course of action.

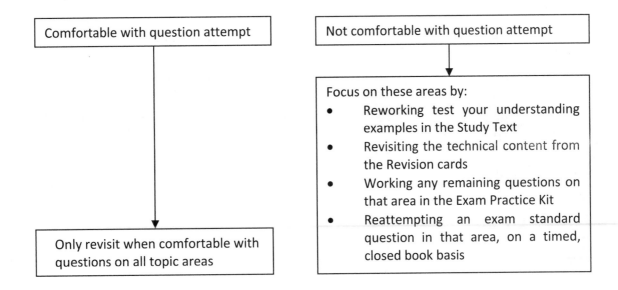

Note that:

 The "footsteps questions" give guidance on exam technique and how you should have approached the question.

Stage 3: Final pre-exam revision

We recommend that you **attempt at least one three hour mock examination** containing a set of previously unseen exam standard questions.

It is important that you get a feel for the breadth of coverage of a real exam without advanced knowledge of the topic areas covered – just as you will expect to see on the real exam day.

Ideally a mock examination offered by your tuition provider should be sat in timed, closed book, real exam conditions.

THE DETAILED REVISION PLAN

Module 1: Introduction to Financial Strategy and Investment Appraisal

Topic	Study Text Chapter	Questions to attempt	Tutor guidance	Date attempted	Self assessment
Verbs	1	–	Before you start, remind yourself of the meaning of the key verbs you are likely to encounter. This will ensure that you always provide the level of detail that the examiner is looking for.		
Objectives	2	9	The difference between the objectives of private and public sector entities is a key exam topic.		
Investment, financing and dividend policies	2	13	These policies and the links between them underpin the whole syllabus, so learn the points well.		
Basic investment appraisal	9	62	Payback, ARR, NPV and IRR should be familiar from previous studies. NPV in particular is a key topic at this level too. MIRR addresses the weaknesses of the standard IRR – make sure you learn the strengths of MIRR.		
Other aspects of investment appraisal	10, 14	69	Capital rationing, sensitivity and equivalent annual cost are tested infrequently, so go through them quickly. Don't neglect the discursive topics – real options and post completion audits are often tested.		
International investment appraisal	11	58	When you have mastered NPV, move on to Chapter 11 on foreign NPV.		
Module 1 Revision Test	–	*17* *55* *63* *65*	*Attempt these questions to cover a variety of topics from the whole of Module 1.*		

Module 2: The Cost of Capital and Gearing

Topic	Study Text Chapter	Questions to attempt	Tutor guidance	Date attempted	Self assessment
WACC (DVM)	6	–	The most common method of computing the WACC is by using the Dividend Valuation Model (DVM). As you go through the Study Text, notice that many of the formula are given on the exam formula sheet. Make sure you identify the ones which need to be remembered. The section at the end of the chapter on "when can WACC be used as a discount rate?" is an important discursive area.		
WACC (CAPM and M+M)	6, 7	22 (parts a and b), 33, 49	In Chapter 7, you'll see many important discursive points on gearing, but also notice that M+M produced formulae which can be used to derive cost of capital. In Chapter 6, you'll see the basic CAPM model.		
Risk adjusted WACC	7	11	This is a really important topic. You must learn the step by step approach explained in the chapter.		
Module 2 Revision Test	–	*39* *60*	*Attempt these questions to cover a variety of topics from the whole of Modules 1 and 2.*		

Module 3: Financing Options and Business Valuation

Topic	Study Text Chapter	Questions to attempt	Tutor guidance	Date attempted	Self assessment
Financing options and the role of treasury	4, 8	Specimen paper Q2 and Q4	These chapters contains several key topics. Break the chapters down into manageable chunks. The calculations on rights issues and lease v buy are important, but so are the long lists of different types of financing options. Much of the chapters are about learning rather than application of methods, so if you work hard to learn the points, you'll be rewarded with some easy marks in the exam.		
Business Valuation	12	42 45 47	A typical question on business valuation will ask you to calculate several valuation methods and comment on the features of each method. It is therefore critical that you understand both the calculations and the discursive elements within this chapter.		
Mergers and acquisitions	13	52	Alongside valuation calculations, you may well be tested on strategic issues covered in Chapter 13.		
Module 3 Revision Test	–	*38 50*	*Attempt these questions to cover a variety of topics from the whole of Modules 1, 2 and 3.*		

Module 4: Working Capital Management, Ratio Analysis and Section A question practice

Topic	Study Text Chapter	Questions to attempt	Tutor guidance	Date attempted	Self assessment
Working capital management (short term finance)	5	23 34 40	It is important to learn the main working capital ratios, and how they combine in the working capital cycle. Past exam questions have often featured discussions on aggressive v relaxed approaches to working capital management.		
Performance measurement (ratio analysis)	3	12	Much of this chapter is revision of prior knowledge. However, whenever it is tested at this level the examiner is critical of students' performance. Make sure you learn the formulae carefully, and understand the implication of each ratio increasing or decreasing.		
Section A practice	–	3 5	You will receive the pre-seen case material in advance of the exam date. Then, on the exam date you will receive the unseen material and the requirement. To practise the skills which you will need to develop for this, look at the pre-seen material for one of the Exam practice kit section A type questions. Make notes and analyse any accounting information to familiarise yourself with the scenario. Then look at the unseen material and the requirement and try to answer the question in timed conditions (one and a half hours, to simulate the real exam).		
Module 4 Revision Test	**–**	**4 6**	**Attempt these questions to cover a variety of topics from the whole of Modules 1, 2, 3 and 4.**		

Note that not all of the questions are referred to in the programme above. The remaining questions are available in the Kit for extra practice for those who require more questions on some areas.

Formulae and tables

Present value of 1.00 unit of currency i.e. $(1 + r)^{-n}$ where r = interest rate, n = number of periods until payment or receipt.

Periods (n)	Interest rates (r)									
	1%	2%	3%	4%	5%	6%	7%	8%	9%	10%
1	.990	.980	.971	.962	.952	.943	.935	.926	.917	.909
2	.980	.961	.943	.925	.907	.890	.873	.857	.842	.826
3	.971	.942	.915	.889	.864	.840	.816	.794	.772	.751
4	.961	.924	.888	.855	.823	.792	.763	.735	.708	.683
5	.951	.906	.863	.822	.784	.747	.713	.681	.650	.621
6	.942	.888	.837	.790	.746	.705	.666	.630	.596	.564
7	.933	.871	.813	.760	.711	.665	.623	.583	.547	.513
8	.923	.853	.789	.731	.677	.627	.582	.540	.502	.467
9	.914	.837	.766	.703	.645	.592	.544	.500	.460	.424
10	.905	.820	.744	.676	.614	.558	.508	.463	.422	.386
11	.896	.804	.722	.650	.585	.527	.475	.429	.388	.350
12	.887	.788	.701	.625	.557	.497	.444	.397	.356	.319
13	.879	.773	.681	.601	.530	.469	.415	.368	.326	.290
14	.870	.758	.661	.577	.505	.442	.388	.340	.299	.263
15	.861	.743	.642	.555	.481	.417	.362	.315	.275	.239
16	.853	.728	.623	.534	.458	.394	.339	.292	.252	.218
17	.844	.714	.605	.513	.436	.371	.317	.270	.231	.198
18	.836	.700	.587	.494	.416	.350	.296	.250	.212	.180
19	.828	.686	.570	.475	.396	.331	.277	.232	.194	.164
20	.820	.673	.554	.456	.377	.312	.258	.215	.178	.149

Periods (n)	Interest rates (r)									
	11%	12%	13%	14%	15%	16%	17%	18%	19%	20%
1	.901	.893	.885	.877	.870	.862	.855	.847	.840	.833
2	.812	.797	.783	.769	.756	.743	.731	.718	.706	.694
3	.731	.712	.693	.675	.658	.641	.624	.609	.593	.579
4	.659	.636	.613	.592	.572	.552	.534	.516	.499	.482
5	.593	.567	.543	.519	.497	.476	.456	.437	.419	.402
6	.535	.507	.480	.456	.432	.410	.390	.370	.352	.335
7	.482	.452	.425	.400	.376	.354	.333	.314	.296	.279
8	.434	.404	.376	.351	.327	.305	.285	.266	.249	.233
9	.391	.361	.333	.308	.284	.263	.243	.225	.209	.194
10	.352	.322	.295	.270	.247	.227	.208	.191	.176	.162
11	.317	.287	.261	.237	.215	.195	.178	.162	.148	.135
12	.286	.257	.231	.208	.187	.168	.152	.137	.124	.112
13	.258	.229	.204	.182	.163	.145	.130	.116	.104	.093
14	.232	.205	.181	.160	.141	.125	.111	.099	.088	.078
15	.209	.183	.160	.140	.123	.108	.095	.084	.074	.065
16	.188	.163	.141	.123	.107	.093	.081	.071	.062	.054
17	.170	.146	.125	.108	.093	.080	.069	.060	.052	.045
18	.153	.130	.111	.095	.081	.069	.059	.051	.044	.038
19	.138	.116	.098	.083	.070	.060	.051	.043	.037	.031
20	.124	.104	.087	.073	.061	.051	.043	.037	.031	.026

Cumulative present value of 1.00 unit of currency

This table shows the present value of 1.00 unit of currency per annum, receivable or payable at

the end of each year for n years $\dfrac{1-(1+r)^{-n}}{r}$.

Periods (n)	Interest rates (r)									
	1%	2%	3%	4%	5%	6%	7%	8%	9%	10%
1	0.990	0.980	0.971	0.962	0.952	0.943	0.935	0.926	0.917	0.909
2	1.970	1.942	1.913	1.886	1.859	1.833	1.808	1.783	1.759	1.736
3	2.941	2.884	2.829	2.775	2.723	2.673	2.624	2.577	2.531	2.487
4	3.902	3.808	3.717	3.630	3.546	3.465	3.387	3.312	3.240	3.170
5	4.853	4.713	4.580	4.452	4.329	4.212	4.100	3.993	3.890	3.791
6	5.795	5.601	5.417	5.242	5.076	4.917	4.767	4.623	4.486	4.355
7	6.728	6.472	6.230	6.002	5.786	5.582	5.389	5.206	5.033	4.868
8	7.652	7.325	7.020	6.733	6.463	6.210	5.971	5.747	5.535	5.335
9	8.566	8.162	7.786	7.435	7.108	6.802	6.515	6.247	5.995	5.759
10	9.471	8.983	8.530	8.111	7.722	7.360	7.024	6.710	6.418	6.145
11	10.368	9.787	9.253	8.760	8.306	7.887	7.499	7.139	6.805	6.495
12	11.255	10.575	9.954	9.385	8.863	8.384	7.943	7.536	7.161	6.814
13	12.134	11.348	10.635	9.986	9.394	8.853	8.358	7.904	7.487	7.103
14	13.004	12.106	11.296	10.563	9.899	9.295	8.745	8.244	7.786	7.367
15	13.865	12.849	11.938	11.118	10.380	9.712	9.108	8.559	8.061	7.606
16	14.718	13.578	12.561	11.652	10.838	10.106	9.447	8.851	8.313	7.824
17	15.562	14.292	13.166	12.166	11.274	10.477	9.763	9.122	8.544	8.022
18	16.398	14.992	13.754	12.659	11.690	10.828	10.059	9.372	8.756	8.201
19	17.226	15.679	14.324	13.134	12.085	11.158	10.336	9.604	8.950	8.365
20	18.046	16.351	14.878	13.590	12.462	11.470	10.594	9.818	9.129	8.514

Periods (n)	Interest rates (r)									
	11%	12%	13%	14%	15%	16%	17%	18%	19%	20%
1	0.901	0.893	0.885	0.877	0.870	0.862	0.855	0.847	0.840	0.833
2	1.713	1.690	1.668	1.647	1.626	1.605	1.585	1.566	1.547	1.528
3	2.444	2.402	2.361	2.322	2.283	2.246	2.210	2.174	2.140	2.106
4	3.102	3.037	2.974	2.914	2.855	2.798	2.743	2.690	2.639	2.589
5	3.696	3.605	3.517	3.433	3.352	3.274	3.199	3.127	3.058	2.991
6	4.231	4.111	3.998	3.889	3.784	3.685	3.589	3.498	3.410	3.326
7	4.712	4.564	4.423	4.288	4.160	4.039	3.922	3.812	3.706	3.605
8	5.146	4.968	4.799	4.639	4.487	4.344	4.207	4.078	3.954	3.837
9	5.537	5.328	5.132	4.946	4.772	4.607	4.451	4.303	4.163	4.031
10	5.889	5.650	5.426	5.216	5.019	4.833	4.659	4.494	4.339	4.192
11	6.207	5.938	5.687	5.453	5.234	5.029	4.836	4.656	4.486	4.327
12	6.492	6.194	5.918	5.660	5.421	5.197	4.968	4.793	4.611	4.439
13	6.750	6.424	6.122	5.842	5.583	5.342	5.118	4.910	4.715	4.533
14	6.982	6.628	6.302	6.002	5.724	5.468	5.229	5.008	4.802	4.611
15	7.191	6.811	6.462	6.142	5.847	5.575	5.324	5.092	4.876	4.675
16	7.379	6.974	6.604	6.265	5.954	5.668	5.405	5.162	4.938	4.730
17	7.549	7.120	6.729	6.373	6.047	5.749	5.475	5.222	4.990	4.775
18	7.702	7.250	6.840	6.467	6.128	5.818	5.534	5.273	5.033	4.812
19	7.839	7.366	6.938	6.550	6.198	5.877	5.584	5.316	5.070	4.843
20	7.963	7.469	7.025	6.623	6.259	5.929	5.628	5.353	5.101	4.870

VALUATION MODELS

(i)   Irredeemable preference shares, paying a constant annual dividend, d, in perpetuity, where P_0 is the ex-div value:

$$P_0 = \frac{d}{k_{pref}}$$

(ii) Ordinary (equity) shares, paying a constant annual dividend, d, in perpetuity, where P_0 is the ex-div value:

$$P_0 = \frac{d}{k_e}$$

(iii) Ordinary (equity) shares, paying an annual dividend, d, growing in perpetuity at a constant rate, g, where P_0 is the ex-div value:

$$P_0 = \frac{d_1}{k_e - g} \quad \text{or} \quad P_0 = \frac{d_0[1+g]}{k_e - g}$$

(iv) Irredeemable bonds, paying annual after tax interest, i(1 – t), in perpetuity, where P_0 is the ex-interest value:

$$P_0 = \frac{i[1-t]}{k_{dnet}}$$

or, without tax:

$$P_0 = \frac{i}{k_d}$$

(v)   Total value of the geared firm, Vg (based on MM):

$$V_g = V_u + TB$$

(vi) Future value S, of a sum X, invested for n periods, compounded at r% interest:

$$S = X[1+r]^n$$

(vii) Present value of 1.00 unit of currency payable or receivable in n years, discounted at r% per annum:

$$PV = \frac{1}{[1+r]^n}$$

(viii)   Present value of an annuity of 1.00 unit of currency per annum, receivable or payable for n years, commencing in one year, discounted at r% per annum:

$$PV = \frac{1}{r}\left(1 - \frac{1}{[1+r]^n}\right)$$

(ix)   Present value of 1.00 unit of currency per annum, payable or receivable in perpetuity, commencing in one year, discounted at r% per annum:

$$PV = \frac{1}{r}$$

(x)   Present value of 1.00 unit of currency per annum, receivable or payable, commencing in one year, growing in perpetuity at a constant rate of g% per annum, discounted at r% per annum:

$$PV = \frac{1}{r-g}$$

COST OF CAPITAL

(i)   Cost of irredeemable preference shares, paying an annual dividend d in perpetuity, and having a current ex-div price P_0:

$$k_{pref} = \frac{d}{P_0}$$

(ii)   Cost of irredeemable bonds, paying annual net interest i(1 − t), and having a current ex-interest price P_0:

$$k_{dnet} = \frac{i[1-t]}{P_0}$$

(iii)   Cost of ordinary (equity) share capital, paying an annual dividend d in perpetuity, and having a current ex-div price P0:

$$k_e = \frac{d}{P_0}$$

(iv)   Cost of ordinary (equity) shares, having a current ex-div price, P_0, having just paid a dividend, d_0, with the dividend growing in perpetuity by a constant g% per annum:

$$k_e = \frac{d_1}{P_0} + g \quad \text{or} \quad k_e = \frac{d_0[1+g]}{P_0} + g$$

(v)   Cost of ordinary (equity) shares, using the CAPM:

$$k_e = R_f + [R_m - R_f]\beta$$

(vi)   Cost of ordinary (equity) share capital in a geared entity:

$$k_{eg}=k_{eu}+[k_{eu}-k_d]\frac{V_D[1-t]}{V_E}$$

(vii)   Weighted average cost of capital, k_0 or WACC:

$$WACC=k_e\left(\frac{V_E}{V_E+V_D}\right)+k_d(1-t)\left(\frac{V_D}{V_E+V_D}\right)$$

(viii) Adjusted cost of capital (MM formula):

$$k_{adj}=k_{eu}[1-tL]\quad\text{or}\quad r^*=r[1-T^*L]$$

(ix)   Ungear ß:

$$\beta_u=\beta_g\left(\frac{V_E}{V_E+V_D(1-t)}\right)+\beta_d\left(\frac{V_D(1-t)}{V_E+V_D(1-t)}\right)$$

(x)   Regear ß:

$$\beta_g=\beta_u+[\beta_u-\beta_d]\frac{V_D(1-t)}{V_E}$$

(xi)   Adjusted discount rate to use in international capital budgeting (International Fisher Effect):

$$\frac{1+\text{annual discount rate B\$}}{1+\text{annual discount rate A\$}}=\frac{\text{Future Spot Rate A\$/B\$ in 12 months' time}}{\text{Spot rate A\$/B\$}}$$

where A\$/B\$ is the number of B\$ to each A\$

OTHER FORMULAE

(i)   Expectations theory:

$$\text{Future spot rate A\$/B\$}=\text{Spot rate A\$/B\$}\times\frac{1+\text{nominal country B interest rate}}{1+\text{nominal country A interest rate}}$$

where   A\$/B\$ is the number of B\$ to each A\$, and

            A\$ is the currency of country A and B\$ is the currency of country B

(ii)   Purchasing Power Parity (Law of one price):

$$\text{Future spot rate A\$/B\$}=\text{Spot rate A\$/B\$}\times\frac{1+\text{country B inflation rate}}{1+\text{country A inflation rate}}$$

(iii)   Link between nominal (money) and real interest rates:

$$[1+\text{nominal(money)rate}]=[1+\text{real interest rate}][1+\text{inflation rate}]$$

(iv)   Equivalent annual cost:

$$\text{Equivalent annual cost} = \frac{\text{PV of costs over n years}}{\text{n year annuity factor}}$$

(v)   Theoretical ex-rights price:

$$\text{TERP}=\frac{1}{N+1}[(N\times \text{cum rights price})+\text{issue price}]$$

(vi)   Value of a right:

$$\frac{\text{Theoretical ex rights price} - \text{Issue price}}{N}$$

where N = number of rights required to buy one share.

Section 1

SECTION A-TYPE QUESTIONS

M PLC (NOV 11 AND MAR 12 EXAMS) – RELATES TO QUESTIONS 1 AND 2

PRE-SEEN CASE MATERIAL

Introduction

M plc is a long established publisher of newspapers and provider of web media. It is based in London and has had a full listing on the London Stock Exchange since 1983. The company has three operating divisions which are managed from the United Kingdom (UK). These are the Newspapers Division, the Web Division and the Advertising Division.

Newspapers Division

The Newspapers Division publishes three daily newspapers and one Sunday newspaper in the UK. The Division has three offices and two printing sites. Between them the three offices edit the three daily newspapers and the Sunday newspaper. The Newspaper Division has two subsidiary publishing companies, FR and N. FR is based in France within the Eurozone and N in an Eastern European country which is outside the Eurozone. Printing for all the Division's publications, except those produced by FR and N, is undertaken at the two printing sites. FR and N have their own printing sites.

Web Division

The Web Division maintains and develops 200 websites which it owns. Some of these websites are much more popular in terms of the number of "hits" they receive than others. Web material is an increasing part of M plc's business. In the last ten years, the Web Division has developed an online version of all the newspapers produced by the Newspapers Division.

Advertising Division

The sale of advertising space is undertaken for the whole of M plc by the Advertising Division. Therefore, advertisements which appear in the print media and on the web pages produced by the Newspapers Division (including that produced by FR and N) and the Web Division respectively are all handled by the Advertising Division.

Group Headquarters

In addition to the three operating divisions, M plc also has a head office, based in the UK, which is the group's corporate headquarters where the Board of Directors is located. The main role of M plc's headquarters is to develop and administer its policies and procedures as well as to deal with its group corporate affairs.

Mission statement

M plc established a simple mission statement in 2005. This drove the initiative to acquire FR in 2008 and remains a driving force for the company. M plc's mission is "to be the best news media organisation in Europe, providing quality reporting and information on European and world-wide events".

Strategic objectives

Four main strategic objectives were established in 2005 by M plc's Board of Directors. These are to:

1   Meet the needs of readers for reliable and well informed news.

2   Expand the geographical spread of M plc's output to reach as many potential newspaper and website readers as possible.

3   Publish some newspapers which help meet the needs of native English speakers who live in countries which do not have English as their first language.

4   Increase advertising income so that the group moves towards offering as many news titles as possible free of charge to the public.

Financial objectives

In meeting these strategic objectives, M plc has developed the following financial objectives:

(i)   To ensure that revenue and operating profit grow by an average of 4% per year.

(ii)   To achieve steady growth in dividend per share.

(iii) To maintain gearing below 40%, where gearing is calculated as debt/(debt plus equity) based on the market value of equity and the book value of debt.

Forecast revenue and operating profit

M plc's forecast revenue and net operating profit for the year ending 31 March 2012 are £280 million and £73 million respectively.

Extracts from M plc's forecast statement of profit or loss for the year ending 31 March 2012 and forecast statement of financial position as at 31 March 2012 are shown in the appendix.

Comparative divisional performance and headquarters financial information

The following information is provided showing the revenue generated, the operating profit achieved and the capital employed for each division and the operating costs incurred and capital employed in M plc's headquarters. This information covers the last two years and also gives a forecast for the year ending 31 March 2012. All M plc's revenue is earned by the three divisions.

Newspapers Division	Year ended 31.3.2010	Year ended 31.3.2011	Forecast for year ending 31.3.2012
	£ million	£ million	£ million
Revenue external	91	94	94
Revenue internal transfers	90	91	96
Net operating profit	45	46	48
Non-current assets	420	490	548
Net current assets	4	8	(10)

Web Division	Year ended 31.3.2010	Year ended 31.3.2011	Forecast for year ending 31.3.2012
	£ million	£ million	£ million
Revenue internal transfers	55	60	66
Net operating profit	10	13	16
Non-current assets	37	40	43
Net current assets	1	1	(2)

Advertising Division	Year ended 31.3.2010	Year ended 31.3.2011	Forecast for year ending 31.3.2012
	£ million	£ million	£ million
Revenue external	162	180	186
Internal transfers	(145)	(151)	(162)
Net operating profit	10	18	19
Non-current assets	3	6	7
Net current assets	1	1	(2)

Headquarters	Year ended 31.3.2010	Year ended 31.3.2011	Forecast for year ending 31.3.2012
	£ million	£ million	£ million
Operating costs	8	9	10
Non-current assets	37	39	43
Net current assets	1	1	(1)

Notes:

1   The Advertising Division remits advertising revenue to both the Newspapers and Web Divisions after deducting its own commission.

2   The Web Division's entire revenue is generated from advertising.

3   The revenues and operating profits shown for the Newspapers Division include those earned by FR and N. The converted revenue and operating profit from N are forecast to be £20 million and £4 million respectively for the year ending 31 March 2012. FR is forecast to make a small operating profit in the year ending 31 March 2012. The Board of M plc is disappointed with the profit FR has achieved.

Additional information on each of M plc's divisions

Newspapers Division

FR is wholly owned and was acquired in 2008. Its financial statements are translated into British pounds and consolidated into M plc's group accounts and included within the Newspaper Division's results for internal reporting purposes.

Shortly after it was acquired by M plc, FR launched a pan-European weekly newspaper. This newspaper, which is written in English, is produced in France and then distributed throughout Europe. M plc's board thought that this newspaper would become very popular because it provides a snapshot of the week's news, focused particularly on European issues but viewed from a British perspective. Sales have, however, been disappointing.

N, which publishes local newspapers in its home Eastern European country, is also treated as part of the Newspapers Division. M plc acquired 80% of its equity in 2010. At that time, M plc's board thought that Eastern Europe was a growing market for newspapers. The subsidiary has proved to be profitable mainly because local production costs are lower than those in the UK relative to the selling prices.

The Newspapers Division's journalists incur a high level of expenses in order to carry out their duties. The overall level of expenses claimed by the journalists has been ignored by M plc in previous years because it has been viewed as a necessary cost of running the business. However, these expenses have risen significantly in recent years and have attracted the attention of M plc's internal audit department.

There has been significant capital investment in the Newspapers Division since 2009/10. The printing press facilities at each of the two printing sites have been modernised. These modernisations have improved the quality of output and have enabled improved levels of efficiency to be achieved in order to meet the increasing workloads demanded in the last two years. Surveys carried out before and after the modernisation have indicated higher levels of customer satisfaction with the improved quality of printing.

The increased mechanisation and efficiency has reduced costs and led to a reduction in the number of employees required to operate the printing presses. This has led to some dis-satisfaction among the divisional staff. Staff in the other divisions have been unaffected by the discontent in the Newspapers Division. Staff turnover has been relatively static across the three divisions, with the exception of the department which operates the printing presses in the Newspapers Division where some redundancies have occurred due to fewer staff being required since the modernisation.

Web Division

The web versions of the newspapers are shorter versions of the printed ones. There is currently no charge for access to the web versions of the newspapers. Revenues are generated from sales by the Advertising Division of advertising space on the web pages. Some of the websites permit unsolicited comments from the public to be posted on them and they have proved to be very popular. The Web Division is undertaking a review of all its costs, particularly those relating to energy, employees and website development.

The Web Division's management accounting is not sophisticated: for example, although it reports monthly on the Division's revenue and profitability, it cannot disaggregate costs so as to produce monthly results for each of the 200 websites. The Division is at a similar disadvantage as regards strategic management accounting as it lacks information about the websites' market share and growth rates. This has not mattered in the past as M plc was content that the Web Division has always been profitable. However, one of M plc's directors, the Business Development Director (see below under The Board of Directors and group shareholding) thinks that the Web Division could increase its profitability considerably and wants to undertake a review of its 200 websites.

Advertising Division

The Advertising Division remits advertising revenue to both the Newspapers and Web Divisions after deducting its own commission. In addition, the Advertising Division offers an advertising service to corporate clients. Such services include television and radio advertising and poster campaigns on bill boards. Advertisements are also placed in newspapers and magazines which are not produced by M plc, if the client so wishes. An increasing element of the work undertaken by the Advertising Division is in providing pop-up advertisements on websites.

Planning process

Each division carries out its own planning process. The Newspapers Division operates a rational model and prepares annual plans which it presents to M plc's board for approval. The Web Division takes advantage of opportunities as they arise and is operating in a growth market, unlike the other two divisions. Its planning approach might best be described as one of logical incrementalism. Increased capital expenditure in 2010/11 helped the Advertising Division to achieve an 11% increase in revenue in that year. The Divisional Managers of both the Web Division and the Advertising Division are keen to develop their businesses and are considering growth options including converting their businesses into outsource service providers to M plc.

The Board of Directors and group shareholding

M plc's Board of Directors comprises six executive directors and six non-executive directors, one of whom is the Non-executive Chairman. The executive directors are the Chief Executive, and the Directors of Strategy, Corporate Affairs, Finance, Human Resources and Business Development. The Business Development Director did not work for M plc in 2005 and so had no part in drafting the strategic objectives. She thinks that objective number four has become out-dated as it does not reflect current day practice. The Business Development Director has a great deal of experience working with subscription-based websites and this was one of the main reasons M plc recruited her in March 2011. Her previous experience also incorporated the management of product portfolios including product development and portfolio rationalisation.

There are divisional managing directors for each of the three divisions who are not board members but report directly to the Chief Executive.

One of M plc's non-executive directors was appointed at the insistence of the bank which holds 10% of M plc's shares. Another was appointed by a private charity which owns a further 10% of the shares in M plc. The charity represents the interests of print workers and provides long-term care to retired print workers and their dependents. Two other non-executive directors were appointed by a financial institution which owns 20% of the shares in M plc. The remaining 60% of shares are held by private investors. The board members between them hold 5% of the shares in issue. None of the other private investors holds more than 70,000 of the total 140 million shares in issue.

It has become clear that there is some tension between the board members. Four of the non-executive directors, those appointed by the bank, the charity and the financial institution, have had disagreements with the other board members. They are dissatisfied with the rate of growth and profitability of the company and wish to see more positive action to secure M plc's financial objectives.

Some board members feel that the newspapers market is declining because fewer people can make time to read printed publications. Some of the non-executive directors think that many people are more likely to watch a television news channel than read a newspaper.

Editorial policy

M plc's board applies a policy of editorial freedom provided that the published material is within the law and is accurate. The editors of each of the publications printed in the UK and France and of the websites have complete autonomy over what is published. They are also responsible for adhering to regulatory constraints and voluntary industry codes of practice relating to articles and photographs which might be considered offensive by some readers. There is less scrutiny of the accuracy of the reporting in N's home country than in other countries. The Eastern European country in which N is situated has become politically unstable in the last two years. Much of this unrest is fuelled by the public distaste for the perceived blatant corruption and bribery which is endemic within the country's Government and business community. It is well known that journalists have accepted bribes to present only the Government's version of events, rather than a balanced view. There is also widespread plagiarism of published material by the country's newspapers and copyright laws are simply ignored.

Corporate Social Responsibility

A policy is in place throughout M plc in order to eliminate bribery and corruption among staff especially those who have front line responsibility for obtaining business. This policy was established 15 years ago. All new employees are made aware of the policy and other staff policies and procedures during their induction. The Director of Human Resources has confidence in the procedures applied by his staff at induction and is proud that no action has ever been brought against an employee of M plc for breach of the bribery and corruption policy. M plc is trying to reduce its carbon footprint and is in the process of developing policies to limit its energy consumption, reduce the mileage travelled by its staff and source environmentally friendly supplies of paper for its printing presses. The Newspapers Division purchases the paper it uses for printing newspapers from a supplier in a Scandinavian country. This paper is purchased because it provides a satisfactory level of quality at a relatively cheap price. The Scandinavian country from which the paper is sourced is not the same country in which N is situated.

Strategic Development

The Board of Directors is now reviewing M plc's competitive position. The Board of Directors is under pressure from the non-executive directors appointed by the bank, the charity and the financial institution (which between them own 40% of the shares in M plc), to devise a strategic plan before June 2012 which is aimed at achieving M plc's stated financial objectives.

APPENDIX 1

Extracts from M plc's forecast group statement of profit or loss and statement of financial position

Forecast statement of profit or loss for the group for the year ended 31 March 2012

	Notes	£ million (GBP million)
Revenue		280
Operating costs		(207)
		———
Net operating profit		73
Interest income		1
Finance costs		(11)
Corporate income tax	1	(19)
		———
FORECAST PROFIT FOR THE YEAR		44
		———

Forecast statement of the group financial position as at 31 March 2012

	Notes	£ million (GBP million)
ASSETS		
Non-current assets		641
Current assets		
Inventories		2
Trade and other receivables		27
Cash and cash equivalents		2
		___
Total current assets		31
		___
Total assets		672
		___
EQUITY AND LIABILITIES		
Equity		
Share capital	2	140
Share premium		35
Retained earnings		185
Non-controlling interest		16
		___
Total equity		376
		___
Non-current liabilities		
Long term borrowings	3	250
Current liabilities		
Trade and other payables		46
		___
Total current liabilities		46
Total liabilities		296
		___
Total equity and liabilities		672
		___

Notes:

1   The corporate income tax rate can be assumed to be 30%.

2   There are 140 million £1 shares currently in issue.

3   The long-term borrowings include £83 million of loan capital which is due for repayment on 1 May 2013 and the remainder is due for repayment on 1 April 2019.

END OF PRE-SEEN MATERIAL

1   M PLC (NOV 11 EXAM)

UNSEEN CASE MATERIAL

Background

Assume today is 1 December 2011.

The results from M plc's French subsidiary, FR, have been disappointing.

FR was originally acquired at the beginning of 2008 in order to provide M plc with printing capacity in Europe from which to launch a new English language pan European newspaper. FR already printed regional French newspapers but had spare printing capacity that M plc was able to use. After acquisition, FR continued to produce the regional French newspapers and launched the pan European newspaper in the middle of 2008. However, since M plc took over the business there has been a fall in circulation of the regional French newspapers and the pan European newspaper has not been as well received as had been expected.

The Board of M plc has decided that, whilst it believes that a pan European weekly newspaper in English is still a viable concept, it would like to sell FR as a going concern. The most serious interest in FR is from PP which is a large competitor in the newspaper business, based in France and listed on the French Stock Exchange. PP already prints and distributes a European edition of a US newspaper across Europe and so has proven experience in this market and an established distribution network. However, PP is already quite a dominant force in the newspaper industry in France and there is some concern that the proposed takeover of FR by PP might be referred to the competition authorities in France.

The proposed sale of FR would involve the settlement of its intra-group borrowings. The sale price would therefore consist of two parts:

1   EUR 25 million to settle FR's intra-group debt.

2   A second payment to acquire M plc's shares in FR.

FR has no external debt and the purchaser would therefore acquire the net assets of FR on a going concern basis with no debt attached.

The Board of M plc hopes to raise a significant amount of funds from the sale of FR, possibly as much as EUR 75 million (which includes the EUR 25 million required to settle FR's intra-group debt).

Discussion at a recent M plc board meeting regarding possible uses of the funds generated by the sale of FR

The following possible uses of the sale proceeds were identified at a recent board meeting:

- Reinvesting the funds in a new project.

- Repaying debt.

- Rewarding shareholders with a one-off dividend payment.

Financial data for M plc

Extracts from the forecast financial statements for the M plc group for the year ending 31 March 2012 can be found in the pre-seen material. The strategic and financial objectives for M plc are in the pre-seen material.

On 1 December 2011, M plc's share price is GBP 3.50 per share.

Financial data for FR

Book values of FR's assets and debt as at 30 November 2011:

	EUR million	
Non-current assets	50	with a market value of EUR 56 million
Net current assets	2	
Long term liabilities	(25)	which consist of intra-group debt only
	27	

FR's results for the 12 months to 30 November 2011:

	EUR million	
Operating profit	6.7	after charging depreciation of EUR 0.5 million
Finance charge	(1.4)	
Tax	(1.3)	
Earnings	4.0	

The management of FR has established that there needs to be an investment in working capital and non-current assets of EUR 1.8 million per annum in order to maintain the current level of operations. M plc forecasts that FR's free cash flow will grow by just 2% a year for the foreseeable future.

M plc considers that PP has a similar level of business risk to FR and approximately the same level of gearing as M plc and therefore plans to use PP as a proxy when valuing FR using a discounted cash flow (DCF) approach.

Financial data for PP

PP is funded as follows:

	Nominal value	*Today's market value*
Ordinary EUR 1 shares	EUR 50.0 million	EUR 5.80 per share
8% irredeemable EUR 1 preference shares	EUR 20.0 million	EUR 1.35 per share
6% Bond maturing in 3 years' time at par	EUR 120.0 million	EUR 103.0 per EUR 100.0

Other information:

- PP has a published equity beta of 1.5 and a P/E ratio of 13.

- M plc estimates that PP could achieve economies of scale of approximately EUR 0.7 million a year after tax by merging with FR. Note that this figure is not expected to grow from year to year but is expected to remain at EUR 0.7 million a year for the foreseeable future.

Financial data common to all three companies:

- For both the UK and France, assume a risk free interest rate of 3% and a market premium of 5%.

- Assume a debt beta of zero.

- Corporate income tax is charged at 30% on all taxable profits and is paid at the end of the year in which the taxable profit arises in both the UK and France.

- The spot rate on 1 December 2011 is EUR/GBP 0.8900 (that is, EUR 1 = GBP 0.8900) and is expected to remain unchanged for the foreseeable future.

Required:

Assume you are an adviser to M plc and have been asked to write a report in which you:

(a) Evaluate the THREE possible uses of the funds generated by the sale of FR that were identified during the recent M plc board meeting.

(Up to 5 marks are available for calculations.) **(10 marks)**

(b) (i) Calculate, as at 1 December 2011, a range of euro denominated values for FR, both with and without synergistic benefits arising from the acquisition. Your answer should include a discounted free cash flow valuation using PP's weighted average cost of capital (WACC). **(18 marks)**

(ii) Discuss the appropriateness of each of the valuation approaches used in your answer to part (b)(i). **(8 marks)**

(iii) Advise on an appropriate minimum and maximum cash price for the sale of FR. **(5 marks)**

(c) Evaluate the risks that arise from investigations by competition authorities into planned takeovers. Include reference to the proposed sale of FR. **(6 marks)**

Additional marks available for structure and presentation: **(3 marks)**

(Total: 50 marks)

2 M PLC (MAR 12 EXAM)

UNSEEN CASE MATERIAL

Background

Today is 1 April 2012.

The Board of M plc is considering the acquisition of a company that specialises in producing pre-recorded news reports and programmes which are sold to television networks for them to broadcast. Television news has been identified as an area of growth in the media industry and has a different business cycle to that of M plc. That is, at times of increased demand for television news, newspaper sales tend to decline and vice versa.

Synergistic benefits might also arise from a move into television news since M plc's worldwide network of journalists could feed news items into both the newspapers and television news programmes.

The Board of M plc has identified GG as a possible takeover target. GG is a company based in the USA that specialises in producing news programmes and recorded video clips for sale to television networks that broadcast in the English language.

Planned bid offer for GG

Initial plans are for the bid offer to be in the form of a share exchange due to the scale of the takeover.

The Board of M plc believes that there is likely to be a negative response from the Board of GG to a bid offer but cannot yet assess how the shareholders of GG will react. No official announcement has been made to the market concerning the potential takeover. However, in recent weeks there has been significant movement in the share prices of both GG and M plc, which is considered to be largely due to the leaking of information on the proposed bid into the public domain. There has been a 10% increase in GG's share price and a 5% decrease in M plc's share price during this period.

Financial information for M plc and GG

The latest available version of M plc's financial statements as at 31 March 2012 can be found in the pre-seen material. Strategic and financial objectives can also be found in the pre-seen.

Additional financial information as at 1 April 2012:

	M plc	GG
Corporate income tax rate	30%	30%
Published equity beta	1.8	2.5
Last year's earnings	GBP 44 million	USD 30 million
Shares in issue	140 million	40 million
	GBP 1 ordinary shares	USD 1 common stock
		(equivalent to ordinary shares)
Share price	GBP 3.77 per share	USD 7.50 per share
Forecast earnings growth in perpetuity	4% pa	8% pa
Risk free rate	1.1%	3.0%
Market premium	4.0%	4.0%

Additional relevant information:

- GG's free cash flow can be assumed to be approximately 60% of its annual earnings and arise at the end of a year. Free cash flow is defined as cash flow from operations after deducting interest, tax and ongoing capital expenditure.

- GG has approximately the same gearing ratio as M plc.

- It is believed that GG's lenders would accept the change of ownership of GG's business and would reassign GG's borrowings to M plc.

- The GBP/USD spot rate is currently 1.6300 (that is GBP 1 = USD 1.6300). GBP is expected to appreciate against USD by 2% a year in each of the next 3 years. It is not considered to be possible to predict currency movements beyond 3 years and so the spot exchange rate should be assumed to remain constant after 1 April 2015 for the purposes of any evaluation.

Required:

Assume you are the Financial Director of M plc and have been asked to prepare a briefing paper for the Board of M plc regarding the proposed takeover bid for GG in which you:

(a) (i) Calculate the current cost of equity for:

- **M plc.**

- **GG.**

- **M plc adjusted for the business risk of GG.** **(3 marks)**

(ii) **Explain the reasons for the differences in your three cost of equity results in part (a) (i) above.** **(4 marks)**

(b) (i) Calculate a range of values for GG as at 1 April 2012. Note that only one discounted cash flow calculation is required. **(8 marks)**

(ii) Advise on:

- The validity of your results in (b) (i) above as the basis for an initial bid offer for GG.

- An appropriate initial offer value for GG and appropriate share exchange terms. **(10 marks)**

(c) Advise whether M plc should proceed with the bid offer for GG. Your answer should take into account:

- The potential impact of the takeover on the attainment of M plc's financial objectives.

- Other relevant factors affecting the decision.

(Up to 4 marks are available for calculations) **(14 marks)**

(d) Explain:

- The actions GG could take to fight the takeover bid.

- The actions M plc could take to help ensure a positive response to the bid offer. **(7 marks)**

Additional marks available for structure and presentation: **(4 marks)**

(Total: 50 marks)

B SUPERMARKETS (MAY 12 AND SEPT 12 EXAMS) – RELATES TO QUESTIONS 3 AND 4

PRE-SEEN CASE MATERIAL

Overview

Introduction

B Supermarkets (B) was founded as a grocery retailer in a European country in 1963. Its sales consist mainly of food and household items including clothing. B now owns or franchises over 15,000 stores world-wide in 36 countries. The company has stores in Europe (in both eurozone and non-eurozone countries), Asia and North America. B's head office is located in a eurozone country. B has become one of the world's largest chains of stores.

B's Board thinks that there are opportunities to take advantage of the rapid economic growth of some Asian countries and the associated increases in demand for food and consumer goods.

Structure

The B Group is structured into a holding company, B, and three subsidiary companies which are located in each of the regions of the world in which it operates (Europe, Asia and North America). The subsidiary companies, referred to as "Regions" within B, are respectively B-Europe, B-Asia and B-North America.

Store operations, sales mix and staffing

B operates four types of store: supermarkets, hypermarkets, discount stores and convenience stores. For the purpose of this case study, the definition of each of these types of store is as follows:

A *supermarket* is a self-service store which sells a wide variety of food and household goods such as washing and cleaning materials, cooking utensils and other items which are easily carried by customers out of the store.

A *hypermarket* is a superstore or very large store which sells the same type of products as a supermarket but in addition it sells a wide range of other items such as consumer durable white goods, for example refrigerators, freezers, washing machines and furniture. Hypermarkets are often located on out-of-town sites.

A *discount store* is a retail store that sells a variety of goods such as electrical appliances and electronic equipment. Discount stores in general usually sell branded products and pursue a high-volume, low priced strategy and aim their marketing at customers who seek goods at prices which are usually less than can be found in a hypermarket.

A *convenience store* is a small shop or store in an urban area that sells goods which are purchased regularly by customers. These would typically include groceries, toiletries, alcoholic beverages, soft drinks and confectionery. They are convenient for shoppers as they are located in or near residential areas and are often open for long hours. Customers are willing to pay premium prices for the convenience of having the store close by.

B sells food products and clothing in its supermarkets and hypermarkets at a higher price than many of its competitors because the Board thinks that its customers are prepared to pay higher prices for better quality food products. B also sells good quality consumer durable products in its supermarkets and hypermarkets but it is forced to sell these at competitive prices as there is strong competition for the sale of such goods. B's discount stores sell good quality electrical products usually at lower prices than those charged in its supermarkets and hypermarkets, B only sells electronic equipment in its discount stores. Customers have a greater range from which to choose in the discount stores as compared with supermarkets and hypermarkets because the discount stores specialise in the goods which they sell. B's convenience stores do not have the availability of space to carry a wide range of products and they charge a higher price for the same brand and type of goods which it sells in its supermarkets.

Although B owns most of its stores, it has granted franchises for the operation of some stores which carry its name.

Nearly 0.5 million full-time equivalent staff are employed world-wide in the Group. B tries when possible to recruit local staff to fill job vacancies within its stores.

Value statement and mission

In recognition of the strong competitive and dynamic markets in which it operates, B's Board has established an overall value statement as follows: "We aim to satisfy our customers wherever we trade. We intend to employ different generic competitive strategies depending on the market segment in which our stores trade."

The Board has also produced the following mission statement:

"B practises sustainable investment within a healthy ethical and thoughtful culture and strives to achieve customer satisfaction by giving a courteous and efficient service, selling high quality goods at a reasonable price, sourcing goods from local suppliers where possible and causing the least damage possible to the natural environment. By this, we aim to satisfy the expectations of our shareholders by achieving consistent growth in our share price and also to enhance our reputation for being an environmentally responsible company."

Strategic objectives

The following objectives have been derived from the mission statement:

1   Build shareholder value through consistent growth in the company's share price.

2   Increase customer satisfaction ratings to 95% as measured by customer feedback surveys.

3   Increase commitment to local suppliers by working towards achieving 40% of our supplies from sources which are local to where B stores trade.

4   Reduce carbon emissions calculated by internationally agreed measures by at least 1% per year until B becomes totally carbon neutral.

5   Maximise returns to shareholders by employing different generic competitive strategies depending on the market segment in which B stores trade.

Financial objectives

The Board has set the following financial objectives:

1   Achieve consistent growth in earnings per share of 7% each year.

2   Maintain a dividend pay-out ratio of 50% each year.

3   Gearing levels as measured by long-term debt divided by long-term debt plus equity should not exceed 40% based on book value.

Governance

The main board comprises the Non-executive Chairman, the Chief Executive and nine Executive directors. These cover the functions of finance, human resources, corporate affairs (including legal and public relations), marketing, planning and procurement. There is also one executive director for each of the three regions, being the Regional Managing Directors of B-Europe, B-Asia and B-North America. There are also nine non-executive main board members in addition to the Chairman.

The main Board of Directors has separate committees responsible for audit, remuneration, appointments, corporate governance and risk assessment and control. The Risk Assessment and Control Committee's tasks were formerly included within the Audit Committee's role. It was agreed by the Board in 2009 that these tasks should be separated out in order not to overload the Audit Committee which has responsibilities to review the probity of the company. B's expansion has been very rapid in some countries. The expansion has been so rapid that B has not been able to carry out any internal audit activities in some of these countries to date. The regional boards do not have a committee structure.

Each of the Regional Managing Directors chairs his or her own Regional Board. All of the Regional Boards have their own directors for finance, human resources, corporate affairs, marketing, planning and procurement but their structure is different for the directors who have responsibility for the stores. In B-Asia, one regional director is responsible for the hypermarkets and supermarkets and another is responsible for discount stores and convenience stores. In B-North America, one regional director is responsible for the hypermarkets and supermarkets and another is responsible for discount stores (B does not have any convenience stores in North America). In B-Europe there is one regional director responsible for supermarkets and hypermarkets, one for discount stores and one for convenience stores. In all regions the regional directors have line accountability to their respective regional managing director and professional accountability to the relevant main board director. There are no non-executive directors on the regional boards. Appendix 1 shows the main board and regional board structures.

Treasury

Each of B's three regions has a regional treasury department managed by a regional treasurer who has direct accountability to the respective Regional Director of Finance and professional accountability to the Group Treasurer. The Group Treasurer manages the central corporate treasury department which is located in B's head office. The Group Treasurer, who is not a main board member, reports to the Director of Finance on the main board.

Shareholding, year-end share prices and dividends paid for the last five years

B is listed on a major European stock exchange within the eurozone and it wholly owns its subsidiaries. There are five major shareholders of B, including employees taken as a group, which between them hold 25% of the 1.350 million total shares in issue. The major shareholders comprise two long term investment trusts which each owns 4%, a hedge fund owns 5%, employees own 5% and the founding family trust owns 7% of the shares. The remaining 75% of shares are owned by the general public.

The year-end share prices and the dividends paid for the last five years were as follows:

	2007	2008	2009	2010	2011
	€	€	€	€	€
Share price at 31 December	47.38	25.45	28.68	29.44	31.37
Net Dividend per share	1.54	1.54	1.54	1.62	1.65

Planning and management control

B has a very structured planning process. Each regional board produces a five year strategic plan for its region relating to specific objectives set for it by the main board and submits this to the main board for approval. The main board then produces a consolidated strategic plan for the whole company. This is reviewed on a three yearly cycle and results in a revised and updated group five year plan being produced every three years.

B's management control system, which operates throughout its regions and at head office, is well known in the industry to be bureaucratic and authoritarian. Strict financial authority levels for development purposes are imposed from the main Board. There is tension between the main Board and the regional boards. The regional board members feel that they are not able to manage effectively despite being located much closer to their own regional markets than the members of the main Board. The main Board members, on the other hand, think that they need to exercise tight control because they are remote from the markets. This often stifles planning initiatives within each region. This tension is also felt lower down the organisation as the regional board members exercise strict financial and management control over operational managers in their regions in order to ensure that the main Board directives are carried out.

Competitive overview

B operates in highly competitive markets for all the products it sells. The characteristics of each of the markets in which it operates are different. For example, there are different planning restrictions applying within each region. In some countries, B is required to operate each of its stores in a partnership arrangement with local enterprises, whereas no such restriction exists within other countries in which it trades. B needs to be aware of different customer tastes and preferences which differ from country to country. The following table provides a break-down of B's stores in each region.

	B Europe	B Asia	B North America
Supermarkets and hypermarkets	3,456	619	512
Discount stores	5,168	380	780
Convenience stores	4,586	35	

B is one of the largest retailing companies in the world and faces different levels of competition in each region. B's overall market share in terms of retail sales for all supermarkets, hypermarkets, discount stores and convenience stores in each of its regions is as follows:

	Market share
Europe	20%
Asia	1%
North America	1.5%

The following table shows the sales revenue and net operating profit earned by B in each of its regions for the year ended 31 December 2011:

	B Europe € million	B Asia € million	B North America € million
Revenue	89,899	10,105	9,708
Net Operating Profit	4,795	743	673

B is constantly seeking other areas of the world into which it can expand, especially within Asia where it perceives many countries have an increasing population and strengthening economies.

Corporate Social Responsibility (CSR)

B is meeting its CSR obligations by establishing environmental targets for carbon emissions (greenhouse gas emissions), careful monitoring of its supply chain, undertaking sustainable investments and investing in its human capital.

Environmental targets for carbon emissions:

B's main board is keen to demonstrate the company's concern for the environment by pursuing continuous improvement in the reduction of its carbon emissions and by developing ways of increasing sustainability in its trading practices. A number of environmental indicators have been established to provide transparency in B's overall performance in respect of sustainability. These published measures were verified by B's statutory auditor and are calculated on a like-for-like basis for the stores in operation over the period measured.

In the year ended 31 December 2011, B reduced its consumption of kilowatt hours (kWh) per square metre of sales area as compared with the year ended 31 December 2008 by 9%. The target reduction for that period was 5%. In the same period it reduced the number of free disposable plastic bags provided to customers per square metre of sales area, by 51% against a target of 60%. Its overall greenhouse gas emissions (measured by kilogrammes of carbon dioxide per square metre of sales area) reduced by 1% in 2011 which was exactly on target.

B provides funding for the development of local amenity projects in all of the countries where B stores operate. (An amenity project is one which provides benefit to the local population, such as providing a park, community gardens or a swimming pool.)

Distribution and sourcing:

Distribution from suppliers across such a wide geographical area is an issue for B. While supplies are sourced from the country in which a store is located as much as possible, there is nevertheless still a requirement for transportation across long distances either by road or air. Approximately 20% of the physical quantity of goods sold across the group as a whole are sourced locally, that is within the country in which the goods are sold. These tend to be perishable items such as fruit and vegetables. The remaining 80% of goods are sourced from large international manufacturers and distributors. These tend to be large items such as electrical or electronic equipment which are bought under contracts which are set up by the regional procurement departments. B, due to its size and scope of operations, is able to place orders for goods made to its own specification and packaged as under its own brand label. Some contracts are agreed between manufacturers and the Group Procurement Director for the supply of goods to the whole of the B group world-wide.

B's inventory is rarely transported by rail except within Europe. This has resulted in lower average reductions in carbon emissions per square metre of sales area by stores operated by B-Asia and B-North America than for those stores operated by B-Europe. This is because the carbon emission statistics take into account the transportation of goods into B's stores.

Sustainable investments:

B aspires to become carbon neutral over the long term. The Board aims to reduce its carbon emissions by investing in state of the art technology in its new store developments and by carrying out modifications to existing stores.

Human Resources:

B prides itself on the training it provides to its staff. The training of store staff is carried out in store by specialist teams which operate in each country where B trades. In this way, B believes that training is consistent across all of its stores. In some countries, the training is considered to be at a sufficiently high level to be recognised by national training bodies. The average number of training hours per employee in the year ended 31 December 2011 was 17 compared with 13 hours in the year ended 31 December 2010. In 2011, B employed 45% more staff with declared disabilities compared with 2010.

Information systems and inventory management

In order to operate efficiently, B's Board has recognised that it must have up-to-date information systems including electronic point of sale (EPOS) systems. An EPOS system uses computers or specialised terminals that can be combined with other hardware such as bar-code readers to accurately capture the sale and adjust the inventory levels within the store. EPOS systems installation is on-going. B has installed EPOS systems in its stores in some countries but not in all its stores world-wide.

B's information systems are not perfect as stock-outs do occur from time-to-time, especially in the European stores. This can be damaging to sales revenue when stock-outs occur during peak sales periods such as the days leading up to a public holiday. In Asia and North America in particular, B's information technology systems sometimes provide misleading information. This has led to doubts in the minds of some head office staff about just how robust are B's inventory control systems.

As is normal in chain store groups, there is a certain degree of loss through theft by staff and customers. Another way that loss is suffered is through goods which have gone past their "sell-by" date and mainly relates to perishable food items which are wasted as they cannot be sold to the public. In most countries, such food items which cannot be sold to the public may be sold to local farmers for animal feed.

Regulatory issues

B's subsidiaries in Asia and North America have sometimes experienced governmental regulatory difficulties in some countries which have hindered the installation of improved information systems. To overcome some of these regulatory restrictions, B-Asia and B-North America have, on occasions, resorted to paying inducements to government officials in order for the regulations to be relaxed.

APPENDIX 1

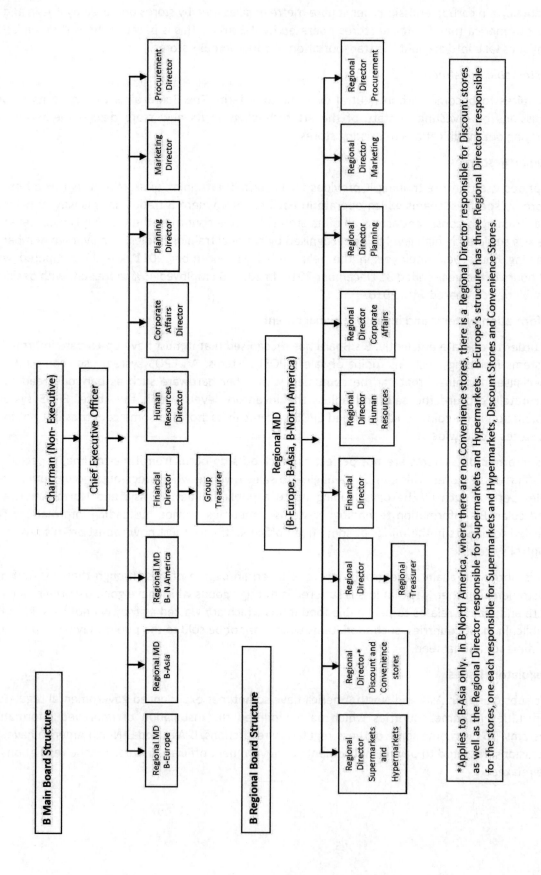

B Main Board Structure

Chairman (Non- Executive)

Chief Executive Officer

Regional MD B-Europe | Regional MD B-Asia | Regional MD B- N America | Financial Director | Human Resources Director | Corporate Affairs Director | Planning Director | Marketing Director | Procurement Director

Group Treasurer

B Regional Board Structure

Regional MD (B-Europe, B-Asia, B-North America)

Regional Director Supermarkets and Hypermarkets | Regional Director* Discount and Convenience stores | Regional Director | Financial Director | Regional Director Human Resources | Regional Director Corporate Affairs | Regional Director Planning | Regional Director Marketing | Regional Director Procurement

Regional Treasurer

*Applies to B-Asia only. In B-North America, where there are no Convenience stores, there is a Regional Director responsible for Discount stores as well as the Regional Director responsible for Supermarkets and Hypermarkets. B-Europe's structure has three Regional Directors responsible for the stores, one each responsible for Supermarkets and Hypermarkets, Discount Stores and Convenience Stores.

APPENDIX 2

B's statement of profit or loss and statement of financial position

Statement of profit or loss for the year ended 31 December 2011

	Notes	€ million
Revenue		109,712
Operating costs		(103,501)
Net operating profit		6,211
Interest income		165
Finance costs		(852)
Corporate income tax		(1,933)
Profit for the year		3,591

Statement of financial position as at 31 December 2011

		€ million
Assets		
Non-current assets		57,502
Current assets		
Inventories		7,670
Trade and other receivables		1,521
Cash and cash equivalents		3,847
Total current assets		13,038
Total assets		70,540
Equity and liabilities		
Equity		
Share capital	1	2,025
Share premium		3,040
Retained earnings		18,954
Total equity		24,019
Non-current liabilities		
Long term borrowings		15,744
Current liabilities		
Trade and other payables		30,777
Total liabilities		46,521
Total equity and liabilities		70,540

Notes:

1   There are 1,350 million €1.50 shares currently in issue. The share price at 31 December 2011 was €31.37.

END OF PRE-SEEN MATERIAL

3   B SUPERMARKETS (MAY 12 EXAM)

UNSEEN CASE MATERIAL

The directors of B are aware that B's results have been slow to recover after the global economic downturn of 2008.   In the medium term, growth prospects for the European business continue to be poor. The group has publicised plans for continued growth and the directors are therefore looking for opportunities for expansion outside of Europe.   In particular, they are exploring the possibility of expanding B's presence in the rapidly growing Asian market in order to counterbalance poor growth prospects in Europe.

Financial data for B

Extracts from the group financial statements for 2011 are provided in the pre-seen material, as are the financial objectives, and the share price and dividend data for the last five years.

Additional data is provided below:

Year	2007	2008	2009	2010	2011
Number of shares in issue throughout the year (million)	1,284	1,284	1,350	1,350	1,350
Earnings for the year (€ million)	3,945	2,818	3,097	3,366	3,591

Expansion strategy into Country A in Asia

One possibility being considered by the directors of B is to establish a presence in Country A, a country in Asia which uses the A$ as its currency.   B has no existing operations in Country A.

In the past, small, family-owned local businesses dominated retail food sales in Country A, with consumers typically shopping on a daily basis. In recent years, however, shopping patterns have moved away from daily shopping and new supermarkets have been successfully opened across the country. These supermarkets operate in much the same way as supermarkets in other countries, selling a combination of both food and household items.

The directors of B have been considering the best strategy for starting to operate in Country A and have concluded that the lowest risk route would be to acquire a small chain of existing supermarkets. These supermarkets would then be rebranded. If the rebranding exercise proved to be successful and produced a profitable return for B within an experimental period of three years, B would consider either purchasing or building additional supermarkets or other types of store in Country A. The potential for growth is considered to be huge in such a large and rapidly developing market and there is a possibility that it could lead to an increase in B's Asian revenue stream to more than four times current levels.

To satisfy this strategy, a company called Alpha Supermarkets has been identified as a potential acquisition target. Alpha Supermarkets operates a small chain of supermarkets in Country A.

Financial data concerning the proposed acquisition and rebranding of Alpha Supermarkets

Alpha Supermarkets is owned and managed as a private family business and comprises 15 small supermarkets in a single region of Country A.

The directors of B are aware that an offer was made recently to the family shareholders of Alpha Supermarkets to buy the whole business for A$960 million. This offer was not accepted but is, nonetheless, considered to represent the fair value of the Alpha Supermarket business in its current form. The main shareholders of Alpha Supermarkets have indicated that they would be prepared to consider an offer from B at a 20% premium above this previous takeover offer price.

The directors of B realise that significant investment would be required to rebrand the Alpha supermarkets after acquisition, including renewing store fittings and changing the types of food and household goods sold.

The following table provides estimated incremental capital and operating cash flows for the first three years of operation for a typical Alpha supermarket following acquisition by B. Estimated financial results of the rebranding exercise for a single supermarket are:

Item	Incremental cash flows A$ million	Timing
Initial capital investment	35	Year 0
Additional operating revenue in year 1, increasing by 12% a year in years 2 and 3	30	
Additional operating costs in year 1, increasing by 8% a year in years 2 and 3	13	
Reinvestment of operating cash flows (OCF)	3	Year 1 and Year 2
Residual value of B's capital investments, including reinvested OCF	30	Year 3

Additional information:

- Country A has a 32% corporate income tax rate.

- Both the initial capital investment and subsequent reinvestment of funds in the business attract immediate 100% tax depreciation allowances. Balancing charges apply to the residual value.

- No additional tax or refunds of tax are due on funds remitted to B.

- The €/A$ spot rate at Year 0 can be assumed to be €/A$7.5000 (that is, €1 = A$ 7.5000).

- B considers that an A$ post-tax discount rate of 15% is an appropriate rate to use when evaluating an investment of this nature.

- All cash flows should be assumed to arise at the end of the year unless stated otherwise and tax should be assumed to be settled at the end of the year in which it arises. However, any tax refunds due will be carried forward and set off against the next tax liability in a future year.

Required:

(a)   For each of the years 2007 to 2011 inclusive:

   (i)   Calculate, in respect of B:

   •   Earnings per share

   •   P/E ratio

   •   Dividend payout ratio   **(8 marks)**

   (ii)   Evaluate B's financial performance. Your answer should include reference to
         the attainment of Financial objective 1.

         Up to 3 marks are available for relevant additional calculations.   **(9 marks)**

   (iii)   Explain the possible rationale behind B's dividend pay-out history.   **(6 marks)**

(b)   Assuming you are the Financial Director of B, write a briefing paper for the Board of
      B regarding the proposed acquisition of Alpha Supermarkets in which you:

   (i)   Calculate the expected financial benefit to B of the rebranding exercise on a
         discounted cash flows basis over a three year time period.   **(10 marks)**

   (ii)   Evaluate the potential risks and opportunities arising from the proposed
         acquisition AND advise whether to proceed.   **(14 marks)**

   Additional marks available for structure and presentation: **(3 marks)**

                                                       (Total: 50 marks)

4   B SUPERMARKETS (SEPT 12 EXAM)

UNSEEN CASE MATERIAL

Today is 1 September 2012.

The directors of B Supermarkets (B) are considering establishing a chain of convenience
stores in the USA following the success of such stores in Europe. Food sales in the USA are
currently dominated by large supermarket chains in out-of-town locations. The general
pattern is for consumers to go shopping for food once a week. However, with increasing
pressure on leisure time, a greater number of single person households and an increasing
preference for fresh food, there is a growing trend for more frequent, local, food shopping.
The Regional Managing Director for North America hopes that by establishing a chain of
convenience stores that B can take advantage of this trend. The aim is to attract customers
by building a reputation for fresh produce and the convenience of ready prepared meals.

An opportunity has arisen for B to purchase and develop 50 empty retail properties. The
properties are considered to be of an appropriate size and location for running small
convenience stores. The price, USD 30 million for all 50 of the retail properties, is also very
attractive.

Details of proposed project

A project team has been set up to manage the project. The project would commence on
1 January 2013 and is to be evaluated over a four year time period from that date.

The stores would be empty when acquired and would need to be re-fitted at an
approximate one-off total cost of USD 10 million for re-fitting all 50 stores.

Both the purchase cost of the properties and the cost to renew the store fittings can be assumed to be paid on 1 January 2013. The store fittings are estimated to have a residual value of USD 4 million on 31 December 2016. There is some uncertainty over the value of the stores themselves on that date. The project team has decided to evaluate the project on the basis that the properties, excluding fittings, could be sold for cash on 31 December 2016 at a price that is 20% greater, in nominal terms, than the original purchase cost.

The Management Accountant has produced some estimates of the total expected revenue and cost figures for the first year of the project as shown below. Note that these are aggregated figures across all 50 stores.

Revenue	USD 90 million
Purchase costs	USD 35 million
Other operating costs	USD 40 million

Each of the above revenue and costs is expected to grow by 12% a year for the duration of the project.

The project team is planning to adopt an aggressive strategy for managing working capital. Target working capital days for the project are given below, together with historical data for B for comparative purposes. Both accounts payable and inventory days are based on purchase costs.

Working capital days	Project	B
Accounts receivable	Nil	Nil
Accounts payable	100 days	139 days
Inventory	30 days	53 days

Additional information:

- Working capital values for accounts payable and inventory at the beginning of each year are to be calculated by applying the target working capital days to the appropriate forecast revenue and/or cost figures for the coming year.

- Working capital adjustments should be assumed to arise at the start of each year.

- The final accounts payable and inventory balances at the end of the project should be assumed to be realised in full at that time.

- After working capital adjustments, project revenue and costs should be assumed to be cash flows and to be paid or received at the end of the year in which they arise.

- Corporate income tax is payable at 33% at the end of the year in which it is incurred. Tax depreciation allowances are available on the store fittings costs on a reducing balance basis at 25% a year. No corporate capital taxes apply to the purchase and sale of the properties.

- The EUR/USD spot rate is expected to be EUR/USD 1.1000 on 1 January 2013 (that is, EUR 1 = USD 1.1000). Interest rates for the EUR and USD are 3% and 5% respectively and the EUR/USD spot rate is expected to move in line with the interest rate differential for the duration of the project.

A discounted cash flow approach is to be used in evaluating the project, based on B's EUR based weighted average cost of capital of 11%.

Required:

Assume you are a member of the project team and are preparing a briefing paper for the local Regional Board of B regarding the proposed project in which you:

(a)   (i)   Describe two possible reasons, other than the use of an aggressive strategy to manage working capital levels, for the differences in working capital days between those expected for the project and historical data for B.   **(3 marks)**

       (ii)   Discuss the benefits and potential drawbacks of the proposed aggressive strategy for managing working capital for the project.   **(6 marks)**

       (iii)   Calculate the forecast accounts payable and inventory balances for each year of the project.   **(5 marks)**

(b)   (i)   Calculate the forecast project net present value (NPV), in EUR, as at 1 January 2013.   **(14 marks)**

       (ii)   Calculate the change in the project NPV if the value of the properties, excluding fittings, on 31 December 2016 is 20% lower than the original purchase cost of USD 30 million.   **(3 marks)**

(c)   Advise whether or not to proceed with the project, taking into account:

- Your results in (b) (i) and (b) (ii) above.

- The reasonableness of the key input variables used in the NPV appraisal.

- The potential risks to B of establishing a new business in a foreign country.

     (16 marks)

Additional marks available for structure and presentation: **(3 marks)**

(Total: 50 marks)

V (NOV 12 AND MAR 13 EXAMS) – RELATES TO QUESTIONS 5 AND 6

PRE-SEEN CASE MATERIAL

V, a private limited company in a European country (SK), which is outside the Eurozone, was founded in 1972. The currency in SK is SK$. V is a travel business that offers three holiday (vacation) products. It has a network of 50 branches in a number of major cities throughout SK.

History of the company

V achieved steady growth until six years ago, when it found that its market share was eroding due to customers increasingly making online bookings with its competitors. Direct bookings for holidays through the internet have increased dramatically in recent years. Many holidaymakers find the speed and convenience of booking flights, accommodation or complete holidays online outweighs the benefits of discussing holiday alternatives with staff in a branch.

V's board had always taken the view that the friendly direct personal service that V offers through its branch network is a major differentiating factor between itself and other travel businesses and that this is highly valued by its customers. However, V found that in order to continue to compete it needed to establish its own online travel booking service, which it did five years ago. Until this point, V's board had never engaged in long-term planning. It had largely financed growth by reinvestment of funds generated by the business. The large investment in IT and IS five years ago required significant external funding and detailed investment appraisal.

Much of V's business is now transacted online through its website to the extent that 60% of its revenue in the year ended 30 June 2012 was earned through online bookings.

Current structure of V's business

V offers three types of holiday product. These are known within V as Package, Adventure and Prestige Travel. V only sells its own products and does not act as an agent for any other travel companies. It uses the services of other companies engaged in the travel industry such as chartered airlines and hotels which it pays for directly on behalf of its customers.

Package

"Package" provides holidays mainly for families with children aged up to their late teens. These typically are for accommodation in hotels (where meals are part of the package) or self-catering apartments (where no meals are provided within the package).

Adventure

"Adventure" caters for people aged mainly between 20 and 30, who want relatively cheap adventure based holidays such as trekking, sailing and cycling or who wish to go on inexpensive back-packing holidays mainly in Europe and Asia.

Prestige Travel

"Prestige Travel" provides expensive and bespoke holidays mainly sold to couples whose children have grown up and left home. The Prestige Travel product only provides accommodation in upmarket international hotel chains in countries across the world.

All three of these products provide holidays which include flights to and from the holiday destinations and hotel or self-catering accommodation. V has its own customer representatives available at the holiday destinations to provide support to its customers. All-inclusive holidays (in which all food and drinks are provided within the holiday price) are offered within each of the three product offerings.

Support products

V supports its main products by offering travel insurance and foreign currency exchange. The travel insurance, which is provided by a major insurance company and for which V acts as an agent, is usually sold along with the holidays both by branch staff and by staff dealing with online bookings.

Currency exchange is available to anyone through V's branches irrespective of whether or not the customer has bought a holiday product from V. A new currency exchange product is provided by V through which a customer purchases an amount of currency, either in SK's home currency (SK$) or else in a foreign currency and this is credited on to a plastic card. The card is then capable of being read by automated teller machines (ATM's) in many countries across the world allowing the customer to withdraw cash in the local currency up to the amount that has been credited on to the card.

Marketing of products

V relies for the vast majority of its business on the literature, available in hard copy and online, which it provides on the holiday products it sells. Exceptionally, V is able to offer some of its existing holiday products at discount prices. These may be offered under any of the three main products offered but they are mostly cut-price holiday deals which are available under the Package holiday product label.

Sales structure

Staff in each of the 50 branches accept bookings from customers and all branches have direct IT access to head office. Online enquiries and bookings are received and processed centrally at head office, which is located in SK's capital city.

Branch managers have some discretion to offer discounts on holidays to customers. V offers a discount to customers who buy holidays through its online bookings. The branch managers have authority to reduce the price of a holiday booked at the branch up to the amount of the online discount if they feel it is necessary to do so in order to make the sale.

Financial information

V's revenue, split across the holiday and support products offered, for the financial year ended 30 June 2012 is summarised as follows:

	Revenue SK$ million
Package	90
Adventure	60
Prestige Travel	95
Support products	5

The overall net operating profit generated in the financial year to 30 June 2012 was SK$35 million and the profit for the year was SK$24 million, giving a profit to sales ratio of just under 10%. V's cash receipts fluctuate because of seasonal variations and also because V's customers pay for their holidays shortly before they depart.

Further details, including extracts from V's statement of profit or loss for the year ended 30 June 2012 and statement of financial position as at 30 June 2012 are shown in Appendix 1.

Financial objectives

V's key financial objectives are as follows:

1   To grow earnings by, on average, 5% a year.

2   To pay out 80% of profits as dividends.

Foreign exchange risk

V has high exposure to foreign exchange risk as its revenues received and payments made are frequently in different currencies. It normally settles hotel bills and support costs, such as transfers between hotels and airports in the local currencies of the countries where the hotels are located. It normally pays charter airlines in the airline's home currency. Scheduled airline charges are settled in the currency required by the particular airline.

V is exposed to fluctuations in the cost of aircraft fuel incurred by airlines which are passed on to travel businesses. It has often been necessary for V to require its customers to make a supplementary payment to cover the cost of increases in aircraft fuel, sometimes after the customer had thought that the final payment for the holiday had been made.

Board composition and operational responsibilities

The Board of Directors comprises five people: an Executive Chairman (who also fulfils the role of Chief Executive), a Finance Director, an Operations Director, an IT Director and a Human Resources Director. The Executive Chairman founded the business in 1972. He has three grown-up children, two of whom successfully pursue different business interests and are not engaged in V's business at all. The third child, a son, is currently taking a "year out" from study and is going to university next year to study medicine.

The branch managers all report directly to the Operations Director. In addition, the Operations Director is responsible for liaising with airlines and hotels which provide the services offered by V's promotional literature. The IT Director is responsible for V's website and online enquiries and bookings. The Finance Director is responsible for V's financial and management accounting systems and has a small team of accountancy staff, including a part-qualified management accountant, reporting to her. The Human Resources Director has a small team of staff reporting to him.

Shareholding

There are 90 million SK$0.10 (10 cent) shares in issue and the shareholdings are as follows:

	% holding
Executive Chairman	52
Finance Director	12
Operations Director	12
IT Director	12
Human Resources Director	12

Employees

V employs 550 full-time equivalent staff. Turnover of staff is relatively low. High performance rewards in terms of bonuses are paid to staff in each branch if it meets or exceeds its quarterly sales targets. Similarly, staff who deal with online bookings receive a bonus if the online bookings meet or exceed quarterly sales targets. V's staff, both in the branches and those employed in dealing with online bookings, also receive an additional bonus if they are able to sell travel insurance along with a holiday product to customers.

Employee development for staff who are in direct contact with the public is provided through updates on products which V offers. Each member of branch and online booking staff undertakes a two day induction programme at the commencement of their employment with V. The emphasis of the induction programme is on customer service not on details relating to the products as it is expected that new staff will become familiar with such product details as they gain experience within V.

Safety

V publicly states that it takes great care to ensure that its customers are as safe as possible while on holiday. To date, V has found that accidents while on holiday are mainly suffered by very young children, Adventure customers and elderly customers. There has been an increase in instances over the last year where customers in resort hotels have suffered severe stomach complaints. This has particularly been the case in hotels located in resorts in warm climates.

Executive Chairman's statement to the press

V's Executive Chairman was quoted in the national press in SK in January 2012 as saying, "We are maintaining a comparatively high level of revenues and operating profit. This is in a period when our competitors are experiencing very difficult trading conditions. We feel we are achieving this due to our particular attention to customer service. He cited V's 40 years of experience in the travel industry and a previous 99% satisfaction rating from its customers as the reasons for its success. He went on to state that V intends to expand and diversify its holiday product range to provide more choice to customers.

Board meeting

At the next board meeting which took place after the Executive Chairman's statement to the press, the Operations Director expressed some concern. He cast doubt on whether V was able to provide sufficient funding, marketing and IT/IS resources to enable the product expansion to which the Executive Chairman referred. The Operations Director was of the opinion that V places insufficient emphasis on customer relationship marketing. The Finance Director added at the same meeting that while V presently remained profitable overall, some products may be more profitable than others.

The Executive Chairman responded by saying that V's high level of customer service provides a sufficiently strong level of sales without the need to incur any other marketing costs. He added that since V achieved a high profit to sales ratio, which it has managed to maintain for a number of years, it really didn't matter about the profits generated by each customer group.

Retirement of the Executive Chairman

The Executive Chairman formally announced to the Board in July 2012 that he intends to retire on 30 June 2013 and wishes to sell part of his shareholding in the company. The Board members believe the time is now right for V, given its expansion plans, to enter a new stage in its financing arrangements, in the form of either debt or equity from new providers.

APPENDIX 1

Extracts from V's statement of profit or loss and statement of financial position

Statement of profit or loss for the year ended 30 June 2012

	Notes	SK$ million
Revenue		250
Operating costs		(215)
Net operating profit		35
Interest income		3
Finance costs		(4)
Corporate income tax	1	(10)
Profit for the year		24

Statement of financial position as at 30 June 2012

	Notes	SK$ million
Assets		
Non-current assets		123
Current assets		
Inventories		3
Trade and other receivables		70
Cash and cash equivalents		37
Total current assets		110
Total assets		233

Equity and liabilities
Equity

Share capital	2	9
Share premium		6
Retained earnings		60

Total equity   75

Non-current liabilities

Long-term borrowings	3	50
Revenue received in advance		3

Current liabilities

Trade and other payables		35
Revenue received in advance		70

Total liabilities   158

Total equity and liabilities   233

Notes:

1   The corporate income tax rate can be assumed to be 30%.

2   There are 90 million SK$0.10 (10 cent) shares currently in issue.

3   30% of the long-term borrowings are due for repayment on 30 June 2014. The remainder is due for re-payment on 30 June 2020. There are debt covenants in operation currently which restrict V from having a gearing ratio measured by long-term debt divided by long-term debt plus equity of more than 50%.

End of Pre-seen Material

5   V (NOV 12 EXAM)

UNSEEN CASE MATERIAL

Assume today is 22 November 2012.

The Board of Directors of V has recently met to discuss ambitious plans to expand the business and to float the company on the local Stock Exchange by means of an IPO (initial public offering). An IPO would help give V access to large amounts of additional funding, at a time when new bank funding and capital market issues are difficult to achieve due to restricted credit conditions in the financial markets.   In addition, an IPO would give existing shareholders, the current directors, the opportunity to realise part or all of their investment.   With his imminent retirement, the Executive Chairman, in particular, is eager to realise part of his investment. There has been positive feedback following preliminary discussion with market analysts regarding the possibility of an IPO.

Details of the proposed IPO

Certain directors of V wish to sell some of their shares as part of the IPO. In addition, the Board has decided to offer a further 10 million new 10 cent shares in V as part of the IPO.

The number of shares to be sold by each director is as follows:

Executive Chairman	8 million shares
Finance Director	1 million shares
IT Director	3 million shares
Human Resources Director	1 million shares

A total of 23 million shares would therefore be sold under the IPO if the issue is fully subscribed. Further sales of shares by current directors will be permitted after pre-defined time periods. The Operations Director has no plans to dispose of any shares as part of the IPO. It was agreed that, in the event that the IPO is undersubscribed, the sale of shares held by directors would take priority over the issuing of new shares.

Activities in July 2012

An Investment Bank was appointed in July 2012 to help with the IPO process.

The Board of V considered that, based on financial information for V as at 30 June 2012, a reasonable target price per share for the IPO would be SK$ 3.40. It was then agreed that, under the IPO, offers for the purchase of shares should be requested on a tender basis in the guide price range of SK$ 2.90 to SK$ 3.60 per share. Under the tender bid, potential investors are asked to specify the number of shares they wish to purchase and the maximum price that they are prepared to pay for those shares.

Financial information for V

The statement of profit or loss and statement of financial position for V for the last financial year can be found in the pre-seen material.

Additional relevant financial information as at 30 June 2012:

- Net operating profit for V for the year ended 30 June 2012 has been arrived at after charging depreciation of SK$ 3 million.

- Capital expenditure for V in the year ended 30 June 2012 was SK$ 5 million, which is typical of the level of annual capital expenditure needed to maintain operations.

- The market value of V's non-current assets is estimated to be SK$ 150 million.

- V pays corporate income tax of 30% on taxable profits and tax is paid in the year in which the taxable profit arises.

- V is estimated to have an equity beta of 1.9.

- The risk free rate is 2% and the market return is 6% in Country SK, the country in which V is based.

There have not been any recent private transactions in V's shares that could be used as a guide to the value of V. However, a review of the financial statements of competitor companies has shown that industry P/E ratios tend to be between 11 and 14.

The travel business in which V operates is highly cyclical but an underlying trend can be identified by adjusting for the cyclical nature of the business cash flows. Until now, the business has shown consistent but unspectacular nominal growth in after-tax cash flows of approximately 2% per annum after adjusting for cyclical effect. However, it is hoped that expansion plans would result in an increased nominal annual growth rate of 3% in the 2 years to 30 June 2014 and then 5% from 1 July 2014 for the foreseeable future. It is estimated that an upfront investment of SK$ 50 million would be required to finance the expansion plans; this would partly be funded by proceeds from the IPO.

Outcome of the tender offer

An open invitation to submit offers to subscribe for shares in V under a tender bid was published on 1 October 2012 with a deadline for submission of offers by 15 November 2012.

Interim results for the quarter ended 30 September 2012 were published on 20 October 2012 and indicated lower growth than had been forecast in the information published at the launch of the tender offer and resulted in a lower than expected demand for shares.

The tender offers actually received by the deadline date are summarised below:

Maximum price offered (SK$ per share)	Number of shares requested at this price (millions)
2.90	4
3.00	3
3.10	2
3.20	3
3.30	3
3.40	6
3.50	5
3.60	4

In the light of the disappointing response, the following two alternative pricing strategies in respect of the IPO are being considered by the Board of V:

Pricing strategy A:

Set the selling price at the original target price of SK$ 3.40 per share and accept that the offer will then be undersubscribed and a lower value of new finance raised.

Pricing strategy B:

Set the selling price at a level at which the issue is fully subscribed.

Required:

Assume you are the Finance Director of V and have been asked to write a report to the Board of V in which you:

(a) Describe the role of an Investment Bank in an IPO by tender bid. **(4 marks)**

(b) (i) Calculate a range of possible values for the equity of V based on financial information as at 30 June 2012. **(13 marks)**

(ii) Discuss the validity of each method used in (i) above as a basis for valuing the equity of V. **(6 marks)**

(iii) Discuss:

- The nature and extent of V's intangible assets. **(4 marks)**

- The implications of a large value of intangible assets on setting a target offer price. **(2 marks)**

(iv) Advise whether the target share price of SK$ 3.40 was set at an appropriate level based on financial information as at 30 June 2012. **(6 marks)**

(c) Evaluate the implications of each of the pricing strategies A and B, based on the offers for shares received by 15 November 2012, on:

- The directors of V.

- The new shareholders of V.

Up to 7 marks are available for relevant calculations. **(12 marks)**

Additional marks available for structure and presentation: **(3 marks)**

(Total: 50 marks)

6 V (MAR 13 EXAM)

UNSEEN CASE MATERIAL

Today is 1 March 2013.

The directors of V have recently met to discuss the best way forward in response to the Executive Chairman's announcement of his retirement plans. In particular they are discussing the need to enable him to realise at least part of his investment in the company either immediately or in a few years' time.

Recent results have been disappointing due partly to weak economic conditions, but also because of V's poor competitive position.

As a result, this is not considered to be a good time at which to sell the company or float it on the Stock Exchange. Even if an interested party could be found, it is estimated that the equity would only be worth approximately SK$180 million (that is, SK$ 2.00 per ordinary share) at the present time which is considered to understate the true value of the company.

The poor competitive position is due to a marked decline in the popularity of the types of holiday that V offers. The directors therefore believe that it is important for V to invest in new holiday products in order to attract new customers and improve its market position. They are particularly interested in expanding into building and operating 'holiday villages', comprising a central hotel plus individual holiday chalets in a campus containing a wide range of sporting and other leisure facilities and activity programmes for children. This appears to be a rapidly expanding holiday sector and could help support future growth.

The directors of V are considering working towards an Initial Public Offering (IPO) in 5 years and accepting finance from a venture capitalist in order to support growth in the intervening period.

This would involve a two-stage plan, outlined below:

Stage 1: *Invite X, a venture capitalist, to invest in the company and collaborate to develop the business, including building three holiday villages.*

Stage 2: *Float the company on an SK Stock Exchange via an IPO.*

X would be asked to contribute SK$ 50 million on 1 July 2013 for use in building three holiday villages.

The Finance Director believes that the most suitable form of funding from X would be a convertible bond with the following terms:

- Issued at par and non-tradable.

- Annual coupon of 2%.

- Option for X to convert to 55 ordinary 10 cent shares in V per SK$ 100 nominal at the time of the IPO.

- If not converted before, the bond would be repayable in full at face value on 30 June 2020.

Director A has expressed surprise that a bond is likely to carry such a low coupon, when V could only borrow at a pre-tax rate of 5% at the present time and the directors estimate V's cost of equity to be 9.5%.

X is likely to expect V to float on an SK stock exchange via an IPO within five years, by 30 June 2018 at the latest. The target price for an IPO on 30 June 2018 is SK$ 4.00 per ordinary 10 cent share in V. This target price is considered to be achievable if the business plans are successfully implemented. At the very least, the directors are confident of raising SK$ 3.00 per share in an IPO.

Financial data for V

The statement of profit or loss for the year ended 30 June 2012 and the statement of financial position as at 30 June 2012 for V can be found in the pre-seen material. The financial objectives of V can be found in the pre-seen material.

Required:

Assume you are the Finance Director of V and have been asked to write a report for the main Board of V in which you:

(a) (i) **Calculate, at future IPO prices of BOTH SK$ 3.00 and SK$ 4.00 per share:**

- **The conversion premium for the convertible bond.**

- **The gross yield to maturity for the convertible bond up to and including conversion.**   **(9 marks)**

(ii) **Explain the benefits and drawbacks to V of accepting funding from a venture capitalist in the form of a convertible bond. In your answer, include reference to Director A's comments.**   **(6 marks)**

(b) **Advise on the likely effect on V's financial objectives of:**

- **Accepting the involvement of X (a venture capitalist) in the business.**

- **Becoming a public listed company in 5 years' time.**   **(11 marks)**

(c)   **Evaluate the proposed plan to involve X in the business, ultimately leading to an IPO, from the viewpoint of:**

- **V's Directors.**

- **X.**

- **V's other stakeholders.**

    Up to 9 marks are available for calculations.   **(15 marks)**

(d)   **Advise on two possible alternative exit strategies, not involving a venture capitalist, which would enable the Executive Chairman to achieve a disposal of shares at or soon after his retirement.**   **(6 marks)**

Additional marks available for structure and presentation: **(3 marks)**

                    (Total: 50 marks)

T RAILWAYS (MAY 13 AND SEPT 13 EXAMS) – RELATES TO QUESTIONS 7 AND 8

PRE-SEEN CASE MATERIAL

Background

Country T is a small landlocked European country which is outside the eurozone. Its currency is T$ which currently exchanges at GBP/T$ 1.5000 and EUR/T$ 1.2500, (that is, GBP 1 = T$ 1.5000 and EUR 1 = T$ 1.2500).

Unlike many other countries, Country T has a nationalised railway system known as T Railways. Before the system was nationalised two separate companies operated the railways.

The growth of road haulage transport and the increasing number of passengers wanting to travel by rail meant that by 1970 fare paying passengers replaced freight transport as the railway companies' main source of income. In 1975 Country T's Government took the view that the two railway companies were not operating in the public interest and they were nationalised; that is taken into public ownership. The Government bought out the two railway companies and established T Railways.

As the transport infrastructure developed, diesel trains gradually replaced steam trains and electric powered trains are now replacing the diesel trains as T Railways carries out electrification of its network.

In 1975, the Board of T Railways formed wholly owned subsidiaries which operated at arm's length from the Board. For example, it formed T Railways Engineering which was responsible for all the engineering works on the T Railways network. The T Railways Board retained a number of functions itself such as responsibility for the T Railways Transport Police Service and T Railways Property. However, this led to much duplication of resources and so in 1998 T Railways adopted a new management structure with T Railways as the holding company for three subsidiary companies as follows:

- T City-Link (TCL) to run passenger rail services.

- T Freight Railways (TFR) to run freight services.

- T Property and Track Services (TPTS) to manage the track, property, transport police and related services.

This structure still exists today with T Railways' corporate governance undertaken by the T Railways Board.

The activities of T Railways

Further details on the activities of each of the three subsidiary companies owned by T Railways is provided below.

TCL:

TCL is responsible for all passenger rail services within Country T and operates on average 1,800 passenger train services per day between Monday and Saturday with fewer services on Sundays. The services offered are between all towns and cities within Country T which are connected to the railway network. In addition, some of TCL's services cross national borders enabling travel from Country T to other countries, some of which are in the eurozone. It also provides some services to remote country locations which originally were not accessible by road. Recent improvements in the road network have resulted in some of these country lines being discontinued by T Railways as demand for the railway service has diminished. Most of TCL's locomotives are now electric as the lines between the major cities within Country T have already been electrified.

TFR:

TFR is solely concerned with railway haulage of freight. In this context, freight is defined as goods transported in bulk, for example, coal, petroleum, industrial products such as steel and concrete, cars and, increasingly, retail goods for supermarkets and large retail shops. TFR does not offer any passenger services. It hauls freight right across the network within Country T and across national borders into other countries, some of which are situated within the eurozone.

Most of TFR's trains are old diesel locomotives but it has recently invested in a number of electric trains which are less harmful to the environment. On average, TFR operates 600 freight services per day, including weekends but excluding national public holidays. In the year ended 31 December 2012, TFR provided 40% of T Railways' total revenue and its share of the freight haulage market in Country T was approximately 10%. Freight carried by road accounts for approximately 80% of the total freight haulage market in Country T. In the last 15 years, total freight carried by rail has increased by about 25% due to increased congestion on T's roads. T's Government considers that road congestion has had a major adverse impact upon the country's productivity.

TPTS:

TPTS replaced T Railways Property and has responsibility for all other services including maintenance and upgrade of track and all of T Railways' property. It operates 200 railway stations, rents space out within the stations for retail purposes as well as running some of its own cafes. TPTS also operates 11 maintenance depots.

T Railways' organisational structure

A strong bureaucratic culture has developed over time within T Railways. The T Railways Board uses a classical rational planning system in which strategic planning decisions are made in a regularised and formal way.

The Chairman of the T Railways Board reports to senior civil servants in T Government's Ministry of Transport. Ownership of T Railways rests entirely with the Government. There is a formal annual meeting with senior Government officials at which the financial statements of T Railways are approved. There are also occasional meetings between members of T Railways Board and Government officials, particularly when Country T's Minister of Transport needs to present information on railway transport to Country T's parliament.

Rail regulator

Country T now has a rail regulatory organisation whose senior staff are appointed by the Government. The Rail Regulator is empowered to make recommendations directly to the Minister of Transport in respect of all issues relating to the operation of T Railways.

The role of the Rail Regulator is to ensure that the railway service is delivered in Country T in a safe and efficient manner. It aims to help the T Railways Board meet future challenges in the provision of an efficient railway service which provides high levels of satisfaction to all rail users and the improvement of safety for staff and passengers. In essence, the Rail Regulator provides an independent review of T Railways' activities. Mindful of the need to show that T Railways fully recognises the role of the Rail Regulator, the Chairman of the T Railways Board recently said that:

"T Railways is committed to providing an excellent service to its customers and work is ongoing to improve our time keeping. Investment in improving railway stations is continuing and accessibility to railway services is increasing with new car parks being built at many stations in the network. Other service amenities are being improved such as better access ramps for disabled customers and the levelling of the height of platforms at many stations so that customers can access and alight from trains without having to a take a large step up or down to the platform. This will reduce the incidence of accidents which occur at stations where the platform infrastructure was developed for a bygone era of railway carriages."

Monitoring the levels of carbon dioxide emissions from rail transport is also an important area of work for the Rail Regulator. (See the section headed "Environmental considerations".)

T Railways' strategic objectives

T Railways' overall strategic goal is to deliver efficient, cost effective, safe and reliable rail services to help facilitate the Government's vision of sustained economic growth and the reduction of carbon emissions in the country as a whole. The T Railways Board has set two strategic objectives, following consultation with its stakeholder groups which are:

(i)   To deliver reliable, safe and punctual rail services to customers efficiently and cost effectively thereby helping to achieve economic growth in Country T by reducing congestion on its roads

(ii)   To continually reduce its level of carbon emissions to help provide an environmentally friendly transport infrastructure.

Financial objectives for T Railways

The Government's aim and the T Railways Board's main financial objectives are that:

(i)   T Railways should at least cover its operating costs from the revenue it earns

(ii)   T Railways should provide value for money.

Financial data for T Railways

The Government requires T Railways to prepare its accounts according to internationally recognised accounting principles so that it can show how it is performing in a commercial environment. The policy of the T Railways Board is not to re-value its non-current assets. Extracts from the latest set of financial statements according to internationally recognised accounting principles are shown in Appendix 1.

The revenue earned and operating costs of the three subsidiaries for the year ended 31 December 2012 are shown below:

	Revenue	*Operating costs*
	T$ million	T$ million
TCL	680	630
TFR	516	494
TPTS	95	80

Notes:

(i)   The total head office operating costs of the T Railways Board are allocated and apportioned to the three subsidiaries.

(ii)   The total operating costs of TPTS was T$842 million in 2012 after the allocation and apportionment of head office operating costs referred to in note (i). All of these costs except for the T$80 million which relate to the revenue earning activities of TPTS, were allocated and apportioned to the other two subsidiaries.

Financing T Railways

The Government of Country T invested T$100 million when it formed T Railways in 1975. This is the only "share" capital that has ever been invested in T Railways. The financing model which has developed is that T Railways costs are guaranteed. This means that any overall operating deficit T Railways incurs on an annual basis is recovered by the T Railways Board through additional Government revenue funding.

Recognising that T Railways would need large amounts of funding to upgrade its infrastructure, the Government initially provided loans to cover capital expenditure. The loan facility was established to emphasise that any Government funding is a liability of T Railways and that T Railways must pay interest on the loan. The intention is that T Railways will also pay back the full amount of the Government loans in due course. The Government loans have no fixed repayment dates and are made to T Railways at a fixed rate of interest of 4% per year. This was the only source of capital funding for T Railways at its formation. However, following Government approval, the T Railways Board is now seeking to widen its sources of finance by, for example, obtaining loans from the banking and commercial sectors.

Key Performance Indicators (KPIs)

In order to plan their activities to meet T Railways' strategic objectives, its three subsidiaries operate a traditional accounting-led approach to strategic planning and management. All of the strategic planning and management activities of the three subsidiary companies are based upon meeting T Railways' strategic objectives. A number of Key Performance Indicators have emerged to evaluate T Railways' overall performance in achieving its strategic objectives.

Examples of KPIs relating to TCL:

•   The results of the national customer survey of all forms of public transport in Country T.

•   The number of customer complaints received. These are reported on T Railways' website every three months for the previous quarter.

Examples of KPIs relating to TFR:

•   Train capacity utilisation, which measures the actual train load capacity utilised per journey against the total available load capacity for that journey.

- The number of trains arriving at their destination on time, measured as a percentage of total journeys made.

- Carbon emissions generated. The analysis of carbon emissions in freight transport is expressed in carbon dioxide emissions as a ratio of tonne per kilometre. That is, kilograms of carbon dioxide divided by weight transported multiplied by the distance travelled.

Examples of KPIs relating to TPTS:

- Number of delays per month to services due to signalling failure.

- Number of complaints per month relating to station cleanliness.

There are also KPIs relating to safety issues which are shown below under the heading of Health and Safety.

Health and safety

T Railways concentrates a great deal of effort on the management of particular risks such as Signals Passed at Danger (SPAD) and customer and staff injuries. T Railways has a Safety Committee which meets regularly and monitors performance against its annual safety targets which have been agreed with the Ministry of Transport. Examples of the KPIs specifically relating to safety which are used by T Railways are:

- The number of customer movement accidents per million passenger kilometres, for example accidents caused due to the motion of trains.

- The number of customer non-movement accidents per million passenger journeys, for example slips and falls while on T Railways' property.

- The number of accidents or injuries sustained by staff per million kilometres travelled.

The KPIs relating to safety issues are reported in T Railways' annual report which accompanies its financial statements.

Environmental considerations

The transport industry's carbon emissions are responsible for between 20% and 25% of all carbon emissions in Country T. In response to initiatives developed by the Rail Regulator, T Railways is increasing its efforts to reduce its levels of carbon emissions. T Railways is committed to reducing its carbon emissions by a third between now and 2015. In addition, all TCL and TFR drivers receive eco-driving training on an ongoing basis. (Eco-driving is driving in a manner that minimises fuel consumption.) TPTS is progressing work on making stations and depots energy efficient by improving lighting and heating systems including the use of intelligent lighting which automatically increases or decreases light output depending on the amount of natural light feeding into the sensors.

All three subsidiaries are keen to reduce waste and to increase the amount of waste they recycle. Each subsidiary is committed to helping to meet an overall target set by the T Railways Board of recycling 85% of T Railways' total waste by 2015.

Development of T Railways

The T Railways Board is constantly seeking ways of generating additional sources of revenue. Consideration is being given to a number of possible initiatives. Some ideas under consideration include:

- structural changes such as splitting T Railways up into its constituent parts and running the three subsidiaries as completely separate entities

- expansion of the network

- diversifying the portfolio through operating other forms of transport

- outsourcing some or all of the current provision of passenger, freight, track, property or retail related services or privatising parts of the business.

The Government has considered privatising the whole of T Railways but so far has been wary of the British experience where ownership and operation of the rail network became very fragmented after privatisation and operations were split across more than 100 companies. However, possible privatisation of T Railways continues to be discussed within Government and Country T's Prime Minister has never ruled it out.

APPENDIX 1

Extracts from T Railways' statement of profit or loss and statement of financial position

Statement of profit or loss for the year ended 31 December 2012

	Notes	T$ million
Revenue		1,291
Operating costs		(1,204)
Net operating profit		87
Finance costs		(72)
Profit before tax		15
Tax	1	(5)
Profit for the year	2	10

Statement of financial position as at 31 December 2012

	Notes	T$ million
Assets		
Non-current assets	3	2,763
Current assets		
Inventories		12
Trade and other receivables		96
Cash and cash equivalents		202
Total current assets		310
Total assets		3,073

Equity and liabilities

Equity

Share capital from Country T's Government	4	100
Retained earnings		900

Total equity		**1,000**

Non-current liabilities

Long-term borrowings from Government	5	1,800

Current liabilities

Trade and other payables		273

Total liabilities		**2,073**

Total equity and liabilities		**3,073**

Notes:

1   The corporate income tax rate is 30%.

2   The agreement with the Government in Country T is that any losses after tax are charged back to the Government.

3   The non-current assets have not been re-valued.

4   The Government's initial investment in T Railways was T$100 million. Subsequent investment by the Government has been in the form of long-terms loans.

5   The long-term Government borrowings are undated.

End of Pre-seen Material

7   T RAILWAYS (MAY 13 EXAM)

UNSEEN CASE MATERIAL

T Railways, via its division TPTS, operates cafes in approximately 50% of its 200 stations. The cafes sell hot and cold drinks and light refreshments to take away or consume on the premises.

The Board of T Railways is keen to outsource the operation of some or all of the cafes since they have never made large profits. Indeed, some of the cafes in smaller stations have been making losses after having been allocated a share of the station overheads.

The Board has been approached by Mr C who is interested in operating the station cafes in five railway stations (which are situated within a 20 mile radius of each other) within a newly formed company, CCC. CCC would pay rent in return for the use of the premises and permission to take over the cafe business and all associated revenues and costs. T Railways estimates that the rent received from CCC when operating these five station cafes would be greater than the head office overheads that are currently reallocated to those cafes.

The cafe project

The contract to operate the five cafes would be for an initial period of three years starting on 1 January 2014. There would also be an option for CCC to extend its services to twenty additional railway stations at the end of the third year and the remainder by the end of 2023, if the project proves to be successful in the first five locations. However, the option to extend the contract to additional stations is subject to high customer satisfaction scores in relation to quality of food and drink, standard of décor and level of service provided.

Investment appraisal

Mr C has drawn up the following estimates to forecast operating cash inflows for a single cafe in the first three years of the project:

Year to 31 December	2014	2015	2016
Number of passengers per station per day	3,600	3,700	3,800
Proportion of passengers using the cafe	9%	12%	15%
Average spend per customer	T$ 3.0	T$ 3.4	T$ 3.6

The railway operates 360 days a year.

Additional information collated by Mr C:

- Operating cash outflows can be divided into:

    – Variable costs per cafe, estimated to be 70% of cash inflows.

    – Fixed costs per cafe, including rent and advertising costs, are forecast to be, on average, T$ 90,000 in 2014 and then increase by 7% a year thereafter.

- Staff costs have been included in operating cash outflows but no provision has been made to pay Mr C a salary as he only intends to claim a nominal salary, allowing profits to be retained in the business or paid out as dividends. Due to the amount of time that Mr C will need to spend running the station cafes, he would not also have time to run his existing cafe business and so would need to employ a manager to run these for him at a salary of T$ 50,000 a year in 2014, increasing by 7% a year thereafter.

- An investment of T$ 200,000 per cafe in fixtures and fittings is required on 1 January 2014, with an estimated residual value of T$ 100,000 per cafe on 31 December 2016.

- Tax depreciation allowances are available on the investment in fixtures and fittings at a rate of 25% per annum on a reducing balance basis.

- Corporate income tax is charged at 30% on taxable profits and, in Country T, is paid at the end of the year in which the taxable profit arises.

- All revenues and costs should be assumed to be cash flows and arise at the end of the year unless otherwise stated.

- The risk free rate is 3% and the premium on market return is 5%.

- A national chain of cafes that is 100% equity financed has a published equity beta of 1.28. Mr C intends to use this information to calculate a cost of equity for CCC.

Financing the project

Mr C is planning to finance the project partly from savings and partly from a fixed term bank loan, at an annual rate of interest of 5.7%, with a debt beta of 0.54. Half of the financing is to be provided in cash and half from a bank loan. One of the next stages of the process is for Mr C to make a formal request to his usual bank for funding for CCC. If the bank is not willing to provide funding, Mr C has sufficient personal resources to be able to finance the initial stage, that is, the investment in the first five cafes.

T Railways

Extracts from T Railways' statement of profit or loss and statement of financial position are found in the pre-seen material. T Railways' strategic and financial objectives are given in the pre-seen material.

Required:

(a)   Advise T Railways of:

- The ways in which the financial objectives of a private enterprise such as CCC are likely to differ from those of T Railways.

- The potential benefits and risks for T Railways of allowing CCC to operate the station cafes. **(9 marks)**

(b)   Assume you are a management consultant reporting to Mr C. Write a report in which you:

(i)   Calculate the following measures in respect of the proposed investment by CCC in five cafes for the initial three year contract as at 1 January 2014:

- Net Present Value (NPV)

- Internal Rate of Return (IRR)

- Payback

Your answer to this section should assume that bank finance is available and should ignore real options. **(19 marks)**

(ii)   Evaluate the potential financial benefit of the project to Mr C. Your answer should consider your results in (b)(i), real options and other relevant factors. **(12 marks)**

(iii)   Advise Mr C on the challenges that CCC might face in obtaining a bank loan to finance the project. **(7 marks)**

Additional marks available for structure and presentation: **(3 marks)**

(Total: 50 marks)

8   T RAILWAYS (SEPT 13 EXAM)

UNSEEN CASE MATERIAL

The Government of Country T has been coming under increasing pressure to reduce Government borrowing. All businesses owned by T Government have been reviewed to identify which could be privatised, either in part or in whole to raise funds. The sales proceeds would be used to reduce T Government's borrowing.

As a result of this review, TPTS was identified as a possible candidate for privatisation. TPTS is a wholly owned subsidiary of T Railways and manages T Railways' track, railway property, transport police and related services.   T Railways would use the sale proceeds to repay funds borrowed from T Government.

The most likely scenario is that TPTS would be sold to company UT, a listed utility company involved in electricity generation and distribution. An initial public offering (IPO) was considered previously but that idea was dismissed in favour of selling TPTS to UT.

If TPTS were to be sold to UT, T Railways would need to pay UT for use of the track, railway property and transport police to enable it to continue running its passenger and freight rail services. Formal service agreements would need to be drawn up and agreed between UT and T Railways. The Rail Regulator would be heavily involved in these negotiations in order to help ensure minimum standards of maintenance and policing and that a fair price is agreed which is sufficient to cover UT's costs in providing such facilities and services.

Financial data for TPTS assuming TPTS remains under T Railways' ownership

Forecast operating cash flows for TPTS for the year ending 31 December 2014:

Table 1: TPTS owned by T Railways	Notes	Track T$ million	Cafes T$ million	Stations T$ million	Total T$ million
Operating cash inflows					
External	1		38	62	100
Internal (from TCL and TFR)	2	783			783
Operating cash outflows					
Costs incurred directly by TPTS		718	30	47	795
Head office costs allocated to TPTS		65	2	4	71
		783	32	51	866
Net operating cash flow	3	0	6	11	17

Notes to Table 1:

Note 1:   Revenue from stations relates to rental income from retail outlets located in stations.

Note 2:   TPTS recharges the full cost of maintaining the track to TCL and TFR without any margin or mark-up.

Note 3:   Net operating cash flow is forecast to grow by 2% a year in perpetuity. Net operating cash flow is subject to corporate income tax at 30%, payable in the year in which it is incurred.

All operating cash flows can be assumed to arise at the end of the year.

Financial data for TPTS assuming it is sold to UT

From the viewpoint of T Railways:

It is estimated that T Railways would pay UT an amount of the order of T$ 800 million in the year ending 31 December 2014 for the use of the track, railway property and transport police in that year. This is expected to increase steadily at an estimated rate of 2% a year thereafter.

In addition, T Railways would no longer benefit from the net operating cash flows generated by the cafes or stations.

T Railways' head office costs that are currently allocated to TPTS would need to be re-allocated to TCL and TFR, increasing the level of head office costs that these two subsidiaries incur. However, the directors of T Railways estimate that total head office costs could be reduced by approximately T$ 25 million a year as a result of the disposal of TPTS.

In assessing the financial impact of the sale of TPTS, the directors of T Railways have decided to apply a cost of capital of 4% to discount the post-tax cash flow impact. This is the hurdle rate set by T Government for use by Government departments and businesses owned by T Government when evaluating investments. It approximates to T Government's cost of borrowing.

From the viewpoint of UT:

Forecast operating cash flows for TPTS for the year ending 31 December 2014 prepared by UT assuming that UT acquires TPTS on 1 January 2014:

Table 2: TPTS owned by UT	Notes	Track	Cafes	Stations	Total
		T$ million	T$ million	T$ million	T$ million
Cash inflows – revenue	1	800	51	73	924
Operating cash outflows		745	32	51	828
Net operating cash flow	2	55	19	22	96

Notes to Table 2:

Note 1: The revenue figure for track is the fee payable to UT by T Railways annually for use of track, railway property and transport police, starting at T$ 800 million in the first year. Revenue from stations relates to rental income from retail outlets located in stations.

Note 2: Net operating cash flow is expected to grow by 2% a year in perpetuity. Net operating cash flow is subject to corporate income tax at 30%, payable in the year in which it is incurred.

All operating cash flows can be assumed to arise at the end of the year.

On 31 December 2013, TPTS is forecast to have property and track at a book value (based on historical cost) of T$ 1,500 million and a replacement cost of T$ 1,990 million. Working capital is forecast to be T$ 2 million.

UT considers 8% to be an appropriate post tax cost of capital to use in discounted cash flow analysis.

Required:

(a)   Compare and contrast the following approaches to the privatisation of TPTS:

- Sell TPTS to utility company UT (an electricity generation and distribution company).

- Sell TPTS to the public via an IPO.   (5 marks)

(b)   From the viewpoint of T Railways:

(i)   Prepare a schedule showing the likely impact of the sale of TPTS on T Railways' post-tax, pre-financing cash flows for the year ending 31 December 2014.   (5 marks)

(ii)   Calculate the value of TPTS to T Railways as at 1 January 2014 based on the present value of the impact of the sale of TPTS on T Railways' post-tax, pre-financing cash flows.   (3 marks)

(iii) Discuss whether 4% is an appropriate discount rate for T Railways to use to value TPTS.   (6 marks)

(c)   From the viewpoint of UT:

(i)   Calculate values for TPTS as at 1 January 2014 using both discounted cash flow analysis and asset bases.   (7 marks)

(ii)   Advise on the validity of the methods and results obtained in (c)(i) for use by UT to set an offer price for TPTS.   (7 marks)

(d)   (i)   Advise on the maximum price that UT is likely to offer for TPTS AND whether this would be acceptable to T Railways.   (4 marks)

(ii)   Recommend whether or not T Railways should proceed with the sale of TPTS, taking both the financial and strategic implications of privatisation into account.   (10 marks)

Additional marks available for structure and presentation: (3 marks)

A report format is not required for this question.

(Total: 50 marks)

SECTION B-TYPE QUESTIONS

FORMULATION OF FINANCIAL STRATEGY

9   CCC (NOV 06 EXAM)

(a)   CCC is a local government entity. It is financed almost equally by a combination of central government funding and local taxation. The funding from central government is determined largely on a per capita (per head of population) basis, adjusted to reflect the scale of deprivation (or special needs) deemed to exist in CCC's region. A small percentage of its finance comes from the private sector, for example from renting out City Hall for private functions.

CCC's main objectives are:

- to make the region economically prosperous and an attractive place in which to live and work

- to provide service excellence in health and education for the local community.

DDD is a large listed entity with widespread commercial and geographical interests. For historic reasons, its headquarters are in CCC's region. This is something of an anomaly as most entities of DDD's size would have their HQ in a capital city, or at least a city much larger than where it is.

DDD has one financial objective: To increase shareholder wealth by an average 10% per annum. It also has a series of non-financial objectives that deal with how the entity treats other stakeholders, including the local communities where it operates.

DDD has total net assets of $1.5 billion and a gearing ratio of 45% (debt to debt plus equity), which is typical for its industry. It is currently considering raising a substantial amount of capital to finance an acquisition.

Required:

Discuss the criteria that the two very different entities described above have to consider when setting objectives, recognising the needs of each of their main stakeholder groups. Make some reference in your answer to the consequences of each of them failing to meet its declared objectives.   **(13 marks)**

(b)   MS is a private entity in a computer-related industry. It has been trading for six years and is managed by its main shareholders, the original founders of the entity. Most of the employees are also shareholders, having been given shares as bonuses. None of the shareholders has attempted to sell shares in the entity so the problem of placing a value on them has not arisen. Dividends have been paid every year at the rate of 60 cents per share, irrespective of profits. So far, profits have always been sufficient to cover the dividend at least once but never more than twice.

MS is all-equity financed at present although $15 million new finance is likely to be required in the near future to finance expansion. Total net assets as at the last balance sheet date were $45 million.

Required:

Discuss and compare the relationship between dividend policy, investment policy and financing policy in the context of the small entity described above, MS, and DDD, the large listed entity described in part (a).   **(12 marks)**

(Total: 25 marks)

10   STR (MAY 07 EXAM)

STR is a well-established marketing consultancy in a country with a low interest rate. STR is a successful business which has experienced rapid growth in recent years. There are 20 million $1 ordinary shares in issue. These ordinary shares are quoted on a recognised stock exchange and 40% are owned by the founders of the business. Dividends were 40 cents per share in 20X3 and grew by 5% per annum between 20X3 and 20X6. This pattern is expected to continue beyond 20X6. Dividends are paid in the year in which they are declared.

Extracts from the financial statements for the past three years are as follows:

	20X4	20X5	20X6
	$million	$million	$million
Profit before tax	21.6	24.4	26.7
Tax expense	7.7	2.6	4.3
Net cash generated after deducting interest, tax and net capital expenditure, but excluding ordinary dividends	19.2	(7.1)	18.8

Additional information:

*   The opening cash balance in 20X4 for cash and cash equivalents was $6 million

*   The opening book value of equity in 20X4 was $60 million

*   Long-term borrowings remained at $50 million throughout the three years and the annual gross interest cost on the borrowings was $1 million

*   There were a number of disposals of non-current assets in 20X4 and an exceptionally high level of capital expenditure in 20X5.

The directors have noticed the build-up of cash and cash equivalents. They are concerned that this might not be in the best interest of the shareholders and could have an adverse effect on the share price. Various proposals have been made to reduce the level of cash and cash equivalents.

Required:

(a) Calculate the following financial information for STR for each of the years 20X4 to 20X6:

  - Closing cash balance

  - Closing book value of equity.   **(3 marks)**

(b) Analyse and discuss the financial performance of the entity from the viewpoint of both the lenders and shareholders, referring to the information calculated in part (a) above and making appropriate additional calculations. Up to 6 marks are available for calculations.   **(10 marks)**

(c) (i) Discuss the comparative advantages and disadvantages of a share repurchase versus a one-off dividend payment.   **(7 marks)**

  (ii) Advise the directors of STR on alternative financial strategies that they could consider that would reduce the level of surplus cash.   **(5 marks)**

(Total: 25 marks)

11   ABC (NOV 07 EXAM)

ABC is an entity based in the UK with diverse international interests. Its shares and bonds are quoted on a major international stock exchange.

ABC is evaluating the potential for investment in the production and distribution of films, an area in which it has not previously been involved. This investment will require £600 million to purchase premises, equipment and provide working capital. An alternative approach would be to acquire a small entity in this field, but a preliminary search has revealed none suitable.

Extracts from the most recent (20X2) statement of financial position (balance sheet) of ABC are shown below:

	£ million
Assets	
Non-current assets	1,920
Current assets	1,880
	———
	3,800
	———
Equity and liabilities	
Equity	
Share capital (Shares of £1)	300
Retained earnings	1,000
	———
	1,300
Non current liabilities	
8.4% Secured bond repayable 20X7	1,100
Current liabilities	1,400
	———
	3,800
	———
Current share price (pence)	800
Bond price (£100)	105
Equity beta	1.2

ABC proposes to finance the £600 million investment with a combination of debt and equity as follows:

- £260 million in debt paying interest at 8% per annum, secured on the new premises and repayable in 20X9

- £340 million in equity via a rights issue. A discount of 15% on the current share price is likely.

A marginally positive NPV of the proposed investment has been calculated using a discount rate of 15%. This is the entity's cost of equity plus a small 'premium', a rate judged to reflect the risk of this venture. The Chief Executive of ABC thinks this is too marginal and is doubtful whether the investment should go ahead. However, there is some disagreement among the Directors about how this project was evaluated, in particular about the discount rate that has been used.

Director A: Suggests the entity's current WACC is more appropriate.

Director B: Suggests calculating a discount rate using data from XYZ, a quoted entity, the main business of which is film production. Relevant data for this entity is as follows:

- Shares in issue: 400 million currently quoted at 373 pence each

- Debt outstanding: £350 million variable rate bank loan

- Equity beta: 1.6.

Other relevant information

- The risk-free rate is estimated at 5% per annum and the return on the market 12% per annum. These rates are not expected to change in the foreseeable future.

- ABC pays corporate tax at 30% and this rate is not expected to change in the foreseeable future.

- Assume both ABC's and XYZ's debt has a beta of zero.

- Issue costs should be ignored.

You are a financial advisor working for ABC's bankers.

Required:

(a)   Discuss the appropriateness of the two Directors' suggestions about the discount rate when evaluating the proposed investment and recommend an appropriate rate to use. You should support your discussion and recommendation with calculations of two separate discount rates – one for each Director's suggestion. Show all your workings.   **(18 marks)**

Calculations count for up to 12 marks.

(b)   Discuss how ABC's market capitalisation might change during the week the proposed investment becomes public knowledge. No calculations are required for this part of the question.   **(7 marks)**

A report format is not required for this question.

(Total: 25 marks)

12   CRM (MAY 09 EXAM) *Walk in the footsteps of a top tutor*

CRM is a UK-based manufacturer of electronic components. Its shares are listed on the UK's Alternative Investment Market. The founder-directors of the entity still own the majority of shares. A combination of private and institutional investors own the remainder of the shares.

CRM has one wholly-owned subsidiary based in Asia. CRM has three on-going financial objectives, which are:

- Provide a total return to shareholders of at least 15% per annum
- Provide a dividend yield comparable with the industry average
- Generate a return on net assets of 30% per annum.

In addition, it has two specific financial objectives for the year to 31 March 20X9. Based on figures for the year to 31 March 20X8 these are:

- Increase revenue by 15%
- Increase earnings per share by 10%.

It has a further financial objective to double revenue in sterling terms in its Asian subsidiary within the three years to 31 March 20Y2.

Extracts from the entity's financial statements for the past two years are shown below. The group figures include those for the subsidiary. Figures are for a full 12 month period ending on 31 March.

Statement of profit or loss

	Group		Asian Sub.	
	20X8	*20X9*	*20X8*	*20X9*
	£ million	£ million	A$ million	A$ million
Revenue	325	355	295	365
Cost of sales	145	156	135	165
Administrative costs	75	82	80	90
Profit before interest and tax	105	117	80	110
Interest payable	9	9	11	11
Taxation payable	27	31	17	20
Earnings	69	77	52	79
Dividends	21	24	0	0

Statement of financial position (balance sheet)

	Group		Asian Sub.	
	20X8	*20X9*	*20X8*	*20X9*
	£ million	£ million	A$ million	A$ million
Assets				
Non-current assets	174	190	137	157
Current assets	167	191	105	121
	341	381	242	278
Equity and liabilities				
Total equity	157	210	85	164
Non-current liabilities				
Secured 9% bond 20Y5	100	100	–	–
Long-term loan from parent	–	–	92	92
Current liabilities	84	71	65	22
	341	381	242	278
Number of shares in issue (million)	125	125	100	100

CRM's share price as at:

31 March 20X8	641.0 pence
31 March 20X9	721.8 pence

The entity's equity beta is not available, but for a similar entity quoted on the main stock exchange it was 1.4 for the whole two year period and is not expected to change. The expected risk free rate is 4% and the return on the AIM is 12%. All figures are post-tax.

Selected industry data:

As at 31 March:	*20X8*	*20X9*
Dividend yield:	2.8%	3.0%
P/E ratio	8.2	9.0
Gearing (Book values of long term debt to total long terms funds)	44%	46%
FTSE AIM all share index	849	925

Average exchange rates	*Exchange rate* Asian $ to £
12 months to 31 March 20X8	6.3
12 months to 31 March 20X9	6.5

Inflation is forecast to average 5.5% per annum in the Asian country and 3.5% per annum in the UK for the foreseeable future.

—

Required:

Assume you are a newly-recruited financial manager with CRM. You have been asked to prepare a report for discussion at the next Board of Directors meeting that analyses the entity's financial performance over the two year period to assess whether it has attained its financial objectives as stated.

Your report should also provide:

- **Recommendations for corrective action by the entity if necessary**

- **Advice about the appropriateness of the stated objectives.**

You should carefully select and calculate appropriate ratios and performance measures for your analysis. Calculations should be shown in an appendix using sensible roundings.

(Calculations account for up to 15 marks)

(Total: 25 marks)

13   HJK (MAY 11 EXAM)

HJK is a long established, family owned and run, IT consultancy company. The company has experienced rapid growth in recent years.

Recent financial history for HJK:

Year ending 31 December	Profit for the year after interest and tax	Investment in projects or capital expenditure	Dividend paid
	EUR million	EUR million	EUR million
20X6	6	–	3
20X7	7	10	2
20X8	10	–	5
20X9	11	15	2
20Y0	16	–	8

In recent years, investment has been funded by cash held generated by the business but HJK now requires additional funds to finance significant expansion. The Directors have considered additional bank finance but their preference is for an initial public offering (IPO), that is, an offer for sale of shares to the public. However, the Directors are concerned about the implications of an IPO on the financial strategy of the company in the areas of dividend, financing and investment.

Required:

(a)   **Evaluate the current dividend policy of HJK.**   **(6 marks)**

(b)   (i)   **Describe the process involved in an IPO.**   **(3 marks)**

(ii)   **Advise on the potential risks with an IPO and what action can be taken to minimise such risks.**   **(4 marks)**

(c)   **Discuss the concerns of the Directors regarding the possible implications of becoming a listed company on dividend, financing and investment strategies and the interrelationship between them.**   **(12 marks)**

A report format is not required for this question.

(Total: 25 marks)

14   TTT (NOV 11 EXAM)

TTT is a public listed company based in Germany with the euro (EUR) as its functional currency. The company is an energy supply company, operating a number of electricity generating facilities and electricity grids both in Germany and other European countries (some of which are outside the eurozone). It has a central treasury function based in Germany.

TTT has defined its three financial objectives as follows:

1   To increase dividends by 10% a year.

2   To keep gearing below 40% (where gearing is calculated as debt/(debt + equity)).

3   To expand by internal growth and/or by horizontal integration via acquisition of companies operating in the same industry sector.

TTT has identified a potential takeover candidate, company WWW, which operates three electricity generating stations in Sweden and has the Swedish Krona (SKR) as its functional currency. TTT is considering a cash offer for WWW of approximately SKR 23,000 million but it has not yet been decided whether this would be financed by debt (at an after tax cost of 5% per annum) or equity. If equity were used then shares would be issued on the open market at the current share price of EUR 2.90 per share.

Extracts from TTT's latest financial statements are as follows:

	EUR million
Long term borrowings	9,500
Share capital (EUR 1 shares)	5,000
Retained reserves	4,000

Last year TTT paid a dividend of 16 cents per share, representing a dividend pay-out ratio of 40%. Earnings have grown by 8% a year on average over the last 5 years and the dividend pay-out ratio has been between 30% and 50% over the period.

WWW has a current market capitalisation of SKR 20,000 million and the current EUR/SKR spot rate is EUR/SKR 9.2000 (that is, EUR 1 = SKR 9.2000). WWW has a P/E ratio of 10 and earnings are expected to grow at 6% a year in future years.

Required:

(a)   **Advise the directors of TTT on:**

   (i)   **The extent to which the company meets its financial objectives both before and after the proposed acquisition of WWW.**   **(11 marks)**

   (ii) **The appropriateness of the stated financial objectives for TTT AND how they could be improved.**   **(7 marks)**

(b)   **Describe THREE roles that the central treasury function of TTT might play in the evaluation and/or implementation of the proposed acquisition of WWW. (7 marks)**

   A report format is not required for this question.

                                                                          (Total: 25 marks)

15   QRR (MAR 12 EXAM)

Assume today is 1 April 2012.

QRR is a bank located and listed in India. Today's exchange rate for the Indian Rupee (INR) is GBP/INR 76.9231 (that is, GBP 1 = INR 76.9231).

In recent years, QRR has experienced a fall in profits as a result of the credit crunch which has weakened the capital base of the bank. Although revenue has risen by 6.3% in the past year, operating profits have fallen by 19% and earnings per share by 9%. In the past QRR has paid regular quarterly dividends.

Due to the credit crunch and the downturn in the global economy, the Indian banking regulator (together with banking regulators around the world) is in the process of introducing higher capital and liquidity requirements for all banks, which will be a legal requirement in twelve months' time. Currently, QRR would not satisfy these new capital and liquidity requirements.

The board of QRR has recently met to discuss how best to improve capital and liquidity in order to be able to meet the new requirements. The following two suggestions were made by Board members regarding the next quarterly dividend:

- Director A has suggested that no dividend should be paid.

- Director B has suggested that the normal cash dividend be replaced with a scrip dividend (that is, a bonus issue of shares).

Under the proposed scrip dividend, QRR would issue shareholders with the right to subscribe for ordinary shares at zero cost in the proportion of 1 new bonus share for every 50 shares held. The rights to receive bonus shares would be issued on 15 May 2012, with the new shares being issued on 31 May 2012. A shareholder would have to choose between the following actions:

1   Sell the rights in the open market for cash at the latest market price for the rights between the dates 15 May 2012 and 31 May 2012.

2   Hold onto the rights until 31 May 2012 and receive new shares in the proportion 1 share for every 50 held on that date.

QRR has 4,300 million INR 100 (nominal) ordinary shares in issue. The market price for selling the rights is expected to be in the order of INR 7 per existing share under the rights. Assume that a typical shareholder in QRR holds 1,000 ordinary shares of nominal value INR100 each and that today's share price is INR 396.

Required:

(a)   **Discuss the likely impacts on QRR's share price of an announcement that no dividend will be paid, as suggested by Director A.**   **(8 marks)**

(b)   **Evaluate which of the following actions would be more beneficial to a typical shareholder if Director B's suggestion is implemented:**

  (i)   **Accepting the shares offered under the scrip dividend.**

  (ii)   **Selling the rights under the scrip dividend in the market.**

> Your answer should include an estimate of the change in shareholder value in each case based upon today's share price. **(8 marks)**

(c) Recommend which, if either, of the strategies suggested by Director A and Director B, QRR should adopt. **(5 marks)**

(d) Identify alternative financial strategies (other than changing the dividend policy) that could help improve QRR's liquidity position. **(4 marks)**

A report format is not required for this question.

(Total: 25 marks)

16 SPORT (SEPT 12 EXAM)

SPORT is a UK-based charity, a 'not for profit' organisation which does not have any shareholders. Its main objective is to provide specialised low cost sports equipment to people with disabilities living in the UK to help them participate in a range of sporting activities. The charity raises funds through an extensive network of its own charity stores, by individual donations and by special fund raising events. The stores sell clothing and other goods which have been donated by the public and are largely staffed by volunteers. All of the store premises are leased rather than owned by SPORT.

SPORT has recently appointed a new Finance Director (FD), who previously worked in the commercial sector for a large sports equipment retailer. The FD is currently reviewing the objectives of SPORT and, in order to assist with this process, the FD has compiled the following list of objectives based on a review of the annual reports of various retail companies which supply sports equipment in the 'for profit' sector.

Extract financial and non-financial objectives for 'for profit' sports equipment retailers:

Financial objectives	Non-financial objectives
Increase earnings per share by 5% a year	High customer satisfaction
Achieve steady growth in dividends	Retain market position in top 3 suppliers
Maximum debt to debt plus equity of 50%	Reduce carbon footprint

The Chair of the Trustees has suggested that the charity considers issuing a GBP 10 million bond in order to finance an ambitious expansion of its retail and fundraising operations. The proceeds of the issue would be used to open a further 100 stores across the UK. Currently, SPORT has 300 stores. The FD has reacted favourably to this proposal and he has been quoted in the press as saying: 'Charities should be run on commercial lines to maximise social good'.

Required:

(a) Describe the main differences between the overall objectives of 'for profit' organisations and 'not for profit' organisations. **(4 marks)**

(b) (i) Advise on the extent to which each of the financial and non-financial objectives listed above could be adapted for use by SPORT. **(9 marks)**

   (ii) Discuss what additional objectives might be appropriate for SPORT.

(5 marks)

   (iii) Advise whether the proposed bond issue to finance an increase in charity stores is appropriate for a charitable organisation such as SPORT. Include reference to the recent press comment from the FD in your answer. **(7 marks)**

A report format is not required for this question.

(Total: 25 marks)

17   BBD (NOV 12 EXAM)

BBD is a listed company, based in Canada, which specialises in extracting natural gas for sale to national distribution networks. Wholesale gas is priced globally in US dollars.

A possible new project to build four new gas drill rigs is being considered. The rigs would use fracking, a relatively new and controversial method of extracting natural gas.

Fracking involves drilling a well hundreds of metres into the ground and pumping it full of water, sand and chemicals to fracture the rock and release gas for sale. There have recently been some reports of fracking causing small earthquakes which result in damage to properties nearby the drill rigs. There is also some concern about the possibility of pollution of the water supply as a result of fracking.

BBD is confident of being able to raise sufficient debt finance for the project based on forecast future earnings from selling the extracted gas. The company is already relatively heavily geared, with a gearing ratio of 50% (debt/debt + equity). 80% of the equity is owned by 6 major institutions, including 2 pension funds.

BBD has recently been the subject of a review by a major rating agency which has unexpectedly put the company on 'negative outlook', implying that there is a high chance that its rating could be reduced. Further discussion has revealed that the rating agency is concerned about the risk involved in the new project and about the increase in gearing that this would create.

A rating downgrade could have major implications for BBD. Therefore the directors have been discussing and investigating courses of action open to them in respect of the planned project in light of the threat of a credit downgrade. The following three possible responses have been identified:

A   Cancel the project.

B   Proceed with the project and accept the risk of a downgrade.

C   Cancel this year's dividend and use the cash saved to help finance the project, thereby hoping to avoid a credit downgrade.

Required:

(a)   **Discuss the potential exposure of BBD's financial results to external factors such as economic variables, market prices and external constraints.**   **(7 marks)**

(b)   (i)   **Advise BBD on the possible implications for the company of a credit downgrade.**   **(5 marks)**

(ii)   **Evaluate each of the three possible responses A, B and C identified by the directors from the viewpoint of shareholder wealth.**   **(9 marks)**

(iii)   **Recommend which possible response A, B or C should be adopted by BBD.**   **(4 marks)**

A report format is not required for this question.

(Total: 25 marks)

18   SRP (MAR 13 EXAM)

Today is 1 March 2013.

SRP is a market leader in the design, manufacture and installation of large scale equipment to customer-specified performance criteria. Although it sells its products worldwide, all its manufacturing capacity is in the UK and its shares are listed on a UK stock exchange.

SRP was formed by the amalgamation of three smaller companies in 1979 and many of its current shareholders previously owned shares in those companies. Small, individual investors own around 30% of the total shares in issue. Approximately 65% of the shares are owned by large institutional investors such as pension funds and the remaining 5% are owned by the directors and employees of SRP.

Financial objectives

SRP's principal financial objective is to maximise shareholder wealth. It also has the following additional specific financial objectives:

- Annual increase in earnings per share (EpS) and dividend per share (DpS) of at least 3% on average over a rolling 3 year period.

- Maintain gearing, based on book values, below 30%.

Gearing is defined as net debt to net debt plus equity where net debt is long term borrowings less surplus cash.

Forecast financial information in respect of the year to 31 March 2013

SRP's forecast statement of financial position as at 31 March 2013 before taking into account the dividend of GBP 89.6 million that is due to be paid on 10 March is shown below:

	GBP million
ASSETS	
Non-current assets	1,650
Current assets	
Cash and cash equivalents	215
Other	210
Total assets	2,075
EQUITY and LIABILITIES	
Equity	
Share capital (GBP1 ordinary shares)	350
Reserves	950
Non-current liabilities	
Secured 7% loan	550
Current liabilities	225
Total equity and liabilities	2,075

Additional information:

- Forecast revenue and earnings for SRP for the year ending 31 March 2013 are GBP 2,500 million and GBP 280 million respectively

- SRP's shares are currently trading at GBP 4.78 per share cum div and the underlying ex div price is not expected to change before 31 March.

- The secured loan is from a consortium of banks and is not traded. It is repayable at par on 31 March 2017.

Surplus cash

The company has been highly profitable in recent years having successfully tendered for a number of very large contracts around the world. As a consequence, SRP has substantial amounts of cash either on deposit or invested in short term securities (shown in the financial statements as cash equivalents). Even after the planned dividend, the directors consider that a significant portion of the forecast cash and cash equivalents balance as at 31 March 2013 is surplus to requirements and are considering how to deal with this surplus cash.

Three proposed strategies for dealing with surplus cash are as follows:

1   Continue to hold the surplus cash in a bank account and/or as short-term securities.

2   Arrange a programme to repurchase a proportion of the company's shares.

3   Pay bonuses on a one-off basis to directors and employees.

For this purpose, surplus cash is defined as all forecast cash and cash equivalents as at 31 March 2013 after paying the planned dividend and setting aside GBP 15 million for the support of on-going operations. Returns on short-term cash can be assumed to be negligible.

Required:

(a)   **Calculate forecasts of the following for SRP, after paying the dividend but before disposing of surplus cash remaining:**

- **EpS and DpS for the year ending 31 March 2013.**

- **Gearing based on book values as at 31 March 2013.**

- **Gearing based on market values as at 31 March 2013.**   **(7 marks)**

(b)   **Calculate the likely impact on EpS, DpS, and gearing of each of the three proposed strategies for dealing with surplus cash.**   **(8 marks)**

(c)   **Evaluate each of the three proposed strategies for dealing with surplus cash. In your answer, take into account likely impact of each strategy on:**

- **Attainment of financial objectives.**

- **Shareholder wealth in both the short and long term.**   **(10 marks)**

   A report format is not required for this question.

(Total: 25 marks)

19   KK (SEPT 13 EXAM)

Assume today's date is 28 December 2013.

KK is a manufacturing company based in Country K. KK is a listed company that is wholly equity financed. 25% of the shares are held by members of an extended family group. KK has adopted 31 December as its financial year end.

Dividend decision

In previous years, KK has maintained a dividend pay-out rate of 80% of earnings. However, some board members have recently questioned whether such a policy is appropriate. Some board members support the 80% pay-out but others have suggested that a lower dividend is necessary in order to help finance expansion in manufacturing capacity to take advantage of new markets that are opening up in Asia.

It is too late to change the dividend for the current financial year, 2013, since the dividend for the year is about to be paid. The first time that a change in dividend policy could be adopted is in 2014.

Additional financial information for KK:

- It is standard practice for KK to pay dividends once a year based on forecast earnings for that year.

- Dividends are paid at or shortly before the end of the year.

- A dividend of K$ 0.50 in respect of the current financial year (2013) has already been declared. This was based on the historical pay-out rate of 80% of forecast earnings for 2013 of K$ 12.5 million.

- Historically, KK has achieved a return on reinvested funds of 16%.

- KK has a cost of equity of 14.7%.

- There are currently 20 million shares in issue.

- Today's share price is K$ 5.00 (cum div).

Possible reduction in dividend pay-out

The board of KK is considering cutting the regular dividend pay-out rate from 80% to 50% of earnings with effect from 2014. If agreed, this would be made public by an announcement on 1 January 2014.

The board is aware that there would be a delay of 12 months between cutting the dividend pay-out rate and realising any benefit in terms of higher earnings as a result of the higher level of reinvested funds.

Discussions regarding a possible change in the dividend pay-out rate have so far been internal and only known by the management team at KK. No announcement has yet been made about a possible change in dividend policy and the share price does not yet reflect the possibility of a cut in pay-out rate.

Growth formula

$g = r \times b$

Where	g	=	annual growth
	r	=	return on reinvested funds
	b	=	proportion of funds retained

Required:

(a) **(i)** Calculate the following performance measures for KK for both years 2014 and 2015 assuming a reduction in KK's dividend pay-out to 50% of earnings from 2014 onwards:

- Growth rate using the growth formula provided.

- Earnings.

- Dividend per share. **(8 marks)**

(ii) Calculate the expected change in KK's share price on 1 January 2014, the day of the planned announcement of the reduction in pay-out rate. Use the dividend growth model and assume that the cost of equity does not change.
(7 marks)

(b) Advise KK on the key factors that affect the optimum level of dividend for the company in 2014. Your answer should include reference to your results in (a)(ii) above as well as any other relevant factors. **(10 marks)**

A report format is not required for this question.

(Total: 25 marks)

FINANCING DECISIONS

20   MNO (MAY 06 EXAM)

MNO is a private toy distributor situated in the US with a US customer base and local suppliers. There is a central manufacturing base and several marketing units spread across the US. The marketing units are encouraged to adapt to local market conditions, largely acting independently and free from central control. These units are responsible for all aspects of local sales, including collecting sales revenues, which are paid across to Head Office on a monthly basis. Funding is provided by Head Office as required.

Figures for last year to 31 December 20X5 were as follows:

Revenue	$10 million
Gross profit margin	40% of revenue
Accounts receivable days	minimum 20, maximum 30 days
Accounts payable days	minimum 40, maximum 50 days
Inventories	minimum 50, maximum 80 days
Non-current assets	$8 million

Accounts receivable, accounts payable and inventories can all be assumed to be the same on both 31 December 20X4 and 31 December 20X5, but fluctuate between those dates.

The Financial Controller is carrying out an analysis of MNO's working capital levels, as requested by the Treasurer. He is assuming that the peak period for accounts receivable coincides with the peak period for inventories and the lowest level of accounts payable.

MNO is currently in consultation with a potentially significant new supplier in Asia, who will demand payment in its local currency.

Required:

(a) (i) Calculate the minimum and maximum working capital levels based on the Financial Controller's assumption regarding the timing of peaks and troughs in working capital variables and discuss the validity of that assumption.

(6 marks)

(ii) Using the figures calculated in (i) above, calculate and draw a chart to show the short-term and long-term (permanent) financing requirements of MNO under each of the following working capital financing policies:

- moderate policy, where long-term financing matches permanent net current assets

- aggressive policy, where 30% of permanent net current assets are funded by short-term financing

- conservative policy, where only 40% of fluctuating net current assets are funded by short-term financing. (7 marks)

(b) Discuss the advantages and disadvantages of an aggressive financing policy and advise whether or not such a policy would be appropriate for MNO. (6 marks)

(c) Advise MNO whether a profit or cost centre structure would be more appropriate for its treasury department. (6 marks)

(Total: 25 marks)

21 LEELOR (MAY 07 EXAM)

LEE is a manufacturing entity located in Newland, a country with the dollar ($) as its currency. LOR is a leasing entity that is also located in Newland.

LEE plans to replace a key piece of machinery and is initially considering the following two approaches:

- Alternative 1 – purchase the machinery, financed by borrowing for a five-year term

- Alternative 2 – lease the machinery from LOR on a five-year operating lease.

The machinery and maintenance costs

The machinery has a useful life of approximately 10 years, but LEE is aware that the industry is facing a period of intense competition and the machinery may not be needed in five years' time. It would cost LEE $5,000 to buy the machinery, but LOR has greater purchasing power and could acquire the machinery for $4,000.

Maintenance costs are estimated to be $60 in each of years 1 to 3 and $100 in each of years 4 and 5, arising at the *end* of the year.

Alternative 1 – purchase financed by borrowing for a five year term

$ interbank borrowing rates in Newland are currently 5.5% per annum. LEE can borrow at interbank rates plus a margin of 1.7% and expects $ interbank rates to remain constant over the five year period. It has estimated that the machinery could be sold for $2,000 at the end of five years.

Alternative 2 – five year operating lease

Under the operating lease, LOR would be responsible for maintenance costs and would charge LEE lease rentals of $850 annually *in advance* for five years.

LOR knows that LEE is keen to lease rather than buy the machine and wants to take advantage of this position by increasing the rentals on the operating lease. However, it does not want to lose LEE's custom and requires advice on how high a lease rental LEE would be likely to accept.

Tax regulations

Newland's tax rules for operating leases give the lessor tax depreciation allowances on the asset and give the lessee full tax relief on the lease payments. Tax depreciation allowances are available to the purchaser of a business asset at 25% per annum on a reducing balance basis. The business tax rate is 30% and tax should be assumed to arise at the end of each year and be paid one year later.

Alternative 3 – late proposal by production manager

During the evaluation process for Alternatives 1 and 2, the production manager suggested that another lease structure should also be considered, to be referred to as 'Alternative 3'. No figures are available at present to enable a numerical evaluation to be carried out for Alternative 3. The basic structure would be a five-year lease with the option to renew at the end of the five-year term for an additional five-year term at negligible rental. LEE would be responsible for maintenance costs.

Required:

(a) (i) **Use discounted cash flow analysis to evaluate and compare the cost to LEE of each of Alternatives 1 and 2.**   **(9 marks)**

(ii) **Advise LOR on the highest lease rentals that LEE would be likely to accept under Alternative 2.**   **(4 marks)**

(b) **Discuss both the financial and non-financial factors that might affect LEE's choice between Alternatives 1, 2 and 3. No further calculations are required in part (b).**
                                                                                       (12 marks)

                                                                                       (Total: 25 marks)

22   DAN'S PORTFOLIO (MAY 08 EXAM)   *Walk in the footsteps of a top tutor*

You are a financial adviser working for a large financial institution. One of your clients, Dan, has a portfolio currently worth £100,000. He has invested in good quality stocks that are spread over diversified industries with an average beta of 1.2; a risk profile he is happy with. He holds other assets, such as property and bank deposits, worth approximately £150,000 (excluding his own home, on which he has a 75% mortgage).

He has recently inherited £40,000 which he intends to invest in equities. He has done some research himself and is considering investing in the following entities in equal proportions.

Entity A is a large, listed entity in a mature industry. Dan already has 15% of his equity investments in this industry sector.

Entity B is a relatively small entity whose shares have been listed on the UK's Alternative Investment Market for the past three years. Its main area of operations is bio-technology, a sector in which Dan has no investments.

Market data for the shares of the two entities are as follows:

Entity	Current share prices (buy price)	Beta	P/E ratio
A	250 pence cum rights	1.1	10
B	500 pence cum dividend	N/A *	20

* Your financial institution estimates a return of 15.8% is required on this stock.

Your transaction charges will be 2.5% of the capital amount.

Financial strategies of the two entities

Entity A is planning a rights issue. The terms will be 1 new share for every 4 held at a cost of 200 pence.

Entity B will allow investors registered at 30 June 20X8 the option of taking a dividend of 45 pence a share or a scrip dividend of 1 share for every 10 shares held.

The policy of Entity B has been to offer scrip dividends as an alternative to cash dividends since its shares were first listed three years ago.

The risk free rate is 5% and the return on the market is 11%. These rates are not expected to change in the foreseeable future.

Required:

(a) Calculate the risk and expected return of Dan's equity investment portfolio if he goes ahead with his proposed investments. Work to a maximum of 2 decimal places in your calculations. **(5 marks)**

(b) (i) Explain the difference between systematic risk (or market risk) and unsystematic risk (or specific risk) and, briefly, the meaning of beta and how it is measured. **(4 marks)**

(ii) Discuss how and to what extent the beta of Entity A and the implied beta of Entity B:

- Might affect Dan's investment decision

- Could be of interest to the directors of single entities such as A and B. **(6 marks)**

(c) Evaluate the implications for shareholder value of Entity A's and Entity B's proposed financial strategies and advise Dan on how these strategies might affect his investment decisions. Include appropriate calculations. **(10 marks)**

(Including up to 6 marks for calculations)

A report format is not required in this question.

(Total: 25 marks)

23 MAT (MAY 08 EXAM)

MAT is a manufacturer of computer components in a rapidly growing niche market. It is a private entity owned and managed by a small group of people who started the business 10 years ago. Although relatively small, it sells its products world-wide. Customers are invoiced in sterling, although this policy is being reviewed. Raw materials are purchased largely in the UK although some are sourced from overseas and paid for in foreign currencies, typically US$.

As the newly-appointed Financial Manager, you are reviewing MAT's financial records to identify any immediate or longer-term areas of risk that require immediate attention. In particular, the entity's forecast appears to be uncomfortably close to its unsecured overdraft limit of £450,000.

Extracts from last year's results (20X6) and the forecast for the next financial year are as follows:

	Last year £000	Forecast £000
Non-current assets	3,775	4,325
Current assets		
Accounts receivable	550	950
Inventory	475	575
Cash and marketable securities	250	100
Total current assets	1,275	1,625
Total assets	5,050	5,950
Total equity	3,750	4,050
Non-current liabilities		
Secured bond repayable 20X8	850	850
Current liabilities		
Accounts payable	450	625
Bank overdraft	0	425
Total current liabilities	450	1,050
Total equity and liabilities	5,050	5,950
Revenue	4,500	5,750
Cost of goods sold	1,750	2,300
Profit before tax	1,050	1,208

Required:

Prepare a report to the Finance Director of MAT advising on whether the entity could be classified as 'overtrading' and recommending financial strategies that could be used to address the situation.

Your advice and recommendations should be based on analysis of the forecast financial position, making whatever assumptions are necessary, and should include brief reference to any additional information that would be useful to MAT at this time.

(Up to 14 marks are available for calculations)

(Total: 25 marks)

24 BZ (MAY 09 EXAM)

BZ is a textile wholesaler based in a country in the Euro zone. Summary financial information is as follows:

- Revenue and earnings last year were €121 million and €23.5 million respectively

- BZ's shares are not listed but they occasionally change hands in private transactions. The shares most recently traded a month ago at €4 per share. There are 39 million shares in issue

- BZ also has €121.5 million of undated debt on its balance sheet. This debt is secured on the entity's assets and carries an interest rate of 8%. The current cost of debt to an entity such as BZ is 9% before tax

- BZ estimates its cost of equity at 11%

- BZ operates an overdraft facility for short-term financing requirements.

The entity currently sells its products in the USA via a distributor. However, its sales in this market are increasing to the extent that BZ is considering setting up its own distribution network in the USA. A State in the south of the USA has offered BZ financial support to establish a base there. BZ management thinks this is not the ideal location but an attractive financing package might persuade them otherwise.

The financing package currently on offer from the State in the south of the USA would take the form of a US$50 million loan at a subsidised interest rate of 3.5% per annum. Interest would be payable at the end of each year and the principal repaid at the end of five years.

The current rate of exchange is US$1.2 = €1. This rate is not expected to change in the foreseeable future.

The marginal corporate tax rate in both countries is 28%.

Required:

(i)   Calculate BZ's current WACC using market values and the cost of equity in the scenario. Assume the current debt ratio remains the same.   **(5 marks)**

(ii)   Advise the board of BZ about how to determine an appropriate discount rate to use when evaluating the proposal to establish a subsidiary in the USA.   **(6 marks)**

(iii)   Discuss the advantages and disadvantages of using government subsidies in any international investment decision. Include a calculation of the value of the subsidy implied in the US State loan.   **(8 marks)**

(iv)   Discuss and recommend to the board of BZ how its US business operations might be financed when the US State loan is repaid.   **(6 marks)**

Note: A report format is not required for this question.

(Total: 25 marks)

25   GREGORY AND GEORGE (NOV 09 EXAM)

Gregory

Gregory, a listed entity based in Europe, provides private medical care through private hospitals. Additional funds are required to fund the construction of a new medical support unit. This was already public knowledge in August 20X9

A rights issue was announced in a press statement on 1 September 20X9. Ordinary shares are to be issued at a discount of 20% on market price and the issue is expected to raise a total sum of €29.3 million.

Gregory already has 40 million €1 ordinary shares in issue. The share price on 1 September 20X9 before the press statement was released was 458 cents.

Mr X holds 200,000 €1 ordinary shares in Gregory and is wondering whether or not to take up the rights being offered.

Required:

(a)   (i)   **Calculate the number of ordinary shares to be issued under the rights issue.**

(2 marks)

(ii)   **Calculate the theoretical ex-rights price.**   **(3 marks)**

(iii)   **Calculate the expected trading price for the rights.**   **(2 marks)**

(iv)   **Evaluate and discuss the impact of the rights issue on the personal wealth of shareholder Mr X for each of the following three alternative responses to the rights offer:**

- **does not take up the rights**

- **takes up the rights**

- **sells just enough rights to provide the funds needed to purchase the remaining rights**   **(10 marks)**

George

George, a competitor of Gregory, is also based in Europe and operates in the medical services industry. It has been highly successful in recent years and has accumulated a large amount of surplus cash representing 10% of total equity value. It now wishes to return this surplus cash to shareholders. Gearing is defined as net debt to net debt plus equity where net debt is debt after deduction of surplus cash.

Current market values:	€ million
Debt	37
Surplus cash	7
Equity	70

The entity is considering the best method to achieve the return of surplus cash to the shareholders, preferably also reducing the cost of capital but not changing the balance of share ownership.

The two main methods being considered are:

(i)   share repurchase

(ii)   one-off special dividend

Required:

(b)   **Compare and contrast the advantages to George of each of the two proposed methods of returning surplus cash to shareholders and recommend which of these methods George should use.**   **(8 marks)**

(Total: 25 marks)

26   CLAUDIA (NOV 09 EXAM)

Claudia is based in Asia and is considering installing a new computer system in order to upgrade the web-based sales system to bring it in line with that of Claudia's main competitors. The cost of $10 million is payable up front but the new system will take a full year to implement. Increased pre-tax operating earnings of $770,000 a year are expected from year 2 onwards indefinitely to reflect increased operational efficiencies and increased revenue from web-based sales.

Claudia is currently funded by ordinary shares and an irredeemable bond as follows:

	Nominal value	Market value
20 million ordinary shares	$1 each	$2.50 each
5.4% irredeemable bond	$33 million	trading at par

Additional debt finance of $10 million will be taken out (also at 5.4%) if the project is approved.

Additional information:

Cost of equity is 6.2%

The project is not expected to have any impact on either the current cost of equity or the cost of debt.

The share price is expected to react very quickly on announcement of the project to reflect the anticipated NPV of the project.

Business tax is payable and refundable at 35% in the year in which it is incurred.

No tax depreciation allowances can be claimed

Assume earnings equal net cash inflow

Cash flows arise at the end of a year

Required:

(a)   **Calculate the current WACC of Claudia (before taking the project into account).**

(3 marks)

(b)   **Evaluate the project using the current WACC calculated in part (a).**   **(4 marks)**

(c) Calculate the post-project WACC for Claudia after adjusting for the NPV of the project and the increased debt, and discuss your results. Discuss and advise whether the pre-project WACC was an appropriate discount rate for Claudia to use in this scenario. **(6 marks)**

(d) Discuss the key factors that Claudia should take into account in respect of this project when:

    (i) assessing customer requirements

    (ii) drawing up an implementation plan **(12 marks)**

(Total: 25 marks)

27 PIC (MAY 10 EXAM)

PIC is a furniture retailing company in a developed country in Asia. It has 15 stores spread around the country. Each store has some freedom to adapt its buying patterns to local market conditions although around 80% of its products must be obtained through central purchasing. Sales receipts are paid to head office on a monthly basis. PIC offers 60-day credit to a few key high-profile and agency customers who account for a substantial proportion of sales by value. However, the majority of customers pay immediately by cash.

The treasurer has observed that working capital levels fluctuate quite substantially from month to month. Based on forecast revenue for next year, the average days and minimum and maximum working capital levels for next year are likely to be as follows:

	Average Days	Minimum A\$ million	Maximum A\$ million
Inventories	105	17.26	29.59
Accounts receivable	15	1.64	3.29
Accounts payable	60	7.40	14.79

At present PIC follows an aggressive policy for financing net current assets. All fluctuating net current assets and 20% of permanent net current assets are funded by overdraft. PIC currently has an overdraft facility of up to A\$20 million, secured as a floating charge on the entity's current assets. Interest is charged at 7% (pre-tax) on daily balances. Over the past year PIC has used its maximum overdraft facility. The treasurer thinks this is too risky a policy in present economic conditions and is proposing a more conservative policy where 100% of permanent net current assets and 20% of fluctuating net current assets are financed by medium or long term finance. To achieve this, PIC is proposing to issue a bond, redeemable at par in 5 years' time, with an annual coupon of 8%. Interest would be paid annually at the end of each year. Other similar corporate bonds have a yield to maturity of 9%.

PIC's shares are listed on a secondary market. The market value of the shares is currently A\$350 million and its cost of equity is 10%. PIC also has long term debt in issue with a market value of A\$100 million at an average pre-tax cost of 8.125%. PIC pays corporate tax at 20%.

Required:

(a) (i) Calculate the short-term and long-term (permanent) financing requirements of PIC under the aggressive policy for financing net current assets that is currently being used and also under the proposed new conservative policy.

(5 marks)

(ii) Calculate the implied issue price per A$100 nominal of the bond being considered by the treasurer.

(3 marks)

(iii) Calculate the weighted average cost of capital (WACC) of PIC at present and discuss, briefly, the likely effect on WACC if PIC changes its policy for financing net current assets.

(4 marks)

(b) (i) Evaluate PIC's proposal to change from an aggressive to a conservative policy for financing net current assets.

(9 marks)

(ii) Advise PIC, briefly, on alternative approaches to financing net current assets that it should consider.

(4 marks)

(Total: 25 marks)

28   CIP (MAY 10 EXAM)

CIP is a family-controlled company. The family owns 80% of the shares. The remaining 20% is owned by a number of non-family shareholders, none of whom owns more than 1% of the shares in issue. The Board of Directors has convened a special Board meeting to review two investment opportunities and, at the request of the new Finance Director, decide on an appropriate discount rate, or rates, to use in the evaluation of these investments. Each of the two investments being considered is in a non-listed company and will be financed 60% by equity and 40% by debt.

In the past, CIP has used an estimated post-tax weighted average cost of capital of 12% to calculate the net present value (NPV) of all investments. The Managing Director thinks this rate should continue to be used, adjusted if necessary by plus or minus 1% or 2% to reflect greater or lesser risk than the "average" investment.

The Finance Director disagrees and suggests using the capital asset pricing model (CAPM) to determine a discount rate that reflects the systematic risk of each of the proposed investments based on proxy companies that operate in similar businesses. The Finance Director has obtained the betas and debt ratios of two listed companies (Company A and Company B) that could be used as proxies. These are:

	Equity Beta	Debt Beta	Debt ratio (debt: equity)
Company A (proxy for Investment 1)	1.3	0.3	1:3
Company B (proxy for Investment 2)	0.9	0	1:6

Other information:

The expected annual post-tax return on the market is 8% and the risk-free rate is 3%.

Assume the debt that CIP raises to finance the investments is risk-free.

All three companies (CIP, Company A and Company B) pay corporate tax at 25%.

CIP has one financial objective, which is to increase earnings each year to enable its dividend payment to increase by 4% per annum.

The Managing Director and the other Board members are confused about the terminology being used in the CAPM calculation and do not understand why they are being asked to consider a different method of calculating discount rates for use in evaluating the proposed investments.

Required:

(a)   Discuss the meaning of the terms "systematic" and "unsystematic" risk and their relationship to a company's equity beta. Include in your answer an appropriate diagram to demonstrate the difference between the two types of risk.   **(6 marks)**

(b)   Using the CAPM and the information given in the scenario about CIP and Companies A and B, calculate for each of CIP's proposed investments:

  • An asset beta.

  • An appropriate discount rate to be used in the evaluation of the investment.
                                                                                       (6 marks)

(c)   Evaluate the benefits and limitations of using each of the following in CIP's appraisal of the two investments:

  • CIP's WACC.

  • An adjusted WACC as suggested by the Managing Director.

  • CAPM-derived rates that use proxy (or surrogate) companies' betas.
                                                                                       (6 marks)

(d)   Discuss, briefly, how an asset beta differs from an equity beta and why the former is more appropriate to CIP's investment decision. Include in your discussion some reference to how the use of the CAPM can assist CIP to achieve its financial objective.   **(7 marks)**

                                                                          (Total: 25 marks)

29   TM (MAR 11 EXAM)

Today's date is 4 March 20X1.

TM is a privately owned company which manufactures children's toys and is based in a country in Asia which has the A$ as its currency. In the financial year to 31 December 20X1 (assuming that there are no policy changes) it is expected that approximately 70% of TM's revenue will be from sales to companies in its home market. The other 30% of revenue will be from sales to companies in a foreign country which has the euro (EUR) as its currency. Export sales are currently priced in A$.

Approximately 10% of TM's home customers are cash buyers, the other 90% are on credit. Export sales are all on credit. Some customers in both the home and export markets regularly exceed their agreed credit period. TM makes no charge for this but refuses repeat orders if customers regularly make late payments beyond their agreed credit period.

In order to increase export sales, TM is planning to make the following policy changes with effect from 1 April 20X1:

1   Relax its credit terms in its export market by offering 90 days credit, an increase of 30 days on its normal terms in this market.

2   Invoice in euro rather than A$, converting the A$ price list to produce a euro price list at the current exchange rate of A$/EUR 0.4000 (A$1 = EUR 0.4000). This euro price list will then be used for pricing export sales for the remainder of the year.

It is expected that these policy changes will result in an increase in export sales of one-third between the first and second quarters of 20X1.

Provisional forecast results for TM (including both home and export sales) for the first two quarters of 20X1, after taking into account the planned policy changes and using the exchange of A$/EUR 0.4000, are shown below:

	First quarter 20X1 (1 January to 31 March) A$ thousands	Second quarter 20X1 (1 April to 30 June) A$ thousands
Revenue	5,750	6,325
Cost of goods sold	3,163	3,529
Purchases	2,150	2,350

	Balances at 31 March 20X1 A$ thousands	Balances at 30 June 20X1 A$ thousands
Accounts receivable	5,000	7,000
Accounts payable	1,800	2,600
Inventory		
Raw materials	1,500	1,700
Work in Progress	740	860
Finished goods	420	500

Additional relevant information is given below:

• All purchases were, and will continue to be, sourced in the home country and paid for in A$.

• Net current assets are currently financed by an overdraft. This policy is under review.

There is concern that the value of the euro against the A$ may fall to A$/EUR 0.4600 at the beginning of the second quarter of 20X1. However, other exchange rate forecasters predict that the exchange rate will remain unchanged. If the exchange rate were to change, the directors do not expect to be able to increase TM's euro prices to reflect the devaluation of the euro in view of the current poor economic environment in Europe.

Required:

(a)   Evaluate the likely impact of the movement in exchange rates from A$/EUR 0.4000 to A$/EUR 0.4600 on 1 April 20X1 on the results for the second quarter of 20X1, assuming that the exchange rate remains unchanged for the remainder of the quarter.
                                                                                                   (6 marks)

(b) (i) Calculate the operating cycle of TM for:

- The first quarter of 20X1.

- The second quarter of 20X1 using an exchange rate of A$/EUR 0.4000 as proposed in the policy change.

- The second quarter of 20X1 using an exchange rate of A$/EUR 0.4600 throughout the second quarter. **(9 marks)**

(ii) Briefly discuss whether the changes in any of the component parts of the cycle give cause for concern. **(3 marks)**

(c) Advise the directors of TM on an appropriate financing structure for net current assets and explain the benefits and potential problems of using euro denominated finance. **(7 marks)**

A report format is not required for this question.

(Total: 25 marks)

30 RED (MAR 11 EXAM)

RED is a family run and owned company based in the United Kingdom which designs and manufactures state-of-the-art vacuum cleaners. It has grown steadily during the eight years since it was founded and the directors consider that the company is now of a suitable size to be listed on the Alternative Investment Market (AIM), which is a market for the shares of smaller companies.

The company is currently in the early stages of development of a new product that it is hoped will be highly successful and will significantly increase the company's share of the vacuum cleaner market. Information about the product's development will be made public at various stages during 20X1. Information may also become public knowledge through other means as more people and organisations become involved in the testing and implementation of production of the new product.

Significant amounts of new funding will be required to finance the final development, production and launch of this product but the existing shareholders are now not able to provide this. Therefore the directors of RED are planning to raise the necessary funds by means of a bond issue followed by an IPO (initial public offering). The bond issue is planned for the middle of 20X1 and the IPO towards the end of the year.

Required:

(a) Compare and contrast the features of a private placing and a public issue for the bonds and advise the directors of RED which method would be most appropriate. **(12 marks)**

(b) (i) Describe the three forms of the efficient market hypothesis and state which form is most likely to apply in practice. **(4 marks)**

(ii) Advise the directors of RED on what steps can be taken to improve the chances of a successful IPO issue and a high share price after the issue. Your answer should include reference to the efficient market hypothesis.

(9 marks)

A report format is not required for this question.

(Total: 25 marks)

31   DCD (NOV 11 EXAM)

DCD is a manufacturer of heavy construction equipment. It has manufacturing facilities around the world.

DCD's Ordinary Share Capital has a nominal value of $70 million ($0.50 shares) and the current market price per share is $6.00. The market price per share three months ago was $5.40.

DCD has experienced rapid growth in demand in recent years and expects revenues to continue to grow in future years. The current manufacturing facilities are already operating close to full capacity.

Proposed new manufacturing facility

The Board is planning to build a new manufacturing facility and has already identified a suitable site and prepared a schedule of forecast cash flows arising from the project. It is expected that the proposed new facility would be fully operational within a year of the initial investment and that the project would generate a rate of return on funds invested of 20%. This is greater than the return on existing funds of 15% due to the greater efficiency of the new manufacturing facility.

Rights issue

The Board has decided to use a rights issue to finance the initial investment of $250 million. The rights issue will be underwritten. The exact costs of underwriting are not known but average underwriting costs in the market are estimated to be 2% of the monies raised. The underwriting costs will be paid out of DCD's existing funds rather than out of the funds raised in the rights issue.

A Board meeting has been called to agree the terms of the rights issue. A decision has to be made as to whether the new shares will be issued at a discount of either 25% or 40% on current market price.

Director A is concerned that a 40% discount will result in a reduction in share price which would adversely affect the value of shareholder wealth. He is supporting the lower discount of 25% as he feels that the impact would be reduced.

Director B is recommending a higher discount of 40% as she believes this will improve take up of the rights issue.

Director C is concerned about the impact of a rights issue on future dividend policy. DCD has traditionally operated a stable dividend policy and she is questioning whether this can be sustained following the proposed rights issue.

Next month, after the Board meeting, a press statement will be released in which the project and related rights issue will be made public.

Required:

(a)   Calculate:

    (i)   The terms of the rights issue (to the nearest whole number of shares) at a discount of both 25% and 40%. **(3 marks)**

    (ii)   The yield adjusted theoretical ex-rights price per share at a rights discount of both 25% and 40%. **(4 marks)**

(b) Demonstrate the likely impact of the proposed project together with the related rights issue on the wealth of a shareholder with 100 ordinary shares. Your answer should consider a rights discount of both 25% and 40%. **(4 marks)**

(c) Recommend an appropriate discount, if any, for the rights issue. Your answer should address the concerns raised by each of the Directors A, B and C.

(No further calculations are required in part (c)). **(8 marks)**

(d) Advise the Directors of DCD on factors that are likely to affect the company's share price both before and after next month's planned press statement. **(6 marks)**

A report format is not required for this question.

(Total: 25 marks)

32 CBA (MAR 12 EXAM)

Assume today is 1 April 2012.

CBA is a manufacturing company, operating in the United Kingdom (UK), whose shares are listed on the main UK stock exchange. The board needs to raise GBP 250 million to fund a number of planned new investments and is considering issuing either a convertible bond or additional shares.

CBA currently has 280 million GBP 1 ordinary shares in issue and today's share price is GBP 3.60 per share. It also has GBP 195 million (nominal) of undated 6% preference shares. The preference shares each have a nominal value of GBP 1 and are currently quoted at GBP 1.05 per share. CBA currently has no debt.

Financial position prior to new investment or new financing

Earnings per share for the last financial year ended 31 March 2012 are 45 pence per share and the dividend pay-out ratio has been maintained as close as possible to 50% of earnings. Assume that the dividend for the year ended 31 March 2012 has just been paid and was based on 50% of estimated earnings for the year.

The proposed convertible bond

The convertible bond would be issued at a 7% discount to its nominal value and carry a coupon rate of 3% per annum. The bond would be convertible into ordinary shares in 4 years' time at the ratio of 23 ordinary shares per GBP 100 nominal of the bond.

Forecast position after issuing the convertible bond and making the new investments

Assuming the new investments are undertaken and financed by convertible debt, CBA expects its earnings to grow by 5% per annum for the foreseeable future and to maintain its dividend pay-out ratio at 50%. The share price is expected to rise by 6% per year over the next four year period.

Other information

- CBA pays corporate income tax at a rate of 30% on taxable profits and tax is payable at the end of the year in which the taxable profit arises.

- CBA has sufficient taxable profits to benefit from any tax relief available.

Required:

(a) Calculate the following values assuming that the proposed convertible bond is issued on 1 April 2012:

    (i) The forecast conversion value for the convertible bond in four years' time.

                  (2 marks)

    (ii) The post-tax cost of debt for the convertible bond based on its yield over the next four years up to and including conversion. **(5 marks)**

    (iii) CBA's post-tax weighted average cost of capital (WACC). For the purpose of this calculation, assume no change in the market value of the ordinary and preference shares as a result of the convertible bond issue. **(6 marks)**

(b) Advise on the benefits and limitations to CBA of issuing a convertible bond rather than new equity. **(7 marks)**

(c) Explain the role of CBA's treasury department in evaluating and implementing the convertible bond issue. **(5 marks)**

A report format is not required for this question.

                  (Total: 25 marks)

33 FF (MAY 12 EXAM)

FF is a company that specialises in the manufacture, supply and installation of fixtures and fittings for offices. It uses F$ as its currency. FF is currently evaluating a project to build a new distribution and sales centre.

The company is currently wholly equity funded and has 30 million shares in issue. The share price is F$11 per share before announcing the proposed project and the ungeared cost of equity is 9%. FF pays corporate income tax at 25%.

The proposed project requires an initial capital investment of F$80 million. The present value of future cash flows following this initial investment is estimated to be of the order of F$110 million, based on a discount rate of 9%. The F$30 million forecast increase in entity value is expected to be fully reflected in the share price immediately the project is announced.

There has been some discussion amongst the directors of FF about how the F$80 million capital investment should be funded. Any new equity would be raised through a rights issue and any borrowings would be at a pre-tax cost of 7%. Both would be required indefinitely. Three alternative financing structures are being considered as follows:

A: F$80 million equity funding.

B: F$80 million borrowings.

C: F$48 million equity plus F$32 million borrowings.

Required:

(a)   Calculate the following, based on Modigliani and Miller's (MM's) capital theory with tax and assuming the project goes ahead:

    (i)   The total value of FF (before deducting debt) on a discounted cash flow basis for each of the financing structures A, B and C.   **(6 marks)**

    (ii)   FF's WACC for each of the financing structures A, B and C.   **(6 marks)**

    Note that MM formulae are provided on the formula sheet.

(b)   Explain your results in (a) above with reference to MM's capital theory with tax, illustrating your answer by drawing graphs of your results in (a) above. Use the graph paper provided.   **(9 marks)**

(c)   Advise, with reasons, which financing structure FF should adopt.   **(4 marks)**

A report format is not required for this question.

                                                        (Total: 25 marks)

34   KK (MAY 12 EXAM)

Today is 24 May 2012.

KK is based in Europe and has the euro (EUR) as its functional currency. KK manufactures specialised computer parts for sale throughout Europe and has experienced rapid growth in recent years. Much of this growth has been as a result of launching new products.

Despite rapidly increasing revenues, KK has experienced liquidity pressures as evidenced by a growing overdraft. KK is now dangerously close to breaching its overdraft limit of EUR 9.0 million.

Extracts from management accounting information for KK for the 12 months of trading up to 30 April 2012 are given below:

Results for 6 months to:	30 April 2012 EUR million	31 October 2011 EUR million
Revenue	12.6	9.5
Cost of sales	9.6	7.1
Other costs (all settled as incurred)	2.0	1.5

Balances as at:	30 April 2012 EUR million	31 October 2011 EUR million
Accounts receivable	7.1	4.8
Accounts payable	3.2	2.7
Inventory	5.6	3.9
Overdraft	8.5	6.0

Working capital days as at:	30 April 2012 Days	31 October 2011 Days
Accounts receivable	103	92
Accounts payable	61	69
Inventory	106	100

For the purposes of this question, taxation should be ignored.

Required:

(a) (i) Calculate what the overdraft requirement would have been on 30 April 2012 if working capital days for the period had remained at 31 October 2011 levels. **(5 marks)**

(ii) Explain the particular pressures faced by companies in times of rapid expansion in respect of working capital and profit margins. Illustrate your answer with reference to KK. **(8 marks)**

(iii) Recommend strategies that KK should consider in order to reduce the amount of funds tied up in working capital. **(5 marks)**

(b) Discuss the key factors that a potential lender is likely to consider when assessing the creditworthiness of a business which is experiencing rapid growth. **(7 marks)**

A report format is not required for this question.

(Total: 25 marks)

35   LL (SEPT 12 EXAM)

Today is 1 September 2012.

LL is a company based in Asia which uses L$ as its functional currency. The company has adopted International Financial Reporting Standards.

LL is currently preparing a bid for a government contract to operate a train service on a new high-speed rail link between the capital city and another city in the same country. The investment appraisal of the project has been completed and shows that the project is financially beneficial. The focus of attention has now shifted to considering how best to finance the initial investment required in the new rolling stock (that is, locomotives and carriages) that is needed to run on the line.

The rail link would be operated by LL for a period of ten years commencing on 1 January 2013. The new rolling stock required would cost L$50 million if bought outright.   There is an active market in second hand rolling stock and it is estimated that the rolling stock could be sold at the end of the ten year period for L$22 million.

The following two alternative financing approaches are being considered:

•   Bank borrowing from its primary bank for a ten year term together with the outright purchase of the rolling stock.

•   A ten year operating lease provided by the supplier of the rolling stock.

Bank borrowing and outright purchase:

•   LL would buy the new rolling stock on 1 January 2013.

•   LL can borrow from its primary bank at a 2.5% credit margin above the bank's published base interest rate. The bank's base rate is currently set at 3.5% but can be expected to change in line with changes in market interest rates.

•   Maintenance costs are expected to be of the order of L$1.5 million per year if LL purchases the rolling stock outright.

Operating lease:

- An initial up-front payment of L$5.8 million would be payable at the start of the lease on 1 January 2013.

- Ten further lease payments of L$5.8 million each would be payable on 31 December in each year starting on 31 December 2013.

- The lessor retains responsibility for maintaining the rolling stock throughout the period of the lease and has included the cost of maintenance services within the lease payments.

Additional information:

- LL's financial year runs from 1 January to 31 December.

- LL pays corporate income tax at a rate of 33%, payable annually at the end of the year following that in which the tax charge or tax saving arises.

- 100% tax depreciation allowances are available at the time of acquiring an eligible asset such as rolling stock.

- Lease payments made by LL would be allowable for tax when they are incurred.

Required:

(a)   Evaluate, using a discounted cash flow approach as at 1 January 2013, whether it would be cheaper for LL to buy and borrow or enter into an operating lease for the new rolling stock.   **(12 marks)**

(b)   Advise on the impact of each of the two alternative financing approaches on LL's statement of financial position.   **(4 marks)**

(c)   Advise LL which type of financing approach to choose, taking into account:

- Your findings in (a) and (b) above.

- Other relevant factors.   **(9 marks)**

A report format is not required for this question.

(Total: 25 marks)

36   XRG (NOV 12 EXAM)

Assume today is 1 October 2012.

XRG is a long established manufacturer of paper and plastic products, mainly for use in the packaging industry. XRG is based in the UK, where it is the market leader, but it sells worldwide. Its shares are listed on a UK stock exchange.

XRG has three financial objectives:

- Gearing at or below 50% (calculated as the ratio of debt to debt plus equity and based on book values).

- Earnings per share of at least GBP 0.30.

- Dividend per share of at least GBP 0.10.

XRG needs to refinance GBP 1,250 million of 5% secured borrowings that mature on 1 January 2013. The board of XRG has been discussing whether to renegotiate the debt and continue with a relatively high level of gearing or, alternatively, to issue shares via a rights issue and use the proceeds of the issue to repay the debt on 1 January 2013.

In summary, the two alternative financing strategies being considered are:

Financing strategy 1

Renew the debt for 10 years at an interest rate of 6%. As before, it would be secured on the company's non-current assets.

Financing strategy 2

Issue new shares at a discount of 25% on today's share price of GBP 3.33 by means of a rights issue.

Forecast equity and debt balances for XRG as at 31 December 2012:

	GBP million
Equity	
Share capital (50 pence ordinary shares)	500
Reserves	1,550
Debt	
5% secured, maturing 1 January 2013	1,250
7% unsecured, undated	1,250

Additional information:

- The new financing strategy will be implemented on 1 January 2013.

- Profit before interest and tax for the year ended 31 December 2013 is forecast to be GBP 650 million.

- Corporate income tax is payable at 30% of the profit before tax figure.

- The dividend payout ratio will be maintained at 35% of earnings.

- Industry average gearing is 40%.

Required:

(a) **For EACH of the two alternative financing strategies under consideration, construct:**

- **A forecast statement of profit or loss for the year ending 31 December 2013.**

- **A forecast schedule of equity and debt balances as at 31 December 2013.**

(8 marks)

(b) **Evaluate the impact of EACH of the two alternative financing strategies 1 and 2 on:**

(i) **The likely attainment by XRG of each of its three financial objectives.**

(9 marks)

(ii) **XRG's shareholders and debt providers.** **(8 marks)**

A report format is not required for this question.

(Total: 25 marks)

37   PPT (MAR 13 EXAM)

PPT is a private manufacturing company. The company owns patents for certain luxury skin care products which it manufactures and sells to the wholesale market. It is also actively involved in research and development (R&D) of new products. PPT has a pre-tax cost of debt of 3.0% and gearing (debt/debt + equity) of 40%, based on its best estimate of the market values of debt and equity.

PPT is currently considering a number of different possible investment projects, proposed by both the R&D and manufacturing departments.

When evaluating proposed investments, PPT has previously always used a discount rate of 10% to discount expected future cash flows. However, the new Financial Director (FD) has challenged this and has suggested that the company should derive a weighted cost of capital (WACC) using the capital asset pricing model (CAPM). This WACC could then be used as the discount rate in future investment appraisal decisions. The Managing Director (MD) has asked the FD to justify this proposal and to calculate a more appropriate WACC for PPT.

The FD of PPT has identified a company, TT, which operates in the same industry. TT has an equity beta of 2.4 and gearing (debt/debt + equity) of 30% based on market values.

Additional information:

- The long term market risk premium can be assumed to be 4.0%.

- The risk free rate is 1.0%.

- Corporate income tax is charged at 35%.

- Debt betas for both PPT and TT can be assumed to be zero.

Required:

(a)   **Calculate a WACC for PPT using TT's beta.**   **(6 marks)**

(b)   **Explain:**

- **The difference between systematic and unsystematic risk.**

- **The components of the CAPM formula.**

- **The theoretical relationship between these components shown by the CAPM formula.**   **(12 marks)**

(c)   **Advise PPT on the benefits and drawbacks of using the WACC calculated in part (a) above as the discount rate in investment appraisal.**   **(7 marks)**

A report format is not required for this question.

                                                                                   (Total: 25 marks)

38 PPP (MAY 13 EXAM)

PPP is a quoted company which specialises in metal working involving expensive metal forge machines. One of the machines is due to be replaced on 30 June 2013. An investment appraisal exercise has recently been completed which confirmed that it is financially beneficial to replace the machine at this point. PPP is now considering how best to finance the purchase of a replacement machine.

The vendor has offered to structure the sale in the form of a finance lease. Alternatively, the machine could be purchased outright, funded by bank borrowings. However, PPP is already heavily geared.

Buy versus lease evaluation

A trainee accountant has started to draft an evaluation of the two finance proposals (shown below) but has only completed the first three years. However, there appear to be a number of problems with the approach that need to be sorted out before the evaluation can be completed for the full 15 year term of the lease. All figures are given in thousands of Z$.

Line	30 June:	2013	2014	2015	2016
	Buy				
1	Initial investment	500.0			
2	Tax relief on initial investment	(150.0)			
3	Maintenance		(18.0)	(18.0)	(18.0)
	Versus lease				
4	Lease payment		(45.0)	(45.0)	(45.0)
5	Tax relief on lease payment			13.5	13.5
6	Accounting depreciation (W1)		(33.3)	(33.3)	(33.3)
7	Tax relief on accounting depreciation (30% tax rate)			10.0	10.0
8	Implied interest on lease (W2)		(14.0)	(11.6)	(9.4)
9	Tax relief on implied interest (30% tax rate)			4.2	3.5
	Net cash flow	350.0	(110.3)	(80.2)	(78.7)
10	Discount factor (5% discount rate)	1.0	0.952	0.907	0.864
	Present value for first three years	350.0	(105.0)	(72.7)	(68.0)

Workings:

W1: Accounting depreciation

11	Machine costs Z$ 500,000 and is depreciated over 15 years. (33.3 = 500/15)		33.3	33.3	33.3

W2: Implied interest in the lease

12	Opening balance (where 350.0 = 500.0 – 150.0)		350.0	291.0	234.4
13	Less implied interest on lease (4% interest rate)		(14.0)	(11.6)	(9.4)
14	Less lease payment		(45.0)	(45.0)	(45.0)
	Closing balance		291.0	234.4	180.0

Additional information used to compile the lease versus buy evaluation:

- The finance lease would provide finance for the Z$ 500,000 capital equipment required on 30 June 2013. The lease would involve a payment of Z$ 45,000 each year, with the first payment due on 30 June 2014.

- Fixed rate bank borrowings are available for the full initial investment of Z$ 500,000 on 30 June 2013 at an interest rate of 5%. The borrowings would be secured on the capital equipment purchased.

- PPP pays corporate income tax at a rate of 30%, payable annually at the end of the year following that in which the tax charge or tax saving arises. There are sufficient taxable profits within PPP to benefit from any tax savings.

- PPP would account for depreciation on the capital expenditure required to buy the new machine on a straight line basis over its estimated 15 years of useful life.

- PPP would be able to claim 100% tax depreciation allowances in the financial year in which capital expenditure is incurred.

- For leases, both accounting depreciation and the implied interest charge are tax deductible.

- Whether leased or purchased outright, future maintenance would remain the responsibility of PPP and would be in the order of Z$ 18,000 per annum.

Except for the initial investment, all cash flows should be assumed to arise at the end of the year to which they relate.

Required:

(a) Demonstrate that the implied interest in the lease is 4%. **(3 marks)**

(b) (i) Identify which of the numbered lines of data:

- Should not have been included in the evaluation.

- Contain an error. **(8 marks)**

(ii) Produce a corrected version of the evaluation for the same time period.
(8 marks)

(c) Evaluate other factors that are likely to influence PPP's choice between the finance lease and bank borrowings to finance the new machine. **(6 marks)**

A report format is not required for this question.

(Total: 25 marks)

39   BBB (MAY 13 EXAM)

Company BBB is one of Country B's largest house-builders. In 2012, BBB sold over 9,000 houses, ranging from apartment buildings to individual family houses.

Customer satisfaction is considered key to the future success of the business and the company invests considerable resources in planning and delivering new homes to match customer demand. Customer demand depends heavily on property prices and on both the availability and affordability of mortgage finance.

Up-front costs for BBB are considerable. Substantial capital investment is needed between purchasing the land for development and receiving payment for the houses. BBB therefore requires considerable borrowings and equity funding to support its operations.

Over the last ten years, house prices have continued to show steady growth and the house-building industry has generally performed well. This has enabled BBB to reduce its dependence on debt finance.

There has, however, been some discussion amongst Board members regarding the capital structure of the company. Indeed, management consultants employed to review the company's financial management have recently recommended that BBB increase its gearing to a more efficient level. This would decrease the weighted average cost of capital (WACC) and hence increase company value.

The consultants have undertaken a full review of historical financial data for both BBB and the wider house-building industry and have estimated that the theoretical gearing level (debt to debt plus equity) at which WACC is minimised is around 60% for BBB

There has been some extensive debate by the Board concerning the consultants' advice. The Finance Director, in particular, is very concerned about increasing gearing at all in the increasingly uncertain economic climate where interest rates are forecast to rise and the banks are reluctant to provide companies with new funding.

Financial data for BBB

BBB has 150 million ordinary B$1 shares in issue (where B$ is the currency in Country B). The shares are currently trading at B$12.83 per share. The cost of equity is estimated to be 8%.

BBB also has the following debt finance:

- B$300 million floating rate bank loan maturing in 8 years' time with annual interest set at 12 month interbank rates plus 2%. The 12 month interbank rate is currently 3% per annum.

- B$500 million of bonds currently trading at B$105 and a quoted yield of 5%.

BBB pays corporate income tax at a rate of 33% on taxable profits.

Required:

(a) (i) **Explain the relationship between WACC and entity value.**   **(3 marks)**

   (ii) **Calculate BBB's current:**

   - **Gearing (based on market values and measured as debt/debt + equity).**

   - **WACC.**   **(5 marks)**

   (iii) **Calculate, using Modigliani and Miller's (MM's) theory with tax, the theoretical reduction in BBB's WACC if gearing were to be increased to 60%.**
                                                                      (6 marks)

(b) **Evaluate the Finance Director's stated opinion that BBB's gearing should not be increased in the current economic climate. Your answer should take into account:**

   - **The risk profile of BBB.**

   - **Practical considerations affecting the optimum choice of gearing.** **(11 marks)**

A report format is not required for this question.

                                                                      (Total: 25 marks)

40   FF (SEPT 13 EXAM)

FF is a retail company which sells large electrical goods. FF is based in Country F in Asia which has the F$ as its currency. FF operates 10 retail stores in Country F. Most sales are for cash but FF also supplies electrical goods on credit to corporate customers.

On 1 July 2013, the Finance Director compiled forecast data for the current financial year ending 30 June 2014 as follows:

	Notes	F$ million
Sales revenue	1,2	725
Purchases	3,4	370
Other costs	5	325
Capital expenditure	6	30
Dividend	7	20

Notes:

1   Retail sales represent 70% of all sales revenue and all retail sales are on a cash basis. The remaining 30% of sales are to corporate customers on credit.

2   Corporate customers are given 60 days credit and largely kept to these credit terms throughout the previous year. At the time of drawing up the forecast data above, there was no reason to assume that this would change in the coming year.

3   Purchases are made on 120 days credit.

4   Inventory value is expected to remain the same throughout the year ending 30 June 2014. Therefore the purchases figure identified above is equivalent to cost of goods sold.

5   Within 'other costs' is depreciation of F$ 40 million. Apart from depreciation, 'other costs' should be assumed to be paid as incurred.

6   Capital expenditure should also be assumed to be paid as incurred.

7   The dividend is to be paid on 20 June 2014.

Additional information:

- On 1 July 2013, opening balances for working capital were as follows:

    - Accounts receivable: F$ 37.2 million

    - Accounts payable: F$ 124.9 million

    - Inventory: F$ 42.0 million

- The opening cash balance was F$ 50 million on 1 July 2013.

- FF has been careful to retain cash resources and has not needed to arrange any back-up bank facilities in addition to its long term bank borrowings.

- Ignore taxation.

Since 1 July 2013 when the forecast was prepared, market conditions have deteriorated. Indeed, a large competitor company recently went into receivership due largely to liquidity issues following demand by key suppliers for cash on delivery. The directors of FF are keen to seek reassurance from their Finance Director that FF has sufficient liquidity to withstand the liquidity pressures created by this type of risk event.

In particular, the Finance Director of FF has been asked to carry out an urgent review of the liquidity impact of each of the following possible scenarios in respect of the year ending 30 June 2014. Assume all other underlying data remain unchanged.

Scenario 1	Scenario 2	Scenario 3
Sales revenue falls to F$ 630 million but the proportion of retail sales remains unchanged. AND Purchases fall to F$ 321 million.	Sales revenue and purchases as for scenario 1. AND Accounts receivable days rise to 100 days.	Sales revenue and purchases as for scenario 1. AND All suppliers demand cash on delivery. **Note:** Accounts receivable days remain unchanged at 60 days.

Required:

(a) Prepare a cash flow forecast for the year ending 30 June 2014 based on the forecast financial data available on 1 July 2013. **(6 marks)**

(b) Evaluate the impact on the borrowing requirement of FF for each of scenarios 1, 2 and 3 given above. Up to 7 marks are available for calculations. **(10 marks)**

(c) Advise FF how the liquidity challenges it faces might affect its approach to:

- The management of working capital.

- Financing working capital and other short term liquidity requirements.

- Long term financial strategy. **(9 marks)**

A report format is not required for this question.

(Total: 25 marks)

41 RR (SEPT 13 EXAM)

RR is a manufacturing company based in the USA and uses the USD as its functional currency. It has just successfully completed the development of a new product, product X. RR plans to put product X into production shortly. No public announcement has yet been made about product X and the research and development activities related to product X have also been kept secret so far.

Financial information for RR

RR has equity as at 30 September 2013 of:

	USD million
USD 0.50 ordinary shares	375
Reserves	1,725
	————
	2,100

Production of product X

In order to start production of product X, RR needs to acquire equipment costing USD 500 million which will be paid for on 1 January 2014. In the first five years of production, beginning 1 January 2014, RR forecasts operating cash flows attributable to product X as follows:

Year	1	2	3	4	5
	USD million	USD million	USD million	USD million	USD million
Cash inflows	260	275	305	340	350
Cash outflows	250	250	250	250	250

Corporate income tax is charged at 30% and is paid at the end of the year in which it is incurred. The initial equipment cost of USD 500 million is eligible for 25% tax depreciation allowances on a straight line basis.

In year 6, RR expects product X to generate net after tax cash inflows of USD 70 million, declining at a rate of 5% a year in perpetuity thereafter.

At RR's weighted average cost of capital (WACC) of 10%, the net present value (NPV) of the forecast cash flows in perpetuity arising from the production of product X is USD 44.6 million.

Rights issue to finance the production of the new product

RR plans to raise the USD 500 million needed to acquire the new equipment by means of a 1 for 5 rights issue at a discount of 30% to the current share price of USD 4.80. The rights issue will be announced shortly, at the same time as the new product. RR's share price is expected to rise straight away to reflect an increase in the value of the company equal to the expected NPV of the project.

Theoretical Ex-Rights Price (TERP) formulae

(1)   TERP $= \dfrac{1}{N+1} [(N \times \text{cum rights price}) + \text{issue price}]$

(2)   Yield-adjusted TERP $= \dfrac{1}{N+1} [(N \times \text{cum rights price}) + \text{issue price} \times (\text{Ynew/Yold})]$

Required:

(a)   Calculate the TERP using formula (1) opposite and incorporating the project NPV for the production of product X of USD 44.6 million.   **(4 marks)**

(b)   (i)   Demonstrate that the forecast cash flows in perpetuity arising from the production of product X have an internal rate of return (IRR) of approximately 11.3%.   **(8 marks)**

       (ii)   Calculate the yield-adjusted TERP using formula (2) opposite and the project's IRR of 11.3%.   **(4 marks)**

(c)   Advise how you would expect the share price to move following the announcement of the imminent production of product X and the rights issue to finance the plan. Your answer should include reference to:

   •   The efficient market hypothesis.

   •   Your TERP results in parts (a) and (b)(ii), including the relative validity of the two results.

   •   Other relevant factors.   **(9 marks)**

A report format is not required for this question.

                    (Total: 25 marks)

INVESTMENT DECISIONS AND PROJECT CONTROL I – ACQUISITIONS AND MERGERS

42   AB PLC AND YZ PLC *Walk in the footsteps of a top tutor*

AB plc is a firm of recruitment and selection consultants. It has been trading for 10 years and obtained a stock market listing four years ago. It has pursued a policy of aggressive growth and specialises in providing services to companies in high-technology and high-growth sectors. It is all-equity financed by ordinary share capital of £50 million in shares of £0.20 nominal (or par) value. The company's results to the end of June 20X2 have just been announced. Profits before tax were £126.6 million. The Chairman's statement included a forecast that earnings might be expected to rise by 4%, which is a lower annual rate than in recent years. This is blamed on economic factors that have had a particularly adverse effect on high-technology companies.

YZ plc is in the same business but has been established much longer. It serves more traditional business sectors and its earnings record has been erratic. Press comment has frequently blamed this on poor management and the company's shares have been out of favour with the stock market for some time. Its current earnings growth forecast is also 4% for the foreseeable future. YZ plc has an issued ordinary share capital of £180 million in £1 shares. Pre-tax profits for the year to 30 June 20X2 were £112.5 million.

AB plc has recently approached the shareholders of YZ plc with a bid of 5 new shares in AB plc for every 6 YZ plc shares. There is a cash alternative of 345 pence per share.

Following the announcement of the bid, the market price of AB plc shares fell 10% while the price of YZ plc shares rose 14%. The P/E ratio and dividend yield for AB plc, YZ plc and two other listed companies in the same industry *immediately prior* to the bid announcement are shown below. All share prices are in pence.

	20X2				
High		Low	Company	P/E	Dividend yield %
425		325	AB plc	11	2.4
350		285	YZ plc	7	3.1
187		122	CD plc	9	5.2
230		159	WX plc	16	2.4

Both AB plc and YZ plc pay tax at 30%.

AB plc's post-tax cost of equity capital is estimated at 13% per annum and YZ plc's at 11% per annum.

Assume you are a shareholder in YZ plc. You have a large, but not controlling, shareholding and are a qualified management accountant. You bought the shares some years ago and have been very disappointed with their performance. Two years ago you formed a 'protest group' with fellow shareholders with the principal aim of replacing members of the Board. You call a meeting of this group to discuss the bid.

Required:

In preparation for your meeting, write a briefing note for your group to discuss. Your note should:

(a) evaluate whether the proposed share-for-share offer is likely to be beneficial to shareholders in *both* AB plc and YZ plc. You should use the information and merger terms available, plus appropriate assumptions, to forecast post-merger values. As a benchmark, you should then value the two companies using the constant growth form of the dividend valuation model   (13 marks)

(b) discuss the factors to consider when deciding whether to accept or reject the bid and the relative benefits/disadvantages of accepting shares or cash   (8 marks)

(c) advise your shareholder group on what its members should do with their investment in YZ plc, based on your calculations/considerations.   (4 marks)

(Total: 25 marks)

43   TAKEOVER BID (MAY 07 EXAM)

Country Y

Country Y is a large industrialised country with strong motor vehicle and construction industries. The glass industry supplies glass to these industries as well as to specialist users of glass such as contact lens manufacturers. There are five major glass manufacturing entities, each with market coverage in Country Y of between 5% and 40%.

Entity Q

Entity Q is a quoted entity and a major player in the glass industry. It has a market share in Country Y of approximately 35%. It is an old, well-established entity with a number of factories used to manufacture glass both locally and abroad. It has a stable, but unexciting, growth rate of 3% per annum and is facing increasing competition from new glass manufacturing entities setting up in its key markets. However, Q's high earnings levels of earlier years have resulted in relatively low levels of debt.

The head office building of Q is in the far north of Country Y in a remote geographical area. It is a considerable distance from the capital city and major centres of population in the south of the country. The building is much larger than the entity requires and several floors are unoccupied.

The management team of Q is highly experienced; the majority of the senior managers have worked for Q for the whole of their working lives.

The computer systems of Q were written especially for the entity, but are in need of replacement in favour of something more flexible and adaptable to changing circumstances.

Entity Z

Entity Z, with a market share in Country Y of 10%, is a comparatively new and small, but fast growing unquoted family-owned entity. It specialises in certain niche markets for high security and extra heat resistant glass. The patents for this specialist glass were developed by the founder owner who now acts as Managing Director. The development of the business has largely been funded by high levels of borrowings at rates of interest well above standard market rates. In addition, the directors have often been required to provide personal guarantees against personal assets.

The management team of Z works in the capital city of Country Y, which is in the more prosperous southern part of the country. Z has a manufacturing base on the outskirts of the capital city.

The management team of Z is enthusiastic to grow the business, but is continually frustrated by a lack of financial and human resources and marketing network that would enable Z to expand into international markets. Also, on a personal level, many of the senior managers own a substantial number of shares in Z and are keen to realise some of their capital gains and become financially more secure.

The computer systems of Z consist of a basic accounting package and an internal network of PCs. Spreadsheet packages are widely used for budgeting and other financial reporting.

Takeover bid

The directors of Q have approached the directors of Z with a view to making a takeover bid for Z. A condition of the bid would be the retention of the current management team of Z, who have vital knowledge of the specialist manufacturing techniques required to manufacture the product range of Z. The directors of Z have been initially quite positive about the bid.

Both parties are concerned that the deal may be referred to Country Y's Competition Directorate, which regulates the country's competition policy, for approval and that conditions may be imposed that could make the takeover less attractive.

Required:

(a)   Explain the role of competition authorities such as Country Y's Competition Directorate.   **(6 marks)**

(b)   Advise the directors of Q and Z on the potential problems of merging the management structure and systems of the two entities and how these could be minimised.   **(9 marks)**

(c)   Discuss whether the choice of capital structure for the new combined entity is likely to affect the overall value of the entity. Include references to Modigliani and Miller's (MM's) theory of capital structure in your answer.   **(10 marks)**

(Total: 25 marks)

44   GG (MAY 07 EXAM)

GG, a large engineering and project management group, has announced plans to sell its wholly-owned telecommunications subsidiary, BB, so that it can concentrate on its core business of major infrastructure developments.

HH, an entity with diverse business interests, has expressed an interest in making a bid for BB, but the directors of HH are aware that there are likely to be several other interested parties.

News of the possible sale has been well received in the financial markets and GG has seen its share price rise by 15% in the last two months. HH expects to be able to use its good reputation and strong market presence to enhance the prospects of BB by improving BB's annual earnings by 10% from the date of acquisition.

Financial information as at today, 23 May 20X7, ignoring any potential synergistic benefits arising from the possible acquisition of BB by HH:

•   Profit after tax for BB for the year ended 30 April 20X7 is estimated as $1 million

- BB's profit after tax has increased by 7% each year in recent years and this trend is expected to continue

- The gearing level of BB can be assumed to be the same as for GG

- The business tax rate is 30%

- Estimated post-tax return on the market is 8% and the risk free rate is 3% and these rates are not expected to change in the foreseeable future

- Assume a debt beta of zero

	HH	GG	Proxy entity for BB in the same industry
Number of ordinary shares in issue	8 million	4 million	–
Current share price	613 cents	800 cents	–
P/E ratios today	11	14	13
Dividend payout	40%	50%	50%
Equity beta	1.1	1.4	1.4
Gearing (debt : equity at market values)	1 : 2	1 : 2.5	1 : 4
Forecast earnings growth	5%	6%	–

Required:

(a) Calculate an appropriate cost of equity for BB based on the data provided for the proxy entity. **(3 marks)**

(b) (i) Calculate a range of values for BB both before and after any potential synergistic benefits to HH of the acquisition. **(8 marks)**

   (ii) Discuss your results in (b) (i) and advise the directors of HH on a suitable initial cash offer for BB. **(7 marks)**

(c) Advise the directors of GG on both the potential benefits and potential drawbacks arising from the divestment of its subsidiary, BB. **(7 marks)**

(Total: 25 marks)

45 SB PLC (NOV 08 EXAM)

SB plc (SB) is an unquoted entity that provides technical advisory services and human resources to the oil exploration industry. It is based in the UK, but operates worldwide. It has been trading for 15 years. The four founding directors work full time in the business. Other employees are a combination of full time technical consultants and managers, and experts retained for specific contracts. Recruiting and retaining qualified consultants is a challenge and SB has to offer very competitive remuneration packages.

The market for the type of services that SB offers is growing. The large multinational oil entities are currently looking at exploration possibilities in the Caribbean. This will open up substantial new opportunities for SB which will require additional funding. However, the concessions for operating in this region are still under discussion with the various Caribbean governments and the oil multinationals have not yet started formal bidding.

In recent years, SB has been informally approached by some of its competitors and also its major customers to sell out. The directors have so far rejected these approaches but are now re-considering the possibilities. An alternative also being considered is an Initial Public Offering (IPO), that is, a stock market flotation.

Assume today is 1 January 20X3

Current financial information

- Revenue in the year to 31 December 20X2 was £40,250,000 and earnings (profit after tax) were £20,188,000. There are five million shares in issue owned equally by the four directors. No dividends have been paid in any year to date.

- Net book value of buildings, equipment and vehicles plus net working capital is £22,595,000. The book valuations are considered to reflect current realisable values.

- SB is currently all equity financed.

Forecast financial information

- Sales revenue for the year to 31 December 20X3 is expected to be £52,250,000.

- Growth in revenue in the years to 31 December 20X4 and 20X5 is expected to be 20% per annum.

- Operating costs, inclusive of depreciation, are expected in the future to average 60% of revenue each year.

- Assume that book depreciation equals tax depreciation and that profit after tax equals cash flow.

- The marginal rate of tax is expected to remain at 28% per annum, payable in the year in which the liability arises.

- Assume from 20X6 onwards that the 20X5 pre-discounted cash flow will grow at 6% per annum indefinitely. This assumes that no new long-term capital is raised. If the entity is to grow at a faster rate, then new financing will be needed.

Industry statistics

The average P/E ratio for the industry, using a very broad definition, is 12 with a range of 9 to 25. The average cost of capital for the industry is 12%. Cost of capital figures by individual entity are not available.

Required:

Assume you are a financial advisor to SB.

(a) (i) Calculate a range of values, in total and per share, for SB.

   (ii) Advise the directors of SB on the relevance and limitations of each method of valuation to an entity such as theirs, and in the circumstances of the two alternative disposal strategies being considered.

   (iii) Recommend a suitable valuation figure that could be used for a trade sale or an IPO.

   Use whatever methods of valuation you think appropriate and can be estimated with the information available.

   Note: Calculations in part (i) count for up to 10 marks.   **(18 marks)**

(b) Advise the directors of SB on the advantages and disadvantages of a trade sale compared with a stock market flotation at the present time, and recommend a course of action.   **(7 marks)**

A report format is not required for this question.

                                                                (Total: 25 marks)

46   LP (MAY 09 EXAM)

LP's shares are listed on the London Stock Exchange. The directors of LP have made an offer for 100% of the shares in MQ. MQ's directors have rejected the bid. If the bid eventually succeeds, the new combined entity will become the largest in its industry in the UK.

Relevant information is as follows:

	LP	MQ
Share price as at today (20 May 20X9)	305 pence	680 pence
Share price one month ago	310 pence	610 pence
Shares in issue	480 million	130 million
Earnings per share for the year to 31 March 20X9	95 pence	120 pence
Debt outstanding as at 31 March 20X9 (book value)	£350 million	£105 million

- 30% of LP's debt is repayable in 20Y2; 30% of MQ's in 20Y3

- LP's cost of equity is 10%

- LP has cash available of £330 million. MQ's cash balances at the last balance sheet date (31 December 20X8) were £25 million.

Terms of the bid

LP's directors made an opening bid one week ago of 2 LP shares for 1 MQ share. The entity's advisers have told the directors that, in order to succeed, they must consider a cash alternative to the proposed share exchange. If a cash alternative is offered and the bid eventually succeeds, 40% of shareholders are expected to accept the share exchange, and 60% the cash alternative.

Required:

Assume you are a financial manager with LP.

(a)   **Discuss and advise the directors on the likely success of the bid based on the current offer and current market data. Recommend, if necessary, revised terms for the share exchange.**   **(9 marks)**

(b)   (i)   **Discuss the advantages and disadvantages of offering a cash alternative to a share exchange. You should include the following calculations in your answer:**

- **The amount of cash that would be needed based on your recommendation of revised terms in part (a) above**

- **The impact of the proposed finance on the combined entity's gearing (debt to debt plus equity).**   **(11 marks)**

(ii)   **Recommend how the cash alternative might be financed.**   **(5 marks)**

Note: A report format is not required for this question.

(Total: 25 marks)

47 RV (MAY 09 EXAM) *Walk in the footsteps of a top tutor*

RV is a private entity based in the UK and operating in a service industry. It has been trading for five years. All the directors and most of the employees are shareholders. None of them has attempted to sell shares in the entity so the problem of placing a value on them has not arisen. It has one external shareholder, which is a venture capital trust. This trust owns 15% of the share capital.

Revenue and profit before tax last year (20X7) were £109 million and £10 million respectively. RV pays corporate tax at 30%. The book value of total net assets as at the last balance sheet date was £25 million.

The entity is currently all-equity financed. The ordinary share capital of the entity is £4 million in shares of 20 pence par value. Dividends have been paid each year since 20X3 at a fixed payout ratio of 25% of earnings. In the current year (20X8) earnings are likely to be slightly lower than in 20X7 by approximately 5%. However, RV's directors have decided to pay a dividend of the same amount per share as in 20X7.

The directors are evaluating investment opportunities that would require all the entity's free cash flow for 20X8 plus long term borrowings of £20 million carrying an interest rate of 8% before tax. If the entity does not borrow to invest, growth in earnings and dividends will be zero for the foreseeable future. If it does borrow and invest, then growth in earnings and dividends are expected to be an average of 6% per annum from 20X9 onwards.

RV's cost of equity is currently 12%. This is expected to rise to 13% if borrowing takes place.

Required

(a) (i) Calculate, in total and per share, a value for equity under each of the following two bases:

- Using the dividend valuation model and assuming no new investment

- Using Modigliani and Miller's theory of capital structure/gearing and assuming the entity borrows and invests. **(8 marks)**

(ii) Discuss the limitations of the two methods of valuation you have just used and advise RV on a more appropriate method. **(7 marks)**

(b) Assuming some of the employees, who between them own 5% of the share capital, wish to sell their shares:

- Advise RV's directors whether either of the values you have calculated in part (a) would be an appropriate valuation for these small shareholdings as compared with a valuation for the whole entity. Include some discussion about how dividend policy might affect the valuation of an entity such as RV.

- Explain how and to whom the shares might be sold. **(10 marks)**

Note: A report format is not required for this question.

(Up to 14 marks are available for calculations)

(Total: 25 marks)

48   XK (MAY 10 EXAM)

XK is a multinational manufacturer of household electrical goods. Its headquarters and main manufacturing base are in the USA. Each manufacturing operation is usually established as a separate wholly-owned subsidiary. The larger electrical appliances tend to carry higher margins and there is a general move away from manufacturing smaller appliances.

Extracts from XK Group's latest statement of financial position at 30 April 20X0:

	US$ millions
ASSETS	
Non-current assets	2,250
Current assets	700
Total assets	2,950
EQUITY AND LIABILITIES	
Equity	
Share capital (Common shares of US$1)	375
Retained earnings	1,150
Total equity	1,525
Non-current liabilities	
Secured 7.5% bonds repayable 20Y0	1,000
Current liabilities	425
Total liabilities	1,425
Total equity and liabilities	2,950

Notes:

- XK's bonds are secured on its non-current assets.

- The current liabilities include overdraft of US$150 million. The conditions of the overdraft require XK to maintain a current ratio of at least 1.5 : 1.

- Group earnings for the year to 30 April 20X0 were US$510 million.

- XK pays corporate tax at 25% per annum.

- XK's share price has risen 5% over the past 3 months to its present level of US$8.75. The stock market price index has fallen by 3% in the same period.

The XK Board is discussing the divestment of one of its US subsidiaries, Company Y, which manufactures smaller appliances. Historically, the subsidiary company, Y, has accounted for 6% of group earnings. XK's accountants, with some input from the subsidiary's management team, have determined a net present value (NPV) to be placed on Company Y of US$325 million. The Executive Directors of Y believe they can transform the business if they have the freedom to respond to market challenges and are considering a management buyout (MBO).

Financing the MBO:

The financing of the MBO will be by a combination of funding from the Executive Directors of Y, an investment bank and a Venture Capitalist.

The Executive Directors of Y expect to be able to raise US$5 million between themselves as equity.

The investment bank will lend a maximum of 90% of the non-current assets of the business secured on those non-current assets, which are valued in the accounts at US$220 million. The interest rate will be 6% and the principal will be repayable in 5 years' time. This rate compares with current prime, or base, rate of 2% and commercial bank secured lending rates of between 3% and 4%.

The venture capitalist will supply the balance of the funding required. The venture capitalist expects a return on its investment averaging 25% per annum (on a compound basis) by 31 March 20X5 and requires all earnings to be retained in the business for 5 years. Some of the MBO team are not happy with this requirement.

Required:

(a)   Evaluate the interests of the various stakeholder groups in both XK and its subsidiary Company Y, and how these might be affected by the divestment.

(7 marks)

(b)   Discuss the economic and market factors that might impact on the negotiations between XK and the various financiers of the divestment (the Executive Directors of Y, the investment bank and the venture capitalist).   (7 marks)

(c)   Evaluate the advantages and disadvantages of the proposed buyout structure, and recommend alternative financing structures for the buyout.

Up to 5 marks are available for calculations   (11 marks)

(Total: 25 marks)

49   ADS (NOV 10 EXAM)

ADS operates a number of large department stores based in a developed country in Asia. Its shares are listed on an Asian stock exchange. It has shown year-on-year growth in earnings and dividends every year since it became a listed company ten years ago. Some years have shown better growth than others but even in a relatively poor year earnings in real terms have been higher than in the previous year. It is currently all-equity financed. Approximately half of its shareholders are institutional investors; the other half is made up of large holdings by the original founding family members and small investors including many employees of ADS.

The directors of ADS are proposing to raise A$250 million to invest in new, smaller stores. This investment will carry similar risk to ADS's current business. It is proposed that the investment will be financed by an issue of an undated bond carrying 5% interest pre-tax. This rate is deemed to reflect the returns required by the market for the risk and duration of the bond. Some of the directors are reluctant to agree to debt finance as they think it will lower the value of equity and this might be a matter of concern for shareholders. The investment is planned for the end of 20X0.

The following information is relevant:

- Earnings for ADS are forecast to be A$127.1 million in 20X1. This forecast assumes that the new stores are already fully operational at the start of 20X1. From the year 20X2 onwards, earnings are expected to increase at a rate of 4% per annum indefinitely.

- The corporate income tax rate is 25%. This is not expected to change.

- The cost of equity for ADS as an all-equity financed company is 9%.

- There are 300 million shares in issue, currently quoted at A$8.50.

One of ADS's directors has recently read an article about company valuation and the differences between Modigliani and Miller (MM) models and the 'traditional' view.

Required:

(a) **Discuss:**

- **How the MM models, both with and without corporate taxes, differ from the 'traditional' view of the relationship between gearing and cost of capital. Accompany your discussion with appropriate graphical illustrations.**

- **The limitations of MM models in 'real world' situations.** **(10 marks)**

(b) **(i)** **Calculate the value of ADS's equity using discounted cash flow techniques, assuming that the new stores are financed by equity.** **(2 marks)**

(ii) **Calculate, assuming that the new stores are financed by the undated bond and using the MM model with corporate taxes, the following:**

- **The value of ADS's equity**

- **The expected cost of equity**

- **The weighted average cost of capital (WACC).** **(6 marks)**

(c) **Explain your results in (b) above and advise the directors whether their concern about lowering the value of equity is valid.** **(7 marks)**

A report format is not required for this question.

(Total: 25 marks)

50 WW (MAY 11 EXAM)

Today's date is 26 May 20X1.

WW is a publishing company that is listed in an Asian country, Country A, which uses the A$ as its currency. WW operates as three separate divisions according to type of publication as follows:

- Public Division – magazines and journals that are widely available in retail stores for purchase by the general public.

- Specialist Division – specialist magazines for particular industry sectors which are only available for delivery by post.

- In-house Division – company in-house journals for circulation to its own staff members.

WW has been disappointed with the recent performance of the Specialist Division and is considering selling that division. WW manages the company's debt centrally and measures the performance of the divisions on the basis of EBIT (earnings before interest and tax).

XX, a book publishing company, has expressed an interest in purchasing the Specialist Division. XX is also located in Country A and is confident that it has the expertise required to improve the performance of the Specialist Division. XX would purchase the net assets employed in the division (that is, non-current assets plus working capital). All borrowings would remain with WW.

There has been some discussion amongst the Directors of XX as to the most appropriate method to use to value the Specialist Division.

- **Director A** has suggested that an asset-based valuation should be used.

- **Director B** has proposed that the valuation should be based on the future operating cash flows of the division, adjusted for tax and discounted by XX's existing weighted average cost of capital (WACC).

- **Director C** has suggested that the WACC used in the valuation should be derived from a proxy company. He has identified YY as a possible proxy for the Specialist Division. YY's sole activity is publishing specialist magazines in a similar market to the Specialist Division.

- **Director D** has suggested that the earnings valuation model should be used based on an estimated cost of equity for the Specialist Division.

Financial data for WW's Specialist Division

The management of WW have provided XX with the following financial data for the Specialist Division:

- The net assets employed in the division had a book value of A$ 15.0 million and an estimated replacement value of A$ 20.0 million on 31 March 20X1.

- Operating cash flows adjusted for tax were A$ 2.5 million in the year ended 31 March 20X1.

- Operating cash flows are forecast to grow by only 1% per annum in perpetuity if the division remains within WW.

Financial data for XX and YY

	XX	YY
Equity beta	1.5	0.8
Gearing ratio (debt/(debt plus equity))	40%	25%
Pre tax cost of debt	6%	7%
Market capitalisation	A$ 150 million	A$ 30 million

Additional relevant information for all companies WW, XX and YY:

- Corporate income tax rate is 30%.

- Risk free rate is 5%.

- The premium over the risk free rate by the market is 6%.

- Debt betas are zero.

Required:

(a) Calculate:

    (i)   XX's existing cost of equity.   **(1 mark)**

    (ii)   XX's existing weighted average cost of capital (WACC).   **(2 marks)**

    (iii)   A suitable WACC for the Specialist Division based on proxy YY, adjusted for XX's gearing.   **(5 marks)**

(b)   (i)   Calculate a range of values for the Specialist Division based on the different methods suggested by Directors A, B and C (but not Director D).   **(5 marks)**

    (ii)   Discuss the validity of the methods suggested by each of the four Directors A, B, C and D.   **(8 marks)**

    (iii)   Advise XX on an appropriate price for the purchase of the Specialist Division.   **(4 marks)**

A report format is not required for this question.

(Total: 25 marks)

51   **MMM RECRUITMENT (SEPT 11 EXAM)**

MMM is a recruitment agency. It has seen rapid growth in recent years and obtained a stock market listing 3 years ago. However, recent profits have been disappointing, largely as a result of poor economic conditions leading to limited employment opportunities.

MMM is planning a takeover bid for JJJ, a rival recruitment agency in a specialist, growing market that has not been affected to such an extent by the poor economic conditions. JJJ has an advanced information technology and information system which was developed in-house and which MMM would acquire the rights to use. MMM plans to adopt JJJ's information technology and information system following the acquisition and this is expected to be a major contributor to the overall estimated synergistic benefits of the acquisition, which are estimated to be in the order of $8 million.

MMM has 30 million shares in issue and a current share price of $6.90 before any public announcement of the planned takeover. MMM is forecasting growth in earnings of 6% a year for the foreseeable future.

JJJ has 5 million shares in issue and a current share price of $12.84. It is forecasting growth in earnings of 9% a year for the foreseeable future.

The directors of MMM are considering 2 alternative bid offers:

Bid offer A – Share based bid of 2 MMM shares for each JJJ share.

Bid offer B – Cash offer of $13.50 per JJJ share.

Required:

(a)   Assuming synergistic benefits are realised, evaluate bid offer A and bid offer B from the viewpoint of:

    (i)   MMM's existing shareholders.

    (ii)   JJJ's shareholders.

    Up to 7 marks are available for calculations.   **(11 marks)**

(b)   Advise the directors of MMM on:

(i)   The potential impact on the shareholders of both MMM and JJJ of not successfully realising the potential synergistic benefits after the takeover.

Up to 5 marks are available for calculations.   **(8 marks)**

(ii)   The steps that could be taken to minimise the risk of failing to realise the potential synergistic benefits arising from the adoption of JJJ's information technology and information system.   **(6 marks)**

A report format is not required for this question.

(Total: 25 marks)

52   YY GROUP (SEPT 11 EXAM)

Assume today is 1 October 20X1.

YY Group is a manufacturer of consumer electronic appliances and its shares are listed on a major stock exchange. The functional currency of the YY group is the $.

The Board of YY is considering the disposal of a wholly-owned subsidiary, TS, that manufactures telecommunications equipment. The CEO of YY thinks this subsidiary is not central to the group's main financial objective and strategic direction and utilises valuable resources that could be more profitably employed in its core businesses. TS, while profitable, has consistently reported lower growth rates than the group as a whole and therefore the CEO is recommending the disposal of the subsidiary.

The Finance Director of YY is not convinced of the need for disposal. He has correctly noted that this subsidiary continues to make a contribution to profits. He thinks that unless an opportunity can be identified that requires this level of investment and can better aid the achievement of the group's objective, YY should not sell TS. His estimate is that TS is worth just under $1 billion ($1,000 million).

The senior managers of TS have indicated they are interested in pursuing a management buyout (MBO). The Board of YY is willing to consider this but some Board members, who agree with the divestment of TS in principle, think a trade sale would be a better alternative.

A meeting of the management team of TS has been called by Mr A, the Managing Director of TS, to discuss a range of issues that need to be considered if they are to launch an MBO. The following views have been expressed by various members of the management team of TS.

Mr A – Managing Director of TS

"I am convinced that we, the management team, can add value to TS. We need to identify how and why, under our own control, we can achieve greater returns from the business than under YY's control. We also need to be able to convince the Board of YY that selling the business to us by means of an MBO is more attractive for them than a trade sale."

Ms B – Financial Manager of TS

"Financing will be a major problem if the Finance Director of YY is correct in his valuation. The TS management team and employees would be able to raise no more than 20% of this value. I have therefore had informal discussions with a venture capital organisation. It is very interested and has money available. However, before starting formal negotiations, I would like to know more about the advantages and disadvantages of venture capital financing in our situation and also whether there are any realistic alternatives."

Mr C – Marketing Manager of TS

"Ms B has explained to me that the $1 billion ($1,000 million) valuation produced by the Finance Director of YY is based on YY's P/E ratio. I have three questions:

1   How is the $1 billion ($1,000 million) calculated? This seems excessive as the net asset value is substantially less than this.

2   Is the net asset value the one we should be focussing on?

3   Are there any other, more appropriate, valuations or methods of valuation?"

Summary financial data

	YY Group (inc TS)	TS
Earnings in the financial year ended 31 August 20X1 ($ million)	1,260	75
Book value of net assets as at 31 August 20X1 ($ million) (Net assets are stated after deducting borrowings.)	8,050	735
Shares in issue on 31 August (unchanged at 1 October 20X1)	525 million	25 million
Share price on 31 August 20X1 ($)	31.20	n/a
Share price on 1 October 20X1 ($)	31.50	n/a

The P/E ratios of companies in the telecommunications industry in the region generally range from 8 to 25. The average P/E ratio is 15.

Required:

Assume you are an independent advisor retained and paid by the management team of TS to advise on the proposed MBO. Prepare briefing notes for a forthcoming meeting with the management team of TS in which you evaluate the concerns raised in respect of the proposed MBO by the following people:

(a)	**Mr A – Managing Director of TS**	**(7 marks)**
(b)	**Ms B – Financial Manager of TS**	**(7 marks)**
(c)	**Mr C – Marketing Manager of TS**	**(11 marks)**

Up to 4 marks are available for calculations in part (c).

A report format is not required for this question.

(Total: 25 marks)

53 TNG (MAR 13 EXAM)

Today is 1 March 2013.

TNG is a group, listed on a European stock exchange, which provides a comprehensive range of equipment and services to the oil industry. Its Head Office is in a country in the Eurozone, with subsidiaries based all around the world.

One of TNG's wholly owned subsidiaries, known as TNG Logistics and Procurement (L&P) offers maintenance and support services for the equipment which is supplied by other TNG subsidiaries. L&P is based in a country in the Eurozone. However, its revenues are always invoiced in USD. Some suppliers to L&P submit invoices in USD but others invoice L&P in EUR.

The main board of TNG has been considering divestment of L&P for some time and has recently received an informal approach from GNT, one of L&P's main competitors. The directors of TNG are now interested in ascertaining an appropriate price for the sale of its shares in L&P and are considering using both a Discounted Cash Flow (DCF) method and a Calculated Intangible Value (CIV) method to establish a value for L&P's equity.

Relevant information for the DCF valuation

Forecast operating cash flows in respect of the year starting on 1 April 2013 are shown below.

Cash inflows (revenue):	USD 155 million
Cash outflows (costs):	
Invoiced in USD	USD 35 million
Invoiced in EUR	EUR 40 million

Additional information:

- L&P is funded wholly by equity.

- It is anticipated that the forecast operating cash flows for the year starting on 1 April 2013 will increase by 10% per annum for the next two years and then by 5% per annum in perpetuity thereafter.

- L&P is committed to a contract to acquire a piece of machinery for EUR 30 million which will need to be paid for in full on 1 April 2013. This machinery is likely to be used in the business for a significant number of years and will thus have a residual value of zero. Special tax depreciation allowances are available on this type of machinery on a straight line basis over three years.

- It is anticipated that EUR 5 million (net of any tax relief) will be spent annually on ongoing investment in non-current assets and working capital necessary to maintain L&P's operations. This will first be incurred in the year ending 31 March 2014 and will then grow at 5% per annum in perpetuity.

- All cash flows, other than the initial purchase of the machinery can be assumed to occur at the end of the year to which they relate.

- The spot exchange rate is forecast to be EUR/USD 1.3000 (that is, EUR 1 = USD 1.3000) on 1 April 2013. The EUR is expected to strengthen against the USD by 1% per annum over the next three years. It can be assumed that exchange rates remain constant from the end of year 3 onwards.

- The weighted average cost of capital can be assumed to be 14% for TNG and 10% for L&P.

- The corporate income tax rate applicable to L&P is 30%. Tax is paid in EUR in the year in which the tax is incurred.

CIV valuation

The directors of TNG have already calculated a value for L&P's intangible assets using the CIV method. This calculation is given below. All averages relate to results over the last three years.

	EUR million
Average profit before tax for L&P	44.10
Industry average return on tangible assets of 11% multiplied by average L&P tangible assets of EUR 325m (= 11% × EUR 325 million)	(35.75)
Value spread	8.35
Less tax at 30%	(2.51)
Post tax value spread	5.84

The post tax value spread is then discounted at L&P's weighted average cost of capital of 10% to give a CIV value of EUR 58.40 million (= EUR 5.84 million/0.10).

A value for L&P is obtained by adding the CIV value of intangible assets to L&P's tangible net asset value of EUR 295.00 million to give a total value of EUR 353.40 million.

(Where EUR 353.40 million = EUR 58.40 million + EUR 295.00 million.)

Required:

(a) Calculate a value for L&P in EUR as at 1 April 2013 based on discounted cash flow analysis. **(12 marks)**

(b) Explain:

- The types of intangible asset that L&P is likely to hold.

- The rationale behind the CIV method of valuing intangible assets. **(6 marks)**

(c) Compare and contrast the validity of the DCF and CIV valuations of L&P for the purpose of establishing an appropriate asking price for the sale of L&P. **(7 marks)**

A report format is not required for this question.

(Total: 25 marks)

54   NN (MAY 13 EXAM)

NN is a listed US international sports clothing and footwear manufacturer that specialises in the high-tech end of the market.   NN owns various sports brand names and manufactures sports clothing products by contract with companies in the Far East.   NN then distributes the products and sells them through wholesale and retail outlets worldwide, including its main high- tech brands N1, N2 and N3 in its expensive main stores in London, Paris, New York and Tokyo.

Brand N4

As well as the high-tech brands, NN also owns brand N4 which was acquired a few years ago. In the year ended 31 March 2007, the year that N4 was acquired, N4 had total revenue of USD 246 million. Despite investment and marketing campaigns, N4 has failed to show consistent growth in revenue and profit since it was acquired. Indeed, in the year ended 31 March 2013, annual revenues were lower than 2006/2007 levels, at just USD 190 million, and N4 had an after tax loss of USD 41 million in the year after charging central overheads of USD 21 million. NN expects this level of loss to continue for the foreseeable future.

Potential sale of N4 to QQ

At the start of 2013, NN announced that it was interested in selling the N4 brand name and company QQ immediately expressed an interest in buying it.

QQ operates in a different type of market to NN. The brands that it owns are mostly at the low-price end of the sports clothing market and are marketed through less prestigious retail outlets such as hypermarket stores in cheaper out of town locations.   These low-price stores focus on selling large quantities of goods at the lowest price possible. The stores keep costs low by spending less on display and marketing and being located in cheaper out-of-town areas. Their customer base largely comprises lower income families but the stores also attract higher earners who are looking for goods at a bargain price.

QQ focuses on minimising costs and also allocates a much smaller amount than NN to spend on advertising and promotion of its brands and does not maintain costly main stores in key capital cities.

QQ's valuation of N4

The directors of QQ have conservatively estimated that, under QQ's cost structure and management, N4 can be expected to generate free cash flow of USD 22 million per annum, with zero growth in real terms.

Financial data for both NN and QQ as at close of business on 30 April 2013

NN position:

- 6,000 million ordinary USD 0.50 (nominal) shares in issue.

- Estimated 'real' weighted average cost of capital (WACC) of 8%.

- Gearing of 40% (debt/debt plus equity, market values).

QQ position:

- 1,800 million ordinary USD 1.00 (nominal) shares in issue.

- Estimated 'real' WACC of 6%.

- Gearing of 50% (debt/debt plus equity, market values).

The issued share capital for both NN and QQ remained unchanged on 1 May 2013.

Details of sales agreed on 1 May 2013

After a period of negotiation and due diligence, QQ submitted an offer to NN on 1 May 2013 to purchase N4 at an offer price of USD 150 million. By prior arrangement, this offer was accepted on the same day. Details of the sale were immediately released into the public domain, including the price agreed.

On that same day, 1 May 2013, the day that the offer became public, NN's shares moved up 6 cents in New York, closing at USD 87.23 per share, and QQ's shares gained 1.5%, closing at USD 15.53 per share.

Mr Q's queries

Mr Q is a newly appointed non-executive director of QQ and he has a list of concerns about the proposed purchase of N4 which the Finance Director of QQ needs to address. These concerns are listed below:

1   How is it possible that the share price of both QQ and NN increased on the day that the sale was announced?

2   How can QQ expect to generate higher profits from N4 than NN was able to?

3   What courses of action are open to QQ if it fails to generate sufficient returns from N4?

Required:

(a)   (i)   **Calculate the value of N4 from the viewpoint of both NN and QQ based on discounted cash flow (DCF) analysis as at 1 May 2013.**   **(4 marks)**

       (ii)   **Evaluate the market's reaction to the proposed sale in comparison with your results in (a)(i) above. Your answer should include a calculation of the increase in market capitalisation for both NN and QQ on 1 May 2013.**

(9 marks)

(b)   **Produce a response to Mr Q, assuming you are the Finance Director of QQ, in which you address each of Mr Q's three queries.**   **(12 marks)**

A report format is not required for this question.

(Total: 25 marks)

INVESTMENT DECISIONS AND PROJECT CONTROL II – PROJECT APPRAISAL

55   CTC TECHNOLOGY COLLEGE (MAY 05 EXAM)

CTC Technology College (CTC) is a non-profit making institution located in Ireland, where the national currency is the euro. The college is funded by a combination of student fees and government grants.

The number of students enrolled on the part-time Information Technology course at CTC has fallen over recent years due to competition from other colleges and the wide range of different courses available. The number of students enrolling on the current course, ITS (IT Skills) has stabilised at around 150 students per annum and there are currently 20 computers surplus to requirements which CTC plans to sell for an estimated €100 each; the current book value of each computer is €200. However, this sale will not occur if the college goes ahead with its plan to replace the current ITS course with an updated course, as it is expected that a new course would result in a significant increase in student numbers.

CTC realises that the financial viability of switching courses is highly dependent on the number of students that the college can attract onto the new course and has commissioned some market research, at a cost of €10,000, into the best course content and likely increase in student numbers. The results of this research indicate that an ITC (IT Competence) course would be the most popular and lead to a significant increase in student enrolments at the college. It is also estimated that there could be an additional benefit to the college of average net revenues of €20 per additional student over and above 150 as a result of those students being attracted to the college and taking other courses at the college at the same time as the ITC course.

The new ITC course would be run by existing staff currently working on the ITS course at a cost of €50,000 per annum. If, however, the numbers of students on ITC were to rise above 200 per annum, an additional part-time member of staff would be needed at a cost of €10,000 per annum, payable in advance. If ITC is adopted, several computers would need to be upgraded at a total one-off cost of €15,000.

Other relevant data is as follows:

	ITS	ITC
	€	€
Fee for the course (per student, payable in advance)	350	360
Directly attributable course costs (per annum, payable in arrears)	1,000	2,000
Books and consumables per student, payable in advance	50	60
Apportionment of college overheads (excluding staff costs) (per annum, charged at the end of the year)	20,000	25,000
Staff training and course development (initial set-up cost)	0	30,000

The planning horizon for the college is four years and projects are evaluated using a discount rate of 8% and on the basis of a zero terminal value at the end of the four-year period. Each course is of one year duration and student enrolments should be assumed to remain constant throughout the four-year period, with ITS attracting 150 students each year.

Taxation and inflation should be ignored.

Required:

(a) Evaluate the number of student enrolments required on the ITC course in order for it to be financially beneficial, on a net present value of cash flow basis, for the college to replace the ITS course with the ITC course. **(15 marks)**

(b) Advise the governing body of the college on the following issues:

(i) how to monitor and control the costs and revenues of the project from the decision to introduce the new course to the start date of the course.

(5 marks)

(ii) options available if only 150 students enrol on the new ITC course by the enrolment deadline two weeks before the beginning of the course by which time all other course preparations will have been completed. **(5 marks)**

(Total: 25 marks)

56   RST (MAY 06 EXAM)

RST is a publicly owned and funded health organisation based in the Far East. It is reviewing a number of interesting possibilities for new development projects in the area and has narrowed down the choice to the five projects detailed below. RST is aware that government budget restrictions may be tighter in a year's time and so does not want to commit to a capital budget of more than $30 million in year 1. In addition, any project cash inflows in year 1 may be used to fund capital expenditure in that year. There is sufficient capital budget remaining in year 0 to enable all projects to be undertaken. Under government funding rules, any unused capital in year 0 cannot be carried over to year 1 and no interest may be earned on unused capital. No borrowings are permitted.

RST assesses capital projects at a hurdle rate of 15% based on the equity beta of health-based companies in the private sector.

	Cash outflows		Cash inflows	
	Year 0	Year 1		
Project	$ million	$ million	$ million	
A	9	16	4	from year 1 in perpetuity
B	10	10	4	from year 2 in perpetuity
C	10	12	5	in years 1 to 10
D	8	5	6	in years 3 to 7
E	9	8	{ 2	in years 1 to 5
			{ 5	in years 6 to 15

Notes

- The projects are not divisible.
- Each project can only be undertaken once.
- Ignore tax.

Required:

(a)   Advise RST on the best combination of projects based on an evaluation of each project on the basis of both:

(i)   **NPV of cash flows**

(ii)   **a profitability index for use in this capital rationing analysis.**   **(15 marks)**

(b)   **Discuss:**

(i)   **whether or not capital rationing techniques based on NPV analysis are appropriate for a publicly owned entity such as RST**   **(5 marks)**

(ii)   **as a publicly owned entity, what other factors RST should consider and what other analysis it should undertake before making a final decision on which project(s) to accept.**   **(5 marks)**

(Total: 25 marks)

57   GHI (MAY 06 EXAM)

GHI is a mobile phone manufacturer based in France with a wide customer base in France and Germany, with all costs and revenues based in euro (€). GHI is considering expanding into the UK market and has begun investigating how to break into this market and is designing a new phone specifically for it. A small project committee has been formed to plan and control the project.

After careful investigation, the following project cash flows have been identified:

Year	£ million
0	(10)
1	5
2	5
3	4
4	3
5	3

The project is to be funded by a loan of €16 million at an annual interest rate of 5% and repayable at the end of five years. Loan issue costs amount to 2% and are tax deductible.

GHI has a debt : equity ratio of 40 : 60 based on market values, a pre-tax cost of debt of 5.0% and a cost of equity of 10.7%.

Tax on entity profits in France can be assumed to be at a rate of 35%, payable in the year in which it arises. UK tax at 25% is deductible in full against French tax in the same time period under the terms of the double tax treaty between the UK and France. The initial investment of £10 million will not qualify for any tax relief.

Assume the current spot rate is £1 = €1.60 and sterling (£) is expected to weaken against the euro by 3% per annum (so that in year 1 it is worth only 97% of its value in euro (€) in year 0).

Required:

(a)   Advise GHI on whether or not to proceed with the project based on a calculation of its adjusted present value (APV) and describe the limitations of an APV approach in this context.   **(15 marks)**

(b)   Explain the function of the project committee of GHI in the following stages of the project:

(i)   determining customer requirements and an appropriate product design for the UK market, and   **(5 marks)**

(ii)   controlling the implementation stage of the project.   **(5 marks)**

(Total: 25 marks)

58   CD FURNITURE MANUFACTURER (NOV 06 EXAM)

CD is a furniture manufacturer based in the UK. It manufactures a limited range of furniture products to a very high quality and sells to a small number of retail outlets worldwide.

At a recent meeting with one of its major customers it became clear that the market is changing and the final consumer of CD's products is now more interested in variety and choice rather than exclusivity and exceptional quality.

CD is therefore reviewing two mutually exclusive alternatives to apply to a selection of its products:

Alternative 1

To continue to manufacture, but expand its product range and reduce its quality. The net present value (NPV), internal rate of return (IRR) and modified internal rate of return (MIRR) for this alternative have already been calculated as follows:

NPV	=	£1.45 million using a nominal discount rate of 9%
IRR	=	10.5%
MIRR	=	Approximately 13.2%

Alternative 2

To import furniture carcasses in 'flat packs' from the USA. The imports would be in a variety of types of wood and unvarnished. CD would buy in bulk from its US suppliers, assemble and varnish the furniture and re-sell, mainly to existing customers. An initial investigation into potential sources of supply and costs of transportation has already been carried out by a consultancy entity at a cost of £75,000.

CD's Finance Director has provided estimates of net sterling and US$ cash flows for this alternative. These net cash flows, in real terms, are shown below.

Year	0	1	2	3
US$m	−25.00	2.60	3.80	4.10
£m	0	3.70	4.20	4.60

The following information is relevant:

- CD evaluates all its investments using nominal Sterling cash flows and a nominal discount rate. All non-UK customers are invoiced in US$. US$ nominal cash flows are converted to Sterling at the forward rate and discounted at the UK nominal rate.

- For the purposes of evaluation, assume the entity has a three-year time horizon for investment appraisals.

- Based on recent economic forecasts, inflation rates in the US are expected to be constant at 4% per annum. UK inflation rates are expected to be 3% per annum. The current exchange rate is £1 = US$1.6.

Note: Ignore taxation.

Required:

Assume that you are the Financial Manager of CD.

(a) Calculate the net present value (NPV), internal rate of return (IRR) and (approximate) modified internal rate of return (MIRR) of alternative 2.   **(12 marks)**

(b) Briefly discuss the appropriateness and possible advantages of providing MIRRs for the evaluation of the two alternatives.   **(4 marks)**

(c) Evaluate the two alternatives and recommend which alternative the entity should choose. Include in your answer some discussion about what other criteria could or should be considered before a final decision is taken.   **(9 marks)**

Note: A report format is NOT required for this question.

(Total: 25 marks)

59   UVW (NOV 07 EXAM)

UVW is a manufacturer of specialist components for the motor trade. Most of the entity's business is 'to order'; very little is manufactured for inventory. The components are sold to customers worldwide but, to date, have been manufactured solely in the UK. The Directors of UVW are reviewing the opportunity to establish a manufacturing base in Asia. There would be some loss of productivity, especially in the first year of operations, but the long-term cost savings would outweigh this.

Two senior managers from the UK will be sent to the Asian country to establish the overseas operation and remain there for the first 12 months. The cost of their salaries, travel and accommodation while in Asia is budgeted at £250,000 for the year.

This cost is included in the figures below.

Capital equipment purchased in UK for the Asian project:	£2 million
Premises and equipment purchased in Asia:	Asian $100 million

Operating cash flows are (year):	One	Two	Three
Costs of Asian operation (Asian $million)	−70	−65	−60.0
Comparable costs of UK operation (£million)	−1.5	−4.5	−4.75

Other information available:

- Assume all cash flows are after tax and that operating cash flows occur at the end of each year.

- The year three cost advantage in sterling is assumed to maintain from year four until year eight. UVW does not evaluate investments beyond eight years.

- The current spot rate is Asian $20 to £1.

- A feasibility study has been carried out in the Asian country at a cost of Asian $1.2 million.

- Expected inflation rate in the Asian country is 8% per annum. In the UK, it is 4% per annum. The risk-free rate in the UK is 3%.

- UVW uses a discount rate of 10% for all its investment decisions.

The entity's Finance Manager does not think 10% adequately reflects the risk of this project. He believes the cost advantage of the Asian operation could fall short of the evaluated DCFs by as much as 20% in year one, 25% in year two, and 30% from year three onwards. His rough calculations suggest that, using his estimates, the project shows a substantial negative NPV.

Required:

(a) (i) **Calculate the sterling NPV of the project both with, and without, adjusting for certainty equivalents.** **(12 marks)**

(ii) **Discuss briefly other internal factors the entity should consider before deciding whether the project should proceed. You are not required to discuss external economic factors or hedging techniques. Include comments on the use of certainty equivalents and why the Finance Manager's 'rough calculations' might have been wrong.** **(6 marks)**

Calculations count for up to 12 marks.

(b) **Advise the Directors of UVW whether or not the management of working capital should be carried out in the Asian country compared with maintaining a centralised function in the UK.** **(7 marks)**

A report format is not required for this question.

(Total: 25 marks)

60 CM LIMITED (MAY 08 EXAM) *Walk in the footsteps of a top tutor*

CM Limited (CM) is a private entity that supplies and distributes equipment to the oil industry in the UK. It is evaluating two potential investments. Investment 1 would expand its operations in the UK, Investment 2 would establish a base in Asia that would allow it to market and sell its products to entities in a wider geographical area. The currency in the Asian country is the $.

CM does not wish to undertake both investments at the present time. Investment 1 would require less capital expenditure than Investment 2, but its operating costs would be higher. Profit forecasts for the two investments are as follows:

Year:	1	2	3
Investment 1 – all figures in £000s			
Revenue	375	450	575
Production costs (excl. Depreciation)	131	158	201
Depreciation	267	267	266
Profit/(loss) before tax	(23)	25	108
Investment 2 – all figures in A$000s			
Revenue	1,300	1,450	1,650
Production costs (excl. Depreciation)	260	290	330
Depreciation	967	967	966
Profit/(loss) before tax	73	193	354

Additional information:

1   The capital expenditure required for **Investment 1** is £1.1 million with an expected residual value at the end of year three of £300,000. The capital cost of **Investment 2** will be A$2.9 million with no residual value.

2   CM depreciates the estimated net cost of its assets (initial cost less estimated residual value) straight line over the life of the investment.

3   Tax depreciation is available on the equipment purchased for **Investment 1** at 40% per annum on the reducing balance basis. Capital expenditure for **Investment 2** can be written off for tax purposes in the year in which it is purchased.

4   Corporate tax rate in the UK is 25%. There are tax concessions in the Asian country. The net effect is that CM would pay tax on profits generated in the Asian country at 10%. No additional tax would be payable in the UK. Tax would be refunded or paid on both investments at the end of the year in which the liability arises.

5   **Investment 1** would be financed by internal funds. **Investment 2** would be financed by a combination of internal funds and loans raised overseas.

6   Assume revenue and production costs excluding depreciation equal cash flows.

7   The cash flow forecasts are in nominal terms. The entity's real cost of capital is 8% and inflation is expected to be 2.75% per annum constant in the UK.

8   CM evaluates all its investments over a three-year time horizon.

9   Cash flows are assumed to occur at the end of each year except the initial capital cost which is incurred in year 0.

10 Operating cash flows for Investment 2 are in A$. The current exchange rate is £1 = A$2. Sterling is expected to weaken against the A$ by 4.5% per annum over the next three years.

11 CM's expected accounting return on investment is 15%, calculated as average profits after tax as a percentage of average investment over the life of the assets.

Required:

(a)   For each of the two investments, calculate:

(i)   The average annual accounting return on investment using average profit after tax and average investment over the life of the assets   **(9 marks)**

(ii)   The NPV using an appropriate discount rate calculated from the information given in the scenario.   **(9 marks)**

(Note: You should round the calculated discount rate to the nearest whole number).

(b)   Recommend, with reasons, which, if either, of the investments should be undertaken. Discuss any non-financial factors that might influence the choice of investment.   **(7 marks)**

A report format is not required for this question.

(Total: 25 marks)

61   DOMINIQUE (NOV 09 EXAM)

Dominique is a multinational group. The head office and parent entity are based in Country D which uses currency D$. The group runs a chain of supermarkets both in Country D and in neighbouring countries. Dominique sources its supplies from its home country D, neighbouring countries and also from some more distant countries.

Dominique is funded by a mix of equity and long-term borrowings. The borrowings are largely floating rate bonds denominated in D$.

Proposed new project

The proposed new project is to open a number of new supermarkets in Country T, a neighbouring country, which uses currency T$. Market research has already been undertaken at a cost of D$ 0.3 million. If the proposed project is approved additional logistics planning will be commissioned at a cost of D$ 0.38 million payable at the start of 20X0.

Other forecast project cash flows:

Initial investment on 1 January 20X0	T$ million	150
Residual value at the end of 20X4	T$ million	40
Net operating cash inflows		
20X0	T$ million	45
20X1 and 20X2	growing at 20% a year from 20X0 levels	
20X3 and 20X4	growing at 6% a year from 20X2 levels	

Additional information:

On 1 January 20X0, the spot rate for converting D$ to T$ is expected to be D$1 =T$ 2.1145. Dominique has received two conflicting exchange rate forecasts for the D$/T$ during the life of the project as follows:

Forecast A   A stable exchange rate of D$1 = T$2.1145

Forecast B   A devaluation of the T$ against the D$ of 5.4% a year

Business tax is 20% in Country T, payable in the year in which it is incurred.

Tax depreciation allowances are available in Country T at 20% a year on a reducing balance basis

All net cash flows in Country T are to be remitted to Country D at the end of each year

An additional 5% tax is payable in Country D based on remitted net cash flows net of D$ costs but no tax is payable or refundable on the initial investment and residual value capital flows.

The project is to be evaluated, in D$, at a discount rate of 12% over a five year period.

Required:

(a)   **Calculate and discuss the D$ NPV of the project cash flows as at 1 January 20X0 using each of the two different exchange rate scenarios, Forecast A and Forecast B. Briefly advise Dominique whether or not it should proceed with the project.**

(18 marks)

(b)   **Discuss the likely impact of changes in exchange rates and tax rates on the performance of the Dominique group as a whole and how this is likely to influence the financial strategy of the group. No further calculations are required.   (7 marks)**

(Total: 25 marks)

62   MR (SEPT 10 EXAM)

MR is a large retail chain of retail stores operating in the USA. It sells top-of the-range, expensive clothes to a wealthy clientele throughout the country. Currently, MR only operates in the USA. Its current market capitalisation is US$760 million and the current market value of debt is US$350 million.

At last month's management meeting the marketing director explained that sales volume had increased slightly in the previous year, largely due to heavy discounting in most of its stores. The finance director expressed concern that such a strategy might damage the image of the company and reduce profits over the longer term.

An alternative strategy to increase sales volume has recently been proposed by the marketing department. This would involve introducing a new range of clothing specifically aimed at the middle-income market. The new range of clothing would be expected to be attractive to consumers in Canada and Europe, giving the possibility of opening stores in Canada and possibly Europe in the longer term.

Assume you are a financial manager with MR and have been asked to evaluate the marketing department's proposal to introduce a new range of clothing. An initial investigation into the potential markets has been undertaken by a firm of consultants at a cost of US$100,000 but this amount has not yet been paid. It is intended to settle the amount due in three months' time. With the help of a small multi-department team of staff you have estimated the following cash flows for the proposed project:

- The initial investment required would be US$46 million, payable on 01 January 20X1. This comprises US$30 million for non-current assets and US$16 million for net current assets (working capital).

- For accounting purposes, non-current assets are depreciated on a straight line basis over three years after allowing for a residual value of 10%. Tax depreciation allowances can be assumed to be the same as accounting depreciation.

- The value of net current assets at the end of the evaluation period can be assumed to be the same as at the start of the period.

- Net operating cash flows (before taxation) are forecast to be US$14 million in 20X1, US$17 million in 20X2 and US$22 million in 20X3 and should be assumed to arise at the end of each year.

The following information is also relevant:

The proposed project is to be evaluated over a three-year time horizon.

MR usually evaluates its investments using a after-tax discount rate of 8%. The proposed project is considered to be riskier than average and so a risk-adjusted rate of 9% will be used for this project.

Corporate tax is payable at 25% in the same year in which the liability arises.

MR would need to borrow 50% of the initial investment cost.

Ignore inflation.

MR's primary financial objectives are:

1   To earn a return on shareholders' funds (based on market values) of 11% per annum on average over a three- year period.

2   To keep its gearing ratio, (debt to debt plus equity based on market values), at below 35%.

Required:

(a) (i) Calculate the net present value (NPV), internal rate of return (IRR) and (approximate) modified internal rate of return (MIRR) as at 01 January 20X1 for the proposed project. **(13 marks)**

(ii) Discuss the advantages and limitations of MIRR in comparison with NPV and IRR. **(6 marks)**

(b) Evaluate the likely impact of the project on MR's ability to meet its financial objectives assuming the project goes ahead. **(6 marks)**

(Total: 25 marks)

63 PEI (NOV 10 EXAM)

PEI is a privately-owned college of higher education in the UK. It competes directly with other private and government-funded schools and colleges. The college directors are considering two investment opportunities that would allow the college to expand in the UK (known as Projects A and B) and a third opportunity to set up a satellite training centre in a foreign country (known as Project C). Ideally, it would invest in all three projects but the company has only GBP 25 million of cash available (where GBP is British Pounds). PEI currently has borrowings of GBP 50 million and does not wish to increase indebtedness at the present time. PEI's shares are not listed.

The initial capital investment required (on 1 January 20X1) and likely net operating cash inflows arising from the investments in each project are as follows.

Project	Initial Investment (GBP million)	Net Operating Cash inflows (after tax)
A	15.50	GBP 1.75 million each year from year 1 indefinitely.
B	10.20	GBP 1.15 million in year 1, and GBP 3.10 million a year in years 2 to 7.
C	9.50	A$ 9.30 million each year for years 1 to 5.

Notes:

(1) The projects are not divisible.

(2) Project B has a residual value of GBP 2.5 million. The other projects are expected to have no residual value.

(3) Projects A and B are to be discounted at 8%. The Finance Director considers that a GBP discount rate of 9% is more appropriate for Project C as it carries slightly greater risk.

(4) The GBP/A$ exchange rate is expected to be GBP/A$ 2.00 on 1 January 20X1 (that is, GBP 1 = A$ 2.00). The A$ is expected to weaken against GBP by 1.5% per annum for the duration of the project.

(5) Assume cash flows, other than the initial investment, occur at the end of each year.

Required:

(a) (i) Calculate the NPV and PI of each of the THREE projects based on the GBP cash flows. **(8 marks)**

(ii) Evaluate your results and advise PEI which project or combination of projects to accept. **(7 marks)**

(b) Explain the alternative method of evaluating Project C using an A$ discount rate, illustrating your answer with a calculation of an appropriate A$ discount rate.

(4 marks)

(c) Discuss the key financial factors, other than the NPV decision, that should be considered before investing in a project located in a foreign country rather than the home country. **(6 marks)**

A report format is not required for this question.

(Total: 25 marks)

64 GOH (MAR 11 EXAM)

GOH is a local government organisation in Gohland, a country that has the G$ as its currency.

GOH is currently evaluating a proposed investment involving the construction and operation of a new health centre in the local region. Some fees will be collected from users of the centre but the majority of services will be provided free of charge.

The Gohland Government sets down strict guidelines to be used by all local government organisations in their appraisal of projects. In relation to investment projects of this nature the guidelines are that:

- A discount rate of 4% should be used as this is the rate specified by the government for use in evaluating such projects.

- Projects of this nature should be evaluated over a 15 year time horizon.

- Discounted cash flow analysis should take into account both the capital investment and the opportunity cost of the land that is required by the project.

- All costs, income and other benefits of the project should be identified and included in the appraisal. These should include the estimated value of benefits to society in terms of health impacts and also any environment and social impacts.

Financial figures for the proposed project

The capital cost of the investment (buildings and equipment) is estimated at G$950 million and would be payable on 1 April 20X1.

The health centre is to be built on a portion of land already owned by GOH. A developer has expressed an interest in buying the land at a price of G$250 million. This is considered a reasonable market value by GOH's Estates Department.

The residual value of the land, buildings and equipment at the end of 15 years is difficult to forecast but the Estates Department thinks at that time the land will be worth approximately G$600 million and the buildings and equipment G$150 million.

Net future benefits (income and other benefits net of costs) for the new regional health centre for use in the NPV analysis are forecast to be as follows:

Year ending 31 March	20X2	20X3	20X4	20X5 to 20Y6
G$ million	90	110	120	130 per year

GOH's financial director has just joined GOH from a private-sector company and has proposed that instead of using a discount rate of 4% a more commercial discount rate should be used based upon a private sector organisation.

He has identified a private health care company, JKL, which operates a number of health centres in Gohland, to be used as a proxy company for calculating a comparable private sector discount rate for GOH.

JKL is currently funded as follows:

Equity:

24.5 million shares quoted on the local market at G$13.00. JKL's cost of equity is estimated at 9%.

Debt:

G$100 million of long dated bonds issued at par and paying a coupon rate of 5.5%. The debt is currently trading at G$95 per G$100 nominal.

Additional information:

- The corporate income tax rate is 30% in Gohland.

- Net future benefits should be assumed to occur at the end of the year.

Required:

(a)   (i)   **Calculate the weighted average cost of capital of JKL.**   **(4 marks)**

(ii)   **Advise on the appropriateness of using the WACC of JKL as the discount rate in GOH's project appraisal, including reference to the differences in the financial and non-financial objectives between the public sector and private sector.**   **(8 marks)**

(b)   (i)   **Calculate the project NPV following Gohland government's guidelines.**

(5 marks)

(ii)   **Advise GOH on other issues that need to be taken into account before deciding whether or not to proceed with the proposed project.**   **(8 marks)**

A report format is not required for this question.

(Total: 25 marks)

65   CIP MANUFACTURING (SEPT 11 EXAM)

Assume today is 1 October 20X1.

CIP is a manufacturing company based in an Eastern European country, which has the euro as its currency. The CIP board is evaluating a potential project which involves the launch of a new product that has a limited life of six years and which will require an initial investment in specialised machinery.

Project cash flows:

The specialised machinery will cost EUR 6.5 million and will be installed and paid for on 1 January 20X2. The Management Accountant has forecast that the net after tax cash flows associated with the new product will be as follows:

Year to 31 December	20X2	20X3	20X4	20X5 – 7
Net after tax cash flows (EUR 000)	750	950	1,400	2,100

The project will have no residual value as the specialised machinery cannot be used elsewhere or sold at the end of the project. The net after tax cash flows can be assumed to arise at the end of the year to which they relate.

Financing the project

The proposed investment is in a development region of the country and the local government is offering subsidised borrowing for 40% of the initial capital investment at an annual interest rate of 1% to encourage investment. A further 20% of the capital required will be raised by bank borrowing, at an annual interest rate of 6%, which is the same as CIP's pre-tax cost of debt.

The duration of the borrowings will match the duration of the investment with the full amount of the borrowings repayable at the end of the six year term. The corporate income tax rate is 30% and tax is payable or recoverable at the end of the year to which it relates. There are sufficient taxable profits within CIP to benefit in full from the tax relief available on interest payments.

CIP has sufficient cash to fund the remaining 40% of the capital expenditure.

Other information:

CIP's current market debt: equity ratio is 1:3.

Administrative costs of arranging the two borrowings are expected to be 1% of the amounts raised.

CIP's current WACC (weighted average cost of capital), which it typically uses for investment appraisal, is 10%. The proposed project is in a market which is expected to be riskier than its normal operations and therefore some of the board of CIP are unsure whether 10% is an appropriate rate at which to appraise the investment. The Management Accountant has suggested that either a risk adjusted WACC should be used as a discount rate (based upon a cost of equity reflecting the business risk of the project and CIP's existing gearing) in an NPV (net present value) evaluation or, alternatively, an APV (adjusted present value) approach should be adopted. He has identified PPP as a company that operates exclusively in the market of the proposed project. PPP's equity beta is 1.95 and it has a current market debt:equity ratio of 1:4. The post-tax risk free rate of return and market rate of return are expected to be 4% and 9% respectively for the foreseeable future.

Required:

(a) **Calculate, as at 1 January 20X2:**

    (i)   **The NPV of the project at CIP's existing WACC of 10%.**   **(2 marks)**

    (ii)   **The NPV of the project at a risk adjusted WACC using PPP as a proxy company in respect of business risk.**   **(5 marks)**

    (iii)   **The APV of the project.**   **(8 marks)**

(b) **Evaluate the potential financial benefits of the project. Your answer should include discussion on the appropriateness of each of the methods used in part (a) to appraise the project.**   **(8 marks)**

(c) **Advise the directors of CIP whether they should proceed with the project.**

    (2 marks)

A report format is not required for this question.   **(Total: 25 marks)**

66   CMEC (NOV 11 EXAM)

Assume today is 1 January 2012

CMec

CMec is a major retail chain that specialises in household products and is based in the UK. It has retail stores throughout the UK which sell a wide range of household products with well-known brand names. It also sells under its own brand label. These goods are produced and packaged by leading manufacturers in the UK on behalf of CMec as CMec does not have its own manufacturing facility.

Proposed investment

The Board is considering expanding CMec's operations into a country in Asia, Country A, which has the A$ as its currency. The expansion would be achieved by acquiring a number of stores from a supermarket chain operating in Country A. This is the first time that CMec has invested in a foreign country.

The cost of purchasing the stores is A$415 million, payable on 1 January 2012. The cost of re-branding and fitting-out the stores has been estimated at A$170 million. For the purposes of evaluation these costs can be assumed to be paid on 1 January 2012. After three years, the stores are expected to be worth A$450 million.

The new stores will require an investment in working capital of A$150 million at the start of the first year and the working capital requirement is expected to grow by 10% a year for the foreseeable future but is expected to be fully recoverable at the end of the project.

The net operating cash flows for the new stores for the first three years of operation are expected to be:

Year to 31 December:	2012	2013	2014
Operating cash flows			
Arising in Country A (A$ million)	200	250	350
Arising in the UK (GBP million)	(14)	(14)	(14)

Due to the risky nature of the project, CMec has decided to evaluate the project on the basis that the new stores will only be operational for three years and the stores are sold at the end of the project.

The following additional information applies:

- CMec operates an accounting year that runs from 1 January to 31 December.

- GBP/A$ spot is expected to be GBP/A$ 1.3000 on 1 January 2012 (that is, GBP 1 = A$1.3000).

- The risk free rate of interest is 7.5% in Country A and 2.0% in the UK.

- CMec uses a GBP discount rate of 10.0% to evaluate UK investments.

- Cash flows, other than the initial investment and refit costs can be assumed to occur at the end of the year to which they relate.

- All funds are remitted to the UK at the end of each year.

For the purposes of this question, taxation can be ignored.

Required:

(a) Calculate, showing full workings, the GBP net present value (NPV) of the proposed investment as at 1 January 2012 based on a three year period, by:

   (i) Discounting GBP cash flows at CMec's GBP discount rate.

   (ii) Discounting A$ cash flows at a corresponding A$ discount rate. **(10 marks)**

(b) Explain why you would expect the NPVs in (a)(i) and (a)(ii) above to be the same.

(3 marks)

(c) Advise how the project evaluation could be adapted to take into account the additional risks involved in foreign investments. **(6 marks)**

(d) Discuss to what extent a post completion audit report prepared by CMec for a previously completed UK project might be useful when planning the implementation of this proposed investment in a foreign country. **(6 marks)**

A report format is not required for this question.

(Total: 25 marks)

67 RST (MAR 12 EXAM)

Assume today is 1 April 2012.

RST is a privately owned specialist equipment supply and support company based in Sydney, Australia with a strong local customer base. RST made a profit of 20 million Australian dollars (AUD) in the last financial year and relies heavily on debt finance.

The company is considering setting up an operation in Perth, Australia, a five hour plane journey from Sydney. It would be the first time that RST has operated outside Sydney. Perth is currently experiencing rapid growth due to the development of the mining industry which has created new opportunities for supplying specialist equipment.

The new operation in Perth would supply specialised mining equipment to the local mines and also provide maintenance support. RST would lease office space in Perth for a five year period and hire new local sales people and technicians. A significant proportion of the lease premium will need to be paid on the first day of the lease period. In all, it is anticipated that the new operation will require an initial investment of AUD 25 million.

If successful, this new operation would increase the size of RST significantly and also provide an opportunity for establishing a permanent operation in Perth. However, it involves a considerable amount of risk and uncertainty, largely because of the new location. In addition, the new operation will be targeted at the mining industry which is a new type of industry sector for RST. As a result, the business risk of this new operation in Perth will be different from that of the current operations in Sydney.

RST's finance department has produced information on likely future cash flows for the Perth operation on the basis of three possible out-turn scenarios. Net present value (NPV) calculations have been undertaken based on an appropriate WACC for RST. The cost of equity used in the WACC was based on the beta of a proxy company located in Perth that operates in a similar industry sector. The results are given below:

Out-turn scenario	Probability of occurrence	NPV (AUD million)
Best case	30%	54
Average case	50%	30
Worst case	20%	48

This gives an overall expected NPV of AUD 21.6 million. The finance manager is happy with this level of return and is prepared to recommend the new operation on the basis of its expected NPV.

There have been some lengthy discussions amongst Board members on the results of the NPV evaluation and on how best to finance the new operation if it goes ahead.

Director S supports the idea of debt finance because the NPV calculations could then be re-performed at the lower cost of debt, making the new operation even more attractive. However, she has some concerns about the risks involved in increasing gearing any further. Director S has also pointed out that the USD has a lower interest rate than the AUD and has therefore suggested that RST use USD denominated debt rather than AUD denominated debt.

Required:

(a) Advise the board of RST on the validity of:

   (i) The appraisal approach adopted (including the use of CAPM and NPV).

   (4 marks)

   (ii) The conclusion reached by the finance manager that RST should proceed with the investment in Perth. (4 marks)

(b) Explain, using examples from the scenario, what "real options" are AND what impact they might have on an investment decision. (9 marks)

(c) Evaluate the comments made by Director S. (8 marks)

A report format is not required for this question.

(Total: 25 marks)

68   PP (MAY 12 EXAM)

PP is a large architectural partnership based in the USA. Its client base ranges from large corporations to an extensive range of smaller companies and individuals.

Much of PP's marketing and client liaison efforts to date have focussed on the larger corporations because there tends to be repeat business from such clients. However, a recent client survey has revealed that 75% of new business results from referrals from satisfied smaller clients. PP is therefore keen to improve its marketing efforts within the smaller client market. Improvements in the information technology (IT) systems currently used by PP are considered to be essential to such a development, to enable increased visibility of the company and its achievements across the whole client base and help promote new business.

PP's current annual revenue is USD 10 million.

Proposed IT project for a new Customer Relationship Management (CRM) system

PP is considering introducing a new Customer Relationship Management (CRM) system to help maintain more regular and better targeted communication with both current and potential new clients. The project is to be appraised over a four year time horizon.

An initial investment of USD 600,000 is required on 1 July 2012, with no residual value at the end of the four year period. It is estimated that there would be on-going system maintenance costs of USD 50,000 a year but no other annual incremental costs attributable to the project. In terms of savings, it is planned that staff numbers would be reduced by one person at an annual saving of salary costs of USD 80,000 and also a saving of other costs of USD 20,000 per annum. However, redundancy pay and costs involved with redundancy arrangements would be approximately USD 200,000, payable on 1 July 2012. Unless stated otherwise, all costs and revenue should be assumed to be paid or received at the end of the year in which they arise.

The partners of the practice are unsure how much new business would be generated by the new CRM system. The number of different unknown variables involved has made it very difficult to arrive at a firm answer. However, it is anticipated that any new business generated as a result of the CRM system would give rise to an increase in net cash inflows in each year that is equivalent to 52% of the annual cash inflow generated by new business. Assume that the additional net cash inflow generated by new business is the same in each of years 1 to 4.

PP evaluates IT projects using a conventional discounted cash flow approach based on costs and benefits that can be quantified with a degree of confidence. The partnership's cost of capital of 12% is to be used as the discount rate.

For the purposes of this question, taxation should be ignored.

Required:

(a) (i) Calculate the net present value (NPV) of the proposed IT project as at 1 July 2012, ignoring the additional cash flows that might arise from new business.
(5 marks)

(ii) Calculate the additional annual cash inflow from new business that is required in order to achieve a breakeven result. Use your answer from part (a) (i) as the starting point for your calculation. **(6 marks)**

(b) Discuss the appropriateness of using a conventional discounted cash flow approach to appraise an IT project. **(6 marks)**

(c) Advise what other financial and strategic factors should be considered when deciding whether to proceed with this project. **(8 marks)**

A report format is not required for this question.
(Total: 25 marks)

69 WIDGET (SEPT 12 EXAM)

WIDGET is a listed group which operates a number of manufacturing facilities within its home country, Country F. The currency of Country F is the F$.

WIDGET has F$700 million funds available for capital investment in new product lines in the current year. Most products have a very limited life cycle. Four possible projects have been identified, each of which can be started without delay.

Initial calculations for these projects are shown below:

Project	Initial investment (F$ million)	Net annual cash inflows after the initial investment (F$ million)	Project term (years)	PV of cash flows arising after the initial investment (F$ million)	NPV (F$ million)
A	100	151.2	1	135	35
B	150	82.3	4	250	100
C	300	242.6	2	410	110
D	350	124.0	6	510	160

Notes:

1 The projects are non-divisible and each project can only be undertaken once.

2 Apart from the initial investment, annual cash flows are assumed to arise at the end of the year.

3 A discount rate of 12% has been used throughout.

4 Ignore taxation.

Required:

(a) (i) Prioritise the projects according to each of the following measures:

- Net present value (NPV)

- Profitability index (PI)

- Payback (undiscounted) **(5 marks)**

(ii) Explain the strengths and weaknesses of each of the prioritisation methods used in (a)(i) above as the basis for making investment decisions in the context of capital rationing for non-divisible projects. **(9 marks)**

(b) (i) Advise what combination of projects maximises shareholder wealth within a maximum total initial investment of F$700 million. **(3 marks)**

(ii) Explain how the optimal combination of projects would need to be reassessed under EACH of the following circumstances:

- 'Soft' rather than 'hard' single period capital rationing applies.

- The same level of capital rationing and range of projects is expected in the following year. **(8 marks)**

A report format is not required for this question.

(Total: 25 marks)

70 APT (NOV 12 EXAM)

APT is a manufacturing company based in a country in the eurozone. The company's shares are listed on a European stock exchange and its current market capitalisation is EUR 1,200 million. APT's debt funding comprises a secured bond of EUR 250 million carrying interest at 6.5% and repayable in 2020.

APT is considering a new product line that would require initial investment in machinery and working capital totalling EUR 500 million. The residual value of the machinery and working capital is expected to be EUR 170 million in total at the end of the project. Net annual cash flows for the proposed project, after tax, for the five years of the project are forecast as follows:

Year	1	2	3–5
Net after tax cash flows (EUR million)	70	100	115

50% of the new capital required would be raised by a loan from a banking consortium. This loan would carry interest at 7% and a floating charge on the project's assets. The duration of the borrowing would match the duration of the investment, with the full amount of the borrowing repayable at the end of the five year term. APT has sufficient cash to fund the other 50% of the capital expenditure.

The proposed project is in a market which has a different risk profile from APT's current operations. YYY is a company that operates exclusively in this market. YYY's market capitalisation is currently EUR 660 million and it has EUR 250 million of outstanding debt.

Other information:

1   APT's current weighted average cost of capital (WACC) is 11%.

2   Equity betas for APT and YYY are 1.6 and 1.3 respectively. The risk free rate of return and market rate of return are expected to be 4.5% and 9.5% respectively for the foreseeable future.

3   Assume both APT and YYY have a debt beta of 0.2.

4   The market value of APT's bond can be assumed to be the same as its face value.

5   All initial capital expenditure occurs at the beginning of the project. Assume all other cash flows occur at the end of each year.

6   The corporate income tax rate applicable to the taxable profits of both APT and YYY is 28%. Tax is paid at the end of the year in which the taxable profit arises. There are no tax depreciation allowances available for the investment in machinery.

Required:

(a)   **Calculate the Net Present Value (NPV) of the project being considered by APT at the following discount rates:**

   (i)   **APT's current weighted average cost of capital (WACC).**   **(3 marks)**

   (ii)   **A project specific risk adjusted discount rate based on the gearing of the project.**   **(8 marks)**

(b)   **Calculate the Adjusted Present Value (APV) of the project being considered by APT.**
                                                                                 (6 marks)

(c)   **Advise APT on the appropriateness of each of the valuation methods used in (a) and (b) above to value this project.**   **(8 marks)**

A report format is not required for this question.

                                                                    (Total: 25 marks)

Section 3

ANSWERS TO SECTION A-TYPE QUESTIONS

1   M PLC (NOV 11 EXAM)

Key answer tips – extracted from the Examiner's "Post Exam Guide"

In part (a), evaluate the three possible uses of the funds and accompany your evaluation with calculations of the effect on gearing of each of the three possible uses. Calculation of growth in revenue and profits between 2011 and 2012 could also be provided.

In part (b)(i), calculate PP's WACC and value FR using the following approaches:

- Net assets (note no deduction of debt).

- Earnings based using both M and PP's P/E ratios.

- DCF basis using free cash flow approach.

In part (b)(ii), discuss the appropriateness of each of the valuation methods you have identified in part (bi).

In part (b)(iii), advise on an appropriate range of prices within which M would be prepared to negotiate with PP. Include specific reference to difficulties of achieving synergistic benefits and whether M's hopes for a price of EUR75 million are likely to be attainable.

Finally, in part (c), identify the main risks that might arise from investigation by a competition authority into a planned takeover - in general terms and with specific reference to the proposed sale of FR.

(a)   Three alternative uses of the funds have already been suggested by the Board of the Newspaper Division. These are:

- Reinvest in a new project.

- Repay debt.

- Pay a one-off dividend.

Investments, funding and dividend decisions are the main financial decisions facing all companies and are closely interrelated as each decision affects the others.

Reinvest in a new project

Reinvestment of the funds into a new project that has a positive NPV would help M plc achieve its growth targets as stated in its financial objectives. As we know from the pre-seen material, the key shareholders (that is, the bank, charity and financial institution) are putting pressure on the Board to devise a strategic plan aimed at achieving M plc's stated financial objectives.

Growth in revenue and profits between 2011 and 2012 met profit growth targets but not revenue growth targets as the following analysis shows:

	2011	2012	Growth achieved	Target growth per financial objectives
Revenue	274	200	2.2%	4.0%
Operating profit	68	73	7.3%	4.0%

A company such as M plc is likely to have a wide range of projects with positive NPVs to consider. These need to be assessed as to their contribution towards meeting M plc's financial and strategic objectives.

With the disposal of FR, M plc will lose control over the pan European newspaper that FR produces and which helps to meet one of its strategic objectives (strategic objective number 3). M plc may therefore wish to consider whether it is possible to provide a news service to native English speakers over a wide geographical spread (strategic objective number 2) by some other means and evaluate projects that might help meet those objectives. For example, M plc could consider launching a web version to reach this readership group.

Reduce debt levels

We know from the pre-seen material that £83 million of loan capital is due for repayment on 1 April 2013, that is, in 16 months' time. The sale proceeds could therefore be retained and invested for use in repaying the loan capital at that time or at an earlier date if early redemption is allowed without penalty.

Alternatively, other debt could be repaid now and separate arrangements made to repay the loan capital of £83 million due in 16 months.

The current gearing level of M plc based on the latest forecast statement of financial position is 33.8%. This is reasonably comfortably within the gearing target of 40% and so there is no urgent need to repay debt in order to keep within the gearing target.

Workings:

Market capitalisation is GBP 490.00 million = 140 × GBP 3.50.

So gearing (D/D+E) is currently 33.8%, (0.338 = GBP 250/(250 + 490).

If the full value of the anticipated proceeds of EUR 75 million were to be used to repay debt, and assuming M plc's share price were to remain unchanged at £3.50, M plc's gearing level would fall to 27.2%. However, this would reduce shareholder returns due to loss of tax relief on debt interest and heavier reliance on more expensive equity capital.

Workings:

New gearing (D/D+E) = 0.272 = (250.00 − 66.75)/(250.00 − 66.75 + 490.00)

where 66.75 = 75 × 0.8900

Note that all these calculations assume no change in the share price as a result of changes in gearing. This is unlikely in practice due to changes in risk and return required to debt and equity holders arising from a change in gearing.

Another important consideration is the likely success of rollover negotiations regarding the borrowings due for repayment in a year's time. If the company is considered to be likely to face refinancing risk, the sales proceeds should be retained to help meet the forthcoming debt repayment.

Pay one-off dividend

At first sight, this may appear to be an attractive option from the point of view of the shareholders, providing an immediate cash benefit. However, this is only a short term view and is likely to lead to comparatively lower shareholder wealth over the longer term due to the higher cost of capital that would result (as discussed above).

A one-off dividend would only be beneficial to shareholders in the longer term if the funds can be invested at higher returns by the shareholders than by the company. Funds should only be returned to shareholders if they cannot be reinvested in the business to produce a higher return than the shareholders could create themselves. Indeed, a one-off dividend might send a signal to the market that there are no profitable investment opportunities available and hence the share price could actually fall.

An added risk is that paying a one-off dividend may create an expectation that dividends will also be higher in the future. This would create problems in the future if M plc is not in a position to satisfy such expectations.

Conclusion

In this scenario, the highest priority would appear to be to reinvest in positive NPV projects in order to boost future earnings streams.

(b)   (i)   **PP's bond cost of debt**

	Time	CF	DF	PV	DF	PV
		EUR	5%		3%	
MV	0	−103.00	1	−103.00	1	−103.00
Net interest						
(6% × (1 − 0.70)	1 to 3	4.20	2.723	11.44	2.829	11.88
Redemption	3	100.00	0.864	86.40	0.915	91.50
				−5.16		0.38

So the current post tax cost of the bond is 3.1%   (= 3% + 2% × (0.38/(5.16 + 0.38)))

Examiner's note:

A calculation based on total values is equally acceptable and produces the same result.

	C cost of capital	MV value (EUR m)	C × MV	
Bond	3.10%	123.6	3.83	W3
Preference shares	5.93%	27.0	1.60	W4, W5
Ordinary shares	10.50%	290.0	30.45	W1, W2
		440.6	35.88	
So WACC is	8.143%		(= 35.88/440.6 × 100%)	

Workings

(W1) Cost of equity is 3% + 1.5 × 5% = 10.5%

(W2) Market capitalisation is 50 million × EUR 5.80 = EUR 290.0 million

(W3) MV of bonds is 120 million × EUR 103/100 = EUR 123.6 million

(W4) Cost of preference shares is EUR 8.0/EUR 135 × 100% = 5.93%

(W5) MV of preference shares is EUR 1.35 × 20.0 million shares = EUR 27.0 million

Valuation of FR

Net assets	EUR million
Non current assets	56
Net current assets	2
Value	58

Note: no deduction for debt is necessary as the net assets of FR are being acquired, free of debt.

Earnings valuation based on P/E

Using M's P/E ratio:

Equity:	EUR 44.6m	= 4 × 11.14	Using M's P/E of 11.14 (= 3.50 × 140/44)
Total value:	EUR 69.6m	after adding debt of EUR 25 million to obtain the combined debt plus equity value of FR	

Using PP's P/E ratio:

Equity:	EUR 52.0m	= 4 × 13	Using PP's P/E of 13 given in the question
Total value:	EUR 77.0m	after adding debt of EUR 25 million	

DCF of pre-interest and post-tax free cash flows at WACC

Free cash flow (FCF) is:	*EUR million*
Earnings	4.0
Add back finance charge	1.4
Deduct tax relief on finance charge (at 30% of 1.4)	−0.4
Add back depreciation	0.5
Deduct funds reinvested	−1.8
FCF pre-financing cash flows	3.7

Giving a value of EUR 61.4m (= 3.7(1.02)/(0.08144 − 0.02)) at a WACC of 8.144% and growth rate of 2%

Alternative approach to calculating FCF:

Free cash flow (FCF) is:	*EUR million*
Operating profit	6.7
Deduct tax charge	−1.3
Deduct tax relief on finance charge (at 30% of 1.4)	−0.4
Add back depreciation	0.5
Deduct funds reinvested	−1.8
FCF pre-financing cash flows	3.7

Additional value from synergistic benefits

Annual benefit of EUR 0.7 million after tax

That is, a total PV of EUR 8.6 million (= EUR 0.7 million/0.08144 where 0.08144 is the value of WACC calculated earlier) taking future years into account.

The expected value of the synergistic benefits can then be added to each of the valuations already obtained above.

Summary of range of values of the assets employed in FR (that is, assuming that the assets employed in FR are sold without debt attached):

	Pre-synergistic benefits	*Post-synergistic benefits*
	EUR million	EUR million
Net assets	58.0	66.6
P/E ratio – M plc	69.6	78.2
P/E ratio – PP	77.0	85.6
DCF	61.4	70.0

Examiner's note:

Note that it is the net assets employed by FR, without debt attached, that are being sold in this scenario. That is, the price paid must cover the value of both the equity AND the debt in this case. Therefore:

— *Net assets have been calculated without deduction of debt.*

— *Debt has been added back to the standard P/E ratio valuation (which values the equity alone).*

— *No adjustment has been made to the DCF calculation since, in this example, this was based on the cash flows attributable to all providers of finance, both lenders and shareholders. The DCF calculation specified in the requirement was based on pre financing cash flows discounted at the (combined) weighted cost of capital.*

(ii)   **Net asset valuation**

The net asset valuation based on market values gives a value of EUR 58 million.

This is the minimum value that PP should consider paying but gives a useful indication of the assets employed in the business.

However, this valuation is not relevant when acquiring a company as a going concern, with the intention of retaining the assets and continuing to operate the business, as is the case here.

The value underestimates the value of the business as it does not take into account intangible assets such as the newspaper brand name that clearly have a value, despite the disappointing recent results.

Earnings valuations

There are two main issues to consider when valuing FR based on earnings:

• Choice of earnings figures.

• Choice of P/E ratio.

We have used historic earnings from a single year in the valuation and do not have sufficient information with which to judge whether or not these are representative of sustainable future earnings.

We have been given two different P/E ratios in the question and have used each of these in the earnings valuation:

• Using M plc's P/E ratio, FR has a value of EUR 69.6 million.

• Using PP's P/E ratio gives a much higher value of EUR 77.0 million.

It is likely that PP's P/E ratio is more appropriate than M plc's P/E ratio in this scenario as we know that PP operates in the same market as FR whereas M plc operates in a number of different market sectors and geographical locations that are likely to have a different earnings and risk profile.

In applying PP's P/E ratio, we are assuming that PP can produce the same rate of return from FR as from its current business activities. The validity of this valuation therefore largely depends on to what extent the relatively poor recent performance of FR is due to poor management by M plc rather than the popularity and future growth potential of the newspaper titles themselves. The indication is the former – that M plc acquired foreign titles that it was not able to develop to their full potential, possibly due to lack of local knowledge or sufficient management supervision. The valuation of FR using PP's P/E ratio is based on the assumption that PP's management can turn round FR's performance and achieve the same returns as PP's current business. It also assumes that PP and FR carry the same level of risk.

DCF valuations

DCF valuations are generally considered to be the most appropriate method of valuation as they are based on the actual forecast free cash flows (before interest) of the business. These have been discounted at PP's WACC adjusted for risk on the assumption that M plc has a similar gearing ratio to PP and give a valuation of EUR 61.4 million.

Note that the DCF approach gives a lower value than the P/E approach, raising further doubts over the validity of applying M or PP's P/E ratio to FR.

Note that using WACC and pre-financing cash flows is superior to using cost of equity and post-financing cash flows because FR's gearing ratio is determined by M plc in line with the group's requirements rather than being representative of how this type of business would be financed. In any case, without a quoted share price for FR it is not possible to determine FR's WACC.

(iii)   In terms of negotiating a price, PP would be expected to offer a reasonable price at the bottom end of the valuation range in order to maximise profits and give room for manoeuvre. This gives an indication of the likely minimum price that M plc is likely to achieve.

The price should not be lower than the net assets value (before synergies) of EUR 58 million.

The DCF valuation gives a slightly higher value of EUR 61.4 million. PP's starting offer is likely to be somewhere between these two valuations.

The maximum price M plc could hope to achieve can be estimated based on the DCF valuation of EUR 61.4 million plus synergistic benefits estimated at EUR 8.6 million. This gives a top price of EUR 70.0 million.

Synergistic benefits are notoriously difficult to achieve in practice and so PP is unlikely to agree to a price as high as EUR 70.0 million even if it is extremely confident that the synergistic benefits can be achieved. This is because PP would expect to take the benefit of the majority of those synergistic benefits.

The price of EUR 75 million that M plc hope to attain would, however, appear to be far too high and unlikely to be achieved. M plc will need to be prepared to accept a lower price.

(c) Competition authorities generally justify intervention in a proposed merger or takeover if they consider it to be against the public interest. For example, if the takeover would restrict competition in the market. As a rule of thumb, competition authorities may investigate an acquisition if it will result in the combined entity acquiring 25% or more of market share. It is highly likely that this will be true in this scenario, although we cannot be certain without additional information regarding PP and FR's share of the French newspaper market.

Investigations can take several months to complete. The result of the investigation may be to allow the acquisition to proceed. However, there is a risk that the authorities could reach a less favourable verdict such as:

• Allow the acquisition to proceed subject to certain conditions designed to help protect the consumer, or

• Block the acquisition altogether.

Conditions imposed by the regulator in this scenario might include limiting the number of additional newspaper titles that PP is permitted to acquire or guaranteeing the continuation of the pan European English language paper.

There is also a risk that the prospect of a substantial delay while the investigation is conducted, together with the time required to cooperate with the investigation, may lead to PP abandoning the bid if the competition authorities decide to conduct an investigation into the bid. The level of interest that PP has in acquiring FR will affect to what extent PP is likely to pursue the bid even if there is an investigation.

Tutorial note – extracted from the Examiner's "Post Exam Guide"

Part (a) was generally answered satisfactorily although frequently candidates' answers failed to recognise the context of the question scenario.

Candidates had the most difficulties with requirements b(ii) and b(iii) in relation to the valuation of a division for disposal. Common errors made by candidates included:

• *Use of book value instead of market values in WACC calculation*

• *Unnecessary de-gearing/re-gearing of proxy company beta*

• *Incorrect calculation of free cash flows*

• *Failure to include synergistic benefit either at all or as a perpetuity*

• *Failure to calculate free cash flow as a growing perpetuity*

• *Weak discussion of the valuation methods.*

In part (c) candidates frequently discussed the general risks of a monopoly arising from the acquisition of the division by an already dominant acquirer instead of the specific risks to a selling company posed by an investigation by the competition commission. Another common error in this part of the question was that many candidates misinterpreted the question requirement as a need to evaluate the risks of takeovers in general rather than the risks arising from investigation into takeovers.

2   M PLC (MAR 12 EXAM)

Key answer tips – extracted from the Examiner's "Post Exam Guide"

Part (a) initially requires the calculation of the existing cost of equity for M plc and the target GG, using the CAPM formula. An adjusted cost of equity for M plc based on the business risk of GG is then required, again using the CAPM formula and recognising the fact that the beta of GG does not need to be adjusted for financial risk as the gearing of both companies is the same. Part (a)(ii) then requires an explanation of the difference between the three figures calculated based upon consideration of the different inputs into the CAPM formulae used in the calculations.

To answer part (b) candidates need to recognise that with limited information only two valuations were sensible in this situation. Firstly the calculation of market capitalisation based upon GG's latest share price and then a DCF valuation using free cash flow and the adjusted cost of equity calculated in part (a). Valuations using the P/E of M plc were not valid in this circumstance because of the different business risk profiles of the companies in question. The validity of these valuations should then be discussed as a basis for making a bid for GG and an appropriate initial bid offer recommended based on this analysis. The calculation of bid terms is also then required on the basis of a share for share exchange.

The next part of the question requires advice on whether to proceed. In order to reach a conclusion on this, the impact of the acquisition on each of the financial objectives of M plc (as detailed in the pre-seen) need to be discussed in turn. Calculations of current gearing, future growth rates and possible control post acquisition are possible and should be used to support the discussion. Other relevant factors should then be discussed with the emphasis on a range of other factors rather than a focus on just one. This section of the report should conclude with a recommendation as to whether the acquisition should be pursued.

The final part of the requirement requires a simple explanation of the actions available to the directors of GG to fight the takeover bid and conversely the actions M plc could take to promote the bid. Answers here need to be brief and to the point.

(a)   **Briefing paper for the board of directors of M plc**

   From: Financial Director

   Date: 1 April 2012

   Purpose:

   To consider issues arising in relation to the proposed takeover bid for GG, including an appropriate bid value and issues relevant to the decision on whether or not to go ahead.

Valuation of GG

(i)   Preliminary cost of capital calculations used as a basis for the discounted cash flow valuation of GG.

Use the formula $k_e = R_f + [R_m - R_f]ß$

So:

M plc's current cost of equity is	1.1% + 4.0% × 1.8	= 8.3%
GG's current cost of equity is 3.0% + 4.0% × 2.5		= 13.0%

Adjusted cost of equity for M plc using GG's beta is

1.1% + 4.0% × 2.5   = 11.1%

Note that It is not necessary to adjust the equity beta of GG for financial risk as both GG and M plc have the same level of gearing and hence face the same financial risk.

(ii)   The difference of 4.7% between the unadjusted costs of equity for the two companies can be subdivided as follows:

- Firstly, a difference of 1.9% arises due directly to the difference in the risk free interest rates in the UK and the USA. It simply represents the difference between a USD discount rate and a GBP discount rate and is eliminated when GG's cost of equity is converted into a GBP basis in the form of the adjusted cost of equity. This highlights the significant exchange risk that M plc is taking on when acquiring GG if GBP/USD exchange rate movements fail to mirror interest rate differentials.

- Secondly, a difference of 2.8% due to the higher returns expected by GG's shareholders due to the more risky nature of GG's business, as indicated by its higher equity beta. This 2.8% difference is equivalent to the difference between M plc's current cost of equity and the adjusted cost of equity based on GG's business risk and is, effectively, the restatement of GG's cost of equity on a GBP basis. It indicates the extent to which GG's business is riskier than M plc's current business.

(b)   (i)   **Valuation based on market capitalisation**

GG: 40 million shares × USD 7.50 = USD 300.0 million

(that is, GBP 184.0 million or **GBP 4.60 per GG share**).

This compares with a market capitalisation for M plc of GBP 527.8 million

(where GBP 527.8 million = 140 million × GBP 3.77) and this takeover therefore represents a huge change of focus for M plc.

Valuation based on discounted cash flow analysis of free cash flow:

Free cash flow = 60% of earnings = 60% × USD 30 million = USD 18 million for last year.

Use M's cost of equity adjusted for GG's beta in the calculation.

Extract taken from EXCEL working (please note that there may be rounding differences).

	Base		1	2	3	from year 4 onwards
			USDm	USDm	USDm	USDm
Free cash flow	8.0%	18.00	19.44	21.00	22.67	
Exchange rate		1.630	1.6626	1.6959	1.7298	1.7298
			GBPm	GBPm	GBPm	GBPm
Sterling CF			11.69	12.38	13.11	
CF in perpetuity						456.74
				$(= 13.11(1.08)/(0.1110 - 0.0800))$		
Discount at	11.10% (Note 1)	1	0.9001	0.8102	0.7292	0.7292
PV			10.52	10.03	9.56	333.02
Total PV	GBP 363.14 million					

Note 1   The appropriate discount is 11.10%, that is, M's risk-adjusted cost of equity based on GG's beta.

At that discount rate, the present value of GG's free cash flows is **GBP 9.08 per GG share.**

Note that:

- There is insufficient information provided in the question to calculate an asset value.

- A P/E bootstrapping approach is not valid in the context of this scenario, since GG is a completely different type of business to M plc and it is unreasonable to expect that M plc will be able to boost the performance of GG to mirror its own P/E ratio. Indeed, the opposite is more likely to be the case due to the lack of experience of M plc management in running a business such as GG.

(ii)   **Validity of results**

Market capitalisation

GG is a listed entity in the US and therefore has a share price. This is likely to be the best indicator of value as it represents the market's current view. One slight note of caution though is that any share price will only reflect the price of a small parcel of shares as typically this is what is bought or sold on the market. Therefore M plc should expect to pay a premium above this market value to reflect the fact that it is buying the whole entity.

Currently GG's share price stands at USD 7.50 (equivalent to GBP 4.60 at the spot exchange rate). The share price has recently risen in speculation of a potential takeover which is typical in a deal of this nature where the market senses that the potential target is unwilling (i.e.: there is anticipation that the shareholders of GG will only sell for potentially an overly high price).

DCF valuation based on free cash flow

A DCF valuation based on free cash flow provides an indication of the underlying value of GG. However, the result cannot be expected to be very accurate in this case as it depends on too many uncertain underlying assumptions. Key input variables such as future business growth rate, future movements in GBP/USD spot rate are only estimates. In addition, the DCF valuation is likely to be overstated since the 1.9% interest rate differential between GBP and USD and anticipated appreciation of GBP against USD has not been taken into account in the exchange rate movements beyond the 3 year time horizon.

Initial offer price

An offer will need to be at a premium in order to:

- Recognise the additional value of the whole business over and above a small parcel of shares.

- Be sufficiently attractive to GG's shareholders.

- Overcome a possible hostile reaction from the Board of GG.

If the takeover ends up being very hostile, the publicity of a hostile response could well flush out unwelcome rival bids and M plc may have to pay an even higher premium. Indeed, there is a risk that M plc could pay too high a price for GG in the end. The DCF valuation indicates a possible value per share as high as GBP 9.08, which is GBP 4.48 higher than the GBP equivalent of the current share price for GG. However, this is based upon bullish growth prospects and a strengthening of British pounds against the US dollar - both of which could well prove to be overly optimistic. It is therefore unlikely that a valuation of GBP 9.08 per share is realistic, and M plc should resist any temptation to negotiate up to that level.

In conclusion, M plc may be best advised to make an initial offer of the order of USD 8.63 (GBP 5.29) per share, representing a premium of 15% on the current share price.

Alternatively, M plc could begin negotiations at a lower price. The danger, however, is that it might need to return with a higher offer at a later date and may then have to go higher than USD 8.63.

Terms of the offer

At an offer based on a value of GBP 5.29 per share for GG's shares and a current market price of GBP 3.77 per share for M plc's shares, a share exchange of 7 M plc shares for every 5 GG shares would appear to be an appropriate starting point.

(c) **Other key issues that might influence whether or not to proceed with the takeover bid**

Impact of the takeover on the attainment of M plc's financial objectives:

- GG has an expected growth rate of 8% but the USD is expected to depreciate by 2% a year, so the net growth rate in sterling terms is only expected to be 6%. However, this is still comfortably 2% above M plc's overall growth target for revenue and profit of 4%. It is therefore likely that GG would help M plc achieve Financial Objective 1.

- With a growth rate for GG above that of M plc, the acquisition of GG would also be expected to help increase dividends.

- The gearing target of 40% should still be met. GG has approximately the same gearing level as M plc of 32% (= GBP 250m/GBP 250m + (GBP3.77 × 140m)) and so M plc should remain within the gearing target immediately following the acquisition of GG assuming the purchase consideration is in the form of a share exchange. The longer term effect on gearing would largely depend on the future success of the acquisition.

Other relevant factors:

M plc would increase its risks significantly due to:

- Increased business risk. Acquiring a new business in an unfamiliar business sector – do the Directors of M plc have the necessary experience and expertise to be able to manage this business effectively?

- Increased beta. GG has a higher beta and hence higher risk than M plc and this will be reflected in an increase in M plc's overall beta following the takeover.

- Increased foreign exchange risk. GG is a US-based business and therefore introduces significant exchange rate exposure to M plc.

Problems may also arise during the implementation stage, when merging systems of management styles/culture, especially as GG is located in an unfamiliar foreign country. All the normal risks associated with setting up in a foreign country apply - such as lack of familiarity with regulations, customer preferences, infrastructure and cost of management support from M plc.

The shareholders of M plc will suffer dilution of control – GG's shareholders will end of with approximately 29% (56/(140 + 56) shares) of the combined business.

M plc shareholders who are not happy about the deal may sell their shares, leading to a significant fall in M plc's share price.

Overall advice:

The proposed takeover carries a huge risk. GG is so large in comparison with M plc, that it would change the whole nature of the group's business. There are major risks that M plc will not be able to manage the new business effectively and that the group could suffer major losses from movements in the value of the US dollar against GB pounds. This could prove to be a very dangerous strategy and best avoided. I would therefore recommend that M plc does NOT proceed with the takeover of GG.

(d) Actions that the Board of GG could take in defence of what it considers to be a 'hostile' bid:

- Appeal to its own shareholders – aggressive publicity to explain the potential future value of the company under its present ownership. This may include good research ideas, management potential, or being made more aware of the company's achievements.

- Attack M plc (the bidder) – criticising M plc's management style, overall strategy, lack of capital investment etc as appropriate in the circumstances – this is especially useful where a share exchange (full or partial) is being offered.

- White Knight strategy – attempt to identify an alternative, more friendly, bidder; for example, a US company with which GG might be more comfortable.

- Counterbid – make a counterbid offer for M plc.

- Competition authorities –get the bid referred to the Competition Authorities in order to delay and, possibly, block the takeover.

Actions that the Board of M plc could take in the face of hostile reception by GG include:

- Use publicity to advertise its strengths.

- Offer a sufficiently high share price to attract less enthusiastic shareholders.

- Include a cash alternative to the share exchange in the offer, although this would have an adverse impact on gearing.

Tutorial note – extracted from the Examiner's "Post Exam Guide"

Many candidates followed a formulaic approach to answering part (b) (i), rather than consider the information available so that only relevant valuations were undertaken. In particular some candidates wasted time discussing a net asset valuation where there was no information – some even tried to calculate such a value. In addition many failed to note that GG was a listed company in its own right and therefore omitted to calculate the market capitalisation. Indeed the vast majority of candidates calculated earnings valuations based on both the P/E of GG and the P/E of M plc. Where the P/E of GG was used this should have resulted in the same answer as the market capitalisation but in many cases didn't due to errors along the way. This was disappointing. Also note that applying the P/E ratio of M plc to GG's earnings was not appropriate in this case since the two businesses operate in quite different businesses and face different levels of business risk. There was also a number of common errors in the NPV calculation, including:

- *Treating the free cash flow as a perpetuity from time 1 rather than adjusting for the different exchange rates in years 1 to 3.*

- *Not growing the perpetuity correctly.*

- *Calculating the perpetuity factor as 1/growth rate.*

- *Not using the correct cost of equity as the discount factor (it should have been the Ke for M plc adjusted for GG's business risk as calculated in part (a) (i)).*

In part (b)(ii) many candidates again followed a formulaic approach and discussed at length net asset valuations, P/E valuations and dividend valuations even though they weren't relevant. This then meant that not enough time was spent critiquing the DCF valuation and hence answers here were weak. Also, many failed to realise that as a listed company the market capitalisation value should be used as the starting point for negotiation and others recognised this important point but didn't suggest that a premium would be required in order to make the bid attractive to the current shareholders of the takeover target.

3   B SUPERMARKETS (MAY 12 EXAM)

Key answer tips – extracted from the Examiner's "Post Exam Guide"

In part (a)(i), calculate EPS, P/E ratios and dividend payout ratios for all five years from information in the scenario.

In part (a)(ii), provide additional calculations of growth in earnings and EPS, and discuss key points (as shown in the marking scheme).

In part (a)(iii), recognise that the dividend objective has always been met and discuss other key points (as shown in the marking scheme).

In part (b), make sure you provide a report structure for this part of the question – report heading, an introduction or purpose of report, and suitable sub headings.

In part (b)(i), provide a suitable layout for the figures (see suggested solutions), and calculate NPV of the 15 stores in A$, converting to EUR at the spot rate given in the question.

Finally, in part (b)(ii)

- Discuss risks and opportunities of the proposed investment, recognising the key points (as highlighted in the marking scheme).

- Provide advice to the Board of B on how to proceed.

(a)   (i)   **Ratios**

	(Given)	(Given)	(Calculate)	(Given)	(Calculate)
Year	Earnings (€m)	Number of shares (m)	Earnings per share (€)	Share price (€)	P/E ratio
2007	3,945	1,284	**3.07**	47.38	**15.4**
2008	2,818	1,284	**2.19**	25.45	**11.6**
2009	3,097	1,350	**2.29**	28.68	**12.5**
2010	3,366	1,350	**2.49**	29.44	**11.8**
2011	3,591	1,350	**2.66**	31.37	**11.8**

	(Given)	(Calculate)	(Calculate)
Year	Dividend per share (€)	Dividend paid (€m)	Dividend pay-out (as % of earnings)
2007	1.54	**1,977**	**50%**
2008	1.54	**1,977**	**70%**
2009	1.54	**2,079**	**67%**
2010	1.62	**2,187**	**65%**
2011	1.65	**2,228**	**62%**

(ii)   **Additional relevant calculations:**

	(Given)	(From part (a)(i))	(Calculate)	(Calculate)
Year	Earnings (€m)	Earnings per share (€)	Increase in earnings	Increase in earnings per share
2007	3,945	3.07	–	–
2008	2,818	2.19	**(29%)**	**(29%)**
2009	3,097	2.29	**10%**	**5%**
2010	3,366	2.49	**9%**	**9%**
2011	3,591	2.66	**7%**	**7%**

General performance – earnings

The analysis of earnings shows a major fall in earnings between 2007 and 2008 of 29%. This coincides with the down-turn in the global economy, probably exacerbated by the shortage of credit and large increases in competition in terms of pricing to attract reluctant consumers.

Earnings recovered slightly in 2009, showing a growth in total earnings of 10% but only 5% growth in earnings per share. Annual growth in earnings subsequently fell back to 9% in 2010 and to just 7% in 2011. Indeed, even in 2011, earnings have still not recovered to 2007 levels.

Market reaction – share price and P/E ratio

The share price fell from €47.38 at the end of 2007 to €25.45 at the end of 2008 reflecting perhaps a lack of confidence in the future prospects of the group. However, since then the share price has steadily improved and now stands at €31.37. Looking at the P/E ratio we can see that it did indeed drop significantly in 2008 and then bounced back a little in 2009 before returning to its 2008 level in 2010 and 2011. It therefore seems to have stabilised, demonstrating continuing confidence in the future prospects of the group despite continuing difficult trading conditions.

Meeting financial objective re growth in earnings per share of 7%

This objective was only met in 2010 and 2011. In 2009, earnings grew by 10% overall but earnings per share only grew by 5% which was, presumably, due to a share issue in that year.

(iii)   In 2008 and 2009, dividend per share was maintained at 2007 levels, despite a major drop in B's earnings. The rationale for such a policy is likely to be to provide stability to shareholders. Indeed, dividend per share remained constant at €1.54 in 2008 despite falling earnings. A much higher dividend pay-out ratio of 70% (20% above the target of 50%) was required in order to maintain a stable dividend payment and continues to be high. There is, however, a risk attached to such a policy as it significantly reduces the value of funds available for re-investment which could damage long term growth prospects. It also increases the possible need for additional debt finance, which is not necessarily very easy to obtain in a period when credit is in short supply due to the economic downturn and increasing capital requirements for banks.

A steady dividend is usually reassuring to investors. However, in the case of B it has not been sufficient to avoid a large drop in share price in 2008. Overall, therefore, shareholders saw negative returns in 2008 after taking the drop in value of shares into account, despite a consistent dividend.

It is not immediately clear why B paid such a small increase in dividends of just 2% in 2011, but this could be partly to allow the dividend pay-out to begin falling back to pre-2008 levels and become closer to the target level of 50%. Such a policy would also help provide capital for the proposed expansion plans.

(b) **Briefing paper for the board of B**

From: **Mr X, Financial Director of B**

Date: **24 May 2012**

Re: Proposed acquisition of Alpha Supermarkets

Purpose

The purpose of this briefing paper is to provide information regarding the potential financial benefit and other opportunities and also risks associated with the proposed acquisition of Alpha Supermarkets.

(i)   **Calculation of added value for an average store:**

Year	0	1	2	3
	A$ m	A$ m	A$ m	A$ m
Investment	(35.00)	(3.00)	(3.00)	30.00
Revenue		30.00	33.60	37.63
Costs		(13.00)	(14.04)	(15.16)
	(35.00)	14.00	16.56	52.47
Tax	11.20	(4.48)	(5.30)	(16.79)
Carry forward tax credit	(11.20)	4.48	5.30	1.42
NCF	(35.00)	14.00	16.56	37.10
Discount factor @ 15%	1.000	0.870	0.756	0.658
PV	(35.00)	12.18	12.52	24.41
NPV (A$ million)	14.11			
Spot rate	7.5000			
NPV (€ million)	1.88			

The added value for a single store is therefore estimated at €1.88 million (A$14.11 million)

For all 15 stores, this gives a total added value of €28.20 million (= 15 × €1.88 million)

(ii)   **Potential risks and opportunities:**

The acquisition of Alpha supermarkets provides a foothold into a new country for B and brings with it both risks and opportunities.

A key point is that the acquisition of Alpha supermarkets on its own is only the first stage and is, in itself, not very material in terms of the size of B Supermarkets. Even if the supermarkets were to lose, say, 50% of their purchase value, this would only create a financial loss for B of the order of €75 million, just 2% of the 2011 annual profit of € 3,591 million. Although significant, this would not have a devastating effect on B.

A major risk however is the potential for damage to B's reputation if this acquisition goes badly wrong, which could have repercussions for its other markets as well as its future plans for expansion in Asia. This risk is difficult if not impossible to quantify.

There are other, lesser risks in developing a business in a new country, even though B already has a presence in other parts of Asia. In summary, these could be:

- Change of ownership: customers might not be happy with a change of ownership, which is a particular risk as B is a 'foreign' owner, and may choose to shop elsewhere.

- Foreign exchange risks. Expansion in the region would bring with it significant exposure to the value of the A$ against the euro, including translation risk (based on the changing value of the net investment in Country A) and actual cash-based transaction and economic risk due to changes in the euro value of remittances to B.

- Political risk – how stable is the current government, what is the risk of government intervention in the project, what is the likelihood of future changes in the tax regime?

- There may also be exchange controls, restricting the amount, if any, of profits that can be repatriated or charging tax on such remittances.

- The unfamiliarity of the market brings added risk of failure, reduced to some extent by starting on a small scale by the acquisition of Alpha Supermarkets.

- Competitor risk may also prove to be important. Local companies operating in the same market may unite to attempt to remove B. For example, there might be price wars or intense competition of other forms from local supermarket chains that could threaten the success of the venture.

- Financing risk. Each stage of the expansion will require access to funds to buy stores or set up new ones and rebrand current stores. There is a risk that this funding is not forthcoming when required, either because of creditworthiness issues of B itself (e.g. high gearing) or lack of willingness or ability of lenders and financial markets to provide sufficient funds.

- Integration risk. Integrating IT systems and management control and reporting systems can cause problems. The co-operation of local staff is essential for success, including a willingness to embrace new systems and corporate culture.

On the other hand, the potential opportunities for future growth in earnings and dividends by further expansion in the region are huge. This supports financial objective 1. The opportunities arise from the follow on options after the acquisition of Alpha Supermarkets.

Advice whether to proceed

B Supermarkets is best advised to go ahead with the acquisition of Alpha Supermarkets. The financial return from these 15 stores themselves is not expected to be very large in the short term, but the benefit from these stores over the longer term and, more importantly still, the potential for further growth in the region is so large that this opportunity is well worth pursuing.

This assumes, of course, that B has sufficient resources (staff and financial) to accommodate the implementation and rebranding and systems changes required. It also assumes that local staff are expected to be willing to co-operate with the required changes and there are no other insurmountable challenges to the success of the takeover.

Note that the likelihood of success is enhanced due to the extensive experience that B already has in foreign expansion and the fact that it already has a presence in Asia.

Tutorial note – extracted from the Examiner's "Post Exam Guide"

This question aimed to test candidates' ability to evaluate financial performance, dividend policy and the financial benefits of a re-branding exercise using DCF/NPV techniques. On the whole this question was very well attempted and a noticeable feature of candidates' answers was a greater use of information from the "pre-seen". The calculations required were particularly well handled and many candidates achieved maximum marks for part (a)(i) of the question. These calculations were fairly straightforward but it has been apparent in past exams that many candidates are unable to "bring forward" knowledge gained on previous subjects and many have been unable to calculate correctly EPS or a P/E ratio so the improvement in May is welcome.

The discussions required in parts (a)(ii) and (b)(ii) were less well answered. In both parts, many candidates failed to recognise the key issues arising from the scenario, focussing instead on general principles of dividend policy (in (a)(ii)) or on the far less important supplementary issues in respect of (b)(ii). Candidates who either wrote very little at all or who focussed exclusively on supplementary issues were unlikely to achieve a pass mark in these sections, with many failing to get more than 30% of the marks available.

4   B SUPERMARKETS (SEPT 12 EXAM)

Key answer tips – extracted from the Examiner's "Post Exam Guide" (note that the comments regarding WORD and/or EXCEL only relate to the COMPUTER BASED papers in March and September each year)

The presentation of answers, in terms of the use of WORD and EXCEL, has improved from previous re-take diets, which is encouraging. In particular the use of EXCEL did show an improvement with clearer audit trails and relatively clearly laid out workings which made it easier for the marker to understand the derivation of each figure. Clearly, repeated comments in previous PEGs have been taken on board.

However, there are still issues that need to be addressed. There were some candidates who did not use WORD at all and presented all of their answers in EXCEL. **This is not to be encouraged** because those candidates using only EXCEL often gave limited answers to the written requirements (presumably because of space). Candidates in certain centres used the page format in EXCEL, which again is not to be encouraged because it makes it harder for the marker to follow workings.

One final point to stress regarding the paper overall is the level of rounding that is expected. In the working capital calculations in part (a), in particular, some candidates did not use any decimal places within their calculations. Even exchange rates were sometimes calculated to just one decimal place. No general rule of thumb is available, but **a sensible level of rounding is expected in order to ensure that a candidate's answer is accurate** as stated. For example, if an answer is to be presented to an accuracy of, say, 3 significant figures, including one decimal place, workings may need to include as many as three decimal places in order to provide such accuracy, especially where discounting or exchange rates are involved rather than just simple addition.

(a)   **Briefing paper**

    To: The main board of B

    From: Mr X, Project team for USA convenience store project

    Date: 1 September 2012

    Investment appraisal as at 1 September 2012

    Purpose: To provide a progress report and initial investment appraisal for the above project and an initial assessment on whether or not to proceed.

Examiner's note:

Answers provided throughout this model answer are direct extracts from EXCEL spreadsheets and so rounding differences may arise when compared to the results obtained using a calculator.

(i) **Working capital strategy**

	USA stores	B group	Difference
Accounts receivables	Nil	Nil	Nil
Accounts payable	100 days	139 days	− 39 days
Inventory	30 days	53 days	− 23 days

The US convenience stores are likely to carry a different profile of goods than the average store operated by the B group. In particular:

- Inventory in the convenience stores will include a greater predominance of fresh foods, which are perishable and therefore require a fast turnover. Inventory days for the convenience stores can therefore be expected to be lower than the average figure for the B group - where a wider range of both perishable and non-perishable products are held in inventory .

- The most likely explanation for the lower accounts payable days estimate for the US stores is that US suppliers are able to demand more favourable payment terms than B is used to being able to negotiate elsewhere. Shorter credit periods may also reflect the higher service level required in order to maintain inventory levels at all times in convenience stores.

(ii) An aggressive strategy with regard to the management of working capital levels will mean that inventory will be kept to a minimum and accounts payable maximised to the extent that the particular market will accept (NB: it is presumed for the purposes of this analysis that 100 days is the maximum credit available in the US). The US convenience stores are not expected to have any accounts receivable, so we do not need to consider the benefits and potential drawbacks of an aggressive strategy for managing accounts receivable.

Benefits of an aggressive strategy:

- Cash flow advantages arising from having low investments in inventory in the first place and from paying suppliers as late as possible. This has the benefit of reducing the level of finance needed to support the working capital investment which then leads to lower borrowing costs.

- Reduced costs of holding inventory, although this might be mitigated by additional delivery costs.

Potential drawbacks of an aggressive strategy:

- Higher risk of stock outs from holding low levels of inventory – leading to customer dissatisfaction and possible loss of customers both in the short term and the longer term.

- Dissatisfied suppliers facing payment delays - leading to a higher risk of loss of supply or lowering of quality, especially in times of shortages.

- Attempts by suppliers to charge higher prices in order to compensate for later payment.

(iii) Working capital values

Year	Base data	0 USD000	1 USD000	2 USD000	3 USD000	4 USD000
Purchases, growth:	12%		35,000.00	39,200.00	43,904.00	49,172.48
Accts payable	100 days	(9,589.04)	(10,739.73)	(12,028.49)	(13,471.91)	
Inventory	30 days	2,876.71	3,221.92	3,608.55	4,041.57	
Net balance (for (b)(i))		(6,712.33)	(7,517.81)	(8,419.95)	(9,430.34)	0.00
Movement (for (b)(i))		(6,712.33)	(805.48)	(902.14)	(1,010.39)	9,430.34

(b) (i) Investment

Workings: tax depreciation

Year	Base data	0 USD000	1 USD000	2 USD000	3 USD000	4 USD000
Capex and b/f balance	10,000	10,000.00	10,000.00	7,500.00	5,625.00	4,218.75
Tax depreciation	25%		(2,500.00)	(1,875.00)	(1,406.25)	(218.75)
C/f balance	4,000		7,500.00	5,625.00	4,218.75	4,000.00
Tax relief at	33%		825.00	618.75	464.06	72.19

DCF calculations

Year	Base data	0 USD000	1 USD000	2 USD000	3 USD000	4 USD000
Buy properties	30,000	(30,000.00)				
Residual value of properties	36,000					36,000.00
Refit		(10,000.00)				4,000.00
Tax depreciation relief			825.00	618.75	464.06	72.19
Subtotal		(40,000.00)	825.00	618.75	464.06	40,072.19
Net operating cash, growing at	12%		15,000.00	16,800.00	18,816.00	21,073.92
Tax at	33%		(4,950.00)	(5,544.00)	(6,209.28)	(6,954.39)
Working capital movement (a)(iii)			6,712.33	805.48	902.14	1,010.39	(9,430.34)
Total in USD000		(33,287.67)	11,680.48	12,776.89	14,081.18	44,761.38
Exchange rate EUR/USD	1.1000	1.1000	1.1214	1.1431	1.1653	1.1880
		EUR000	EUR000	EUR000	EUR000	EUR000
Total in EUR000		(30,261.52)	10,416.36	11,177.08	12,083.42	37,679.27
NPV at 11% in EUR000 (using EXCEL NPV function)	21,850					

(ii) **Change in NPV resulting from change in final property value**

The cash flow in respect of the value of the properties at time 4 would change from USD 36 million to USD 24 million (i.e.: USD 30 million × 80%) – a difference of USD 12 million

Incremental approach:

Reduce NPV by

USD 12 million/1.1880 × 0.659 = EUR 6,657,000

Giving a revised NPV value of

EUR 15,193,000 (= EUR 21,850,000 – EUR 6,657,000)

Examiner's note:

As this exam was sat on PC, we demonstrate below an alternative approach that can be achieved simply using EXCEL by saving a 2nd copy of the EXCEL sheet and then changing a single cell representing the residual value of the properties. This gives a slightly different result due to rounding differences.

Year		0	1	2	3	4
	Base data	USD000	USD000	USD000	USD000	USD000
Buy properties	30,000	(30,000.00)				
Residual value of properties	24,000					24,000.00
Refit		(10,000.00)				4,000.00
Tax depreciation relief			825.00	618.75	464.06	72.19
Subtotal		(40,000.00)	825.00	618.75	464.06	28,072.19
Net operating cash growing at	12%		15,000.00	16,800.00	18,816.00	21,073.92
Tax at	33%		(4,950.00)	(5,544.00)	(6,209.28)	(6,954.39)
Working capital movement (see (a)(iii))		6,712.33	805.48	902.14	1,010.39	(9,430.34)
Total in USD000		(33,287.67)	11,680.48	12776.89	14,081.18	32,761.38
Exchange rate EUR/USD	1.1000	1.1000	1.1214	1.1431	1.1653	1.1880
Total in EUR000		(30,261.52)	10,416.36	11,177.08	12,083.42	27,577.90
NPV at 11% in EUR000	15,196					

(c)   **Financial implications**

The project is expected to generate a significant return with a net present value of EUR 21,850,000. Purely on this basis the project to set up 50 new convenience stores in the USA should be undertaken.

However, the DCF results depend heavily on the reliability of the input variables, as is demonstrated by the results of the sensitivity analysis in (b)(ii). Just by changing the assumption relating to the value of the properties on 31 December 2016 from a 20% increase to a 20% decrease, the NPV would fall by EUR 6,657,000 to EUR 15,193,000 (using the result obtained from the incremental approach), a fall of 30%. Given that property prices are volatile and past experience shows that values can fall significantly, then it could be argued that an evaluation based on a 20% drop in value would be more prudent for decision making purposes.

Other input variables that may prove to be unreliable estimates include:

- The Growth rate (which appears to be highly optimistic at 12%, although this is, presumably, a money rate, including any inflationary expectations, but may well be unsustainable at that level).

- Revenue (which depends heavily on having the correct business model to meet customer preferences).

- Costs (which depend on correct estimates of required staffing levels and salary costs).

- Exchange rates (see below).

- The cost of capital used of 11% is the rate applicable to B as a whole and may not be appropriate for this investment, especially as the project is overseas.

- It would also be more prudent to assume that annual working capital investment/cash release occurs at the end rather than at the beginning of each year since cash is released from working capital rather than absorbed in each financial year until the final year.

Expanding in a foreign country carries additional risks in terms of the following (key issues only listed below but these would be expected to be developed in a candidate's answer):

- Foreign exchange risk

- Understanding customer preferences – especially given that this is a different type of store than previously operated in the USA.

- Local regulatory environment including taxation and reporting, plus health and safety etc.

- Managing the business and the people from a distance and/or relocating UK staff to help set up and manage the business, at least at the start.

- Adapting the culture of the business to fit with B's culture while being sensitive to local differences in culture that need to be retained and working within these.

- Local resistance from customers to foreign ownership.

- Communication difficulties across different time zones.

- Understanding the demands of government and any steps required to avoid government intervention.

- Integrating different systems.

- Conducting business in a different business environment – understanding local protocol and business practices.

- Financial management in a different environment (e.g. working round the absence of credit interest on bank accounts in the US).

Foreign exchange risks may be significant. The investment appraisal has been based on forecast exchange rates derived from the interest rate differential. These are likely to be highly unreliable predictors of future exchange rates. The outturn result could therefore differ significantly from that shown. This may not be a problem, however, if, as is likely, shareholders have invested in B group with full knowledge of its major exposure to the US and, indeed, many other regions of the world. Investors may have deliberately chosen to invest in B group in order to obtain exposure to a diverse range of currencies and expect results to reflect exchange rate movements in the year.

Conclusion

On basis of this analysis, the project appears to be worthwhile pursuing on a trial basis. The greatest risk to success is probably the business plan itself in terms of whether the convenience store concept will be successful in the USA. Opening a few stores may be the only way of confirming that such stores will be welcomed and have the potential to be run on a profitable basis.

Tutorial note – extracted from the Examiner's "Post Exam Guide"

This was a compulsory case study style question involving the evaluation of the working capital requirements of a retail operation in part (a) and the evaluation of a proposed retail development in a foreign country in parts (b) and (c). The calculations in parts (a) and (b) were generally well answered. More problems arose with the written elements which were sometimes excellent but, in other cases, failed to focus on the question set, especially in part (a). In part (c), answers often lacked sufficient breadth and depth in terms of the number of issues raised and the amount of valid discussion around each issue.

5 V (NOV 12 EXAM)

Key answer tips – extracted from the Examiner's "Post Exam Guide"

You should begin your answer by providing a report structure. This should be a report heading, a brief introduction that explains the purpose of the report or terms of reference and suitable subheadings, which typically would follow the wording of the question requirements. Ensure the numerical parts of your answer are presented in a logical and tidy manner.

Part (a)

This part of the question requires description rather than discussion. You need therefore to provide brief details only of the key roles of an investment bank.

Part (b)(i)

In this part of the question it is first necessary to determine what possible values might be calculated. These could be jotted down in an answer plan with brief notes on how each valuation might be performed. The most common valuation methods, and ones that apply here, are: asset value, earnings (or P/E) basis, and DCF/NPV approach. Calculate each in turn, as follows:

Asset value – recognise it is net asset values that are relevant.

P/E basis – using the range of industry P/E ratios given in the scenario.

DCF/NPV – calculate as follows:

Total free cash flow (PAT plus depreciation less capital expenditure)

Cost of equity using the CAPM

DCF/NPV using the constant growth version of the DVM.

Part (b)(ii)

Discuss the appropriateness of each of the methods you have used as they relate to V. Each method should be a sub-sub heading in your report.

Part (b)(iii)

Identify the nature of the intangible assets present in V's valuations. Recognise that many of these can be grouped together, which adds to the risk and uncertainty of the true value of V.

Part (b)(iv)

Provide a table of valuations based on the various issue prices given in the scenario. The valuations should be based firstly on the number of shares currently in issue AND also after the IPO. They should be presented in a table as suggested in the solutions below.

Advise V whether the target price set is appropriate when compared with the values you have calculated in part (b)(i). In particular recognise the impact of V's growth projections.

> **Part (c)**
>
> Note that up to 7 marks are available for additional calculations. Decide therefore what extra calculations should be relevant. For directors, it would be logical to see how much each director would gain under each pricing strategy.
>
> Evaluate the likely viewpoints of directors and new shareholders under each pricing strategy. Provide a concluding paragraph summarising your main observations.

Report to the board of V

From: Finance Director

To: The directors of V group

Date: XX November 2012

Purpose: To consider the possible reasons for the poor uptake of the tender offer and how best to price the offer based on the tender offers received.

(a)   Describe the role of an Investment Bank in an IPO by tender bid

Key aspects to address:

- Advising V on the process involved.

- Advising V on an appropriate issue price.

- Advising on the appointment of other specialists (e.g. lawyers).

- Advising on stock exchange requirements.

- Assisting with the drawing up the prospectus and publicising the IPO.

- The Investment Bank might also underwrite the offer.

(b)   (i)   Valuation of V's equity using different methods

Asset based approach

Net asset value: SK\$ 102 million

Workings:

Book value of net assets	75
Uplift to market values of non current assets	27 (= 150 – 123)
Net asset value:	102

Alternative approach:	
Non current assets at market value	150
Current assets	110
Deduct liabilities	(158)
Net asset value:	102

P/E based approach

(based on post-tax earnings of SK$ 24 m)

	Value of V (SK$m)	Value per share (SK$)
At P/E of 11	264 (= 11 × 24 m)	2.93 (= 264m/90m)
At P/E of 14	336 (= 14 × 24 m)	3.73 (= 336m/90m)

DCF approach

Calculation of free cash flow:	SK$ million
Profit after tax	24
Add back depreciation	3
Capital expenditure (on-going requirement)	(5)
Free cash flow for year ended 30 June 2012	22

Calculation of cost of equity: 9.60% using Ke = rf + beta x (rm − rf)

where beta = 1.9, rf = 2% and rm = 6%

DCF valuations (assuming investment goes ahead)

Using a discount rate of 9.6%:

	30 June 2012 SK$ million	30 June 2013 SK$ million	30 June 2014 SK$ million	30 June 2015 SK$ million
Free cash flow (after tax)	(50.00)	22.66 = 22 × (1 + 3%)	23.34 = 22.66 × (1 + 3%)	
Cash flow in perpetuity				532.76 $= \dfrac{23.34 \times (1 + 5\%)}{(9.6\% - 5\%)}$
Discount at 9.6%	1.000	$(1 + 9.6\%)^{-1}$	$(1 + 9.6\%)^{-2}$	$(1 + 9.6\%)^{-2}$
PV	(50.00)	20.68	19.43	443.52

Total NPV: SK$ 433.6 million

Alternative workings using a discount rate of 10%:

	30 June 2012 SK$ million	30 June 2013 SK$ million	30 June 2014 SK$ million	30 June 2015 SK$ million
Free cash flow (after tax)	(50.00)	22.66 = 22 × (1 + 3%)	23.34 = 22.66 × (1 + 3%)	
Cash flow in perpetuity				490.14 $= \dfrac{23.34 \times (1 + 5\%)}{(10\% - 5\%)}$
Discount at 10%	1.000	0.909	0.826	0.826
PV	(50.00)	20.60	19.29	404.86

Total NPV: SK$ 394.8 million

Ignoring the planned investment gives a lower DCF valuation of:

SK$ 295.3 million   = 22 million × (1 + 2%)/(9.6% – 2.0%)

The expansion is therefore worthwhile, assuming that suitable finance is available.

Dividend valuation method (DVM)

Use dividend at Time 0 of SK$ 19.2 million (= SK$ 24 million × 80%).

At 2% growth, the DVM gives a value of equity of SK$ 257.7 million

(= 19.2 million × (1 + 2%)/(9.6% – 2%))

To apply an initial growth rate of 3% followed by 5% in perpetuity requires the same approach as used in the DCF calculation above, and is not repeated here since DCF gives the better answer.

DVM can also be applied using a single growth rate of either 3% or 5%, but this ignores the forecast sequence of growth rates given in the question.

(ii) **The validity of each result**

An asset valuation is based on book values of assets but, more importantly, it ignores intangibles. In the case of V, intangibles are likely to be very large - there will be significant value in its trading names and reputation. An asset valuation without taking intangibles into account is therefore not appropriate here. The P/E valuations are more useful. But only valid if the P/E used is truly representative of the industry as a whole and V's business profile is typical for the industry. A DCF approach is the most correct approach technically. This approach has the advantages of:

- Taking the time value of money into account.

- Taking the cost of capital into account and measuring returns against that base.

- Being based on the specific circumstances of V itself rather than on a proxy or industry average.

However, the DCF valuation is only as good as the data on which it is based and so:

- Could prove to be unreliable if cash forecast data is, itself, unreliable.

- Could be unreliable as it is based on very uncertain future growth prospects which are very hard to predict.

DVM is an acceptable approach. However, a DVM calculated using a simple or growing perpetuity at a single growth rate of 3% or 5% was inadequate given the forecast change in growth rate. Given the extensive information provided to calculate and discount free cash flows, a DCF valuation was a better approach in this instance.

(iii) **Extent and impact of intangibles and implications for setting a target offer price**

As mentioned above, V is likely to have a high value of intangible assets derived from its trading names and reputation built up over many years.

Relevant types of intangibles that candidates could discuss include:

- Experience and skills of branch staff.

- Reputation of holiday reps and other support services while on holiday in case of difficulty.

- Contact details of past customers and others who have shown an interest in V's holidays in the past for use for marketing purposes.

- Reputation for high customer satisfaction.

- Network of hotels who are willing to do business with V.

- Reputation for resolving disputes and compensating dissatisfied customers.

However, unlike non-current assets, intangibles such as a reputation for, say, high quality holidays and delivery can be eroded very quickly in the face of adverse publicity. This adds an element of risk and uncertainty to the true value of the company and on the attainable offer price in the tender bid.

(iv) **Appropriateness of original target price**

The Investment Bank target price of SK$ 3.40 values the company prior to the IPO and project at SK$ 306 million (= 90 million x SK$ 3.40), before taking into account either the shares issued or the funds received as part of the IPO.

Comparison to P/E valuations

The target price of SK$ 3.40 gives a valuation that is at the middle to high end of P/E valuations derived from the industry P/Es of between 11 to 14.

Comparison to DCF valuations

The valuation of SK$ 306 million at the target price of SK$ 3.40 is:

- Significantly lower than the DCF valuation of SK$ 434 million at a discount rate of 9.6% (or SK$ 395 million using 10%) that was compiled assuming that the proposed investment goes ahead and produces the high growth forecast.

- Higher than the DCF valuation of SK$ 295 million assuming 2% growth and no investment.

Note, however, that the DCF valuations are heavily dependent on the growth forecasts used.

Comparison to DVM valuation

DVM is not considered further here since DCF is considered to provide superior results.

Conclusion

The target price of SK$ 3.40 per share therefore appears to be slightly bullish but not unreasonable on the basis of a review of the P/E and DCF valuations based on financial data as at 30 June 2012, assuming that at least some of the potential for growth is realised on becoming a listed company.

The target price reflects a P/E ratio of approximately 13 times, which is considered to be at the high end of industry averages. The DCF valuation is also slightly above V's perceived current value before taking expansion plans into account but below the DCF valuation that is based on the assumption that the investment goes ahead.

We now know, however, that the first quarter results showed lower growth than had been used in the DCF valuation. If the company had been aware of falling profits between 30 June 2012 and 1 October 2012, the date the prospectus was published, the target price should have been adjusted to reflect this new information.

(c) **Evaluation of pricing strategies A and B**

Price per share SK$	Number of shares requested at this price (millions)	Cumulative (millions)	Findings/observations
2.90	4	30	
3.00	3	26	
3.10	2	23	Sell all 23 million shares if set price at SK$ 3.10.
3.20	3	21	
3.30	3	18	
3.40	6	15	Only sell 15 million shares if set price at SK$ 3.40.
3.50	5	9	
3.60	4	4	

Pricing strategy	Share price post IPO	Amount raised	Amount for directors	Amount for V
A	SK$ 3.40	SK$ 51.0m (= 15m × SK$3.40)	SK$ 44.20m (= 13 × SK$ 3.40)	SK$ 6.8m (= SK$ 51.0m − SK$ 44.2m)
B	SK$ 3.10	SK$ 71.3m (= SK$3.10 × 23m)	SK$ 40.3m (= 13 × SK$ 3.10)	SK$ 31.0m (=SK$ 71.3m − SK$ 40.3m)

Directors' viewpoint

Those directors selling shares will receive a higher value for their shares under pricing strategy A rather than pricing strategy B. The amount they would raise personally under each of the two pricing strategies is calculated below:

Director	Number of shares being sold	Value at SK$ 3.40 each under pricing strategy A	Value at SK$ 3.10 each under pricing strategy B
Executive Chairman	8m	SK$ 27.2m	SK$ 24.8m
Finance Director	1m	SK$ 3.4m	SK$ 3.1m
IT Director	3m	SK$ 10.2m	SK$ 9.3m
Human Resources	1m	SK$ 3.4m	SK$ 3.1m

The 'bird in hand' principle is likely to encourage these directors to choose pricing strategy A in order to maximise the funds received.

There may be an agency issue here because pricing strategy B raised a greater value of funds for V to invest in new projects and so there may be a conflict of interest between the best interests of the directors and of the company.

On the other hand, the directors may take a longer term viewpoint and realise that the future prospects for the company will ultimately affect the level of future dividends and the share price.

The directors are selling a very small proportion of their shares (even the Executive Chairman) or none at all (the Operations Director). To some extent this is due to conditions written into the IPO which prevent the directors from selling too many shares at the beginning. Additional sales are permitted within defined time periods. All of the directors will therefore be interested in the likely future share price movement as it will affect future proceeds when they sell additional shares at a later date.

On the face of it, pricing strategy A offers the highest price. However, the apparent failure of the IPO to attract subscribers at a price of SK$ 3.40 under pricing strategy A could be expected to lead to a fall in the share price and hence reduce or even eliminate this difference.

Indeed, pricing strategy A raises such a low level of new funds (SK$ 6.8 million) for V to invest on expansion, that the expansion plans might well have to be cancelled if pricing strategy A is adopted and this could also depress the share price and the value of future dividend streams. Whether or not this is a good strategy in view of the recent disappointing results will depend on whether the investment is still a sound prospect or not.

Viewpoint of the new shareholders of V

New investors are most likely to prefer pricing strategy B as they then pay less for the shares they acquire.

In addition, as already discussed earlier, it is highly likely that the share price would fall immediately following the IPO if a price of SK$ 3.40 were to be chosen, under pricing strategy A. This would inevitably create bad feeling amongst the new investors and adverse publicity for V which could have wider negative consequences.

Finally, pricing strategy B provides more funds to V to use for future projects and expansion plans, enhancing the value of the company further.

There is therefore a potential conflict of interest arising regarding the choice of pricing strategy, with current shareholders (directors) likely to prefer the higher price under pricing strategy A in order to maximise the cash received for their shares and the potential for selling additional shares at this higher price. However, new investors and consideration of the long term prospects of the company itself would favour the lower price under pricing strategy B in order to lower the cost of the shares acquired and also provide increased funds for future investment.

Conclusion

Assuming the funds raised can be invested in positive NPV projects and secure the long term prospects of V, pricing strategy B would be the best strategy for all parties. However, if V is considered to have only limited future growth prospects, the directors (who are also the shareholders) may opt for pricing strategy A in order to maximise the wealth of the current shareholders.

Tutorial note – extracted from the Examiner's "Post Exam Guide"

This question was handled well overall and no one part of the question appeared to cause specific difficulty.

Part (a) was generally satisfactorily attempted. The main weakness was to discuss what investment banks do in general terms rather than relate the answer to the tender process. More candidates than might be expected did not know what an investment bank did at all.

The calculations for part (b)(i) were done very well on the whole and many candidates got full or nearly full marks. However, many still cannot arrive at a sensible asset value, making too many variations on the correct answer for any one error to be called "common". Of all the possible valuation calculations available to candidates the free cash flow valuation tended to be the least well attempted and was often missing altogether.

Part (b)(ii) was also answered satisfactorily in the majority of cases.

In part (b)(iii) many candidates did not understand the meaning of "intangible assets" and often discussed non-current assets or even current assets.

Part (b)(iv) was very poorly answered, many missing the point of the question altogether.

In part (c) a sizeable minority had little understanding of the mechanics of a tender process. A common error was that many candidates seemed to think that the bank could apply different prices to different applicants.

The structure and presentation of answers to this question was very variable with some candidates not even providing a report heading.

---

6   V (MAR 13 EXAM)

Key answer tips – extracted from the Examiner's "Post Exam Guide"

Part (a) (i)

To calculate the conversion premium, first calculate the value of the shares obtained per SK$ 100 nominal of bond on conversion. Next, compare this with an IPO value of SK$ 3.00 per share to obtain the conversion premium per SK$ 100 nominal. Repeat this calculation using an IPO value of SK$ 4.00 per share.

To calculate the gross yield to maturity, first schedule the cash flows arising under the convertible bond up to and including conversion. Assume an initial investment of SK$ 100 and a value equal to the conversion value of the bond on the conversion date based on a share price of SK$ 3.00 on that date. It is easiest to work in terms of SK$ 100 nominal of bond but any other nominal amounts are also acceptable. Calculate an NPV of the cash flows at a range of discount rates in order to identify the rate at which the NPV is closest to zero. This is the internal rate of return (IRR) or, in other words, the yield to maturity for the bond based on the conversion value used. Now repeat the calculation assuming a share price of SK$4.00 per SK$ 100 nominal on conversion.

Part (a) (ii)

The answer should focus on the choice of a convertible bond to structure the venture capitalist funding. Identity the key benefits and drawbacks of accepting such finance and then expand each item in more detail. Don't forget to mention the liquidity demands of servicing and repaying the bond if the IPO does not go ahead as planned or the large effective cost if the bond is converted into shares at a high conversion premium in 5 years' time.

Part (b)

Consider each of V's financial objectives in turn, firstly discussing how they are likely to change as a result of X's involvement in the business. Then discuss how they are likely to change following an IPO.

Part (c)

Consider each of the stakeholders listed in turn, evaluating and advising on the impact of the proposed arrangement on each type of stakeholder.

Part (d)

Identify and then advise on two alternative exit strategies.

(a)   (i)   **Conversion premium per SK$100 nominal**

	At SK$ 3.00	At SK$ 4.00
At issue, pay SK$ 100	100.00	100.00
On conversion receive 55 shares worth SK$ 3.00/SK$4.00 each	165.00	220.00
Hence conversion premium of	65.00	120.00

Calculation of yield to maturity at an IPO price of SK$ 3.00

Time	0	1	2	3	4	5	
	SK$	SK$	SK$	SK$	SK$	SK$	
Cash flow	−100	2	2	2	2	167	*(= 165 + 2)*

IRR using IRR function: 12.2%

Alternatively, discount convertible bond cash flows at different discount rates to find the IRR:

Time		SK$	DF at 15%		DF at 10%	
0	Initial	−100	1	−100	1	−100
1 to 5	Interest	2	3.352	6.70	3.791	7.58
5	Conversion value	165	0.497	82.01	0.621	102.47
				−11.29		10.05

From this analysis we can see that the IRR, that is, the yield to maturity of the bond, is approximately 12.4% (= 10% + (5% × 10.05/(10.05 + 11.29))) at an IPO price of SK$ 3.00.

Calculation of yield to maturity at an IPO price of SK$ 4.00

Time	0	1	2	3	4	5	
	SK$	SK$	SK$	SK$	SK$	SK$	
Cash flow	−100	2	2	2	2	222	*(= 220 + 2)*

IRR using IRR function: 18.6%

Alternatively, discount convertible bond cash flows at different discount rates to find the IRR:

Time		SK$	DF at 20%		DF at 15%	
0	Initial	−100	1	−100	1	−100
1 to 5	Interest	2	2.991	5.98	3.352	6.70
5	Conversion value	220	0.402	88.44	0.497	109.34
				−5.58		16.04

From this analysis we can see that the IRR, that is, the yield to maturity of the bond, is approximately 18.7% (= 15%+ (5% × 16.04/(16.04 + 5.58))) at an IPO price of SK$ 4.00.

(ii) **Benefits and drawbacks of convertible bond**

The main benefit to V of structuring the finance in the form of a convertible bond is that the bond carries a low interest rate, below market rates, which has an immediate cash flow benefit   If anticipated growth is insufficient to support an IPO, the bond would be repaid and the effective pre-tax cost of the bond to V would simply be the coupon of 2%. To this extent, Director A is correct in noting that this may be a cheap source of finance for V and lower risk if growth objectives are not achieved.

However, the high conversion premium needs to be taken into account when evaluating the overall cost of the bond if it is converted as part of an IPO. This is potentially very high. Indeed, at IPO share prices of SK$ 3.00 and SK$4.00, the effective pre-tax annual cost is 12% and 19% respectively (as calculated in (a)(i) above). This is clearly much higher than V's cost of debt which is to be expected as it reflects the fact that a venture capitalist would be providing high risk finance which requires the potential for commensurately high returns. This also means that Director A is not correct in assuming that the bond is a cheap source of finance under all circumstances. The actual cost incurred will depend on other factors. In addition, if a significant conversion premium materialises then the directors may feel that they are giving away their own success.

V is also taking on significant risks by accepting funds via a convertible bond. The principal needs to be repaid even if the planned growth and IPO are not realised. It could be very difficult for V to successfully refinance such a large borrowing which would, indeed, double its long term borrowings. It is unlikely that the holiday villages could be sold for as much as they cost to build.

There is also an immediately detrimental impact on gearing with the doubling of long term debt. It is possible that this could lead to the breach of the debt covenant, making the current scheme impossible without either restructuring V's borrowings to give the current lenders priority over interest and capital repayments, or adopting an alternative structure such as convertible preference shares in place of the convertible bond that would achieve the same objective.

(b) **Involvement of X (a venture capitalist)**

Growth target (currently 5% a year target growth in earnings)

X is unlikely to accept a target of 5% per annum growth in earnings. X will require aggressive growth targets in relation to both revenue and earnings which would need to be reflected in revised financial objectives for V.

However, X should recognise that projected growth is likely to be lower in the early years as the project is launched. It will take some time for V to become established in the new "holiday village" market. A cumulative growth target over the whole time period is therefore more likely to be acceptable to X.

Dividend objective (currently a pay-out ratio of 80% of profits)

Capital growth is paramount to X and X is likely to accept much lower dividend or other pay-outs in order to allow any profits to be reinvested in the business and hence support high growth. Indeed, in many cases the original shareholders may have to accept a dividend 'window', receiving no dividends at all in order to share in the risks of the project and prioritise the reinvestment of profits to promote growth and also give priority to paying returns to X.

Listing in 5 years' time.

Growth target (currently 5% a year target growth in earnings).

Once publicly listed on a Stock Exchange, V will be accountable to a wide range of shareholders, both individuals and institutions. Investors prefer a steady dividend stream, which goes hand in hand with steady earnings growth and so a lower growth rate will be sought that is considered to be sustainable over the longer term.

Dividend objective (currently a pay-out ratio of 80% of profits)

Following an IPO, V would become a public company and would be answerable to external parties, including shareholders. Investors in public companies tend to prefer slower, steady growth in earnings and dividends rather than large dividend pay-outs that are unlikely to be sustainable in the longer term. The dividend policy required after an IPO will depend to some extent on the profile of the external shareholders. Large scale institutional investors generally prefer steady but growing dividends, whereas smaller scale investors might accept lower dividends in exchange for the prospect of higher growth, preferring capital gains to income. V should seek stability in its share price, supported by a steady, sustainable dividend policy that matches investor expectation.

(c) **Evaluation of the proposed plan from the viewpoint of different interested parties.**

	Value in Current position	*Value after IPO at SK$ 3.00*	*Increase over current position*	*Value after IPO at SK$ 4.00*	*Increase over current position*
	SK$ million	SK$ million	SK$ million	SK$ million	SK$ million
Executive chairman	93.6	140.4	46.8 (50%)	187.2	93.6 (100%)
4 other directors	21.6 × 4	32.4 × 4	10.8 (50%) each	43.2 × 4	21.6 (100%) each
Venture capitalist		82.5 plus interest of 5	32.5 (65%) plus interest over initial investment of 50	110.0 plus interest of 5	60.0 (120%) plus interest over initial investment of 50
Total	180.0	352.5		470.00	

V's Directors

Inviting X to invest in the company would inevitably create large changes for the directors.

The way that the company is run would need to change. X would expect a seat on the board and to contribute to financial and strategic decisions. The directors could benefit from the expertise and experience of X in turning businesses around and pursuing growth in preparation for an IPO. However, this may also be uncomfortable as X seeks to make changes that may not always be acceptable to the other directors.

Executive Chairman

If the company were to be sold now at SK$ 180 million, the Executive Chairman could expect to be able to retire straightaway and realise his full investment of SK$ 93.6 million (= 52% × SK$ 180 million).

Alternatively, under the delayed IPO strategy, he can expect a 50% - 100% increase in the value of his shares to between SK$140.4 million and SK$ 187.2 million. This equates to a compound annual return of between 8.5% and 14.9% in the intervening 5 years (see workings above and below).

However, the higher price carries some significant drawbacks. The venture capitalist and growth strategy carries significant risk. The success of the planned growth and IPO are by no means guaranteed and the value of his shares could fall instead of rise. In addition, he would have to wait five years for his cash and it is likely that he would only be permitted to sell a first tranche of shares at that point, with further sales permitted at future dates.

Other directors

As for the Executive Chairman, the attractiveness of the proposed plan will largely depend on what extent the other directors prefer certain returns now rather than the possibility of a higher price in 5 years' time, but also the risk that the value falls if the development and IPO were not successful.

The most important factor that they need to take into account is their confidence that the expansion plans and IPO would indeed, be likely to be successful. The directors could see a large fall in the value of their investment were the new development and IPO to fail. Indeed, the drain on financial resources created by needing to redeem the convertible bond could prove to be too much for V and lead to the failure of the company. On the other hand, however, there is the prospect of large financial gain. There is therefore a trade-off here between risk and reward that needs to be carefully assessed before proceeding.

Although it is unlikely that the directors will receive any dividends in the 5 years running up to the IPO, they would benefit from an increase in the share price.

- Under an IPO price of SK$ 3.00 per share, the compound average annual growth rate of the value of a share over the 5 year period running up to the IPO is 8.5% (where $0.0845 = (3.00/2.00)^{(1/5)} - 1$).

- Under an IPO price of SK$ 4.00 per share, the compound average annual growth rate of the value of a share over the 5 year period running up to the IPO is 14.9% (where $0.1487 = (4.00/2.00)^{(1/5)} - 1$).

X

X's primary objective in investing in V would be to obtain an attractive return on his investment.

Due to the risks involved with this venture, X would be looking for the prospect of a significant return, possibly of the order of 20% a year.

Earlier analysis shows that:

- At an IPO share price of SK$ 3.00, X would make an effective annual return on its investment of approximately 12% per annum.

- At an IPO price of SK$ 4.00, the effective annual return rises to approximately 19%.

X is therefore only likely to be interested in the scheme if confident that an IPO would be successful and raise at least SK$ 4.00 per share.

X is in a safer position than the directors since he would obtain repayment of the amount invested via the convertible bond plus some limited amount of interest if the IPO were to fail.

V's other stakeholders

V's other stakeholders include lenders, employees, customers and suppliers.

Lenders

Gearing based on book values

Current: 40% (= SK\$ 50m/(SK\$ 50m + SK\$ 75m))

After investment by X: 57%

= (SK\$ 50m + SK\$ 50m)/(SK\$ 50m + SK\$ 50m + SK\$ 75m)

It is not clear whether the covenant is based on book or market values. If based on book values, the covenant would be breached and would therefore need to be renegotiated before the scheme could be actioned, to give the banks priority over X in the event of default.

It may be better to structure the venture capitalist finance in the form of convertible preference shares rather than convertible bonds to ensure that other lenders retain priority in terms of both interest payments and repayment of capital in the event of the company getting into problems.

Employees

Employees are likely to react to the proposal in one of two ways according to their confidence in the development will be successful. Their future job prospects are also tied up in the success of the scheme.

They may also be concerned about any changes in management style and working conditions that might be pushed through by X in a strive for growth helped by a reduction in costs and increase in efficiency.

Customers

Customers have less to lose by the development as they always have the option of buying holidays from other providers. They would, however, gain from a successful development of new holiday villages if this type of holiday is of interest to them.

Suppliers

Suppliers would be monitoring V closely for signs of a deterioration in credit worthiness due to the extra liquidity pressures on the business following an investment by X. If they had any concerns about the ability of V to meet its commitments to them, they may demand earlier payment for services provided such as block booking of hotel rooms.

(d) Two alternative exit strategies:

Share buy out

The Executive Chairman could seek to sell his shares, to current board members and/or potential new investors. This would involve very little disruption to the business but the other board members may not have access to the large amount of cash required. In addition, they may be reluctant to increase their exposure to V given the current difficult trading conditions.

Sell part of the business

Alternatively, the directors could look at ways of dividing up the business and selling part of the business to a competitor. The proceeds of the sale could be used to repurchase the shares held by the Executive Chairman and the other board members could continue to run the remaining part of the business. However, this could increase the competitive pressure on V and lead to a fall in sales if V's customers prefer to deal with the acquirer or if the acquirer has sufficient financial support to be able to lower prices, temporarily at least, in an attempt to increase their market share.

Tutorial note – extracted from the Examiner's "Post Exam Guide"

Candidates generally had a good understanding of the role of a venture capitalist. However, candidates should note that, at strategic level, the examiner is interested in the ability to apply that knowledge in the context of a given scenario. Good background knowledge is insufficient. So, for example, the requirement in part (a)(ii) focuses on funding from a venture capitalist in the form of a convertible bond. This was not the right place to write an essay on the role of venture capitalists. The focus should have been on the high risk to V of taking on additional debt that required servicing and repayment in the event of non-conversion and which, if converted, would be at a yield to maturity higher than the present cost of equity.

In part (c), the question specifically mentioned that there were up to 9 marks available for calculations. In many instances, no calculations were provided. Simple calculations of the value of the Executive Chairman's shares if sold today against what they would be worth under the two IPO prices provided were essential in order to evaluate the potential benefit to the Executive Chairman of proceeding with the planned venture capitalist investment leading up to an IPO as compared to selling his shares now. Other useful calculations could have included the implied compound growth in the share price that underpins the estimated post IPO share price to see if this appears to be reasonable or achievable.

Other common errors:

- *Inability to calculate either the conversion premium or the yield to maturity for the convertible bond. Some candidates calculated a net present value and then labelled this as a yield to maturity.*

- *A belief that the convertible bond would not affect gearing.*

- *A proposal that the Chief Executive should exit the business by passing shares on to his children, without any mention of how he would receive payment for the shares.*

7   T RAILWAYS (MAY 13 EXAM)

Key answer tips – extracted from the Examiner's "Post Exam Guide"

Part (a) should begin with consideration of the difference between public and private company financial objectives and access to financial resources and how this might impact on the way the cafes are run when under private management. These changes then need to be interpreted in terms of benefits and risks to T Railways.

Part (b)(i) should begin with the calculation of a WACC to use as the discount factor in the NPV calculation. The NPV calculation requires the identification and listing of relevant cash flows. These then need to be listed under the correct time frame, uplifted for growth and adjusted for tax as required. A separate working should be provided in respect of tax depreciation allowances.

Part (b)(ii) should start by considering the results in part (b) (i) and the sensitivity of those results to changes in key variables and to the possibility that bank finance may not be approved. The possibility and impact of 'abandonment' and 'follow on' options can then be evaluated. The evaluation should finish with a conclusion.

Part (b)(iii) requires a change of focus to that of the bank and its assessment of creditworthiness of Mr C in respect of the bank loan required.

(a)   **Advise T Railways**

Differences in financial objectives:

- The primary objective of a private enterprise such as CCC will be to maximise shareholder wealth. In contrast, T Railways' stated financial objectives are:

    – To at least cover operating costs from the revenue earned.

    – To provide value for money.

- T Railways is therefore likely to set a lower target for financial returns than CCC, being content to cover costs rather than pursuing profit.

In addition, T Railways' objective of achieving 'value for money' focuses on operating the current business efficiently and cost effectively but does not encourage growth. In contrast, CCC is likely to be more proactive in managing the business for growth and returns.

Potential benefits and risks for T Railways:

- Assuming that the rent charged to CCC is commensurate to the net cash inflows generated by the business to date T Railways should not lose out financially.

- Indeed, there is the possibility of financial gain if higher usage of the cafes leads to higher profits for CCC and hence allows for the possibility of future rent rises.

- Another benefit is that T Railways can then focus on the core business of running railways, leaving catering in railway stations to a specialist in that field.

- If CCC improves the service to customers, T Railways would benefit indirectly through greater customer satisfaction. Indeed, CCC may have better access to funding needed to invest in the business in order to improve the service provided.

- On the other hand, CCC may not develop the business as expected and could create a reputational risk for T Railways if the level of service provided deteriorates under CCC's management.

- T Railways is also losing a potentially highly profitable income stream. The rental income is likely to be lower than the profits that could be achieved by operating the cafes in a more aggressive, commercial manner.

(b) **REPORT**

From: Management Consultant, Company X

To: Mr C, Managing Director, CCC

Re: Proposed investment in five station cafes in stations that are currently operated by T Railways

Purpose

To appraise the investment and advise on issues relevant to the decision on whether or not to proceed with the investment

(i) Preliminary calculations to obtain a WACC for use as a discount factor in DCF calculations:

Firstly, calculate the ungeared cost of equity:

keu = Rf + [Rm − Rf]ßu

So, keu = 3% + (5% × 1.28) = 9.4%

Next, calculate WACC:

Kadj = Keu (1 − tL) where L = debt/(debt + equity) and Kadj = WACC

So, WACC = 9.4% × (1 − (0.3 × 0.5)) = 7.99%

Alternative method based on geared beta:

Firstly, calculate geared beta

$$ßg = ßu + [ßu − ßd]\frac{V_D(1-t)}{V_E}$$

So ßg = 1.28 + (1.28 − 0.54) × ((0.5 × 0.7)/0.5) = 1.798

Secondly, calculate the geared cost of equity

keg = Rf + [Rm − Rf]ßg

So, keg = 3% + 1.798 × 5% = 11.99%

Finally, calculate WACC

$$WACC = keg \left[\frac{V_E}{V_E + V_D}\right] + k_d[1-t]\left[\frac{V_D}{V_E + V_D}\right]$$

So, WACC = 11.99% × 50% + (5.7% × 0.7) × 50% = 7.99%

NPV and IRR calculations:

	Base data	0	1	2	3
Cash flows		T$000	T$000	T$000	T$000
Operating cash inflows (W1)			1,749.6	2,717.3	3,693.6
Operating cash outflows	70% inflows		(1,224.7)	(1,902.1)	(2,585.5)
Fixed operating costs	7% uplift		(450.0)	(481.5)	(515.2)
Manager's salary	7% uplift		(50.0)	(53.5)	(57.3)
Sub total		0.0	24.9	280.2	535.6
Tax at 30%			(7.5)	(84.1)	(160.7)
Tax relief on tax WDA (W2)			75.0	56.3	18.8
Fixtures & fittings		(1,000.0)			500.0
Net operating cash flow		(1,000.0)	92.4	252.4	893.7
Discount at 8%		1.000	0.926	0.857	0.794
PV at 8% (in T$000)		(1,000.0)	85.6	216.3	709.6
NPV (in T$000)	11.5				
Discount at 10%		1.000	0.909	0.826	0.751
PV at 10% (in T$000)		(1,000.0)	84.0	208.5	671.2
NPV (in T$'000)	(36.3)				

IRR: $\qquad$ 8.48% = 8% + 2% × (11.5/(11.5 + 36.3))

Workings

(W1) Revenue per café

Number of passengers per day	3,600	3,700	3,800
Percentage of passengers using the cafe	9%	12%	15%
Average daily spend per passenger (T$)	3.0	3.4	3.6
Days in year that trains operate	360	360	360
Total revenue (T$) per café	349,920	543,456	738,720
Revenue for five cafes (T$)	1,749,600	2,717,280	3,693,600

(W2) Tax written down allowances

		Tax relief at 30%
Fixtures & fittings	1,000.0	
25% WDA in year 1	(250.0)	75.0
C/f to year 2	750.0	
25% WDA in year 2	(187.5)	56.3
C/f to year 3	562.5	
Final value	(500.0)	
Balancing allowance	62.5	18.8

Payback calculation:	0	1	2	3
	T$000	T$000	T$000	T$000
Net operating cash flow		92.4	252.4	893.7
Balance of investment	1,000.0	907.6	655.2	(238.5)

Hence payback occurs during year 3, at approximately 2 years 8.8 months

(where 8.8 = 655.2/893.7 × 12 months).

(ii) **Potential benefit**

The results in (b)(i) show that the project is expected to generate positive wealth for shareholders.

It has:

- An NPV result of T$ 11,500 at a WACC of 8%.

- An internal rate of return of 8.48%, which is slightly higher than the WACC but lower than the geared cost of equity of 11.99%.

- Payback is achieved approximately 8.8 months into year 3.

Evaluation of results

The results in (b)(i) are highly sensitive to a number of input variables such as the cost of capital and estimates of growth, passenger numbers, variable cost relationships and residual value. Mr C therefore needs to consider how reliable these estimates are. Three of these (customer numbers, residual value and the cost of capital) will be examined in more detail below.

The estimated growth in customer numbers gives a figure of 570 customers a day (or 47 customers per hour in a 12 hour day) by year 3. There needs to be a 'reality check' here to ensure that such numbers appear to be realistic given the size of the cafe premises and the extent of takeaway business. Indeed, for smaller premises these numbers may exceed reasonable capacity and lower growth figures may need to be applied.

The residual value of fixtures and fittings is particularly important. If, say, the RV of the 5 cafes fell 5% to T$ 475,000, the NPV of the project would be -T$2,430 (see workings below). This demonstrates that the residual value would not need to fall much to make the initial project not worthwhile.

Workings (in T$000):

Tax written down allowance becomes 26.25 (= 30% × (562.5 – 475.0))

So cash flows decrease by 17.55 (= (500.0 + 18.8) – (475.00 + 26.25))

So NPV decreases by 13.93 (= 0.794 × 17.55)

To –2.43 (= 11.5 – 13.93)

Perhaps of greater importance here though is the impact of the financing of the project on the NPV. If Mr C is unable to secure the debt funding then the initial acquisition will need to be funded from 100% equity which will impact on the cost of capital. An appropriate all equity cost of capital would be 9.4% (= 3% + 5% × 1.28). Given that the IRR of the project is 8.48%, then this shows how important it is for Mr C to secure bank funding to finance the project. If not, the initial project will not be financially viable.

Similar sensitivity exercises could be carried out for each of the other underlying assumptions.

Real options

The profitability of the cafes is forecast to increase significantly year on year during the three year period due to forecast increase in the number of passengers using the cafes, together with a forecast increase in average spend. Before tax adjustments, forecast net operating cash flows increased ten-fold between year 1 and year 2, increasing from T$24,900 to T$280,200 in that year and almost doubled again in year 3. However, as already commented above, these figures need to be reviewed to see if they are reasonable. The customer numbers predicted at the end of year 3 appear to be close to maximum capacity (or possibly exceed maximum capacity already, depending on the size of the cafes) and this would restrict or eliminate the possibility of future growth. Space constraints need to be taken into account when valuing 'follow on' options.

The 'follow on' option to expand the number of cafes operated within the next three to ten years is, however, still potentially very valuable, even assuming zero growth in customer numbers beyond year 3. However, expanding from 5 to up to 100 cafes would greatly change the nature of the business. CCC would need to develop a more complex management structure and acquire extensive additional finance to be able to expand in this manner.

It is not stated that there is an option to 'abandon' the first five cafes, that is, whether there is a break clause in the rental agreement. Even with a break clause, abandonment is likely to create a large loss given the large upfront investment required to fit out the cafes at the beginning.

There is unlikely to be any possibility of 'delay' to the start of the project. It is likely that T Railways could find other interested parties and Mr C could lose out. No contract has yet been signed. It appears that Mr C has sufficient personal resources to be able to proceed without finance from the bank if the bank refuses to provide a loan.

Conclusion

In conclusion, the project does appear to be worthwhile pursuing assuming that the growth in passenger numbers and of the number of passengers making use of the café is considered to be reliable. The potential profits in the longer term are sufficient to make the experimental run with five cafes to be worthwhile as long as Mr C has sufficient personal financial resources to be able to withstand a possible loss.

(iii) **Challenges that Mr C may face in obtaining bank funding for CCC include:**

- Preparing a convincing, comprehensive business plan. Mr C may not have the necessary expertise to put together comprehensive plans backed up by forecast results and cash flows.

- The bank may not accept the cash forecast. For example, the bank may not consider the customer growth forecast to be realistic.

- Mr C would be well advised to seek help from a qualified accountant in preparing this plan.

- As a business start-up, the bank cannot rely on previous results or credit history for CCC, relying instead on Mr C's own personal reputation.

- The bank may require Mr C (and other directors of CCC, if any) to provide some degree of security for the loan in the form of a charge over their personal assets, which might not be achievable.

- Over reliance of the success and operation of the business lies with just one person (Mr C). This may be considered to be too risky.

The bank will seek reassurance about the management capabilities and experience of Mr C and any other Directors of CCC. In this respect, Mr C should be able to point to his experience of running other cafes previously, assuming that these have been and can be seen to be well run.

Tutorial note – extracted from the Examiner's "Post Exam Guide"

Overall the question was satisfactorily answered, often because of good answers to parts (a) and/or (b)(i).

Part (a)

This part of the question was answered at least satisfactorily by most candidates and very well indeed by many, especially in some overseas centres. Common misunderstandings were:

1   Assuming that private sector firms are not interested in Value for Money.

2   Discussing issues that are unlikely to be relevant, such as that passengers would choose not to travel by train if they didn't like the cafe.

Part (b)(i)

Most candidates scored satisfactory marks on this part of the question and many obtained very high or maximum marks. The main weaknesses were:

- *Providing calculations based on 1 café instead of 5, or mixing up calculations of 1 café and all 5 cafés, for example showing revenue and variable costs for 5 but initial investment costs for only 1 or using T$90,000 for the fixed costs of five cafes*

- *The NPV calculations were generally done well, but many candidates were unable to calculate (either at all or correctly) IRR and/or payback. A problem here was that if the candidates own NPV figure for the first three years showed negative DCFs, the calculations became difficult or impossible. On the "own figure" basis credit was given for a correct comment/attempt.*

- *Tax depreciation allowances were generally handled well although a sizeable minority also showed accounting depreciation and/or interest charges in the cash flows.*

The better candidates correctly calculated a WACC to use as the discount factor based on a geared equity beta. More often the ungeared equity beta of 1.28 was used to calculate a cost of equity of 9.4% which was then either used as the discount rate or used to calculate an incorrect WACC. A surprising number of candidates took 5% as the market return rather than the market premium in the CAPM.

Part (b)(ii)

This part of the question was very poorly answered on the whole. Discussion tended to be little more than very general comments on the NPV, IRR and payback results. Very few candidates indeed discussed IRR being a measure of risk or sensitivity and even fewer recognised that the payback was highly dependent on the residual value.

The requirement to consider real options was often ignored. Those candidates who attempted to answer it either misunderstood completely what real options are or talked about them in the abstract without relating them to the scenario. Candidates in some overseas centres were clearly quite ignorant about the meaning of real options.

Part (b)(iii)

This part of the question was considerably better answered than part (b)(ii) although many candidates failed to recognize that this is a small new company, an individual in fact, needing the loan and provided discussion more appropriate to a large, listed company.

8 T RAILWAYS (SEPT 13 EXAM)

Key answer tips – extracted from the Examiner's "Post Exam Guide"

The answer to part (a) should consider the two alternative privatisation methods listed in the requirement, focussing on a comparison of the methods themselves rather than the impact on TPTS of privatisation per se.

In part (b) (i), the answer should begin by considering all the current TPTS cash inflows and outflows to identify which are lost as a result of the sale of TPTS. Any new cash flows (such as payment to UT for the use of the track and policing services) and any other changes (such as to head office costs) should also be added to the list.

In part (b) (ii), the net change in cash flows identified in part (b)(i) should be discounted by applying the growing perpetuity formula at a growth rate of 2% and a discount rate of 4%.

Finally, in part (b) (iii), the appropriateness of the discount rate of 4% should be considered. Starting with the rationale for its use and then questioning the validity of the use of a discount rate that takes neither risk nor tax into account.

Part (c)(i) should begin by scheduling the relevant cash flows for TPTS once owned by UT. These should then be discounted at 8% using a growth rate of 2%. Asset based valuations should also be provided on both a cost and replacement cost basis.

Part (c)(ii) should consider the validity of each method used in (c)(i), taking each in turn, within the context of the question scenario.

Part (d)(i) should begin by looking at the maximum price that UT would consider based on the results in part (c). This should be compared to the cost of disposing of TPTS from T Railways' viewpoint as calculated in part (b)(ii) and a conclusion drawn.

The answer to part (d)(ii) should firstly consider the financial implications of the sale of TPTS from the viewpoint of both T Railways and its sole shareholder, T Government. Both short and long term financial impacts should be considered. The answers should then widen out to consider the wider strategic benefits and drawbacks of the sale of TPTS, before reaching an overall recommendation.

(a) **Price obtained and speed and risk of completion of the sale**

The IPO has the potential to raise higher sales proceeds than a trade sale to UT by opening the sale up to a wider potential investor group. However, a successful IPO requires a strong demand for shares, reflecting public confidence in the future profitability and government support for the new company.

Although likely to be at a lower price, a sale to UT would be quicker and cheaper to achieve. No underwriting costs would be required and the tighter timeframe would result in lower exposure to a fall in the stock market during the sale process.

Management expertise

In both cases, the sale agreement could include 'lock ins' for the transfer and retention of key staff to ensure continuity in track management and transference of management expertise in this specialist area. A sale to UT would have the added advantage of a main Board of UT who already have expertise in managing an independent services company.

Confidence in the on-going provision and quality of the maintenance of track

A long term view is required when managing track quality. There is some reassurance that UT would be willing to adopt such a strategy as, indeed, the provision of utility services requires a similar long term business and maintenance perspective. The management of UT would also already have the necessary experience and expertise in managing and negotiating service levels with T government in respect of the provision of utilities. This skill is likely to be useful when drawing up a service agreement for provision of the railway track to T Railways.

To summarise, although selling to UT may not raise as high a sales value, it would seem to be a quicker and safer approach to privatisation.

(b) **The sale of TPTS from the viewpoint of T Railways**

(i) **Impact of the sale of TPTS on T Railways' post-tax, pre-financing cash flows**

Changes to T Railways forecast cash flows for the year ending 31 December 2014:

	T$ million	
Revenue from cafes and stations foregone	(100)	where 100 = 38 + 62
Direct operating costs no longer incurred	795	
Benefit from reduction in HO costs	25	
Fees payable for use of track	(800)	
Incremental net operating cash outflow	(80)	

This equates to a post-tax net operating cash outflow of T$ 56.0 million for the year ending 31 December 2014 (= T$ 80 million × (1 – 0.30)).

(ii) **Present value of change in cash flows**

NPV of forecast change in cash flows above

Value at 4% with
2% growth: T$ 2,856 million = T$ 56.0 m × 1.02/(4% – 2%)

(iii) **Validity of 4% discount rate**

Benefits:

- Easy to apply, consistent with other businesses owned by T Government.

- Represents T Government's cost of borrowing which is consistent with the funding structure of T Railways, which is wholly funded by T Government.

Drawbacks:

- The 4% cost of capital has not been adjusted to reflect the beta or risk profile of the railway business. Some adjustment would be reasonable to ensure that a more realistic commercial valuation of TPTS is obtained for use in setting a fair price for the sale of TPTS.

- 4% is the pre-tax cost of debt to T Railways but has been applied to post tax cash flows. This is clearly inconsistent treatment of tax - a post-tax cost of debt would have been more appropriate and used to calculate T Railways' WACC. Alternatively, the pre-tax cost of capital of 4% could have been applied to pre-tax cash flows. This is, arguably, technically more correct since tax is paid across to the sole lender, T Government, and so would be best removed from the calculation altogether due to the circular flow of the tax element.

- Using a non-risk-adjusted cost of capital as the discount rate is likely to over-value TPTS and give T Railways an unrealistic target price for TPTS.

(c) **The sale of TPTS from the viewpoint of UT**

(i) **Valuing TPTS from the viewpoint of UT**

Asset bases	T$ million
Non-current assets at cost	1,500
Add working capital	2
Capital employed at book value	1,502

	T$ million
Non-current assets at replacement value	1,990
Add working capital	2
Capital employed at book value	1,992

DCF basis

NOCF after tax of T$ 67.2 million

(= T$ 96 m × (1 – 0.30) at a discount rate of 8% gives an NPV value of:

T$ 1,142 million at 2% growth (where $1,142 = 67.2 \times 1.02/(8\% - 2\%)$)

(ii)   **Validity of methods used and results obtained**

An asset based valuation is the simplest valuation method available because it simply uses information provided.   However, neither book value nor replacement value is likely to be representative of the underlying commercial value of TPTS. The commercial value of the track is the potential revenues that it can generate. The track has little value for an owner unless it can be used to run trains. Without the railways, it would be worth little more than the value of scrap metal. Even if there were a newly formed railway company which could use the track, it would be unlikely to pay anything near to cost price for second hand track, especially as track systems are constantly evolving technologically.

The DCF valuation is lower than either of the asset based valuations. This is an unusual position but supports the opinion expressed above that the asset based valuations do not give valid results in the context of this scenario. The DCF valuation is more appropriate in this case since it reflects the earning capacity of the track.

However, the validity of the DCF result depends to a large extent on the validity of the inputs to the DCF model.   The cash flow estimates for 2014 are highly subjective. It is not yet clear as to what it might cost to maintain the track nor is it clear how much UT could charge T Railways for use of the track. Also, the business is wholly dependent on one customer and hence UT may demand a lower price because of the risk this creates.

(d)   **Overall assessment and recommendation**

(i)   **Maximum price that UT is likely to offer for TPTS AND whether this is likely to be acceptable to T Railways**

Maximum price

As already discussed above, the DCF valuation obtained in (c)(i) above is considered to be more appropriate than an asset based valuation in this instance. The maximum price that T Railways can expect to obtain for TPTS is therefore T$ 1,142 million.   However, the actual price achieved may be significantly lower depending on UT's perception of the risks involved in taking over the running of the track and the uncertainties surrounding both the future cost of maintaining the track and the fee that could be obtained for the provision of the track to T Railways.

Whether this price is likely to be acceptable to T Railways

Based on the results in (b)(ii) above, the disposal of TPTS is estimated to cost T Railways T$ 2,856 million based on the present value of the net increase in cash outflows in perpetuity at T Railways' discount rate of 4%.

This is more than double the price of T$ 1,142 million that UT might be willing to pay.

T Railways would therefore lose out financially if it were to sell TPTS. The immediate sale proceeds, which would enable it to repay debt, would be more than offset by the loss of revenue and the increase in costs in perpetuity, even after taking the interest saving into account.   Indeed, the interest saving is overstated in the calculation since the discount rate used was the pre-tax cost of capital and would be lower after taking the tax saving on debt interest into account.

(ii)   It is not recommend that T Railways should proceed with the sale of TPTS unless forced to do so by pressure from T Government. It does not benefit T Railways from either a financial or strategic point of view. Indeed, it creates significant risk to the continued operation of the railways by losing direct control over such core and strategic assets as the track, stations and other property and property services.

Looking at the financial angle first:

- As already noted above, T Railways would lose out financially by the sale of TPTS.

- Indeed, T Government, as the sole source of finance for T Railways, would also lose out financially. The short term gain in terms of funds received on repayment of some of T Railways' borrowings would be outweighed by the net increase in funding that T Railways would require in perpetuity. This strategy provides a short term gain in exchange for higher costs in the future. However, T Government might consider that this is a price worth paying on the assumption that financial conditions may improve in the future and that it is more important to address the immediate need of reducing T Government borrowing than to be too concerned about additional costs in the future when public sector borrowing may be less of an issue.

- Another observation is that the current government would gain favourable publicity by reducing public sector borrowing and it will be a different government that has to pick up the added costs at a later date.

There are also significant strategic drawbacks and risks to T Railways (and hence also to the country as a whole) arising from the sale of TPTS. Key issues are considered below:

- Loss of control over the maintenance of the track. If the acquirer does not invest in the track and maintain it at the appropriate standard, this would have a direct impact on the provision of rail services which could undermine T Railways' business.

- Unknown future liability to support UT in the future. If UT were to become unviable due to escalating maintenance costs, it is likely that T Railways would will feel obliged to increase the amount paid for use of the track or otherwise support UT in order to ensure that it is able to continue in business. T Railways cannot provide passenger and freight services without track! In addition, T Railways would not be able to meet its targets for safely and reliability of service (many of which are set by the Rail Regulator) if UT were to be unable or unwilling to maintain the track to an acceptable standard. In other words, by selling TPTS, T Railways would lose all control over how the track is maintained but would retain all the risks inherent in the provision and maintenance of the track.

- Inadequate rail services could have significant knock-on effects for the economy as a whole. Many employees and industries will rely on the rail network to transport people and goods. Environmental targets also depend on greater use of the railways.

In conclusion, the costs and risks outlined above clearly outweigh the benefits to T Railways of the sale of TPTS and it is recommended that T Railways does not proceed with the proposed sale of TPTS. Track and other property are core business assets that are central to T Railways' business and service targets. Selling and hence effectively outsourcing such a vital resource and hence losing direct control over how the track is managed could undermine the whole of T Railways' business. Indeed, the risks extend beyond T Railways as a disruption in the country's rail services would be likely to have much wider implications for the whole economy.

Tutorial note – extracted from the Examiner's "Post Exam Guide"

Overall this question was answered only satisfactorily. Many candidates were ill-prepared to address a question concerning the privatisation of part of T Railways, despite a significant clue in the pre-seen material.

In part (a), candidates often wrote about the advantages and disadvantages of privatisation in general, rather than focus on the choice of privatisation approach. Candidates who did compare and contrast an IPO with a direct sale generally did well.

In part (b)(i) candidates were expected to prepare a schedule showing the impact on T Railways' forecast cash flows for 2014 of TPTS no longer being part of the group. That is, to identify 'relevant' cash flows, a key skill in preparation for an investment appraisal exercise. This simply required identification of those cash flows that would no longer be incurred (such as café and station income and direct operating costs), those which changed (e.g. savings in overhead costs) and any new cash flows. This was not a technically challenging requirement, but was often poorly attempted. In part (b)(ii), most candidates were able to produce reasonable answers and, in particular, deal with the growing perpetuity correctly.

Many candidates only scored one or two marks for requirement b(iii) as they failed to identify the problems with using a risk free and pre-tax discount rate to value risky post tax cash flows.

Answers to part (c)(i) were on the whole good, although a significant number of candidates failed to adjust correctly for net current assets on the asset valuation basis. Part (c)(ii) however, was not as well answered, with often little or no recognition of the specifics of the scenario in answers. Candidates often failed to identify that their net asset valuations were higher than their discounted cash flow valuation or the implications of such a result.

Most candidates correctly identified that the maximum price that UT would pay was the discounted cash flow valuation from part (c)(i). However, a significant number of candidates failed to then go on to advise on the acceptability of this valuation to T Railways as stated in the requirement.

Answers to part (d)(ii) were mixed with some very good answers. The main reason for a poor mark in this section was because of a failure to apply the scenario and to expand beyond a generic answer. Candidates that had worked through the pre-seen material and had a good grasp on the scenario were able to produce good answers.

Overall, the main reason that candidates failed this question was because they did not give comments appropriate for a Government organisation such as T Railways. It must be stressed that this is a strategic level paper and therefore candidates are expected to be able tailor their answers to take into account the specifics of the scenario, rather than simply provide a generic answer.

Section 4

ANSWERS TO SECTION B-TYPE QUESTIONS

FORMULATION OF FINANCIAL STRATEGY

9   CCC (NOV 06 EXAM)

Key answer tips

Part (a) is a tricky question on objective setting that requires a reasonable depth of knowledge of NFPs to score well.

Part (b) is more straightforward but needs good application to the two companies concerned.

(a)   The key criteria that need to be considered when objective setting are as follows:

Stakeholder expectations

All organisations need to identify key stakeholders, examine their expectations and try to set objectives to meet them.

For CCC stakeholders include:

- Local residents want to see the provision of quality health and education services and value for money in response to paying local taxes.

- Local businesses who will be interested in local infrastructure when deciding whether to invest in the area. In particular, CCC may be keen to ensure that DDD does not close its local offices, with resulting job losses, and move to the capital city.

- Central Government committees who make funding decisions based on local population and deprivation.

For DDD stakeholders include:

- Shareholders want to see their wealth increased through a mixture of growing dividends and an increasing share price. DDD has reflected this in the objective to increase shareholder wealth by 10% per annum.

- Customers will expect a certain level of quality and value for money, depending on the nature of products sold.

- The local communities affected by DDD will expect them to be good citizens and operate at high levels of corporate social responsibility.

Stakeholder power

All organisations will find conflicts between stakeholders, so they need to consider how to prioritise them.

For a company like DDD the expectations of shareholders come first for the following reasons:

- This is usually reflected in companies' legislation where directors have a duty in law to put shareholder interests first. Many governance recommendations focus on protecting shareholder interests.

- Failure to deliver shareholder expectations will result in a falling share price and difficulties raising finance. Ultimately, shareholders have the power to remove directors should they feel dissatisfied.

However, this does not mean that other stakeholders' needs are ignored. Clearly, if customers are unhappy, then sales will be lost with a resulting fall in profitability and shareholder wealth.

For CCC the problem is more complex:

- It is much more difficult to prioritise stakeholder expectations. For example, given limited funds, should community health care needs come before educational ones?

- Even individual stakeholder groups have multiple conflicting objectives. For example, residents want to pay less tax and have better provision of services. Thus, even if some groups are satisfied, others may still vote for changes in CCC.

- With companies, customers pay directly for the products they receive, ensuring that customer needs are addressed. With CCC the bulk of its funding comes from central government, not the local community that benefits from CCC's actions. Thus the needs of the funding body may take priority over locals needs, otherwise funding may be cut (**note**: this is less likely here as funding is mainly driven by population size).

Measurement issues

For an organisation like DDD, once shareholders have been prioritised, all decisions can be evaluated by reference to financial measures such as profitability. While non-financial targets will be incorporated as well, the 'bottom line' will be seen as key. Thus financial targets can be set for most objectives.

For CCC it is much more difficult to measure whether it is achieving its stated aims and hence to set targets.

- For example, how do you assess whether somewhere is an 'attractive place to live and work' or whether health and education provision is 'excellent'?

Other issues

All organisations need to ensure that objectives set relate to controllable factors to ensure staff are motivated to meet them.

All organisations need to differentiate between cause and effect and have objectives for both. For example, DDD may have an objective of customer satisfaction, which will need to be translated into objectives for quality, cost, etc.

(b)   As described above, companies make decisions with the primary objective of maximising shareholder wealth.

Investment decisions

Potential investments should thus be assessed using NPV or SVA, rather than ROCE to ensure that shareholder wealth is increased.

This should be the case for both MS and DDD, though the former will have more difficulty determining a suitable discount rate as it is unquoted.

Dividend decisions

Once shareholder value has been created, the firm needs to decide how to return those gains to shareholders – either as dividends or reinvested to enhance the share price further.

Modigliani and Miller argued that, given certain assumptions, dividend policy was irrelevant to shareholder wealth. If a dividend were cut, for example, shareholders could manufacture dividends by selling shares without any overall loss of wealth. Central to their theory was the idea that shareholders had perfect information and would understand why a dividend policy was changed.

In the case of MS, shareholders are also employees so will have full information regarding any change in dividend policy and will not thus perceive any information content in the dividends themselves. However, should the dividend be cut, shareholders who require income will not be able to sell shares to generate cash as the company is unquoted. MS should thus try to continue the stable dividend policy it has adopted to date, even though historical dividend cover is lower than the 'rule of thumb' of two.

In the case of DDD, major institutional shareholders will have good information from the company but may have tax preferences regarding income and capital gains so DDD should adopt a consistent dividend policy to meet their requirements. DDD will probably have attracted a certain clientele of shareholder based on previous policies.

Financing decisions

Both firms need to raise finance in order to undertake new investments to increase shareholder wealth. The issue here is whether the finance used ultimately affects shareholder wealth as well.

From a theoretical point of view, Modigliani and Miller argued that, in the absence of taxation and certain other assumptions, the choice between debt or equity finance was irrelevant. With corporation tax they concluded that debt finance was preferable, due to the benefits of the tax shield. With personal taxes the conclusions depend on the specific circumstances of the company and its shareholders. Incorporating real world factors, many analysts argue that there is an optimal gearing level for each company.

DDD is already at the typical gearing ratio for its industry so it would reasonable to assume that this is its optimal gearing level. Future financing should involve a mixture of debt and equity to maintain this ratio.

MS is all-equity financed at present so it should seek to raise at least some of the $15 million required using debt finance to take advantage of the tax relief and low costs involved.

Interrelationships

All three types of decisions are inter-related, thus the financing decision will affect the cost of capital and, as a consequence, the net benefits obtainable from a particular project, thereby influencing the investment decision, while the financing decision concerning gearing will affect both the other decisions.

The dividend decision, in determining the level of retentions, will affect the cash available for investment, and the extent to which external sources of funds need to be sought in financing to optimise operations.

10 STR (MAY 07 EXAM)

Key answer tips

In part (a) ensure that your workings are clearly set out.

In part (b) it is vital that you discuss any ratios calculated rather than simply presenting the examiner with a set of numbers.

Part (c) is bookwork and a good reminder that you need to be familiar with all aspects of the syllabus.

(a)   **Cash balances**

	20X4 $m	20X5 $m	20X6 $m
Net cash flow before dividends	19.2	(7.1)	18.8
Dividends (W1)	(8.4)	(8.8)	(9.3)
Net cash flow	10.8	(15.9)	9.5
Cash b/f	6	16.8	0.9
Cash c/f	16.8	0.9	10.4

Book value of equity

	20X4	20X5	20X6
	$m	$m	$m
Profit before interest and tax (bal)	22.6	25.4	27.7
Interest	(1.0)	(1.0)	(1.0)
Profit before tax	21.6	24.4	26.7
Tax expense	(7.7)	(2.6)	(4.3)
Profit after tax	13.9	21.8	22.4
Dividends (W1)	(8.4)	(8.8)	(9.3)
Retained profit	5.5	13.0	13.1
Book value of equity b/f	60	65.5	78.5
Book value of equity c/f	65.5	78.5	91.6

(W1) **Dividends**

20X4: dividend = 20 million × $0.40 × 1.05 = $8.4 million

20X5: dividend = $8.4 million × 1.05 = $8.82 million

20X6: dividend = $8.82 million × 1.05 = $9.261 million

(b) **Additional calculations**

	20X4	20X5	20X6
Interest cover	22.6×	25.4×	27.7×
Dividend cover	1.65×	2.48×	2.41×
Earnings per share (cents)	69.5	109	112

Gearing = debt net of cash/(debt + equity)

	20X4	20X5	20X6
Debt	50	50	50
Cash	16.8	0.9	10.4
Debt net of cash	33.2	49.1	39.6
Equity	65.5	78.5	91.6
Debt (net) + equity	98.7	127.6	131.2
Gearing	33.6%	38.5%	30.2%

Return on equity

	20X4	20X5	20X6
Profit after tax	13.9	21.8	22.4
Equity	65.5	78.5	91.6
Return on equity	21.2%	27.8%	24.5%

Return on capital employed, using net debt + equity

	20X4	20X5	20X6
Profit before interest and tax (bal)	22.6	25.4	27.7
Debt (net) + equity	98.7	127.6	131.2
Return on capital	22.9%	19.9%	21.1%

Comments

The financial performance from the shareholders' point of view has generally been encouraging:

- Both earnings per share and the book value of equity have been increasing.

- Dividends have increased.

- Return on equity has consistently been above 20%.

- Financial gearing has fallen in 20X6 and dividend cover is now over two, indicating lower risk attached to the dividends.

The only area of worry, however, is that return on equity fell from 20X5 to 20X6.

The financial performance from the lenders' point of view has been less convincing. On a positive note:

- Interest cover is very high and rising, suggesting a low default risk.

- Gearing fell in 20X6, again suggesting less risk for lenders.

However,

- STR had poor cash flow in 20X5. Lenders may wish to see more detailed analysis of cash flow to determine if any underlying problems persist.

(c) (i) The relative advantages of a share repurchase verses a one-off dividend are as follows:

Share repurchase	One-off dividend
• A repurchase may be more tax efficient than a dividend for some shareholders.	• A dividend may be more tax advantageous for some shareholders.
• A reduction in the number of shares should boost EPS.	• All shareholders are treated fairly.
• Increased gearing as equity is reduced. This is only an advantage if STR is moved closer to its optimal gearing level.	• The amount of cash paid is more certain – with a repurchase it will not be known in advance how many shareholders will choose to sell.
• Does not create an expectation of higher future dividends. On the contrary, less cash will be needed for future dividends due to fewer shares.	

(ii)   Alternative strategies for reducing a cash surplus include the following:

- increase the growth rate of dividends

- long-term equity investments — e.g. acquire other firms and/or buy stakes in rivals, customers, etc

- reduce debt by repaying loans

- increase capital expenditure

- increase investment in research and development — e.g. to enter new markets.

11   ABC (NOV 07 EXAM)

Key answer tips

Part (a) is a straightforward question on cost of capital. Part (b) is more tricky requiring comments on market efficiency and shareholder reaction.

(a)   **A suitable discount rate**

A discount rate must reflect both the business risk and the financial (gearing) risk of a project. The current figure of 15% is only trying to reflect business risk.

Director A

Director A has suggested using ABC's existing WACC of 10.59% (W1). This reflects ABC's existing business and gearing risk so would only be appropriate if

- The new investment had the same business risk as ABC.

    The film venture appears to be much more risky that ABC's existing (diversified) activities as shown by the respective asset betas of 1.374 (W2) and 0.898 (W3).

- It would be financed to maintain ABC's long term gearing level.

    The proposed finance would increase ABC's gearing so this condition is broken. However, this may be viewed as a short term departure from optimum gearing (assuming ABC is at its optimum level) and that the firm will use higher amounts of equity next time to address the balance.

- The project is small

    Compared to a market capitalisation of £2,400 million, the proposed investment of £600 million must be considered significant.

In conclusion Director A's suggestion is not suitable for assessing the project.

Director B

Calculating a rate using a beta from a proxy film company addresses the business risk issues identified above. However, Director B has not given further details regarding whether a cost of equity figure or a WACC type figure should be used and, if the latter, which gearing level to incorporate.

The approach adopted in working 2 uses project gearing to calculate a project WACC of 13.63% (W2). This is the most appropriate discount rate to use and would suggest that the project is worth undertaking, although sensitivity analysis of project cash flows is still recommended before action is taken.

Note:

Both approaches use the CAPM to determine the cost of equity. This is entirely appropriate as ABC's shareholders are likely to comprise well diversified investors who will only be interested in the systematic risk of potential investments.

Workings

(W1) **Director A – company WACC**

Cost of equity (using CAPM):

$$k_e = R_f + \left[R_m - R_f\right]\beta = 5 + (12\text{-}5) \times 1.2 = 13.4\%$$

$V_E = 300 \times 8.00 = £2,400$ million.

Cost of 8.4% bonds

Time	Narrative	CF	DF @4%	PV @4%	DF @5%	PV @5%
		£		£		£
0	Market value	(105)	1	(105)	1	(105)
1–5	Interest net of tax (8.4×0.7)	5.88	4.452	26.18	4.329	25.45
5	Redemption	100	0.822	82.20	0.784	78.40
NPV				**3.38**		**(1.15)**

$$K_d = \text{IRR} = 4 + \frac{3.38 \times (5-4)}{(3.38 - (-1.15))} = 4.75\%$$

$V_D = 1,100 \times 105\% = £1,155$ million

WACC

$$k_0 = k_{eg}\left[\frac{V_E}{V_E + V_D}\right] + K_d\left[\frac{V_D}{V_E + V_D}\right] = 13.4\left[\frac{2,400}{2,400+1,155}\right] + 4.75\left[\frac{1,155}{2,400+1,155}\right]$$

= 10.59%

(W2) **Director B – using XYZ**

Cost of equity for ABC film project

Step 1: de-gear proxy industry beta from XYZ:

$$\beta_u = \beta_g\left[\frac{V_E}{V_E + V_D[1-t]}\right] = 1.6\frac{400 \times 3.73}{400 \times 3.73 + 350(0.7)} = 1.374$$

Step 2: re-gear for ABC project using film project gearing:

Tutorial note

It could be argued that the overall ABC gearing should be used here for the regearing, since that is the gearing which ABC's investors will consider overall.

$$\beta_g = \beta_u \left(1 + (1-t)\frac{V_D}{V_E}\right) = 1.374 \times \left(1 + \frac{260(0.7)}{340}\right) = 2.109$$

Step 3: use CAPM equation:

$$k_e = R_f + \left[R_m - R_f\right]\beta = 5 + (12-5) \times 2.109 = 19.77\%$$

Cost of 8% debt

Given that the debt will be issued and redeemed at par, the cost can be calculated simply as

$$K_d = 8 \times 0.7 = 5.6\%$$

Project WACC

$$k_0 = k_{eg}\left(\frac{V_E}{V_E + V_D}\right) + K_d\left(\frac{V_D}{V_E + V_D}\right) = 19.77\left(\frac{340}{600}\right) + 5.6\left(\frac{260}{600}\right) = 13.63\%$$

(W3) **ABC's asset beta**

$$\beta_u = \beta_g\left(\frac{V_E}{V_E + V_D[1-t]}\right) = 1.2\frac{2,400}{2,400 + 1,155(0.7)} = 0.898$$

(b) The market capitalisation of ABC during the week the investment becomes public knowledge will depend on the following factors:

Investors' reactions to disclosed information

- Investors will respond to information communicated about the company.

- Once they find out about the business area (i.e. film), investors may correctly anticipate the higher risks and demand a higher return to compensate.

- This will then be assessed against expected future cash flows. Unless investors believe that there will be a corresponding increase in returns, then there will be a fall in the share price

- ABC may be reluctant to publish details regarding project cash flows to avoid giving potential competitors useful information.

- In any respect shareholders may not believe forecasts. Without such forecasts the share price will depend to some extent on how much the board are trusted.

- If ABC found an acquisition target instead, then it would be easier for investors to analyse the fundamentals of that target and respond accordingly.

Market efficiency

- Most major stock markets are (almost) semi-strong efficient meaning that share prices will reflect all publicly available information.

- When ABC publishes the new information there may be a slight time lag while investors process and analyse the information before the impact on the share price is fully seen.

- If information about the proposal has already been leaked to the market, then the share price would already have reacted and the official publication would have little impact.

12 CRM (MAY 09 EXAM) *Walk in the footsteps of a top tutor*

Top tutor tips

At first glance this appeared to be a strange question – ratio analysis is more commonly tested in other papers in the syllabus.

However, the consideration of the given objectives, and recommendations for corrective action, brought in some key Financial Strategy topics.

Calculations accounted for 15 of the 25 marks, so a sensible starting point would have been to prepare the Appendix. In deciding which ratios to compute and comment upon, make sure you refer to the given list of 6 key objectives for the firm and its subsidiary.

When writing the report, try to analyse the implications of all the changes in ratios. It is not sufficient to simply state what has happened.

Report to: Board of Directors

From: Financial Manager

Date: 20 May 20X9

Subject: **Analysis of Financial Performance and Attainment of Group Objectives in the period 20X8–20X9**

Introduction

I have prepared this report to analyse the performance of CRM and its Asian subsidiary. I have taken the six stated objectives one by one and assessed whether they have been achieved. Supporting calculations are contained in the appendix at the end of the report.

Objective 1: Provide a total return to shareholders of 15% per annum

The appendix shows that the expected return, based on the CAPM, was 15.2%. The actual return for 20X8–9 was 15.6%. This objective was therefore narrowly achieved.

However, using a beta from an entity listed on the main stock exchange might not be appropriate. AIM listed shares are far less liquid than those on the main market and therefore likely to be more volatile and risky. If the beta is uplifted by, say, 25% to allow for this additional risk then the expected return would be 18%.

It is not clear how CRM determined that it required a return of 15% per annum.

Objective 2: Generate a return on net assets (RONA) of 30% per annum

The RoNA for the group has fallen slightly from 40.9% to 37.7% but this is still comfortably above the 30% target.

Objective 3: Provide a dividend yield comparable with the industry average

The dividend yield has improved slightly in 20X9 over 20X8, but, in both years, this was below the industry average.

The industry average will contain a very broad range of entities. Some will be listed entities on the main market; some might be private entities that have no share listing. Comparison with an industry average is therefore inappropriate. Also, investors in shares in the AIM usually prefer capital gains.

Objectives 4 and 5: Increase revenue by 15% and earnings per share by 10%

	CRM Group	Asian sub
Revenue increase 20X9 over 20X8	9.2%	23.7%
EPS increase 20X9 over 20X8	11.6%	51.9%

The revenue objective was not achieved. The EPS objective was comfortably achieved. The Group performance would have been much worse but for the Asian sub and neither objective would have been met.

Objective 6: Double turnover of Asian sub by 31 March 20Y2 in sterling

Turnover in 20X9 was £56.2 million. To meet this objective, turnover in A$ would need to be approximately A$773 million. If the Asian sub grows at 20X8/9 rates (approximately 24%) there would be a shortfall of A$77 million to approximately A$11 million. The A$ is forecast to depreciate by approx 2% per annum based on forecast inflation rates. This implies a weakening economy so increasing turnover without major new investment would be difficult. However, it must be recognised that theories of interest rate parity and purchasing power parity have not held in recent years and are likely to be even less reliable given the current global economic volatility.

Summary and Recommendations

In summary the Group has met two of its objectives. However, if the figures for the Asian sub are excluded then the overall performance has been poor. If the Asian country's economy is weakening, as suggested above, then the Group needs to take some major decisions to improve its performance if the years to 31 March 20Y0, 20Y1 and 20Y2 are not to be much worse than the previous year.

The main recommendations and advice on objectives are summarised as:

- CRM currently retains all the Asian sub's earnings in that entity, presumably to facilitate the objective of doubling turnover. However, in a weakening economy, the objective should be reconsidered as perhaps the retained earnings from the Asian sub could be more profitably invested elsewhere.

- The objective of achieving a dividend yield comparable with the industry average is inappropriate. It is total returns to shareholders that are more important. How a required total return of 15% has been determined needs to be reviewed.

- CRM's gearing based on book values is below the industry average and falling. While recognising the weaknesses of comparability with industry averages, as discussed above, the Group could consider increasing its borrowings to take advantage of the tax benefits and lower its WACC. If we use market values of equity and assume the book value of the debt equals the market value, then CRM's gearing is only around 10%, which is very low for a manufacturing entity and demonstrates the scope for additional borrowing.

APPENDIX

Key ratios and performance measures of CRM and Asian Sub

	CRM Group	Asian Sub A$
Increase in revenue	9.2%	23.7%
	(355 – 325)/325 × 100	(365 – 295)/295 × 100
Increase in earnings	11.6%	51.9%
	(77 – 69)/69 × 100	(79 – 52)/52 × 100
Return on net assets		
20X8	40.9%	45.2%
	(105/257) × 100%	((80/177) × 100%
20X9	37.7%	43.0%
	(117/310) × 100%	(110/256) × 100%

Calculation of forward rates (average throughout the year)

Top tutor tips

A common mistake is applying the parity formula the wrong way up. Be careful here.

31.3.20X9	6.50	
31.3.20Y0	6.63	(6.5 × 1.055/1.035)
31.3.20Y1	6.75	(6.63 × 1.055/1.035)
31.3.20Y2	6.88	(6.75 × 1.055/1.035)

Key Figures for Asian Sub in Sterling (£m) using average exchange rates

	20X8	20X9
Revenue	46.8	56.2
Earnings	8.2	12.2
Net Assets	28.1	39.4

CRM Group comparison with industry

	CRM Group	Industry
Dividend yield		
20X8	2.62%	2.80%
20X9	2.66%	3.00%
Gearing (debt / (debt + equity), based on book values)		
20X8	38.9%	44%
20X9	32.3%	46%
P/E ratio		
20X8	11.6	8.2
20X9	11.7	9.0

Return to shareholders

Expected return $=$ RF $+ \beta$ (RM–RF) = 4% + 1.4(12%-4%) = 15.2%

Actual return $=$ $[(P_1 - P_0) + Dt]/P_0 \times 100$

$=$ $[(721.8 - 641) + 19.2]/641 \times 100$ = 15.6%

13 HJK (MAY 11 EXAM)

Key answer tips – extracted from the Examiner's "Post Exam Guide"

Part (a)

- Examine the historic dividend figures provided and identify the current dividend policy.

- Identify alternative dividend policies and compare and contrast the features of each.

Part (b)(i)

- Discuss the process involved in an IPO.

Part (b)(ii)

- Consider the potential problems and risks involved in an IPO.

- Discuss what action can be taken to minimise such risks.

Part (c)

Consider each of: dividends, financing and investment in turn, explaining and advising the directors how an IPO might affect each of these three policy areas, and concluding by examining the interrelationship between them.

(a)

Year	Profit for the year after interest and tax	Investment in projects or capital expenditure	Dividend paid	Payout as % of profit	Payout as % of profit less reinvestment
	EUR million	EUR million	EUR million		
20X6	6	–	3	50%	50%
20X7	7	10	2	29%	0%
20X8	10	–	5	50%	50%
20X9	11	15	2	18%	0%
20Y0	16	–	8	50%	50%

The current dividend policy of HJK appears to be as follows:

* In years where there is no major capital investment 50% of available profits are paid as a dividend.

* In years when there is major capital investment a dividend of EUR 2 million is paid out irrespective of the level of profit or cash flow.

This unpredictable and erratic pattern of dividend payouts is typical of a family company where the needs of the business and of individual shareholders can be expected to be major factors behind the dividend payout in each year.

In this case, the history of recent dividend payouts indicates a policy of a constant payout ratio of 50% unless there are strong calls on cash from elsewhere, as there was in 20X7 and 20X9. However, even in those years of high capital expenditure, a minimum dividend of

EUR 2 million was maintained, presumably to provide the minimum annual income required by the major shareholders.

In a private company, shareholders are likely to have a greater influence on dividend policy and so we can conclude that HJK's shareholders are not wholly dependent on large dividend income and are happy for all surplus cash above a certain minimum payout level to be reinvested in the business where suitable reinvestment opportunities exist. Investing in all available projects that carry a positive NPV should, ultimately, maximise shareholder wealth. Unlike a listed company, HJK is likely to be more dependent on the use of retained earnings that are held in the form of cash to finance expansion. Using retained earnings that are available in cash form keeps gearing levels low and also reduces shareholder risk.

(b) (i) An IPO refers to the issue of shares onto the market – which could be the main stock market such as the London Stock Exchange or a smaller scale market such as AIM in the UK.

The issue of shares will be made through an issuing house (usually an investment bank) which acquires the shares and offers them to the public either at a fixed price (known as an offer for sale) or offers them for tender (known as an offer for sale by tender).

(ii)   **Potential risks and remedies:**

- The main risk is that not all of the shares are sold to the public and hence the company does not generate sufficient funds. This could be either because the price was perceived to be too high or because the economic conditions have deteriorated and the market for that company is in decline. It could also arise from bad publicity. The main remedy for this is to have the issue underwritten (which means that a third party will promise to buy any outstanding shares). However this can be very expensive. It could also result in a fall in the share price immediately after the issue.

- Another risk is that the issue is over-subscribed. This could be because the price is set too low and hence becomes a bargain. Whilst the company will generate all the funds that it plans an over-subscription could be damaging to its reputation and credibility. It also has the effect of passing profit to the new investor which, with proper pricing, would have come to the company. Therefore it is important that the price of the issue is set at an appropriate level. The use of a tender issue can help avoid this risk.

(c)   **Implications of a Listing for Dividend Policy**

In listed companies it would be more common to find a policy of paying a stable level of dividend, that is, a constant dividend per share or a dividend per share that is growing at a constant growth rate each year in line with average underlying growth in profits. In general, investors prefer a predictable dividend level that grows at a consistent but sustainable rate.

If HJK were to list, then the profile of its shareholders will change, as will shareholder expectations about dividend levels.

For listed companies dividend policy is seen as an important indicator of where the company is and what its plans are. That is, dividends give signals to the market about the strength of the company. There is a major difference here between listed companies and privately owned companies where shareholders have inside information about the performance of the company and do not need to rely on the signalling effect of dividends. Because of this signalling effect for listed companies a typical dividend policy would be one of constant or constantly growing dividend which does not change much year on year.

HJK is accountable to its shareholders and needs to ensure that the dividend policy matches the expectations of shareholders. Most shareholders will require stable growing dividends year on year and not fluctuating dividends. Major shareholders such as large financial institutions (e.g.: pension funds) also usually prefer regular dividend payouts so that they can plan their cash flows. Other investors may also have chosen to invest in a particular share due to anticipated future dividend levels.

Another consideration is the share price itself. Once listed, HJK would be interested in protecting its share price. The market prefers predictable dividend levels, this helps signal stability and hence improve market confidence in the company. This, in turn, protects or improves the share price.

For all the reasons given above, we can conclude that HJK will need to change its dividend policy to one of stable growing dividends. In the event that changes are needed to this underlying policy, it is also important for HJK to keep the market informed in advance so that future prospects for growth can be reflected in the share price.

Implications for Financing Strategies

Becoming a listed company potentially opens up greater sources of finance to HJK in the future. A listing allows HJK to have a presence and reputation within the capital markets and therefore potentially makes it easier to raise debt in the markets. Once listed it should also be easier for the company to raise new equity in future either through rights issues or new issues of shares.

Implications for Investment Strategies

Once listed every decision that is made within the company will be scrutinised by the market and have either a positive or negative effect on the share price. The market does not like surprises therefore it will be important that the forecast impact of any investment decisions is fed to the market.

Given that greater sources of finance will be available (see before) HJK could be in a position to take on even greater investment in the future.

Interrelationship between dividends, financing and investment

To conclude, an important point to make is that there will be a clear link between dividend, investment and financing decisions as one will affect the other. Funds that are paid out as dividends cannot also be reinvested in projects. Any funds that are paid out and could otherwise have been reinvested will therefore impact on other areas of the business's financial strategy and leave the company with the choice of either reducing its investments or increasing its financing or a combination of the two. Clearly if stable dividends need to be paid then in years where profits are low this could impact on the ability to make investments which could necessitate the need for new finance. Conversely, in good years there could be more cash available for investment without the need for additional funds. The key however, will be to manage market expectations through good information.

All three areas (dividends, investment and financing) are therefore directly interlinked.

Tutorial note – extracted from the Examiner's "Post Exam Guide"

Discussion of the dividend policy, IPO process and consequences of listing for a private, family-owned and managed business was surprisingly poor, even though this was a straightforward question where candidates could have gained good marks.

Most candidates were able to identify the current dividend policy but many failed to recognise that HJK was a family company and thus the dividend policy was likely to reflect that. Many candidates actually discussed the policy as if HJK were already listed.

Part (b) was reasonably well answered – as was part (c).

---

14   TTT (NOV 11 EXAM)

Key answer tips – extracted from the Examiner's "Post Exam Guide"

Part (a)(i)

Prepare preliminary calculations as follows:-

- EPS pre acquisition and post acquisition if funded by debt and

- Gearing pre and post acquisition and provide brief comments on these calculations.

Part (a)(ii)

Advise on the appropriateness of the objectives noting in particular:

- Volatility of dividend pay out

- Unsustainability of the dividend payout objective if earnings growing at only 6% without the acquisition

- That the acquisition will assist growth in EPS and dividend pay out

- Effect on gearing of the acquisition and its method of funding using either market or book values

- Acquisition clearly helps growth objective

Part (b)

Choose three key roles performed by a Treasury Department in evaluation and implementation of the acquisition

Describe the activities that might be performed under each role

(a)   (i)   **Financial objective 1: To increase dividends by 10% a year.**

Before the acquisition, TTT's earnings have grown by 8% per annum on average. The target growth in dividends of 10% is therefore is not sustainable over the long term without significant growth in earnings in the future.

Note that the variation in dividend pay-out between 30% and 50% of earnings may indicate an attempt to smooth dividend levels.

WWW's long term earnings growth prospects are lower than TTT's at 6% per year and so the acquisition risks reducing long term earnings growth.

However, the target earnings growth of 10% can be expected to be achieved in the year of acquisition due to the addition of WWW's earnings. Growth in earnings is expected to be boosted by 4.6% if funded by debt and by 10.85% if funded by equity (see workings).

Note that the impact on earnings per share varies considerably according to how the deal is financed. If financed by equity, earnings per share can be expected to fall as a result of the acquisition due to the greater number of shares in issue.

Workings: Earnings per share calculations

	Earnings	Earnings per share for TTT
Pre acquisition	TTT: EUR 2,000m WWW: SKR 2,000m, or EUR 217m (where SKR 2,000 = 20,000m/10 based on a P/E = 10, and EUR 217m =SKR 2,000/9.2)	Eps: 40 cents = 16 cents/40%
Post acquisition, funded by debt (at 5% post tax interest)	EUR 2,092m, 4.6% increase (2,092 = 2,000 + 217 − (5% × 2,500))	Eps: 41.8 cents, 4.5% increase (0.418 = 2,092/5,000)
Post acquisition, funded by equity (assuming no change in share price)	EUR 2,217m, 10.85% increase (2,217 = 2,000 + 217)	Eps: 37.8 cents, 5.25% decrease (0.378 = 2,217/(5,000 + (2,500/2.90))

Financial objective 2: To keep gearing below 40% (where gearing is calculated as debt/(debt + equity)).

Based on market values the current gearing is 39.6%, which is only just under the target level of 40%. Gearing exceeds the limit if the acquisition is funded by debt (at 45.3%) but falls markedly to 35.8% if funded by equity. (See workings below.)

Using book values of equity, the gearing target is exceeded in all cases. Gearing improves if the acquisition is funded by equity but remains well above the target level of 40%.

Workings: Gearing calculations

	Gearing based on market values (workings in EUR)	Gearing based on book values (workings in EUR)
Pre acquisition	39.6% = 9,500m/ (9,500m + 14,500m)	51.4% = 9,500m/ (9,500m + 5,000m + 4,000m)
Post acquisition funded by debt (at a cost of EUR 2,500m – that is SKR 23,000m/9.2)	45.3% = (9,500m + 2,500m)/ (9,500m + 2,500m + 14,500m)	57.1% = (9,500m + 2,500m)/ (9,500m +2,500m + 9,000m)
Post acquisition funded by equity (assuming no change in share price)	35.8% = 9,500m/ (9,500m + 2,500m + 14,500m)	45.2% = 9,500m/ (9,500m +2,500m + 9,000m)

Financial objective 3: To expand by internal growth and/or by horizontal integration via acquisition of companies operating in the same industry sector.

The acquisition clearly helps towards the growth target. WWW represents horizontal integration in the same broad energy industry sector.

(ii)   The financial objectives are a rather strange combination. Dividend growth is a useful target but appears to be too high at 10% per annum and is not linked to company performance. It may be better replacing this objective with a lower minimum dividend growth figure coupled with a dividend payout target and an earnings or earnings per share growth target.

A dividend growth target without an earnings target could lead to payment of dividends in excess of what the company can afford – it is an easy target to meet if sufficient retained profits and cash are available or investments are cut but is not sustainable over the longer term if not underpinned by earnings growth.

The gearing target objective is reasonable, although it would be better if it defined whether gearing was based on book values or market values. Debt covenants may require this target to be met. Interest cover may also be important to lenders and may be stated in debt covenants. TTT should consider adding an interest cover target to its financial objectives.

The general growth target does not have any numbers attached. An earnings growth target or a growth in market capitalisation target could be added in order to enable this target to be quantified and success measured in financial terms.

(b)

Examiner's note:

Candidate answers should include a full description of any THREE of the following key roles of treasury during the evaluation and implementation of the acquisition:

- Advise on an appropriate discount rate for use in the evaluation of WWW with regard to:

    - Risk appetite of TTT and risk profile of WWW.

    - Currency profile of WWW's cash flows.

    - Cost of capital of TTT.

- Advise on appropriate funding of bid, including:

    - The choice of debt versus equity funding.

    - Choice of actual sources of finance.

- Liaise with 3rd parties:
  - Negotiate with lenders over interest rate, fees and covenants for bank debt.
  - Liaise with intermediaries regarding the issuance of bonds, including costing, publicity and other arrangements.
  - Liaise with intermediaries regarding the costing and arrangements for a rights issue or placement of shares.
  - Controlled release of information to the market.

- Risk management aspects of the proposed acquisition, including:
  - Managing exchange rate risk (for example, through hedging or foreign currency borrowing).
  - Managing interest rate risk (for example, by choice of interest profile and/or interest rate swap).
  - Manage liquidity risk – forecast liquidity needs and ensure that sufficient liquidity is available at all times.

- Assess reaction of the market in terms of:
  - Impact on credit rating and credit worthiness in general.
  - Impact on share price.
  - Impact on debt covenants.

- Integration of WWW into central treasury systems. This might include:
  - Pooling of bank accounts.
  - Standardising bank relationships.
  - Regular cash forecasts.
  - Reporting exchange rate risk.
  - Controlling working capital.

Tutorial note – extracted from the Examiner's "Post Exam Guide"

The main weakness in part (a)(i) was the evaluation of the impact of the acquisition on increasing dividends per share by 10% a year. Candidates tended to concentrate on calculating different levels of gearing and the assessment of impact on growth. These calculations were generally fairly well attempted although many who used book values of equity ignored retained earnings. The question was deliberately vague on whether market or book values should be used in the gearing calculations. Either type of value was acceptable for credit although the better candidates commented on this ambiguity.

Many candidates misunderstood the significance of (a)(ii) and rewrote their answers to (a)(i).

In part (b) candidates often discussed the general roles of treasury departments instead of the question requirement which asked for a discussion of three key roles during the evaluation and/or implementation of the planned acquisition.

15   QRR (MAR 12 EXAM)

Key answer tips – extracted from the Examiner's "Post Exam Guide"

Part (a) requires a straightforward discussion of the likely impact on the company's share price, of an announcement that no dividend is to be paid. Such a discussion should consider both the information processing ability of the market and potential shareholder reaction based on preference and expectation.

The approach in evaluating whether to accept the shares or sell the rights to a potential scrip dividend should be to calculate the overall wealth of a typical shareholder under each alternative and compare the results.

Part (c) requires a brief comparison of a scrip issue with simply not paying a dividend at all and should end with a recommendation. Part (d) should be a straightforward list of possible alternative strategies to improve liquidity to a bank such as QRR.

(a)   If an announcement is made that no dividend is to be paid, there are two aspects to be considered. Firstly, the speed of any reaction and secondly, how the market will react.

- The speed of reaction of the market will be dependent upon its efficiency level. If the market is only weak form efficient then the share price is unlikely to react straight away (because in such a market the share price reacts very slowly to any new information released about a company). If however the market is semi-strong form efficient then the market will react instantly to the announcement of a zero dividend (because, by definition, semi-strong form means that there will be an instant reaction to any new information). If the market is strong form efficient then the market will in effect have already reacted to the news about a zero dividend prior to it being realised and hence there would be no further share price impact. Markets are generally found to be semi- strong form efficient and therefore we would expect the market to react straight away to the announcement.

- In relation to whether the share price will go up, down or stay the same there are a number of considerations to bear in mind:

  - Dividends simply move cash from cash owned by the shareholders in the company to the shareholders' own pockets. Theoretically therefore the value of the company does not change and therefore, all things being equal the share price should not change.

  - From a behavioural finance standpoint, it is known that investors prefer dividends, if they are paid, to be stable or increasing. In most developed markets dividend payments are often seen to signal the health of a company and there is an expectation that for most companies the markets expect to see a stable dividend policy. Therefore if QRR, having previously paid a substantial dividend, announces that it will not pay a dividend this year, it is likely that the market will react unfavourably and hence the share price will fall (possibly quite significantly) as investors sell shares.

      –   However, markets are a little more sophisticated than that and it's possible that given the credit crunch, drop in profits and the expectation of stricter funding requirements for banks in the future, the market may have already built in an expectation of either a zero dividend or a vastly reduced dividend. If this is the case then the drop in share price would be reduced if indeed it drops at all (some investors may even perceive the lack of a dividend as evidence of sound management in such an economic climate which could in fact bolster the market.)

(b)   (i)   **Shareholder who accepts the shares**

A typical shareholder with 1000 shares will receive an entitlement to one new share for every 50 held. That is, the right to acquire 20 new shares (where 20 = 1,000/50). This may give the shareholder the illusion of increased "value" as he now holds 1,020 shares. However, the company itself has not changed in value and so the total value that those shares represent is unchanged.

The share price can be expected to fall to the extent that the 1,020 shares will have exactly the same value as the original 1,000, that is INR 396,000. This implies a fall in the share price to INR 388.24 (= INR 396,000/1,020).

    (ii)   **Shareholder who sells the rights**

If the rights are sold, a typical shareholder should receive INR 7,000 in total (where INR 7,000 = 1,000 × INR 7).

If the remaining 1,000 share are worth INR 388.24 each, the shareholder's total worth can be estimated to be INR 395,240 (= INR 388,240 + INR 7,000).

This is marginally less than in (i) above, indicating that it is better for the shareholder to accept the new shares rather than sell the rights. Note, however, that it is likely that arbitrage activity in the market will close out any discrepancy between (i) and (ii) and so the shareholder should be largely indifferent between the two options.

Again, there is an impression of increased "value" as a result of the INR 7,000 receipt, but this is largely illusory due to the likely corresponding fall in the share price.

(c)   In theory, shareholders should be indifferent between a zero dividend and a scrip dividend and the decision should have no impact on company value. However, it is important for the board of QRR to fully understand how the market is likely to react to the news.

Assuming that the market is already anticipating some change in the dividend policy because of the economic environment (as discussed already in part (a)) then it's possible that it will react better to Director B's suggestion of a scrip dividend rather than no dividend at all, as at least investors feel that they are getting something. However, the larger and more sophisticated the investor the more they will understand that the scrip dividend has no bearing on the overall value of their investment.

Indeed, there are a number of disadvantages with the scrip dividend from QRR's point of view. Firstly, a scrip dividend will incur significant administrative costs whilst a zero dividend will not. Secondly, a greater number of shares in circulation may increase the pressure for dividend payouts in the future as the dividend per share would be lower for the same total dividend payment. Thirdly, a scrip dividend has the effect of moving reserves from distributable to non-distributable by increasing share capital. This reduces the reserves available for distribution as dividends at a future date.

However, despite the drawbacks associated with a scrip dividend, in practice many companies, including banks, have chosen the scrip dividend route in recent years in order to give the impression that they are giving a payout to investors.

(d) Alternatives to a zero dividend or a scrip dividend to improve liquidity include:

- Raising additional equity via a rights issue or a new issue. The success of this though will be very dependent upon the state of the market and the enlarged share capital would require higher dividends in future years in order to maintain the current level of dividend per share.

- Issuing new debt via a bond issue. This might be better than an equity issue, depending on investor risk appetite.

- Reduce costs – for example, make staff redundant

- Sell assets – for example, close branches of the bank

- Raise interest rates offered on investments to encourage more deposits.

Tutorial note – extracted from the Examiner's "Post Exam Guide"

The main weakness with answers to this question was a lack of understanding that the key principle of a scrip issue is that it is simply a transfer of capital and has no overall effect on the value of the firm. Many candidates in part (b) calculated the number of new shares per 1,000 correctly but then simply applied the pre-scrip share price of INR 396 to the total number of shares after the issue rather than adjust the share price down to reflect the fact that overall value would not change. This error in logic was then followed through into the calculations for selling the rights. However an additional error in this calculation was that many candidates applied the sale price of INR 7 to 20 shares rather than 1,000 – despite the fact that the question clearly stated that the selling price for the rights was INR 7 per existing share.

The discussion in part (a) was reasonably well addressed by the majority of candidates and it was encouraging to see so many candidates make the connection that given the credit crunch and restrictions on the banking sector, that the market may already have anticipated a zero dividend payment.

Parts (c) and (d) were typically not as well answered as part (a) and indeed many candidates fell into the trap of discussing generic liquidity measures such as inventory and working capital management in part (d) which obviously do not apply to a bank.

16   SPORT (SEPT 12 EXAM)

Key answer tips – extracted from the Examiner's "Post Exam Guide"

The first part of the question requires a simple description of the differences between the overall objectives of 'for profit' and 'not for profit' organisations. Answers should focus on the differences and reasons for those differences rather than just state what the objectives of such organisations are.

The second part of the question asks for advice on whether the 6 specific objectives identified can be adapted for use by the charity in question. Answers here should address each objective in turn and focus on its suitability and suggest how it might be adapted. The next part of the question then asks for additional objectives that may be suitable (these should be additional objectives and not simply a repeat of previous suggestions.

The last part of the question asks for advice again on the appropriateness of a charity using a bond issue to raise funds to support expansion. Answers here should make reference to the FD's comment that charities should be run on commercial grounds and should focus on the risks and the impact of a bond issue on the main beneficiaries of the charity.

(a)   'For profit' organisations are generally principally run for the benefit of the shareholders who as the owners of the organisation are major stakeholders. The overall objective is therefore likely to be the maximisation of shareholder wealth, measured in terms of returns to shareholders through dividend payments and an increasing share price.

In a 'not for profit' organisation, the overall objectives will be different because the organisation does not have shareholders and so a profit objective is not appropriate. The main purpose is normally some charitable or other non-profit objective such as improvements in the welfare of a certain part of society or the environment at home or abroad and so the key objective will be based on the benefits provided. 'Not for profit' organisations tend to measure their objectives in terms of efficiency, economy and effectiveness rather than profit.

(b)   (i)   **Financial objectives:**

Growth in earnings per share

Clearly, a target based on earnings per share is not appropriate for an organisation such as SPORT which does not have shareholders. However, the principle of increasing revenue and decreasing costs (that underpins growth in earnings) is relevant to SPORT. The commercial activities of SPORT should operate along sound commercial lines in order to maximise the surplus that can be used to subsidise equipment. SPORT might consider adapting the earnings target and redefining it in terms of, for example:

- Increasing donations.

- Reducing costs/increasing income from stores.

Growth in dividends

This is a measure of the benefit derived by shareholders in a commercial context and is therefore not appropriate for SPORT. However, this could be redefined in the context of SPORT in terms of a growth in subsidies provided or, if a fixed subsidy %, a growth in value of subsidised equipment provided.

Gearing target

Gearing level is essentially a measure of risk and applies equally to a 'for profit' and 'not for profit' organisation such as SPORT. SPORT could apply the gearing target to its lease obligations and, if pursued in future, to the bond as well.

Non-financial objectives

To a certain extent the objectives identified could apply equally to a 'not for profit' and 'for profit' organisation.

The customer satisfaction target could equally apply to SPORT in terms of both successful stores and appropriate special equipment supplied.

The objective of retaining market position probably doesn't apply so directly to SPORT, although it is important for SPORT to maintain and grow its profile in the charity sector to ensure a continued stream of donations and support. An alternative might be to achieve the highest level of donations compared to other similar charities (although this level of competiveness might actually be against the ethos of SPORT as ultimately all charity is worthwhile).

The last objective of reducing the carbon footprint is an important objective for all organisations in these times and should be encouraged.

(ii) **Additional objectives**

As with commercial organisations, SPORT will have other stakeholders such as employees, customers, suppliers and the communities in which the stores operate. As a charity, SPORT should be very aware of the social dimension of business and needs to address the requirement to take account of all stakeholders.

Additional objectives that could be considered by SPORT include:

- Providing employees with fair salaries and treating volunteers fairly.

- Providing equal treatment for all employees.

- Providing recipients of reduced cost sports equipment with quality service and ensuring that recipients receive products which are safe and fit for purpose.

- Ensure a high level of service is provided to customers of the charity stores.

- Ensuring that goods sold in the charity stores are of high quality and meet safety regulations.

- Fair treatment of workers in the organisation's supply chain.

- Aiming to expand the range of sporting equipment supplied and/or expanding the range of recipients.

(iii) There is some merit in the FD's comment, certainly in terms of the commercial aspects of the organisation. The concept of what constitutes a charitable organisation needs to encompass social enterprise – organisations run for social benefit, which operate on a commercial basis. There is nothing inherently 'wrong' with trying to operate the stores at a profit and hence maximise funds available for pursuing a charity's main charitable objectives.

However, a charity should not be seen to take excessive risks in order to realise profit that can be used for charitable purposes. It is not unknown for the trading arm of a charity to prove to be unprofitable and, in extreme cases, to fail and pull the charity down with it. Commercial operations need to be conducted in a professional manner – there is an even higher duty of care in the use of donated funds than in the use of shareholders' funds – and so the Trustees need to be absolutely sure that the return on investment of the funds will more than cover the cost of servicing the bond and that sufficient investments can be realised or other provision made to ensure that there is no problem repaying the bond on maturity.

Conclusion: If the trustees are confident that the proceeds from the bond can be used to successfully develop the stores and that the expansion would be successful and lead to an increase in net income without undue risk, then the bond issue and store development should be considered further. Careful risk assessment is required. For example, to determine the maximum extent of loss possible if the project proves to be unsuccessful and therefore new stores need to be closed and the bond repaid, possibly at a time when market rates are unfavourable.

Tutorial note – extracted from the Examiner's "Post Exam Guide"

Part (a):

Most candidates were able to describe the key overall objectives of 'for profit' organisations and 'not for profit' organisations, but a significant minority were unable to describe why these objectives might be different.

Part (b)(i):

Most candidates showed good exam technique in that they considered in turn all 6 of the objectives in the question, however, most answers were superficial in their advice on how each objective could be adapted. Indeed many candidates simply stated whether each objective was suitable for SPORT without then taking the next step and commenting on how it could be changed to fit the charity's aims. There were a few excellent answers where candidates demonstrated well thought out application to the scenario.

Part (b)(ii):

A minority of candidates ignored this requirement altogether and there were very few good answers. If attempted, many candidates repeated what they had already said in part (b)(i) or just listed very vague ideas without formulating them into specific objectives.

Part (b)(iii):

Few candidates scored well regarding the comments made by the FD, however, answers in respect of the bond issue were on the whole much better. Many candidates grasped the fact that the key issue here was the potential introduction of too much risk to the charity and the impact that this might have on the various stakeholders.

17   BBD (NOV 12 EXAM)

Key answer tips – extracted from the Examiner's "Post Exam Guide"

Part (a)

Recognise that this part of the question focuses on exposure to *external* factors that are largely outside BBD's control. In an answer plan, list the key variables that are *relevant* to BBD's situation. Then take each in turn and provide a brief discussion of each.

Part (b)

For part (b)(i) consider the main areas of impact on the company if its credit was downgraded. The main areas that would be affected are availability and cost of finance and its share price. Then advise the board of what the impact might be, an obvious example being that borrowing would cost more, if it is available at all.

For part (b)(ii), evaluate each of the three proposed courses of action in the context of its impact on shareholder wealth, balancing the potential positive and adverse impacts on shareholders.

For part (b)(iii) summarise the key points from your answers to parts (b)(i) and (b)(ii) and conclude with a recommendation. Recognise that there might not be a single ideal course of action but base your recommendation on your own evaluation.

(a)   **Potential exposure of BBD's financial results to external factors**

BBD is exposed to a large number of economic and other variables. Issues that candidates could raise in discussion include:

- Market energy prices, and the price of gas in particular.

- US dollar exchange rate against the Canadian Dollar.

- Global sources of gas – as more are found global supply increases which potentially means that price will fall.

- Global demand for gas – higher demand (e.g. due to economic growth or adverse weather) could push the wholesale price up.

- The risk of loss due to legal action against the company to recover damages for property damage etc.

- Competitor action.

- Government intervention in terms of duties and tariffs imposed on the extraction of natural resources.

- Public sentiment towards the extraction of natural resources.

- Credit standing.

(b) (i) **Possible implications of credit downgrade**

A credit downgrade usually has three major impacts:

Impact on the ability to access funding

- Lenders are more reluctant to lend and, indeed, some may choose not to lend to BBD despite earlier willingness to do so, following a credit downgrade or even indication that a credit downgrade might be imminent.

- BBD is also likely to face difficulties when it is time to re-negotiate existing borrowings and existing lenders may not be willing to renew borrowings.

Impact on cost of funding

- Interest costs will be higher. This may affect current borrowings as well as the cost of new borrowings.

Share price

- A downgrade gives the perception to the market as a whole that the company is potentially in trouble and hence the share price is likely to fall as investor confidence is dented. There is also an increase in critical discussion of the company on financial pages of newspapers, in financial journals and on websites.

Impact on suppliers and customers

- Suppliers may become more reluctant to provide services without up-front payment. Credit terms provided may be reduced.

- If customers have concerns about the long term future of BBD, they may switch supplier.

(ii) **Evaluate each response**

Response A

- It might be simplest to cancel the project until the company is on a more secure financial footing from which to expand. It is certainly the most risk averse option in the short term time horizon.

- However, BBD may depend on this new project to achieve growth and move to a more secure financial footing. This is a judgment call on the importance of the project to the future long term prospects of the company.

- Given the nature of the industry in that there is limited gas available for extraction using traditional methods, there is likely to be an expectation from investors that BBD should continually be seeking new sources and methods of gas extraction.

- Therefore this project is likely to be in line with what investors expect and if it does not go ahead then investors are likely to lose confidence resulting in a reduced share price.

Response B

- The company will need to balance the advantages of proceeding with the project against the downside risks arising from a credit downgrade.

- The added costs and, indeed, the viability of pursuing the project in the face of a credit downgrade need to be assessed.

- If it is considered that the cost of borrowing would become prohibitive, or, indeed, no project finance were available following a downgrade, this would not be a viable option.

Response C

- In theory, if the project earns at least the cost of capital, the shareholder will not lose value.

- However, many shareholders will be institutions or individuals who have planned their portfolio in the expectation of certain levels of income. Such shareholders would clearly prefer to receive a dividend at all costs and there is a risk to BBD that they would rearrange their portfolios in order to achieve higher income levels if it was considered that BBD might repeat such action in the future. There might therefore be a risk of high sales of shares that could deflate the share price.

- However, as mentioned above, response C may still be considered to be the 'least bad' option available and, indeed, the only course of action open to the company if it still wishes to pursue its ambition to exploit the fracking market and is unable to obtain finance for the project in the face of a credit downgrade.

(iii) **Recommendation**

Examiner's note:

Candidates were assessed according to the quality of their supporting arguments and coverage of key determining factors rather than their choice of appropriate response.

Candidates could say that BBD should adopt response C in order to develop this important new market and enhance shareholder wealth over the long term without adding unnecessary risks that would result from adopting response B.

Other candidates may recommend response B on the basis that this also maximised shareholder wealth and that the company is fundamentally strong enough to withstand a credit downgrading, at least in the short term, after which it is hoped that the company will be regarded upwards following a successful new project.

Alternatively, candidates may choose to recommend response A on the basis that it may be considered a good time to 'retrench' until economic conditions improve and environmental concerns have been refuted.

The final choice of response will largely be determined by investor preference and the balance between risk and return for each of the three possible responses.

The final choice of strategy will largely depend on the opinion of the major shareholders following consultation.

Tutorial note – extracted from the Examiner's "Post Exam Guide"

This was a wholly narrative question, which was generally answered well and many candidates who attempted it gained very high marks. However, those who answered it badly tended to misunderstand what "external factors" and "external constraints" mean and discussed internal factors such as staffing issues. Particularly pleasing was that most candidates demonstrated good application of the real world to the scenario.

18   SRP (MAR 13 EXAM)

Key answer tips – extracted from the Examiner's "Post Exam Guide"

Part (a)

Determine the number of shares and the market capitalisation. Use these figures to calculate earnings per share and dividend per share.

Then calculate the book value of equity and net debt and use these figures to calculate gearing at book values.

Finally, calculate gearing using the market value of equity calculated previously.

Part (b)

Calculate the cash that would be repaid and the equivalent number of shares that would be repurchased.

Then recalculate the ratios under each alternative. Note no changes needed for 'retain cash' option.

Part (c)

Consider the implications of each strategy on the attainment of financial objectives, utilising your calculations from part (b). Then consider the implications of each strategy for shareholders, both in the short term (e.g. receipt of cash) and long term (e.g. impact on long term growth prospects).

(a)   **Calculation of EpS, DpS and gearing at both book values and market values**

EpS		Notes/workings
Shares in issue (million)	350	
Earnings in year ended 31.03.13 (GBPm)	280	
EpS	0.800	= 280/50
DpS		
Shares in issue (million)	350	
Dividend paid in year (GBPm)	89.6	
DpS	0.256	= 89.6/350

Gearing at book values

Debt (GBP m)	550.00	
	(110.40)	= 215 – 89.6 – 15
Less surplus cash (GBPm)	————	
Net debt (GBPm)	439.60	= 550 – 110.4
Equity (GBPm)	1,210.40	= 350 + 950 – 89.6
		(Don't forget to adjust equity to take account of the dividend of 89.6.)
Gearing at BV	26.6%	= 439.60/(439.60 + 1,210.40)

Gearing at market values

Debt (GBPm)	550.00	
	(110.40)	= 215 – 89.6 – 15
Less surplus cash (GBPm)	————	
Net debt (GBPm)	439.60	= 550 – 110.4
Equity (GBPm)	1,583.40	= (350 × 4.78) – 89.6
		or 350 × ex div share price of 4.524 (where 4.524 = 4.78 – 0.256)
Gearing at MV	21.7%	= 439.60/(439.60 + 1,583.40)

(b)   **Calculation of likely impact of the three proposed strategies for dealing with surplus cash.**

Assumption

All the surplus cash of GBP 110.40 million is used either to repurchase shares or to pay bonuses. [Alternative assumptions were also acceptable.]

Preliminary workings

Based on an ex div share price of 4.524 (= 4.78 – 0.256), the number of share to be repurchased is 24.40 million (= 110.4m/4.524), leaving 325.60 million shares in issue.

	1 Hold onto cash	2 Repurchase shares	3 Pay bonuses
EpS			
Earnings (GBPm)	No change	280.00	169.60 (= 280 – 110.4)
Number of shares (m)		325.60 (workings)	350.00
New EpS	0.800	0.860	0.485 (single year impact)
Previous EpS	0.800	0.800	0.800
Impact	**nil**	**up 0.06 long term**	**down 0.315 in that year**
DpS			
Dividend (GBPm)	No change	89.6	No change
Number of shares (m)		325.60	
New DpS	0.256	0.275	0.256
Previous DpS	0.256	0.256	0.256
Impact	**nil**	**up 0.02**	**nil**
Gearing at BV			
Net debt (GBPm)	No change	550.00 (No surplus cash)	As for share repurchase
Equity (GBPm)		1,100.00 =350 + 950 – 89.6 – 110.4	
New gearing	26.6%	33.3%	33.3%
Previous gearing	26.6%	26.6%	26.6%
Impact	**nil**	**Up by 6.7%**	**Up by 6.7%**
Gearing at MV			
Net debt (GBPm)	No change	550.00	As for share repurchase
Equity (GBPm)		1,473.00 =(350 × 4.78) –89.6 – 110.4	
New gearing	21.7%	27.2%	27.2%
Previous gearing	21.7%	21.7%	21.7%
Impact	**nil**	**Up by 5.5%**	**Up by 5.5%**

(c) **Evaluate impact on attainment of financial objectives and on shareholder wealth.**

1 **Retain cash**

Three reasons or motives have been advanced for individuals and companies to hold cash – transaction, speculative and precautionary. Each is commented on briefly below:

- The transaction reason – if SRP has sufficient cash to meet day to day transactions it has no need of additional cash for this reason.

- The speculative motive would allow the company to take advantage of opportunities such as buying assets at temporarily favourable prices or making an investment. This would be a logical reason for SRP to hold cash even if it has no potential immediate investment opportunities.

- The precautionary motive would allow SRP to maintain a safety cushion or buffer to meet unexpected cash needs. Given the long term nature of SRP's contracts, its cash flow is fairly predictable so less cash is needed for precautionary needs. However, the surplus cash is approximately equivalent to just one year's dividend payment and so may not seem to be an excessive cash buffer.

On the downside, shareholders are missing out on the income that they could obtain by investing the funds elsewhere. With 5.3% of total assets held in the form of surplus cash (where 5.3% = GBP 110.4 million/GBP 2,075 million × 100%) and therefore earning little or no return, shareholders will prefer to be given the cash back so that they can invest it elsewhere and enhance their returns.

However, if SRP thinks investment opportunities might be available in the not too distant future, shareholders may be willing to forego receiving the cash now in the expectation of even greater returns in the future.

2 Share repurchase

The advantage to shareholders is that selling shares back to the company allows them to raise cash with no transaction costs. Not all will want to sell, but SRP is only aiming to purchase around 7% of the shares in issue.

The make-up of the shareholders is relevant here in terms of the potential success of any repurchase scheme, as institutional investors are far less likely to participate in a share repurchase than smaller scale investors as they tend to be more concerned with regular income. However, 30% of the shares are held by small investors who might welcome the chance to realise their investment.

The advantage to the company in the long term is an opportunity to increase DpS at the same total level of dividend payment or, alternatively, keep DpS at the same level and reduce total dividend payments, retaining cash for future investment. EpS will similarly increase due to the lower number of shares. Shareholder wealth should not be affected, their shareholding will be worth less (reflecting fewer shares) but they are now holding additional cash. If this cash can be invested profitably, this should lead to an increase in shareholder wealth in the medium term. However, there is an almost inevitable trade-off between risk and reward here. The riskiness of the equity will increase due to the higher gearing levels. Gearing will increase from 26.7% to 33.3% based on book values.

The share repurchase is unlikely to have much effect on the overall cost of capital as the increased use of lower cost debt is likely to be offset by higher returns required on equity. The tax benefit of debt is not relevant as there is no impact on gross debt here.

On a practical note, the company's articles of association must be checked to ensure they permit a share repurchase.

3 Bonuses to directors and employees

The payment of bonuses reduces shareholder wealth (and reserves) by the amount paid out. It is of little benefit to shareholders unless it leads to the retention of key employees or leads to higher profits as a result of more highly motivated staff in the future. In either case, a long term bonus plan is likely to be of more benefit to the company than large one-off payments at this time.

The directors' bonuses need to be referred to a remuneration committee before amounts are determined. Indeed, director bonuses need also to be approved by shareholders, something that is not always guaranteed, as has been seen in the UK in the recent past.

Gearing would increase to 33.3% (based on book values and using 31 March 2013 figures) due to an increase in net debt and a decrease in reserves – the same effect as for under the share repurchase.

But for a manufacturing company with substantial assets this is still a modest rate. SRP should consider amending its gearing objective from 30% to, say, 35%.

Tutorial note – extracted from the Examiner's "Post Exam Guide"

There were a surprising number of fundamental accounting errors in part (a), such as deducting the dividend from earnings when calculating EpS and adding retained earnings to the market value of shares when calculating the market value of equity.

However, most candidates made a reasonable attempt at part (a).

Additional common errors in the calculations in part (a):

- *Omitting to first adjust retained earnings and cash by deducting the planned dividend that has not yet been reflected in the forecast information provided in the question.*

- *Omitting to calculate and then deduct surplus cash from debt to obtain a net debt figure for use in the gearing calculations.*

- *Using the cum div rather than the ex div share price when calculating gearing based on market values (or, alternatively, use the cum div share price and then deduct the dividend).*

- *Incorrectly adding retained earnings (of GBP 950 million) to the market value of the shares when calculating equity for use in gearing calculations at market values.*

The requirement in part (b) used the verb 'calculate'. No credit was therefore given for general comments in place of calculations in part (b), although, where appropriate, comments made in part (b) were awarded credit in part (c).

Common errors in the calculations in part (b):

- *Deducting the amount used to repurchase shares from earnings rather than from equity.*

- *Deducting the number of shares rather than the cost of repurchasing the shares from equity.*

- *Omitting to increase net debt by the cost of repurchasing shares.*

- *Stating that bonus payments would have no impact on these performance measures.*

- *Omitting to reduce earnings by the amount paid out in bonuses.*

Part (c) was generally attempted better than part (b). There were some good comments about the benefits and drawbacks of retaining cash in the balance sheet in the context of attainment of financial objectives and of shareholder wealth. There was some confusion over the payment of bonuses, with a number of candidates stating that this would have no impact on shareholder wealth, despite SRP being a listed company with only 5% of shares being held by directors and employees combined.

---

19   KK (SEPT 13 EXAM)

Key answer tips – extracted from the Examiner's "Post Exam Guide" (note that the comments regarding WORD and/or EXCEL only relate to the COMPUTER BASED papers in March and September each year)

Part (a)(i) requires the calculation of the impact of a change in dividend pay-out rate on certain specified variables which are used as key inputs in calculating the impact on share prices in part (b). It is therefore essential to attempt part (a) before moving on to part (b). Remember to take into account the time delay between cutting the dividend and affecting earnings. It may be useful to draw a time line here to help work out the timings involved.

In part (a)(ii), the share price value should be based on the present value of future dividends in perpetuity. It is important to look at each year individually because of the time delay between cutting the dividend and realising the benefit in terms of increased earnings. Only after the third year is it possible to apply a growing perpetuity to finish the NPV calculation. It is therefore not possible to apply the standard DVM formula (based on a perpetuity) straightaway as this is based on a simply growing perpetuity starting at time 0.

The answer to part (b) should begin by interpreting the results in part (a)(ii) and then move on to consider alternative dividend theories.

(a)   (i)

Performance measure	*2013*	*2014*	*Workings*	*2015*	*Workings*
Earnings growth rate	3.2%	3.2%	No change as reinvestment of additional retained earnings not actioned until this year	8%	g = r × b = 16% × 50% = 8%
Earnings(K$ million)	12.5	12.9	= K$ 12.5 million × 1.032	13.932	= K$ 12.9 million × 1.08
Dividend per share(K$)	0.50	0.3225	= 12.9m × 50%/20m	0.3483	= 13.932 × 50%/20 m

where 3.2% = r × b = 16% × 20%

(ii)   At a 50% pay-out rate, the share price can be calculated as the present value of future dividends in perpetuity at a discount rate of 14.7% as at 1 January 2014 as follows:

Date	*31 Dec 2014*	*31 Dec 2015*	*31 Dec 2016 onwards*
Dividend per share	0.3225	0.3483 (= 0.3225 × 1.08)	0.3483 uplifted by 8% a year
PV of all future dividends as at 31 Dec 2015			5.6144 = 0.3483 × 1.08/ (0.147 – 0.08)
Discount factor	0.8718	0.7601	0.7601
	(= 1/1.147)	(= 1/1.147^2)	
PV as at 31 Dec 2013	0.2812	0.2647	4.2675
Total PV	4.81		

Alternative approach, using a multi-columnar table on EXCEL:

Date	31 Dec 2014	31 Dec 2015	31 Dec 2016	31 Dec 2017	Etc
Dividend per share	0.3225	0.3483 (= 0.3225 × 1.08)	0.3762 (= 0.3225 × 1.08^2)	0.3762 (= 0.3225 × 1.08^3)	Etc

Total NPV (using EXCEL NPV function at a discount rate of 14.7%): K$ 4.81

Both approaches give the same result. That is, that the ex div share price is expected to move from K$ 4.50 to K$ 4.81 as a result of the change in dividend pay-out ratio.

(b)   There are many theories surrounding dividend decisions.

The DVM result in (a)(ii) above predicts that reducing the level of dividend would lead to an increase in the share price (moving from K$ 4.50 to K$ 4.81 per share). This is because the increase in retained funds should promote growth and hence increase shareholder wealth. However, the share price will only reflect this theoretical result if investors believe that retaining the funds will, indeed, produce the higher returns forecast by the DVM and act accordingly by increased demand for shares, which pushes the share price up to K$ 4.81 on the stock market.

Note that this result depends on the rate of return on reinvested funds being higher than the investors required rate of return (i.e.: Ke). Indeed if the rate of return on reinvested funds had been lower than the cost of equity then we would expect the share price to actually fall.

We also need to consider more practical considerations affecting the optimum level of dividend.

Firstly, the signalling effect of dividends. A lower dividend could be interpreted by investors as an indication that the company is in financial difficulty rather than that the company is seeking investment opportunities in new markets.

Secondly, all shareholders (including family shareholders) tend to prefer a predictable level of dividends in order to be able to plan ahead. Many shareholders may rely on the dividend stream to provide day-to-day income.

Thirdly, some shareholders may prefer cash (following the 'bird in hand' principle) whereas others may prefer an increase in share price, depending on their perception of the long term stability of the company and their personal tax position. If capital gains are taxed at a lower rate than income, a switch from dividend to capital gain may be advantageous to shareholders. On the other hand, investors who are in that tax position and prefer capital gains to dividends may have invested in other companies with lower pay-out ratios and, therefore will not be current shareholders in KK.

We are not given the full breakdown of the shareholders, but if the shares are concentrated in the hands of a small number of shareholders, personal preferences would also be important. Before making a reduction in dividend pay-out, KK should seek to ensure that major shareholders understand the reasoning behind it and agree to this change in policy.

A residual dividend policy is unlikely to be valid for a public company where shareholders have expectation of regular dividend payments from year to year. A residual dividend policy is where dividends are paid out only after exhausting all available positive NPV projects.

Tutorial note – extracted from the Examiner's "Post Exam Guide"

In part (a)(i) many candidates correctly calculated the new 8% growth rate but applied this to both 2014 and 2015, ignoring the year delay before the new growth rate applied. Where this was the case candidates did score the marks for earnings and dividend per share based on their own figures and therefore were only penalised for an incorrect growth rate in 2014.

Generally, this section was reasonably well answered, although some candidates assumed that the 16% reinvestment rate was the growth rate, demonstrating a lack of understanding.

In part (a)(ii), common errors included the use of earnings instead of dividend cash flows or not adjusting for growth.

In part (b), there were some excellent, full answers. However, other candidates only provided very brief and/or generic answers. Where 10 marks are available, a more in-depth answer is clearly expected. For example, answers should have included reference to the calculations in part (a)(ii), as instructed in the requirement and considered the trade-off between share price and retention levels.

FINANCING DECISIONS

20   MNO (MAY 06 EXAM)

Key answer tips

A straightforward question focusing on working capital policies (moderate, aggressive, conservative).

However, many students seemed unable to perform the calculations in (a) (ii) according to the examiner's comments, so review this carefully.

In part (b) the question asks for a discussion of financing policies, not working capital policies, limiting the scope of your answer.

(a)   (i)   **Working capital levels**

Minimum working capital:

	Period	**Working**	$000
Receivables	20 days	$10m × 20/365	548
Inventories	50 days	$10m × 60% × 50/365	822
			1,370
Payables	50 days	$10m × 60% × 50/365	(822)
			548

Maximum working capital:

	Period	Working	$000
Receivables	30 days	$10m × 30/365	822
Inventories	80 days	$10m × 60% × 80/365	1,315
			2,137
Payables	40 days	$10m × 60% × 40/365	(657)
			1,480

Comments:

The calculations assume that the maximum periods for inventories and receivables coincide with the minimum payables period. This is questionable on the following grounds:

- Higher inventory and receivables would imply a period of higher volumes of business. This would normally correspond to higher payables (and hence period) as well.

- The operating cycle concept implies that there is normally a time lag between additional purchases, higher inventory levels and, finally, higher sales and receivables.

(ii) **Financing of working capital**

Maximum financing requirements:

		$000
Non-current assets		8,000
Permanent net current assets		548
Fluctuating net current assets (max. level)	(1,480 – 548)	932
		9,480

Financing under each policy ($000):

Policy	Working	Long-term finance $000	Max. short-term finance (balance) $000
Moderate	8,000 + 548	8,548	932
Aggressive	8,000 + 70% × 548	8,384	1,096
Conservative	8,000 + 548 + 60% × 932	9,107	373

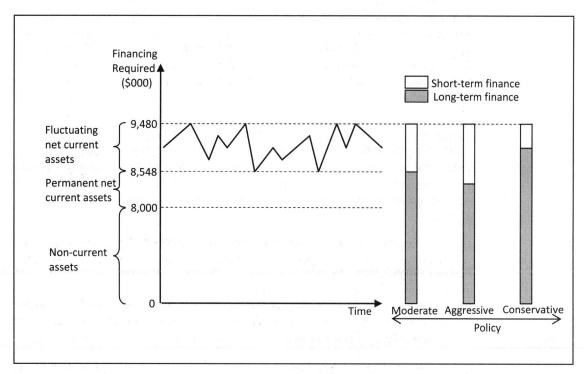

(b)   Advantages of a more aggressive approach:

- Less finance is made up of (more expensive) long-term finance, reducing overall financing costs.

- The lower financing costs should result in better profitability.

- Quicker cash turnover may allow more reinvestment and hence allow the business to expand more quickly.

- Greater flexibility as even a large fall in net current assets would not leave MNO over-financed.

Disadvantages of a more aggressive approach:

- Higher liquidity risk i.e. more risk of the company running out of cash or going into liquidation.

- Greater management time required to manage and renew short-term finance.

- Less relaxed credit policy for receivables may reduce sales.

Appropriateness for MNO:

- The decentralised nature of MNO's operations with an emphasis on local flexibility would suggest that a more aggressive policy would be better. This is further reinforced by the expectation of large fluctuations in net current asset levels.

(c)   Whether treasury should be a cost or profit centre

It is possible to operate the treasury department as a profit centre, charging each division the market value of the services provided, and speculating on risk exposures in pursuit of further profits.

The advantages of having a profit centre are as follows:

- There is the potential for large additional profits if everything goes to plan.

- The treasury will be motivated to provide its services as economically and effectively as possible, otherwise the business units will want to look elsewhere for such advice.

- The business units will have more realistic operating costs, since these costs will include the market value of treasury advice received.

The disadvantages are as follows:

- There is the potential for huge losses if the treasury makes a mess of things. Unhedged speculative positions can rapidly turn loss-making and, rather than admit the problem and realise their losses, there have been several cases in practice where positions have got worse and worse while managers hope for the best.

- Additional administrative costs involved in running a separate profit centre.

- Wasted management time in negotiating the prices of services supplied. The price cancels out in group terms, but may be important in calculating the profit earned by each individual business unit.

- Potential gains are limited given the small size of MNO.

- The decentralised culture of MNO may make it harder to standardise and effectively centralise policies.

On balance a cost centre approach is likely to be appropriate.

21 LEELOR (MAY 07 EXAM)

Key answer tips

A straightforward question focusing on the lease v buy decision. The main area of difficulty is part (a) (ii) in calculating a breakeven lease rental.

(a) (i) **Alternative 1: Buy**

	$t = 0$	$t = 1$	$t = 2$	$t = 3$	$t = 4$	$t = 5$	$t = 6$
	$	$	$	$	$	$	$
Buy / sell machine	(5,000)					2,000	
Tax re WDAs (W1)			375	281	211	158	(125)
Maintenance costs		(60)	(60)	(60)	(100)	(100)	
Tax relief @ 30%			18	18	18	30	30
Net cash flow	(5,000)	(60)	333	239	129	2,088	(95)
DF@ 5%(W2)	1	0.952	0.907	0.864	0.823	0.784	0.746
PV	(5,000)	(57)	302	206	106	1,637	(71)
NPV	**(2,877)**						

Workings

(W1) Capital allowances

	$	Tax relief @ 30%	Timing
Purchase cost	5000		
Year 1 allowances @ 25%	(1,250)	375	t = 2
WDV end Year 1	3,750		
Year 2 allowances@ 25%	(938)	281	t = 3
WDV end Year 2	2,812		
Year 3 allowances@ 25%	(703)	211	t = 4
WDV end Year 3	2,109		
Year 4 allowances@ 25%	(527)	158	t = 5
WDV end Year 4	1,582		
Residual value	2,000		
Balancing charge Year 5	418	(125)	t = 6

(W2) Discount rate

There are a number of different approaches to the lease v buy decision. Here we use the post-tax cost of borrowing to take into account the tax relief LEE would receive on loan interest payments.

- Pre-tax cost = 5.5 + 1.7 = 7.2%

- Post-tax cost = 7.2 × (1 − 0.3) = 5.04%

- For simplicity we shall use 5%.

Alternative 2: Lease

Time	Narrative	CF $	DF@ 5%	PV $
0 − 4	Lease payments	(850)	1 + 3.546 = 4.546	(3,864)
2 − 6	Tax relief − 850 × 30%	255	5.076 − 0.952 = 4.124	1,052
NPV				**(2,812)**

Conclusion:

It is cheaper for LEE to lease the machinery rather than buy it. However, the net benefit is only $65.

(ii) **Breakeven rental**

- Let the lease payment increase to X.

- The new NPV will be = −4.546X + 0.3 × X × 4.124 = −3.309X.

- To be indifferent, the lease NPV cost must increase to 2,877.

- Thus −2,877 = −3.309X.

- The lease payment can thus increase to X = $869.

(b) Alternative 3 appears to be a standard finance lease. In choosing between the three options (buy, operating lease or finance lease), the following factors must be considered:

- **Cost** – the operating lease appears cheaper than buying. However, we do not have figures for alternative 3.

- **Certainty of figures** – most of the figures (e.g. capital cost, lease payments) are certain except for the residual value for the asset and the maintenance costs, which are harder to forecast. Together these give most uncertainty to the buy option.

- **Flexibility to cease sooner** – it is easier to change plans if the asset is bought. Terminating a lease early often involves penalties.

- **Flexibility to extend use** – similarly both the buy option and alternative 3 allow the possibility to continue using the asset beyond five years. Alternative 2 does not. The value of this flexibility will depend on whether the machine (which will last ten years) is still needed after five years.

- **Maintenance** – with the operating lease maintenance is carried out by the lessor. However, with alternatives 1 and 3 it may be easier to schedule maintenance for when the machine is not required as much, reducing downtime.

- **Disposal** – with the leases LEE will not have to dispose of the asset. If the asset is bought then it will be LEE's responsibility.

- **Balance sheet** – the asset will be capitalised under alternatives 1 and 3 and a non-current liability recognised. The operating lease is off-balance sheet finance.

- **Cash flow** – leasing avoids having to raise sufficient cash to buy the asset.

- **Taxation** – depending on Newland's tax regulations, there may be advantages to one of the alternatives.

22 DAN'S PORTFOLIO (MAY 08 EXAM) *Walk in the footsteps of a top tutor*

Top tutor tips

The references to beta and systematic/unsystematic risk in part (b) should have given a clue that the calculations in the question were to be performed using the CAPM model.

Part (c) covered rights issues and bonus issues, and could have been answered independently of the previous parts of the question. Even if you had struggled with the calculations in part (a), with good exam technique you could have scored a pass mark on this question by answering parts (b) and (c) where there were plenty of easy marks.

(a) **Portfolio risk and return**

Dan's proposed portfolio will comprise 3 elements; the current portfolio, Entity A and Entity B. Given that Dan is already well diversified we only need to consider the systematic risk of his investments.

The systematic risk of the portfolio can be measured as the weighted average of the individual elements' beta factors. We are given beta factors for the existing portfolio (1.2) and for Entity A (1.1), but not for Entity B.

Use CAPM to calculate Entity B's beta, given that we know B's required return is 15.8%:

$$k_e = R_f + \left[R_m - R_f\right]\beta$$

$$15.8\% = 5\% + \left[11\% - 5\%\right]\beta$$

$$\beta = 1.8$$

	Value (£)	Beta
Current portfolio	100,000	1.2
New investment – Entity A	20,000	1.1
New investment – Entity B	20,000	1.8
	140,000	

$$\text{Weighted average beta} = \left(\frac{100}{140} \times 1.2\right) + \left(\frac{20}{140} \times 1.1\right) + \left(\frac{20}{140} \times 1.8\right) = 1.27$$

Now, the required return from the portfolio can be calculated using CAPM:

$$k_e = R_f + \left[R_m - R_f\right]\beta = 5\% + (11\%\text{-}5\%) \times 1.27 = 12.62\%$$

(b) (i) Systematic risk is risk caused by market-wide factors, such as interest rate changes, recessions and oil price changes. It affects all companies to some extent and therefore cannot be eliminated, no matter how diversified a portfolio becomes.

Unsystematic risk is risk specific to a particular company or industry. As an investor diversifies his portfolio, the impact of unsystematic risk becomes negligible.

Beta is a measure of the impact of systematic risk on a company. $\beta > 1$ indicates that the company is affected to a greater than average extent by systematic risk factors, whereas $\beta < 1$ indicates lower than average risk.

Beta is measured by monitoring returns on a company's shares over a period. If the company's shares are more volatile than the average returns in the market, a beta of greater than 1 is calculated.

(ii) **The impact of beta values on Dan's investment decision**

If Dan incorporates Entity A's and/or Entity B's shares into his portfolio, the overall beta of the portfolio will become the weighted average of the individual betas.

In this case, Entity A has a lower beta than Dan's portfolio and Entity B has a higher beta. Thus investing in Entity A will reduce Dan's overall portfolio beta but investing in Entity B will increase the overall portfolio beta.

We are told that Dan is happy with the existing risk profile of his portfolio. This means that before investing in Entity B, Dan will need to assess the new (higher) risk profile of the new combined portfolio. It may be that investing in Entity B increases the risk of Dan's portfolio to a level which he is not prepared to tolerate.

The relevance of beta values to the directors

Betas indicate the level of systematic risk and are thus relevant only for well-diversified investors. The directors of the individual entities may not be well-diversified and would see their wealth (e.g. bonuses) dependent on unsystematic as well as systematic risk factors.

However, the directors of a company have a duty to maximise the wealth of their company's shareholders rather than their own wealth. The key issue is thus whether or not the shareholders are well-diversified, not the directors.

Therefore, directors will use the beta value of their companies to calculate required returns for the company's investors. This required return will then be used to calculate a discount rate for project appraisal, to ensure that all projects give sufficient returns to keep investors satisfied.

(c)   **Financial strategies**

Entity A

Entity A is planning to raise new finance through a rights issue.

Theoretical ex-rights price ("TERP") $= \frac{1}{N+1}\left[(N \times \text{cum rights price}) + \text{issue price}\right]$

$$= \frac{1}{5}\left[(4 \times £2.50) + £2.00\right]$$

$$= £2.40$$

Theoretically, the wealth of a shareholder will not change as a direct consequence of the rights issue, as shown below:

Consider Dan's position:

If he invests £20,000 in Entity A, after transaction costs of 2.5% he will buy

$\dfrac{£20,000 \times 97.5\%}{£2.50} = 7,800$ shares, so:

Cum rights wealth:

	£
Shares: 7,800 × £2.50	19,500

In the rights issue, Dan will subscribe for $\dfrac{1}{4} \times 7,800 = 1,950$ new shares, so:

Ex rights wealth:

	£
Shares: (7,800 + 1,950) × £2.40	23,400
Less: Cash paid 1,950 × £2.00	(3,900)
	———
	19,500
	———

In practice, the share price and hence the wealth of a shareholder may change if the rights proceeds are invested in a new project. Here we are not told what the rights proceeds will be invested in. Dan would need to ask about this before deciding whether to invest.

For example, if Entity A used the new finance to fund a positive NPV project, this would have the impact of increasing shareholder wealth, and would make investment in Entity A's shares a more attractive proposition.

Entity B

Entity B is offering a choice between cash and scrip dividends.

Dan's position if he invested in Entity B would be:

$$\text{Number of shares owned} = \frac{£20,000 \times 97.5\%}{£5} = 3,900 \text{ shares}$$

Thus, the choice to Dan would be:

Cash: 45p per share × 3,900 = £1,755

Scrip dividend: 1 for 10 offer, so $\frac{1}{10} \times 3,900 = 390$ shares

Whichever option Dan chose, his overall wealth would not change (the firm has not raised any new finance so has not been able to generate any new shareholder wealth by investing in new projects). This is Modigliani and Miller's Dividend Irrelevance Theory, which showed that the pattern of dividends is irrelevant to shareholder wealth. Dan's choice of cash or bonus shares would be driven solely by his current need for cash.

23 MAT (MAY 08 EXAM)

Key answer tips

This was the shortest question (1 page including requirement). The requirement was not broken down into sub requirements like the other questions in Section B, and as a consequence it may have appeared more daunting.

The key with a question like this is to pick out as many sub headings as possible from the lengthy requirement, to help you structure your answer.

REPORT

To: Finance Director, MAT

From: An External consultant

Date: Today

Subject: Forecast financial position

1   **Introduction**

This report has been prepared to analyse the forecast financial position of MAT.

2   **Overtrading**

In the Appendix I have presented a detailed financial analysis of MAT's current and forecast financial position, in order to assess whether MAT is overtrading.

Overtrading is a problem which often affects small, growing businesses such as yours. As sales grow quickly, the amount of cash needed to fund investment in working capital can grow dramatically and lead to firms having to find external sources of finance.

2.1 Working capital position

MAT's working capital position is forecast to deteriorate. The current cash operating cycle (the length of time between paying out cash for purchases and receiving cash for sales) is 50 days, but it is forecast to increase to 52 days. This does not seem to be a significant change, until we look more closely at the constituent figures.

Receivables days are 45 at the moment, but this is forecast to increase to 60. Perhaps as an enticement to new customers, the company is intending to offer better credit terms to them. This will put MAT at greater risk of default, and is the main reason why the overdraft is forecast to increase so much.

This increase in receivables days is partly offset by improvements in both inventory holding period and payables payment period. However, MAT needs to be careful; payables payment period is 94 days at the moment and is forecast to increase to 99 days. If this is beyond the official period of credit offered by suppliers, there is a danger that they might start reviewing MAT's credit terms. If MAT's credit limits were cut, this would put severe extra financial pressure on the business.

The overall worsening of the firm's working capital position is best shown by the current ratio, which is forecast to move from 2.8 to 1.5 as the overdraft increases dramatically.

2.2 Other financial analysis

Sales are forecast to increase by 27.8% next year, but at the same time, non-current assets are forecast to increase by a relatively small amount (14.6%). This shows that MAT is not really expecting to invest to support the increased level of sales. If the higher level of sales is to be sustainable, further investment in non-current assets must be made.

2.3 Conclusion

MAT does seem to be exhibiting the classic signs of overtrading. Sales are growing dramatically, but the firm is not forecasting to invest sufficiently in non-current assets to support the higher level of sales. Working capital investment is also increasing, and the overdraft is approaching the limit.

3   **Financial Strategies**

In order to address the overtrading problem, MAT will need to implement some or all of the following strategies:

3.1   **Working capital strategies**

- Receivables days are forecast to be 60. As identified above, this is arguably too high. MAT should review the credit terms of competitors to see what the industry standard is. A credit period of 30 days for computer components could well be achievable. Also, once credit periods have been set and communicated to customers, MAT's management need to ensure that customers adhere to the limits. Credit controllers, or even debt factors, could be used to ensure money is collected promptly.

- Inventory holding period is forecast to be 91 days. This seems very high for a firm which sells computer components. Although a Just In Time system would not be appropriate given that many customers and some suppliers are based overseas, better analysis of inventory lines should enable MAT to cut the amount of inventory and hence improve its cash position.

- Payables payment period is currently 94 days and forecast to increase to 99. This means that any discounts for prompt payment are not currently being taken by MAT. Paying earlier and taking discounts where available may save MAT money in the long term.

3.2   **Financing strategies**

- MAT is approaching its overdraft limit. Also, it has an £850,000 secured bond which is repayable shortly (in 20X8). These two factors are causing great concern. MAT needs to arrange a refinancing package with the bank. If possible, MAT should negotiate to convert the current overdraft/bond combination into one new longer term secured loan. The firm has plenty of non-current assets (£4.325m forecast) upon which to secure this new loan.

- If the £850,000 bond and the £425,000 (forecast) overdraft could be replaced by (say) a £2m longer term secured loan, the extra cash raised could be used to invest in some more non-current assets to enable the firm to support its higher level of sales.

- Based on a tax rate of 30% the forecast dividend for next year is £546,000 (see note to appendix 2). Cutting the dividend could contribute substantially to ensuring that the overdraft does not increase excessively.

4   **Further information required**

In order to more fully appreciate MAT's position at the moment, the following information would be useful:

- Industry average figures for cash operating cycle and current ratio – a comparison with these figures would enable us to see whether MAT is under- or over-performing in the context of its competitors.

- Hedging strategies – MAT buys and sells goods overseas. We are told that purchases are denominated in US$, so exchange risk will be a potential problem. Hedging strategies could be used to fix payments and receipts to eliminate the risk of losses.

- Further information regarding sales in the industry – we know that MAT operates in a niche market. It would be interesting to know whether MAT is the market leader, and whether its impressive forecast growth in sales is typical.

Tutorial note

The most efficient way of attacking a question like this is to put all your calculations into an appendix and then refer to them during your report. Don't spend so long on the calculations that you don't leave enough time for the written bits.

Appendix 1 – financial analysis

Cash operating cycle (in days)		*Last year*	*Forecast*
Receivables collection period	$\dfrac{\text{Receivables}}{\text{Sales}} \times 365$	45	60
Inventory holding period	$\dfrac{\text{Inventory}}{\text{Cost of sales}} \times 365$	99	91
Payables payment period	$\dfrac{\text{Payables}}{\text{Cost of sales}} \times 365$	(94)	(99)
Total cash operating cycle (days)		50	52
Current ratio	$\dfrac{\text{Current assets}}{\text{Current liabilities}}$	2.8	1.5
Profit margin	$\dfrac{\text{Profit before tax}}{\text{Revenue}}$	23.3%	21.0%
Growth in revenue		–	27.8%
Growth in profit		–	15.0%
Growth in non current assets		–	14.6%

Appendix 2 – cash flow forecast

	Working	£000	£000
Profit before tax			1,208
Tax and dividends (Note)	(1,208 – 300)		(908)
Changes in working capital			
Receivables	(950 – 550)	(400)	
Inventories	(575 – 475)	(100)	
Payables	(625 – 450)	175	
		____	
			(325)
Changes in non-current assets			(550)
			____
Change in cash and overdraft	(100–250) – (425–0)		(575)
			____

Note:

- Equity is forecast to increase by 4,050 – 3,750 = £300,000. Given profit before tax of £1,208,000, this means that tax and dividends must amount to the difference of £908,000.

- We are not told the tax rate that applies here, but using a figure of 30% , say, we would expect a tax charge of 30% × 1,208 = 362, indicating a dividend of the order of

  908 – 362 = £546,000.

24   BZ (MAY 09 EXAM)

Key answer tips

There were plenty of easy marks in this question.

The calculations should have been within the capabilities of any well-prepared student, given that they covered core syllabus topic areas.

Make sure you tailor your answer to the specific scenario in part (iv). It is not appropriate to simply list different financing options without assessing their suitability to the given circumstances.

(i)   **Calculation of WACC**

Market capitalisation of equity = 39 million × €4   = €156 million

Value of debt   = €121.5 × 0.08/0.09   = €108 million

$$\text{WACC} = \frac{k_e \times E}{D+E} + \frac{k_d(1-T) \times D}{D+E}$$

= 11% × 156/264 +   9% (0.72) × 108/264

= 9.15%

(ii) **Advice on discount rate**

Neither the WACC nor the current cost of equity is entirely relevant to the investment decision here. The WACC could only be used if the investment was not only in the same risk class, but financed in the same way as the entity. The cost of equity could only accurately be used if the new investment was of the same risk as the entity overall.

The rate that should be used is a risk-adjusted cost of capital that reflects the systematic risk of the investment. The CAPM could be used by finding a proxy entity's published beta, adjusting for the differences in gearing and using the formula to calculate a discount rate.

Alternatively, if there is likely to be a change of gearing (financial risk) when undertaking the new project, the Adjusted Present Value technique could be used. Here, the project is discounted using an ungeared cost of equity which reflects only the business risk of the project, and then any costs and benefits associated with the financing of the project are adjusted for separately.

A further issue to consider is whether to apply a US discount rate to US dollar-denominated cash flows, or apply a Euro discount rate to Euro-denominated cash flows.

(iii) **Advantages/disadvantages of government subsidies**

The advantages of using the US state subsidy are:

- The entity obtains cheaper finance;

- The entity does not need to provide security for this loan;

- There may be other advantages such as having the state government as a "partner" might ease issues such as applications for planning permission.

The potential disadvantages are that:

- The domestic rates change downwards over the five-year period, making the savings less attractive;

- The US$ strengthens against the €, making interest payments more expensive;

- The US State government may not honour its commitments;

- The investment fails in less than five years and the entity is tied into a five-year loan agreement (this would also be true of any term loan agreement);

- Conditions attached to the loan might be commercially restrictive;

- Tax laws in both countries need to be examined for any hidden penalties.

Value of the subsidy

The PV of the subsidy is the after-tax benefit over the five-year period, computed at the pre-tax market rate of interest.

		€million
The annual difference of interest payments is:		
$(0.09 - 0.035) \times$ €41.7 million (US$50m/1.2)	=	€2.29
After tax, the annual amount is €2.29 × 0.72	=	€1.65
The PV of the benefits at 9% is 1.65 × 3.89*	=	€6.42

*This is the annuity factor for five years at 9%

Tutorial note

The PV of the benefits has been calculated using the opportunity cost of debt as the discount rate. An argument could be made that, in theory, the WACC is the more appropriate rate, representing as it does the opportunity cost of the benefits. This typically would have the effect of reducing the value. In the case here there would be little difference as the unrounded WACC is only 9.15%. It is however necessary to assume that BZ will be able to offset interest payments against tax.

(iv) **Finance post-subsidy**

Alternative methods that might be considered are:

Long-term bonds

The entity's gearing ratio is 41% (108/264) and it has an overdraft facility. How this compares to the industry average is not known but further debt might be considered too risky, especially for a relatively risky business venture into a new market in a region that might be developing economically given the State aid being offered.

Supplier credit

The scenario does not give details of how BZ sources its raw materials, but it is possible that suppliers would provide some funding if there were business opportunities for their products.

Cash/disposal

BZ clearly has no cash on hand as it is using overdraft facilities. It could review its assets to determine whether there is any surplus that could be disposed of.

Leasing

Finance leases are the equivalent of secured medium-term bank loans and suffer the same disadvantages. Operating leases may be possible for some equipment, but this is an unlikely source in the circumstances.

Equity

The amount required is too small for a new issue, but a rights issue might be a possibility. The scenario does say shares change hands occasionally, which suggests there are more than just family members. This might be an expensive option because of the fees involved.

Venture capital/joint venture

This venture is probably too small for an equity investment by a venture capitalist although venture capitalists do provide debt finance and this might be an option. Some form of joint venture with a US-based entity might also be an option.

Recommendation

All the alternatives carry advantages and disadvantages. In these circumstances, there is no obvious preferred type of finance. The decision will rest with the directors' attitudes to risk and control. Their future objectives for the entire entity, not just their overseas expansion plans, should be established and evaluated. Subsequently, a financing, or possibly re-financing, plan should be discussed with the entity's bankers and, if appropriate, its shareholders.

25 GREGORY AND GEORGE (NOV 09 EXAM)

Key answer tips

The first part of the question was a fairly standard rights issue question. The calculations started very simple and progressed until the final part was quite complex. It was important to explain the impact on shareholder wealth rather than just present calculations.

Part (b) asked you to present the advantages to George of the two options. Simply presenting a generic list, with no application to the firm in question, would not have scored well.

(a) (i) Price of new shares after 20% discount to current price of 458 cents is: 366 cents

(= 458 cents × (1 – 20%))

So, the number of new shares required is: 8.0 million (= €29.3 million/3.66)

		€ million
(ii)	40 million shares @ 458 cents	183.20
	8 million shares @ 366 cents	29.28
		€212.48 million

Divide by the number of new shares: €212.48/ (40 + 8) = 4.427

So T.E.R.P. is 443 cents

(iii) Expected trading price for the rights is the T.E.R.P. of 443 cents less the discounted share price of 366 cents

So the expected trading price for the rights is 77 cents each (443 – 366)

(iv) Mr × will be given the right to buy 40,000 discounted shares

(*New shares offered = 8/40 × current holding of 200,000 = 40,000*)

	€000
Current value of holding	
200,000 shares @ 458 cents	916
Do not take up the rights	
200,000 @ T.E.R.P of 443 cents:	886.0
plus payment from underwriters assumed to be	
equivalent to the value of the rights, that is,	
77 cents × 40,000 =	30.8
Total	**916.8**

The difference here is caused by rounding. The wealth of the shareholder theoretically stays constant in this case, since the reduction in value of the shares is offset by the sale proceeds of the rights.

Take up the rights

Shareholding of 240,000 @ 443 cents: 1,063.2

Less cost of buying discounted shares   (146.4)

(366 cents × 40,000):

Total   **916.8**

Again, the change in wealth is only a rounding difference. Theoretically, the wealth of the shareholder should stay constant if the shareholder takes up the rights.

Sell sufficient rights to provide funds to purchase the remaining rights:

Sell Y rights where

77 × Y = 366 (40,000 – Y)

So   Y = (366 × 40,000)/(77 + 366)

= 33,047

and so take up 6,953 rights (40,000 – 33,047)

So new shareholding of 206,953 @ 443 cents: 916.8

The cost of buying the new shares and the proceeds of selling the rights net off to zero, so once again (except for a small rounding difference) the shareholder's wealth stays constant.

Conclusion and discussion of other factors affecting value in practice:

The calculations are all based on theoretical assumptions, such as the existence of a perfect capital market. In the real world, in a semi-strongly efficient capital market, market sentiment and expectation will also have an effect on the share prices. For example, if the company announces a rights issue but investors are not happy that the funds will be put to good use, the share value might fall below the TERP calculated above.

(b)   **Impact on gearing**

Current gearing: 30:100 = 30% (where 100 = 37 – 7 + 70)

Revised gearing: 37:100 = 37%

(where 37 = original debt of 37, equity is now 63 = 70 – 7 and so D + E = 100 = 37 + 63)

This increase in gearing would occur for both the share repurchase and the special dividend. It would be expected to lead to a decrease in the cost of capital if the company is not approaching debt capacity and 37% is still on the downward sloping part of the WACC curve and so does not affect George's choice.

Other factors

Share repurchase

Advantages over special dividend:

- Enhance earnings per share (as fewer shares in circulation)
- Reduce amount of cash needed to pay future dividends
- Investors taxed as capital gains which may be lower than income tax

Special dividend

Advantages over share repurchase:

- Easier and cheaper to arrange (a share repurchase will require payment of a premium)

- No change in the balance of ownership

Note that both methods reduce the likelihood of unwelcome takeover bids (as there is less cash on the balance sheet)

Conclusion

The impact on gearing and hence cost of capital is the same in both cases and so does not affect the choice. However, only the special dividend will meet George's second objective of keeping the balance of ownership the same and so George may prefer to use a special dividend rather than a share repurchase. The final decision will depend on a review of the other factors listed above and their relative importance to the entity and its shareholders. If the shares are held by a few large shareholders, their views also need to be taken into account.

26   CLAUDIA (NOV 09 EXAM)

Key answer tips

WACC and NPV are core syllabus areas, so the numbers in this question should have caused few problems.

Project planning (covered in part (b)) is often neglected by students who prefer to focus on calculations. However, it is frequently tested, so can be a source of easy marks if you have revised the topic carefully.

(a)   WACC   = $k_e \times MV_e/(MV_e + MV_d) + k_d(1-t) \times MV_d/(MV_e + MV_d)$

Workings

k_e	=	6.2%	(as given in the question)
$k_d(1-t)$	=	5.4% × (1 − 0.35)	= 3.51%
MV_e	=	$2.50 × 20 million)	= $50 million
MV_d	=	$33 million	(trading at par so use nominal value)
Hence, WACC	=	(6.2% × 50/83) + (3.51% × 33/83)	
	=	5.13%	

(b)

$000	Time 0	Time 1	Time 2 onwards
Investment	(10,000)		
Pre tax earnings			770
Tax			(269.5)
Net cash flow	(10,000)	0	500.5
DF @ 5.13%	1	0.951	(1/0.513) × 0.951
PV	(10,000)	0	9,278

The project produces a negative NPV of $722,000

(c) Adjust the WACC for the NPV of the project and the additional debt:

k_e	=	6.2%	(unchanged per question)
$k_d(1-t)$	=	3.51%	(unchanged per question)
MV_e	=	$50 million – $0.722 million	= $49.278m
MV_d	=	$33 million + $10 million	= $43 million
$MV_e + MV_d$	=	$92.278 million	
So, WACC	=	$k_e \times MV_e/(MV_e + MV_d) + k_d(1-t) \times MV_d/(MV_e + MV_d)$	
	=	6.2% × 49.278/92.278 + 5.40 (1 – 0.35)% × 43/92.278	
	=	4.95%	

Suitability of the current WACC in project appraisal:

In general, the current WACC should not be used as a discount rate if the new project causes the capital structure and/or the business risk of the entity to change.

Capital structure

The gearing has increased, and the WACC has fallen slightly from 5.13% to 4.95% but there is insufficient change to invalidate the use of the current WACC in the evaluation of the project.

Risk

There is no indication that the project has a different risk profile to that of the business as a whole. Upgrading IT systems is in line with normal business practice for this company and this business sector.

Therefore the current WACC is considered to be a suitable discount rate with which to evaluate this project.

(d) (i) **Assessing customer requirements**

Understanding customer requirements is critical to the success of any project. For a web-based sales system, it is important that the system is perceived as being user friendly and secure, or Claudia may well lose business to competitors. Also, for a system to be used in Asia, where there are many languages, it is important that Claudia incorporates all necessary languages in the system.

A thorough programme of market research is recommended, along with a detailed review of competitors' systems.

For example, perhaps Claudia could use a market survey at the order point – i.e. ask customers for feedback when they place an order through the website.

Also, to enhance the customer experience, it will be important to link the new sales system to other IT systems such as inventory control, billing and distribution. For example, customers could easily be put off if they were allowed to order goods which were not currently in stock.

(ii) **Drawing up an implementation plan**

The first step in drawing up an implementation plan is to timetable key processes and dates. Gantt charts can be used to highlight deadlines for different phases of the project.

The project manager will allocate key tasks to members of the implementation team, and will continually review progress against the plan to ensure there are no overruns on timing.

Also, the project manager will monitor actual costs and revenues against budget and take remedial action to address any problems arising.

Before live running, it is vital that careful testing of the new system is carried out.

If possible, the project manager should arrange for parallel running of the new system before closing the old system.

After implementation, monitoring should continue, to make sure no unexpected problems arise.

27 PIC (MAY 10 EXAM)

Key answer tips

Several different topics were covered in this question, but the main one was working capital management.

Make sure you understand the difference between aggressive and conservative approaches to working capital management.

In part (a)(i), note that the working capital level will be at a maximum when receivables and inventory are at their maximum levels but payables are at their minimum level.

(a) **Calculations**

(i) Total working capital requirements are calculated as follows:

minimum   (1.64 – 14.79 + 17.26)   = A\$ 4.11m

maximum   (3.29 – 7.40 + 29.59)   = A\$ 25.48m

Thus the fluctuating element of net current assets is A\$21.37m (25.48 – 4.11) and the permanent proportion A\$4.11m.

Short and long-term financing requirements would therefore be:

	Aggressive (A$ million)	Conservative (A$ million)
Short-term, financing (e.g. overdraft)	22.19 = (20% × 4.11) + 21.37	17.10 = (80% × 21.37)
Long-term, financing (permanent)	3.29 = (80% × 4.11)	8.38 = (20% × 21.37) + 4.11
Total	25.48	25.48

(ii)   The issue price of the proposed bond on a "Yield to Maturity" basis can be demonstrated using a unit of A$100. The proposed bond will pay A$100, its face value, at the end of 5 years. The formula is:

Annual interest × (annuity factor for t = 5, r = 9%)

+ A$100 × (discount factor for t = 5, r = 9%)

= (A$8 × 3.89) + (A$100 × 0.650)

= 31.12 + 65.00 = 96.12

The issue price of the bond would therefore be A$96.12 per A$100 nominal.

(iii)   Current WACC is calculated as follows:

Type of security	Market Value A$m	Rate of return %	Proportion of total %	Weighted return %
Equity	350.00	10.0	74.5	7.45
Long term debt	100.00	6.5 (= 8.125% × 0.8)	21.3	1.38
Overdraft	20.00	5.6 (= 7% × 0.8)	4.2	0.24
Total	470.00		100%	9.07

The WACC at present is 9.07% assuming the full amount of short term financing is used continuously as suggested by the scenario in the question. If PIC switched to additional long term financing instead of overdraft the cost of equity and the cost of its remaining overdraft might change. However, the overall effect would be minimal. PIC is re-financing a very small proportion of its total capital structure and the difference in the cost of the two methods being considered is very small. Also, how entities finance net current assets does not attract significant market interest unless it is a very large component of its total capital.

(b)   (i)   **Evaluation of proposed change in policy**

The advantages of PIC's current, aggressive policy are:

- It would generally provide the highest expected return. Short-term financing is (generally) cheaper than long term financing due to the compensation required by long-term lenders for loss of liquidity and greater credit risk of longer term finance.

- Even if net current assets fall below expected "permanent" levels, PIC would not be over-financed.

- PIC faces potentially large fluctuations in net current asset levels so it would benefit from the flexibility that an aggressive financing policy provides.

The disadvantages are:

- The policy carries a higher risk of illiquidity unless overdrafts are backed up by committed bank facilities.

- It involves greater management time to manage and renew short-term financing sources.

Other factors that should be considered are:

- PIC's proposed conservative financing policy involves all non-current assets, the "permanent" proportion of net current assets and 20% of fluctuating net current assets being financed by medium to long-term funding. Short-term finance would continue to be used for part of the fluctuating net current assets. There would be a proportionately high cost involved in issuing a relatively small amount of new medium to long-term bonds.

- PIC is currently using supplier credit to finance much of its fluctuating working capital requirements; accounts receivable (credit given to customers) is an average of 15 days whereas accounts payable (credit taken from suppliers) is on average 60 days. This is the norm in retailing but this does not mean there is no cost involved; PIC might be foregoing early payment discounts.

More information is needed on various factors before accurate advice can be provided on whether it should change its current policy. The main factors to consider are:

- The availability of increased overdraft – PIC currently has a facility of A$20 million but may breach that limit in the current year and needs up to A$22 million if the financing policy is not changed.

- The future cost of overdraft financing.

- The method and interest rate receivable from investing short term cash surpluses.

- More frequent patterns of net current assets levels should be analysed throughout the year. At a minimum these should be forecast monthly but weekly or even daily would be appropriate for a large retailing entity.

(ii)   Alternative approaches to financing net current assets that PIC should consider

Moderate policy – somewhere in between the two extremes of aggressive and conservative. This policy matches the short-term finance to the fluctuating net current assets, and the medium to long-term finance to the permanent part of net current assets plus non-current assets.

Financing methods that are only relevant to receivables:

- Factoring should be considered – where a bank or other financial institution takes over the collection of accounts receivable and pays PIC a discounted value up-front. A bank could offer important additional services such as credit checking and approval of new customers wishing to make use of this credit facility.

- Invoice discounting or other similar type of securitized short-term debt should also be considered. This has the advantage of maintaining a direct relationship between the company and the customer when collecting debts due.

Tutorial note

Other long term methods such as equity or complicated bonds (for example, debt with warrants) are not suitable here.

28 CIP (MAY 10 EXAM)

Key answer tips

An understanding of different types of risk is critical to success in this paper. The definitions and diagram in part (a) should have been very straightforward book work.

The calculation of ungeared/geared betas in part (b) is also a vitally important topic which is covered very frequently in the exam.

(a) **Systematic and unsystematic risk**

Risk that cannot be diversified away is called systematic risk. This risk is due to economic factors which affect the economy as a whole (such as interest rates, recession etc.). Risk that can be reduced by diversifying the securities in a portfolio is unsystematic risk. This risk relates to factors which are unique to a company or of the industry in which it operates.

Total risk is the combination of systematic and non-systematic risk. The total risk of a share can be measured by its standard deviation. Systematic risk of a share is measured by its equity beta.

Beta is the measurement of systematic risk estimated by considering the volatility of an individual share price movement against the movement in the market as a whole. This is usually undertaken by plotting on a graph movements over time of the individual share price on the vertical axis against movements in the market over the same time period on the horizontal axis. Regression analysis is used to estimate the slope of the line, which is then referred to as beta.

An entity with an equity beta greater than 1 would be expected to have systematic risk proportionately greater than the risk of the market. Conversely an equity beta which is less than 1 would suggest systematic risk for that company proportionately less than the risk of the market. However, to use betas it is necessary to assume that betas calculated on the basis of historic information are reliable indicators of current and future risks.

The following diagram illustrates the difference between unsystematic and systematic risk, showing how unsystematic risk can be diversified away but systematic risk will remain even in a fully diversified portfolio.

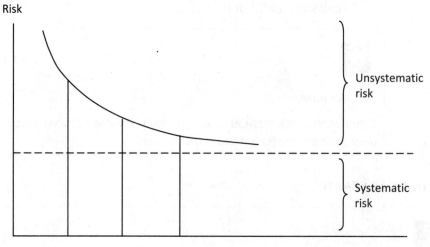

(b)   **Calculations of beta and discount rates**

Investment 1 (proxy company A)

$$\beta_u = \beta_g \left[\frac{V_E}{V_E + V_D(1-t)} \right] + \beta_d \left[\frac{V_D(1-t)}{V_E + V_D(1-t)} \right]$$

$$= \left[1.3 \times \frac{3}{3 + 1(1-0.25)} \right] + \left[0.3 \times \frac{1(1-0.25)}{3 + 1(1-0.25)} \right] = 1.1$$

Now regear this ungeared beta to reflect gearing of 60% E and 40% D (debt beta is zero – debt is risk free)

$$1.1 = \beta_g \times \frac{60}{60 + 40(1-0.25)}$$

So ß$_g$ = 1.65

Now, using CAPM,

$$k_e = R_f + [R_m - R_f]\beta$$

$$= 3\% + (8\% - 3\%) \times 1.65 = 11.25\%$$

So the risk adjusted WACC would be

$$WACC = k_e \left[\frac{V_E}{V_E + V_D} \right] + k_d(1-t) \left[\frac{V_D}{V_E + V_D} \right]$$

$$= \left[11.25\% \times \frac{60}{100} \right] + \left[3\%(1-0.25) \times \frac{40}{100} \right] = 7.65\%$$

Tutorial note

An alternative way of deriving this 7.65% would have been to use the ungeared beta (1.1) in CAPM to give a keu of 8.5%, and then to use the M+M equation

$$k_{adj} = k_{eu}[1 - tL]$$

to give 8.5%[1−(0.25 × 40/100)] = 7.65%

Investment 2 (proxy company B)

$$\beta_u = \beta_g \left[\frac{V_E}{V_E + V_D(1-t)} \right] + \beta_d \left[\frac{V_D(1-t)}{V_E + V_D(1-t)} \right]$$

$$= \left[0.9 \times \frac{6}{6 + 1(1-0.25)} \right] + \left[0 \times \frac{1(1-0.25)}{6 + 1(1-0.25)} \right] = 0.8$$

Now regear this ungeared beta to reflect gearing of 60% E and 40% D (debt beta is zero – debt is risk free)

$$0.8 = \beta_g \times \frac{60}{60 + 40(1-0.25)}$$

So β_g = 1.2

Now, using CAPM,

$$k_e = R_f + [R_m - R_f]\beta$$

= 3% + (8% – 3%) × 1.2 = 9%

So the risk adjusted WACC would be

$$WACC = k_e \left[\frac{V_E}{V_E + V_D} \right] + k_d(1-t) \left[\frac{V_D}{V_E + V_D} \right]$$

$$= \left[9\% \times \frac{60}{100} \right] + \left[3\%(1-0.25) \times \frac{40}{100} \right] = 6.3\%$$

Tutorial note

An alternative way of deriving this 6.3% would have been to use the ungeared beta (0.8) in CAPM to give a keu of 7%, and then to use the M+M equation

$$k_{adj} = k_{eu}[1 - tL]$$

to give 7%[1–(0.25 × 40/100)] = 6.3%

The appropriateness of these rates is discussed further in the answer to part (d).

(c) **Benefits and limitations of possible discount rates**

WACC

Using an estimated WACC is a practical expedient for many companies and understood by many non-finance people. The argument against using the WACC would be (a) theory does not support using WACC for investment appraisal other than in very specific circumstances (equivalent risk to the company as a whole and financed in the same proportions), and (b) here it is estimated – how is not explained but unlikely to be based on a theoretically correct formula (for example CAPM).

Adjusted WACC

These are not theoretically acceptable and suffer from the same problems as the basic WACC. However, as with WACC, they are easily understood by non-finance people and provide a good rule of thumb and at least attempt to reflect in a rough and ready manner the risk of the specific investment against the average investment.

CAPM-derived rates

This is a theoretically acceptable method of determining a discount rate but it has major limitations in the circumstances here:

- CAPM is a single period model, which is being used to calculate a discount rate for, presumably, a number of years. The risk of the investments could well change over their lives.

- It is based on historical data and the variance surrounding beta is large; using the CAPM at all can only provide a rough estimate. It also assumes that past variability with the market will continue.

- CAPM assumes only systematic risk needs to be captured as unsystematic risk has been diversified away. This might not be true in a single, relatively small private company with few shareholders, whereas the proxies are listed companies with, presumably, a large number of unconnected shareholders.

- Comparisons with proxy companies are difficult as they assume close similarity of activities and business risk. No two companies are *exactly* alike and even if the activities seem similar their operations could be quite different in terms of business risk.

(d) **Explanation of asset and equity betas, investment appraisal and objectives**

An equity beta includes the effects of a company's gearing. Therefore, when using a proxy beta of another company, it is important to strip out the effects of gearing which relate to the proxy company's capital structure.

The asset beta is the ungeared beta with the effects of gearing risk removed. It reflects just the underlying systematic business risk of the company.

The asset beta should be used as a starting point in the investment appraisal process, since it reflects just the business risk of the investment.

Then, either:

1   the finance (gearing) risk associated with a new investment decision can be incorporated using the Adjusted Present Value method, after first discounting the project cashflows using a discount rate derived by putting the asset beta into the CAPM equation.

2   the finance risk of the company can be adjusted for by regearing the asset beta to reflect the company's existing gearing position. A risk adjusted WACC, using a cost of equity based on this geared (equity) beta can then be used for discounting.

The key determinant of which method to use is whether the gearing of the company will change when undertaking the new project. If so, the APV method (method 1 above) should be used.

CAPM can help CIP to achieve its financial goals by allowing the firm to set a cost of capital that more accurately reflects the business risks it faces and then by allowing it to work out an appropriate cost of capital.

This will reflect the amount of risk that the firm is exposed to and help it make decisions on projects that comply with their financial objectives to maximise the wealth of the shareholders.

29   TM (MAR 11 EXAM)

Key answer tips – extracted from the Examiner's "Post Exam Guide"

In part (a) candidates should calculate export sales in the 1st quarter as a base line figure then calculate expected sales in the 2nd quarter assuming they are one third higher. Export sales in the 2nd quarter should then be calculated assuming two different exchange rates.

In part (b) candidates should present and/or calculate the base figures on which the components of the operating cycle for quarter 1 and quarter 2 will be calculated. The various components and the operating cycle for the two quarters can then be calculated. Brief comments should then be provided on the figures obtained. The discussion should analyse the figures rather than simply comment on numbers.

In part (c) candidates should identify the key issues of an appropriate financing structure for working capital and the benefits of financing in a foreign currency and then advise on each key issue in turn.

(a) Export sales in the first quarter of 20X1 are forecast at A$ 1,725,000 (= 30% × A$ 5,750,000).

This is equivalent to EUR 690,000 (= A$ 1,725,000 × 0.4000).

Export sales in the second quarter of 20X1 are expected to be one-third higher, that is, EUR 920,000 (= EUR 690,000 × 4/3).

Sales of EUR 920,000 are worth:

- A$2,300,000 at A$/EUR0.4000 (920,000/0.4000)

- A$2,000,000 at A$/EUR0.4600 (920,000/0.4600).

The difference in revenue due solely to exchange rate movements is therefore A$300,000 (which equates to 4.7% of the total revenue of A$ 6.325 million).

Given that credit terms would now be 90 days this means that all of this change in revenue would impact on accounts receivable.

(b) (i) **Calculation of operating cycle**

Days Inventory of raw materials:

Raw materials/Purchases × 365	63.7	(1,500/2,150 × 4) × 365	66.0	(1,700/2,350 × 4) × 365

Less finance from suppliers:

Accounts payable/ Purchases × 365	−76.4	(1,800/2,150 × 4) × 365	−101.0	(2,600/2,350 × 4) × 365
	−12.7		−35.0	

Days Production time

Work-in-progress/Cost of Goods Sold × 365	21.3	(740/3,163 × 4) × 365	22.2	(860/3,529 × 4) × 365
Finished goods/Cost of Goods Sold × 365	12.1	(420/3,163 × 4) × 365	12.9	(500/3,529 × 4) × 365

Days credit given to customers

Accounts Receivable/Revenue on credit × 365	79.3	(5,000/5,750 × 4) × 365	101.0	(7,000/6,325 × 4) × 365

Total operating cycle (Days)	100.0		101.1	

Examiner's note

Other relevant ratios and calculations were given credit as appropriate.

If the A$/EUR exchange rate were to move to 0.4600, revenue would be A$ 300,000 less at A$ 6,025,000. Accounts receivable would also be A$ 300,000 less at A$ 6,700,000. Receivables days would therefore be only marginally higher at 101.5 (6,700/(6,025 × 4) × 365). There would there be no significant change to the operating cycle which would change from 101.1 days to 101.6 days.

(ii) The operating cycle's *total* days has not changed as dramatically as might be expected; from a forecast of 100.0 days in the first quarter to a forecast of 101.1 days in the second quarter. However, two components have changed substantially and more or less cancel each other out.

We would expect accounts receivable days to increase given the change in terms for export sales. We know that the change in terms means that export customers will have an extra 30 days to pay and hence given that for the second quarter of 20X1 export sales are expected to account for approximately 36% of total sales, then we would only expect an increase of approximately 11 days overall. However, accounts receivable days are being forecast to increase from 79.3 to 101.0 days, a rise of approximately 22 days, thus indicating that a potential worsening in customers' ability to pay is being forecast.

The other component to change considerably is accounts payable days which have increased from 76.4 to 101.0, indicating that the increase in accounts receivable days is being financed almost entirely by TM's suppliers. This might be by agreement with suppliers but is unlikely. In any case, it might mean TM foregoing discounts and supplier goodwill.

Credit policy in general should be reviewed in an attempt to prevent customers taking longer to pay than agreed. TM could consider early payment discounts or charging interest on overdue accounts, although both these methods can be difficult to implement, administer and enforce.

All components of days production time have increased, although not substantially. However, the increases should be investigated. Given the concerns noted above, efforts should be made to reduce all three components for example by reviewing production methods, suppliers and suppliers' terms of trade.

(c) The operating cycle is only the time span between production costs and cash returns; it says nothing in itself about the amount of net current assets that will be needed over this period. TM seems to be following an aggressive financing policy, financing all of its net current assets (including permanent and fluctuating elements) with short term debt in the form of an overdraft. This policy generally provides the highest expected return (because short-term debt costs are typically less than long-term costs) but it is very risky. TM should consider a more moderate policy by financing part of its net current assets with medium or long term debt. As the need for more finance is caused by an increase in export sales, TM might consider arranging a medium term borrowing denominated in euro. There would be no need to raise such a borrowing in a foreign country in the euro zone as euro finance is likely to be readily available in TM's home country.

The main benefit of financing overseas investment or expansion with finance raised in the same country is currency matching. A loan in a major world currency such as the euro should not be difficult to raise as there will be an active and ready market in the currency. With euro borrowings, some of the receipts from sales in euro can be used to service the debt. However, aspects to consider are:

- Borrowing in euro is a relatively inflexible approach to hedging currency exposure arising on accounts receivable as it cannot be readily adjusted (without incurring costs) to reflect constantly changing levels of euro denominated accounts receivables.

- Using euro finance only hedges exposure on accounts receivable. The impact on operating profit is likely to be of more importance to TM. Forward contracts are a more appropriate tool to hedge euro cash inflows. If these are used to cover the period up to expected settlement of the amount due, the translation exposure arising on euro accounts receivables will already have been hedged within this approach and euro denominated finance for a portion of net current assets would no longer be appropriate.

Tutorial note – extracted from the Examiner's "Post Exam Guide"

There was some confusion over the required adjustment for exchange rate movements but otherwise the calculations were generally well answered, although it was disappointing that so many candidates failed to recognise that the revenue, cost of sales and purchases figures were given for a 3 month period rather than a year.

There were more problems with the requirement to advise on an appropriate financing structure and explain the benefits and potential problems arising from the choice of euro finance in part (c).

Candidates were expected to recognise that TM was following an aggressive financing policy and to consider the pros and cons of such a policy. A general discussion of financing policies in general without application to TM was not sufficient. Discussion on the use of euro finance tended to be limited to the principle of matching euro cash flows. Consideration of the benefits and limitations of euro finance in terms of managing currency risk was often overlooked.

---

30 RED (MAR 11 EXAM)

Key answer tips – extracted from the Examiner's "Post Exam Guide"

In part (a), firstly compare and contrast the key features of the two methods of raising debt finance under consideration. Then consider the appropriateness of each for RED and conclude with advice on which to choose.

In part (b)(i), explain each of the three forms of EMH in turn and explain which is most likely in practice.

In part (b)(ii), identify key issues and then present each in turn in short, clear paragraphs. Don't forget to include reference to the relevance of the efficient market hypothesis.

(a) **Private placing**

Under a private placing the bond units would not be offered to the public. Instead an issuing house – typically a stockbroker – will arrange for the bonds to be "placed" at an agreed price with institutional clients. A private placing of bonds is quicker and cheaper to arrange than an offer for sale and to some extent less risky as usually the issuing house will be fairly certain its clients will subscribe to the issue before agreeing to a placing.

Public issue

In a public issue, an issuing house – typically a merchant bank – will acquire the bonds and offer them to the public, usually at a fixed price (as compared with tender offers). The offers are usually announced by way of an abbreviated prospectus in a financial newspaper or journal. The main issuing house may involve underwriters if they are unsure of the success rate of the offer.

Other features of offers for sale/public issue are:

- Offers that are oversubscribed may be scaled down on a pre-determined basis.

- Some subscribers may buy simply to re-sell quickly and make a short-term profit, although this is more likely with ordinary shares than bonds.

Advantages of a private placing for RED

- Marketability. A key difference is whether RED and its advisors think there is a ready market for the bonds. Being a private company, the company may not be well enough known for a public issue to succeed in attracting sufficient investors.

- Cost. Private placing is almost certain to be cheaper as there will be no costs of underwriting and this method also largely avoids the cost of extensive 'road shows' to publicise the issue.

- Speed. A private placing is also likely to be completed faster than a public issue for the same reason.

Advantages of a public issue for RED

- Publicity ahead of the IPO. A public issue and accompanying road show would raise the company in the public awareness and therefore help prepare for a successful IPO later in the year.

Conclusion

I would advise that a private placing is used by RED for the issue of the bonds as this is likely to be more successful for an unlisted company than a public issue and would also be a useful first step in helping to raise the market profile of the company in the run up to the planned IPO.

(b) (i) Explanation of the weak, semi-strong and strong forms of the EMH:

Weak form

- EMH in its weak form states that the current share price reflects all the information that could be gleaned from a study of past share prices.

- Therefore no investor can earn above-average returns by developing trading rules based on historical price or return information.

Semi-strong form

- The semi-strong form of the EMH says that the current share price will not only reflect all historical information, but will also reflect all other published information.

- Therefore no investor can be expected to earn above-average returns from trading rules based on any publicly available information.

Strong form

- The strong form of the EMH says that the current share price incorporates all information, including non-published information. This would include insider information and views held by the directors of the entity.

- Therefore people with inside knowledge of the company could not make a profit by using this information; however, this is 'insider trading' and is illegal in many countries and so this form of the theory is difficult to test.

The academic consensus is that the semi-strong form is the most likely to occur in practice.

(ii) The success of the IPO can be improved by:

- An appropriate choice of issue price. To be attractive, this should be slightly below the perceived market value, although there is a risk of under-pricing the offer as current shareholders would then lose out.

- Underwriting (at a significant cost).

- Careful choice of timing in terms of the new product development cycle (i.e.: to ensure that the new product is developed sufficiently, patents obtained, market research available etc).

- Choice of timing in terms of market conditions (to help ensure there is sufficient interest in equity investments in general at the time of the issue).

- Careful/planned communication to prospective investors.

A high share price after issue can be assured by:

- Positive financial performance.

- Publicising that positive financial performance to the market by careful management of share information released to the public (e.g. profit forecasts, quarterly and annual financial statements, information provided in press releases) so that the market can respond in an appropriate manner to this information and, under the semi-strong form of the efficient market, reflect this information in the share price of the company.

Tutorial note – extracted from the Examiner's "Post Exam Guide"

There was a widespread lack of understanding of the process of issuing bonds by private placement and the important factors behind a successful IPO. The minority of candidates who were well versed in this subject area generally achieved high marks in this question.

Common errors in part (a):

- *Presentation of the features of an IPO versus a private placement of shares rather than bond issues.*

- *Lack of understanding that a private issue of bonds would not change ownership control.*

Common errors in part (b):

- *Lack of precision in defining the three forms of the efficient market hypothesis or confusion about the differences between them. In particular many candidates failed to recognise that EMH relates to the impact of information on share prices rather than just the availability of information.*

- *Discussion of dividend policy and dividend signalling – neither of which was relevant in the context of this scenario.*

- *A focus solely on publicity to the detriment of other factors.*

31 DCD (NOV 11 EXAM)

Key answer tips – extracted from the Examiner's "Post Exam Guide"

Part (a)(i)

Calculate conversion terms using discount rates of 25% and 40%

Part (a)(ii)

Calculate yield adjusted theoretical ex-rights price at discount rates of 25% and 40%

Part (b)

Calculate:

- Value before rights issue

- Number of new shares after rights issue

- Value of shareholding after rights issue at both 25% and 40% discount rate and after deducting capital cost of buying new shares

---

Part (c)

Address the concerns of each of the three directors, relating your comments to the calculations provided in part (b). Recommend an appropriate discount rate.

Part (d)

Advise the directors, noting in particular:

- Efficiency of the market

- Market assessment of project v the company's evaluation of the project's benefits

- Market support for rights issue

- Other information re the company that has become public

- General market price movements

(a)　(i)　**Terms of the rights issue**

	Suggested rights issue price	Terms of share issue required (see working)	Funds raised	Totals
25% discount	$4.5	2 for 5	$252m	196
40% discount	$3.6	1 for 2	$252m	210

Workings:

At 25% discount

Number of shares to be issued is $250m/$4.5 = 55.6m rounded to 56m.

This gives terms of 56m/140m = 0.4 to 1 or 2 for 5 and funds raised of 56m × $4.5 = $252m

At 40% discount

Number of shares to be issued $250m/$3.6 = 69.4m round to 70m.

This gives terms of 0.5 to 1 or 1 for 2 and funds raised of 70m × $3.6 = $252m

(ii)　**Yield adjusted TERP calculation**

		Number of shares	Total value of shares ($)	Value per share ($)
At 25% discount	2 new shares at $4.50 × 20/15	2	12.00	
	5 old shares at $6.00	5	30.00	
	Total	7	42.00	6.00
	So yield adjusted TERP =	$6.00		
At 40% discount	1 new share at $3.60 × 20/15	1	4.80	
	2 old shares at $6.00	2	12.00	
	Total	3	16.80	5.60
	So yield adjusted TERP =	$5.60		

(b) Assume a shareholder has 100 shares in DCD:

		$
Before rights issue		
Value of shareholding before rights issue (100 × $6.00):		600

		$
After rights issue at 25% discount		
Existing share value	100 × $6.00	600
New shares	40 × $6.00	240
		840
Less capital to buy shares	40 × $4.50	(180)
Value of shareholding after rights issue:		660

		$
After rights issue at 40% discount		
Existing share value	100 × $5.60	560
New shares	50 × $5.60	280
		840
Less capital to buy shares	50 × $3.60	(180)
Value of shareholding after rights issue:		660

(c) The concerns of Director A seem to be valid as the higher discount of 40% results in the yield adjusted TERP of $5.60 falling below the current market price of $6.00 whilst the current market price would be maintained using the lower discount of 25%. This is because at a 25% discount the impact of this discount on new shares would be exactly offset by the greater return projected from the new investment. However, as demonstrated in part (b) theoretically the level of discount makes no difference to shareholder value.

The point made by Director B has no validity in theory. A higher discount would require a larger number of rights to be issued. The total new investment required from each investor would be identical whichever discount rate is chosen and therefore have no impact on the extent of take up of the offer. However, in practice, a high discount rate can give the impression that the new shares are priced at a bargain level and take up can be higher. This also has implications for underwriting costs that can be lower if rights are issued at higher discount rates.

Director C is also correct in that the choice of discount will impact on the dividend payable per share because it will affect the number of shares in issue. However, the level of discount should have no impact on the total dividend paid to each shareholder (before considering issue costs – see below).

The cost of underwriting the rights issue may also be relevant to the choice of discount. On average this would be expected to be $5.04m (2% of $252m) but the agreed cost will depend on the terms of the issue and the level of discount. A higher discount may result in lower underwriting costs as the risk of the rights issue failing should be lower.

It is recommended that a discount of 25% is used since this avoids a fall in the share price assuming that project returns are achieved as forecast and may allow the company to continue with a more stable dividend policy.

(d) The extent to which the share price is affected immediately before and in the 12 months following the announcement of the investment and the rights issue, will depend upon many factors including:

- The efficiency of the market.

- To what extent the market agrees with the company evaluation of project benefits.

- The degree to which the market supports the rights issue.

The efficient market hypothesis states that if a market is semi strong then it will react immediately to information as it is made public. A market in weak form means that the share price will react very slowly to new information and a market in strong form means that the share price will already reflect all information whether publicly or privately available. It is generally believed that markets are of a semi-strong form.

The share price has increased by 11% in the past three months which could be due to many factors including general market confidence, the release of good results or speculation that an investment needs to be made. Some information concerning the investment may have already leaked into the public domain and be reflected in the share price. The extent to which the share price moves after the announcement depends on the extent to which the impact of the investment has already been anticipated correctly. In the 12 months following the announcement further information about the project will be made publicly available and share prices should adjust to reflect this new information.

There may also be speculation about a potential rights issue and share prices may fall if there are any doubts about whether it will be fully subscribed.

Tutorial note – extracted from the Examiner's "Post Exam Guide"

In part (a) many candidates failed to understand the concept of a yield adjusted TERP. Those who did attempt it often used an incorrect basis for the adjustment.

In part (c), candidates' discussions of the directors' views on the impact or implications of the two discount rates proposed were often confused and frequently ignored the calculations attempted in part (b).

Part (d) was left unanswered by a sizeable minority of candidates. Those who did attempt it tended to answer satisfactorily and address the key issues of market efficiency and market sentiment.

On the whole, technical knowledge of rights issues was poor.

32   CBA (MAR 12 EXAM)

Key answer tips – extracted from the Examiner's "Post Exam Guide" (note that the comments regarding WORD and/or EXCEL only relate to the COMPUTER BASED papers in March and September each year)

The approach to part (a) should be to follow the requirements in order and firstly calculate the conversion premium for the convertible bond based on the expected share price in four years' time and the conversion ratio. The cost of debt calculation first requires the scheduling of the bond's cash flows, these being the initial proceeds of issue adjusted for the discount, the interest cash flow adjusted for tax relief and the conversion premium in four years' time from part (a)(i). A standard IRR approach should then be applied to these cash flows, preferably using the IRR function within EXCEL. To complete the WACC calculation it is first necessary to calculate the cost of equity using the dividend valuation model and the cost of preference shares using the irredeemable debt formula (remember not to adjust for taxation on the dividend). Total market values for equity, preference shares and convertible debt then need to be calculated and put into the WACC formula.

In part (b) the benefits and limitations of convertible debt over a new issue of equity should be discussed, taking care to keep the answer focussed on only these types of finance rather than a general discussion of debt versus equity or convertible debt versus other debt. Part (c) requires answers to be specific to the treasury role in evaluating and implementing the bond.

(a)   (i)   **Premium on conversion:**

Share price now = GBP3.60

Share price in 4 years' time = GBP4.54 (GBP3.60 × 1.06^4)

Forecast conversion value = GBP104.42 (23 × GBP4.54)

(ii)

Year		Cash Flow	DF@7%	DCF	DF@5%	DCF
0	Loan capital	−93.00	1.000	−93.00	1.000	−93.00
1 – 4	Annual Interest	3.00 (0.70)	3.387	7.11	3.546	7.45
4	Capital Redemption	104.42	0.763	79.67	0.823	85.94
Totals				−6.22		0.39

Post tax Kd by interpolation = 5% + 2% [0.39/(0.39+6.22)] = 5.12%

Note: the result will be slightly different depending on the two rates chosen. Here, the NPV at 5% is fairly close to zero so in practice no further calculations would be necessary.

(iii)   **Calculation of WACC**

$$\text{WACC} = \left[k_{eg} \times \frac{E}{D+E+P} \right] + \left[k_d(1-t)\frac{D}{D+E+P} \right] + \left[k_p \times \frac{P}{D+E+P} \right]$$

This is most easily calculated in columnar form as follows:

	Market value GBP m (MV)	Cost of capital (k)	MV × k GBPm
Ordinary shares	1,008	11.56%	116.52
Preference shares	205	5.71%	11.71
Debt	250	5.12%	12.80
TOTAL	1,463		141.03

So WACC is GBP 141.03m/GBP 1,463m = 9.64%

Workings for cost of capital:

Calculation of ke

Formula for cost of equity for a company with constant growth and recently paid dividend is

$$Ke = \frac{d1}{po} + g$$

D1 = (GBP 0.45 × 50% × 1.05) = GBP 0.23625 per share

Ke = (GBP 0.23625/GBP 3.60) + 0.05 = 0.1156 i.e.: 11.56%

Calculation of kp

K_p = (GBP 0.06/GBP 1.05) = 0.0571, i.e.: 5.71%

K_d was calculated earlier.

Workings for market values

Ordinary shares   GBP 1,008m = 280m × GBP 3.60

Preference shares   GBP 205m = GBP 195m × GBP (1.05/1.00)

Debt   Equal to the amount to be raised of GBP 250m

(b)   **Benefits (to CBA) of convertible bond over equity**

- All forms of debt would normally be cheaper than equity for the company because interest carries tax relief, dividends do not. Also, debt is (usually) less risky than equity for the providers of finance and therefore the return required by a debt provider will be less than that for an equity provider.

- There is no immediate dilution of earnings if debt is issued, although debt interest has to be paid before equity dividends are declared and paid. Dilution would occur on conversion but the logic of a convertible bond would be that the money invested would increase earnings to the level where there would be sufficient to pay old and new shareholders without reducing EPS or DPS.

- Costs of issue are likely to be lower with convertible debt than a new issue of equity. It is also likely to be quicker to arrange, although convertible debt might take longer than straight debt.

- Assuming preference shares are classed with debt, gearing is currently low at 17% prior to the issue of the convertible debt. CBA is thus taking no advantage of the tax relief available on any interest payments. In addition given that gearing is so low it is likely that the WACC calculated in part (a) will be lower than the WACC prior to the investments and new finance. This is because it is likely that the effect of the lower cost of debt will outweigh the impact of any increase in the cost of equity as a result of adding debt into the capital structure.

Disadvantages of convertible debt over equity

- Interest has to be paid otherwise the company could be put into liquidation. This is the risk of all forms of debt over equity.

- At high levels of debt the gearing level might rise to an unacceptable level for equity holders, increasing the cost of equity and the overall WACC. This does not seem to be an issue for CBA as gearing is relatively low at present at 17%. If debt is issued this would rise to 31%, still not unreasonable. This gearing would reduce once conversion started to take place, all other things being equal.

Overall evaluation

There is insufficient information in the scenario about economic and market factors and the business risk of CBA to make a full evaluation and recommendation. However, CBA is fairly lowly geared at present and an issue of debt would be unlikely to significantly increase the cost of equity. Assuming investor reaction to an issue of convertible debt is positive then this would appear the most attractive option.

(c) Treasury is likely to be involved in:

- Determining conversion ratio(s) and coupon interest rate on the instrument.

- Managing the relationship with the investment bank or issuing house supporting the bond issue.

- Calculating costs of capital and ensuring that new debt will not adversely affect the value of the company. Ensuring earnings are sufficient to cover interest payments and maintain dividend levels to preference and ordinary shareholders.

- Preparing all paperwork and a timetable for the issue.

Tutorial note – extracted from the Examiner's "Post Exam Guide"

It was disappointing that only a minority of candidates did well in part (a) for this question, given that the calculations required were relatively straightforward. The main errors in the calculations in part (a) were:

- *Failure to calculate the conversion premium – seemingly from a lack of knowledge.*

- *Not using an IRR approach to calculate the cost of the convertible debt.*

- *Even where an IRR approach was adopted the convertible debt cash flows were not always correctly identified e.g.: failure to adjust for the discount on the issue of the bond and failure to adjust for tax relief on the interest cash flow.*

- Calculating the cost of preference shares as the coupon rate rather than adjusting for market value.

- Adjusting for tax relief with the cost of preference share calculation.

- Basing the cost of equity calculation on earnings rather than dividend and not adjusting for growth in dividend.

Part (b) was reasonably well answered – although some candidates did make irrelevant points about convertible debt versus straight debt despite the fact that the question only asked for a comparison of convertible debt and new equity. It is important that candidates read the requirements carefully as credit will only be given for answers that focus on the requirement.

Part (c) again was reasonably well answered – candidates seem well prepared for questions concerning the treasury function.

33 FF (MAY 12 EXAM)

Key answer tips – extracted from the Examiner's "Post Exam Guide"

Part (a)(i)

Calculate the value of FF using each of funding structures A, B and C recognising that MM's formula is required for B and C.

Part (a)(ii)

Calculate the WACC for each of funding structures A, B and C recognising that MM's formula is required for B and C.

Part (b)

Explain the results of your calculations

Provide two graphs; one showing that, according to MM, value increases at different levels of borrowing, the other showing that WACC decreases as gearing increases.

Part (c)

Provide advice about which financing structure maximises shareholder wealth

Briefly explain the limitations of MM's theory

(a)　**Summary**

	A	B	C
Total F$ value	F$ 440 million	F$460 million	F$448 million
WACC	9%	8.61%	8.84%

(i)　**Workings:**

Funding structure A

Entity Value = Original shareholder value + F$110 million value of the project

= F$11 × 30 million shares + F$110 million = F$440 million

Funding structure B

Entity Value (D + E) = V_u + TB = F$460 million

(= F$440 million + (0.25 × F$ 80 million))

Funding structure C

Entity Value (D + E) = V_u +TB = F$448 million

(= F$440 million + (0.25 × F$32 million))

(ii) **WACC:**

Funding structure A

WACC = k_{eu} = 9%

Funding structure B

WACC = $k_{eu}(1 - tL)$ = 9% × (1 − (0.25 × 80/460)) = 8.61%

Funding structure C

WACC = $k_{eu}(1 - tL)$ = 9% × (1 − (0.25 × 32/448)) = 8.84%

(b)

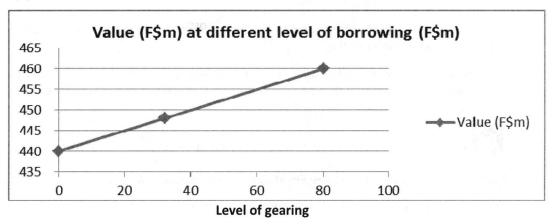

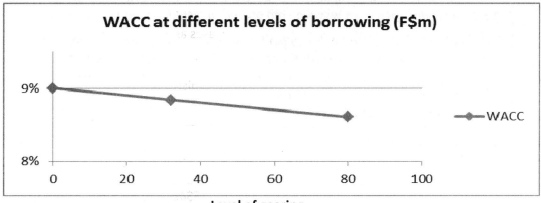

Under MM (with tax), increasing gearing increases the value of the company due to the tax relief available on debt and nothing else. Given that the value of the debt is determinable then the increase in value associated with the tax shield on the debt will flow to the equity providers and hence increase shareholder wealth.

Also, by introducing debt finance, the overall (weighted average) cost of capital falls. This is because the increasing cost of equity resulting from the additional debt being taken on is more than off-set by the impact of the tax shield on that debt.

(c)   I would advise that FF proceed with funding structure B as it gives the greatest value of shareholder wealth value without creating significant danger of financial distress due to the low gearing level created.

The value of FF and hence also shareholder wealth (since the value of debt remains constant) is increased largely due to the tax benefit in perpetuity that arises from the use of debt financing.

MM's theory based on a number of assumptions which do not necessarily hold in practice. These assumptions include:

- MM ignores the impact of financial distress at very high levels of gearing which will push up the cost of equity (and usually the cost of debt) to such an extent that the WACC will increase.

- MM is also based on unrealistic assumptions about perfect capital markets and perfect information.

However, these considerations are not important here as the level of debt being considered is quite small, being just approximately 20% of the value of the company.

Tutorial note – extracted from the Examiner's "Post Exam Guide"

This was not a popular question; presumably the combination of MM and graphs was too daunting. Many candidates appeared to choose this question as a "make weight". However, those who understood what was required tended to gain good marks.

Few candidates could adequately explain MM's capital theory although most recognised the influence of the tax shield on WACC and firm value if financing is with debt. The graphs, when attempted at all, were generally poor and some candidates provided a graph showing the direction of costs of capital using the traditional theory rather than MM's.

---

34   KK (MAY 12 EXAM)

Key answer tips – extracted from the Examiner's "Post Exam Guide"

Part (a)(i)

Calculate the value of: accounts receivable; accounts payable; and inventory if working capital days had remained unchanged,

Calculate what the overdraft would have been.

Part (a)(ii)

Calculate profit margin

Calculate working capital cycles

Discuss the key pressures on the components of working capital

Ensure the answer refers to KK

Part (a)(iii)

Provide recommendations for reducing funds tied up in working capital

(Note – no discussion of the financing of WC is required)

Part (b)

Discuss key factors to assess credit worthiness as shown in the marking guide.

(a)   (i)   If working capital days had remained at the level of 31 October 2011 in the six month period to 30 April 2012, we would have expected accounts receivable, accounts payable and inventory days as follows on 30 April 2012:

The accounts receivable balance would have been EUR 6.4 million (= (92 days × EUR 12.6 million) divided by the number of days in six months, i.e.: 182.5 days).

The accounts payable balance would have been EUR 3.6 million (= (69 days × EUR 9.6 million) divided by 182.5 days.

The inventory balance would have been EUR 5.3 million (= (100 days × EUR 9.6 million) divided by 182.5 days.

Therefore, the total investment in working capital at 30 April 2012 would have been EUR 8.1 million (= EUR (6.4 +5.3 – 3.6) million), compared to EUR 9.5 million (= EUR (7.1 + 5.6 – 3.2) million). This represents a difference of EUR 1.4 million and would have meant an overdraft balance as at 30 April 2012 of EUR 7.1 million rather than EUR 8.5 million.

(ii)   In times of rapid expansion most businesses will face specific pressures on each of the elements of working capital (that is inventories, accounts receivable and accounts payable) and also on profit margins. Each of these is considered in more detail below.

Inventory

KK's inventory has increased from EUR 3.9 million on 31 October 2011 to EUR 5.6 million on 30 April 2012. Even without an increase in inventory days, KK would have required EUR 5.3 million of inventories on 30 April 2012, an increase of EUR 1.4 million from 31 October 2011 levels.

The greater the number of different products manufactured and sold the greater the burden on the inventory management systems. In the case of KK the expansion is as a result of new products and so a significant investment in inventories will be required in order to support the increase in sales.

Accounts receivable

KK's accounts receivable balance has increased from EUR 4.8 million on 31 October 2011 to EUR 7.1 million on 30 April 2012. Even without an increase in accounts receivable days, the 30 April 2012 balance would have been expected to be EUR 6.4 million, an increase of EUR 1.6 million on 31 October 2011 levels.

With the launch of new products, KK is likely to have new business from both new and existing customers. Where additional revenue is from existing customers then there will obviously be an increase in the absolute value of the receivable given the higher volume but, all things being equal, the level of receivable days should stay the same. However, for new customers then potentially there could be additional risk of late payment or bad debt, especially if inadequate creditworthiness checks are made prior to making the sales, as a result of a lack of staffing.

Accounts payable

Expansion will obviously impact on payables, as we see in the case of KK where accounts payable have increased from EUR 2.7 million on 30 October 2011 to EUR 3.2 million on 30 April 2012. The precise impact on the working capital cycle will depend on the credit terms negotiated and taken.

We would have expected an accounts payable balance of the order of EUR 3.6 million on 30 April 2012 due solely to increased cost of sales and assuming accounts payable days remained unchanged. Indeed, KK's accounts payable days have fallen from 69 days on 31 October 2011 to 61 days on 30 April 2012. This is contrary to what would have been expected from increased cost of sales and so it would appear that there has been some relaxation on paying suppliers and an indication that some suppliers have been paid early.

Pressure on profit margins

This is particularly marked in cases where expansion has arisen as a result of a reduction in selling price to improve volumes. In the case of KK, however, this does not seem to be the case. We are told that the expansion has arisen because of the launch of new products. It is entirely possible that the new products are actually able to be sold at a premium to existing prices and therefore the margin could actually have improved. Based on the financial information for KK the gross margin in the six months to 31 October 2011 was 25.3% [(9.5 − 7.1)/9.5]compared to 23.8% [(12.6 − 9.6)/12.6]for the six months to 30 April 2012 − therefore indicating that the new business is actually at a potentially lower margin than the existing business.

Impact on employees

Another general pressure arising from expansion relates to the impact on employees. If rapid expansion is not backed up with a commensurate increase in credit control resources then it's highly likely that there will be issues in the management of working capital. Also, additional staff would need to be trained, which takes time. Therefore there could still be short term challenges in the effective management of working capital.

Pressure on overdraft

From part (a)(i) we have established that had KK been able to maintain its working capital days through good management then the overdraft would only have grown by EUR 1.1 million, rather than EUR 2.5 million. In the face of on-going profits, increase in short term funding requirements together with the worsening of working capital days are classic signs of over-trading.

(iii) It is important to ensure that sound management is in place to manage all aspects of working capital appropriately.

- In terms of inventory management, JIT systems could be set up – although this would require close working with suppliers.

- In terms of receivables management a factoring company could be used to ensure liquidity. Alternatively a prompt payment discount could be offered to customers – although this would obviously have an impact on margins.

- In terms of payables management the key to minimising the cash impact would be to negotiate an extension of credit terms from suppliers, to the extent that is possible without causing any detrimental effect on the supplier relationship.

(b) When assessing the creditworthiness of KK, a potential lender will to a large extent be concerned with KK's future prospects. To that end, the potential lender is likely to consider:

- Any budgets or cash forecasts showing expected growth and its projected impact on profitability and cash flow. If future predictions are detailed, comprehensive and well documented, with sensible assumptions then the potential lender is more likely to extend credit. There may be some suspicion that prices are being dropped to promote sales volumes and that further falls in profit margin could affect the overdraft requirement. It is also important that profit margins are monitored closely and maintained within agreed limits. Note that, if the cost of sales and other costs had been controlled at a 33% increase, the overdraft position would have been improved by a further EUR 0.2 million.

    (**Workings:** *The net profit in the 6 months to 31 October 2011 is EUR 0.9 million, therefore a 33% increase would have increased profits to EUR 1.2 million. The actual profit for the 6 months to 30 April 2012 was EUR 1.0 million, a difference of EUR 0.2 million.*)

- The nature of the new business in terms of its sustainability.

- The state of the economy in general and KK's competitive position within the market place, again to assess the sustainability of the new business and the achievability of the forecasts.

Other factors which will also be considered include:

- The quality of management, both in terms of the success of their past decisions but also in relation to the quality of their forecasts.

- The purpose for which the additional overdraft would be used. Given that an overdraft facility is short term finance then it will be important that it is matched to a short term investment – typically to support the fluctuating element of the working capital investment. If the overdraft is planned to be used for capital investment then the bank is unlikely to sanction the increase in overdraft.

- The existing capital structure and specifically any loans already outstanding. In particular the bank will need to assess any repayment terms and restrictive covenants on such finance to ensure that either a repayment is not due in the immediate future or that covenants will not be breached.

- In addition, the bank will consider short term liquidity measures such as the current or quick ratios and will look to monitor these on a continuous basis.

Lastly, reports from external credit agencies may be sought.

Tutorial note – extracted from the Examiner's "Post Exam Guide"

This question focused on short term funding issues of a company apparently "overtrading" and also how a lender might assess credit worthiness. Although a popular question, many candidates did not attempt part (a)(i) which required re-calculation of an overdraft balance assuming working capital days had remained unchanged over a 6 month period. However, the discussion sections were generally well attempted and most candidates were able to relate their answers to the scenario.

35   LL (SEPT 12 EXAM)

Key answer tips – extracted from the Examiner's "Post Exam Guide" (note that the comments regarding WORD and/or EXCEL only relate to the COMPUTER BASED papers in March and September each year)

The first part of this question is a straightforward buy/borrow vs leasing NPV exercise. Firstly the cash flows appropriate for the borrowing option should be identified (being the purchase of the asset and its residual value at the end of the lease term, the associated tax impacts from owning the asset and the maintenance costs to be borne, net of tax). These should then be discounted at the post tax cost of debt for the company to arrive at the present value cost of the buy/borrow option. Secondly, the cash flows appropriate for the leasing option (being the lease payments and associated tax relief) should be identified and the same post tax cost of debt used to arrive at the present value of the cost of leasing.

The next part of the question asks for advice on the impact of each option on the statement of financial position. The key point here is that the operating lease will in effect be off-balance sheet. Extra marks are available for candidates who indicate that they are aware of possible future changes to the accounting treatment of operating leases that are under consideration at the present time.

The final part of the question asks for advice on which option to choose and should comment on the findings from the first two parts of the question as well as other relevant factors such as the certainty of cash flows, the variability of the interest rate and the position at the end of the contract period.

(a)

Buy/borrow

	L$ million	Time	DF @ 4%	PV
Initial purchase	(50.0)	0	1.000	(50.0)
Tax relief	16.5	2	0.925	15.3
Maintenance	(1.5)	1 to 10	8.111	(12.2)
Tax relief on maintenance	0.5	2 to 11	7.799	3.9
Residual value	22.0	10	0.676	14.9
Tax charge on residual value	(7.3)	11	0.650	(4.7)
Versus operating lease				
Initial lease payment saved	5.8	0	1.000	5.8
Tax relief lost	(1.9)	2	0.925	(1.8)
Subsequent lease payments saved	5.8	1 to 10	8.111	47.0
Tax relief lost	(1.9)	2 to 11	7.799	(14.8)
PV of buy/borrow versus leasing				**3.3**

Showing a net benefit of buy/borrow.

Workings:

The DF of 4% is calculated as:

Gross interest of 6.0% (= 2.5% + 3.5%)

Giving cost of debt net of tax of 4.0% (= 6.0% × (1 − 0.33))

(Or, more accurately, taking into account the year time delay in receiving the tax relief on interest: 4.08% = 6% − 2%/1.04, which could be rounded to 4%.)

The discount factor of 7.799 is calculated as 7.799 = 8.111/1.04

Or, alternatively, it is acceptable to use 7.798 = 8.760 − 0.962 or a discount factor obtained using an appropriate EXCEL function.

(b) The operating lease does not have the same 'grossing up' effect on the financial statements as the buy/borrow alternative, since neither the asset value nor accrued lease payments are shown in the statement of financial position. Whereas both the value of the rolling stock and the value of matching debt will be included if the company were to buy the rolling stock outright and finance the purchase using a bank borrowing.

Using an operating lease therefore has the beneficial effect on the financial statements of lower gearing and lower bank borrowings, which potentially could make it easier for LL to raise finance in the future.

Note that the IASB is currently looking at bringing operating lease commitments onto a company's statement of financial position.

(c)   From a financial point of view and based on current interest rates and estimated future values, the buy/borrowing approach appears to be slightly less expensive than the operating lease approach.

However, the buy/borrow approach has the disadvantage of 'grossing up' the statement of financial position with both the total borrowing and the value of the asset. This could be an important consideration if LL is close to breaching a borrowing covenant.

Other relevant factors affecting the decision include:

- The risk due to the variable rate basis for the interest cost of the bank loan. The actual interest cost is therefore unknown at the beginning of the project and could change the balance of costs between the bank loan and lease.

- Maintenance costs are included in the lease payment and so the lease also provides certainty as to these costs whereas, under the buy/borrow approach, LL will need to retain additional liquidity (e.g. bank facilities) to meet any unforeseen large maintenance payments.

- Any 'follow on' real option might have a major impact on the choice of approach. With the 'buy/borrow' approach, the company already holds the asset and is in a position to carry on trading and follow up new custom. Leasing for an additional period of time could prove to be much more costly.

- Under the lease, the lessor can simply remove the asset if lease payments are not made. The asset may or may not be secured against the bank loan and so the same risk may not arise. However, securing the loan against the assets is likely to reduce the cost of the bank loan.

- Under the 'buy/borrow' approach, the appraisal relies heavily on the residual value of the asset and the ability of the company to sell the asset at the year end for the value expected.

Overall recommendation:

The operating lease approach has major advantages in terms of certainty of future cash flows and improved statement of financial position structure. However, it is slightly more expensive based on these estimated figures, although these are probably not large enough to outweigh the advantage of certainty provided by the lease. However, if there is a high probability of lucrative follow on options, this might swing the decision in favour of the bank borrowing.

Tutorial note – extracted from the Examiner's "Post Exam Guide"

Part (a):

This was the best answered part of the question, which is not surprising as past diets show that candidates often do better in the numerical aspects of questions than written aspects. Here a significant minority of candidates were able to complete the calculations required with few if any errors, which is encouraging. However, many candidates did make errors, the most common of which included:

- *Using a discount rate of 6% (i.e.: pre-tax) rather than the 4% post-tax rate.*

- *Including interest cash flows within the cash flow analysis.*

- *Timing errors with respect to the tax cash flows.*

- *Forgetting the tax impact of the maintenance cash flows or ignoring maintenance altogether.*

Part (b):

Many candidates correctly identified that the buy/borrow option would impact on the non-current assets of LL, but often failed to note that there would also be a corresponding increase in debt. Many also did mention the impact of the operating lease on the statement of profit or loss but failed to mention the impact on the statement of financial position, which is what the question clearly asked for. This indicates that candidates are not always reading the requirements carefully enough.

Part (c):

On the whole this was the least well answered part of the question. In particular the lack of depth in answers was disappointing with some candidates simply stating only one or two factors in little more than bullet point form.

Most candidates commented upon their results from part (a), but few made any reference to the results from part (b), despite this being specifically mentioned in the requirement.

36   XRG (NOV 12 EXAM)

Key answer tips – extracted from the Examiner's "Post Exam Guide"

Part (a)

Construct statements of profit or loss and schedule equity and debt balances under the two financing strategies. Think clearly about the layout of your answer. The format shown below is recommended as it shows the impact of the two strategies on each variable side by side.

Part (b)

The company has three financial objectives. It is first necessary to calculate the impact on each of the objectives under the two alternative financing strategies. You should then evaluate the impact of each of the financing strategies on each of the objectives using your calculations in part (a) to support your arguments.

In part (b)(i) of the question you should simply evaluate the attainment or otherwise of the objectives. In part (b)(ii) you are then required to evaluate the impact on shareholders and debt providers.

(a)   **Preliminary workings**

Amount to be raised   = GBP 1,250 million.

Suggested rights price   = GBP 3.33 × 75% = GBP 2.50 per share.

Shares to issue   = GBP 1,250 million/GBP 2.50 = 500 million 50 pence shares.

There are 1,000 million 50 pence shares currently in issue, so rights issue ratio is 1 for 2.

Increase in share capital is GBP 250 m (=500 m × 50 pence per share).

Increase in share premium account is GBP 1,000m (= 500m shares × (GBP 2.50– GBP0.50)).

Revised statement of profit or loss and equity/debt balances

	Year ending 31.12.2013:	*With debt* GBP m	*With rights* GBP m
1	Profit from operations	650	650
2	Finance costs	(163)	(88)
3	Tax @ 30%	(146)	(169)
4	Earnings	341	393

Calculations of dividends and retained earnings

5	Dividends payable	119	138
6	Retained earnings	222	255

Statement of equity and debt balances

7	Equity:		
	Ordinary shares of 50 pence	500	750
	Share premium and reserves	1,772	2,805
8	Secured debt	1,250	0
9	Unsecured debt	1,250	1,250

Workings/notes

1   Earnings do not change.

2   Finance charges   (1,250 × 6% + 1,250 × 7%)   1,250 × 7%

3   Tax = 30% of earnings – finance charges.

4   Earnings = EBIT – Finance costs – tax.

5   Dividends are 35% of earnings as given in the question.

6   Retained earnings are earnings minus dividends paid.

7   Ordinary share capital remains the same under the debt option as at present. With a rights issue it increases by 50% (1 for 2 are terms of offer). Reserves increase by retained earnings of GBP 222 million under the debt option and by GBP 255 million under the equity option. With a rights issue reserves increase further by the share premium account of GBP 1,000 million.

8   Secured debt remains the same in book value terms under the debt alternative.

9   Unsecured debt remains the same under both alternatives.

(b)   (i)   **Preliminary calculations**

	With debt	With rights
EPS (pence)	34.1 (=341/1000)	26.2 (=393/1500)
DPS (pence) (= EPS × 35%)	11.9	9.2
Gearing (D/(D+E))	52.4%	26.0%

Workings:

With debt refinancing,

gearing = 52.4% (GBP 2,500 million/(GBP 2,500 million + GBP 2,272 million)

With rights issue,

gearing = 26.0% (GBP 1,250 million/(GBP 1,250 million + GBP 3,555 million)

Evaluation of attainment of objectives

Gearing:

The company's gearing objective is not being met even before the refinancing. Gearing using book values is currently 54.9%. It reduces slightly to 52.4% if the re-financing is with debt because another year's profits will have been added to reserves. This level might be considered too high compared with the industry average, which will doubtless have an impact on the company's cost and therefore value of equity. Gearing falls significantly to 26.0% if re-financing is with equity. This might be considered too low a ratio; the company now loses valuable tax relief. If the industry average gearing of 40% is considered "optimum" (and the scenario does not suggest this) then the market might think the company is being too conservative in its financing policies.

EPS:

The EPS objective is met if the re-financing is with debt but will not be met if a rights issue is used. Under the rights issue the actual level of earnings will be higher due to the significantly reduced finance costs, but because this is shared across a greater number of shares, the EPS will fall.

DPS:

DPS of GBP 0.10 per share is only satisfied if refinancing using debt. As with the EPS, the failure of the rights issue to meet this objective is because despite increased earnings and therefore an increased total level of dividend, it has to be shared amongst a greater number of shares.

Additional observations:

1   It is questionable whether the current financial objectives are wholly appropriate for a company such as XRG. For example, the objectives could be improved by measuring gearing on the basis of market values, measuring earnings in absolute terms with some measure of growth from previous years and measuring dividend on the basis of growth or pay-out ratio.

2   A 1 for 2 rights issue would perhaps be seen as demanding. Each shareholder has to increase his investment in this company by 37% (GBP 2.50 for GBP 6.66 currently invested) and find cash accordingly. In this case, as substantially the shares are institutionally held, it may not be critical.

(ii)   **Evaluation from shareholders' perspective**

- If the re-financing is with debt then in effect the status quo is maintained apart from a slight increase in the interest cost (5% debt has been replaced with 6% debt) and therefore the impact on shareholders will be minimal.

- Under the rights issue the shareholders will suffer an immediate drop in share price as a result of the shares being issued at a discount. The theoretical ex-rights price (TERP) will be GBP 3.05 per share (=((GBP 3.33 × 1,000 million) + (GBP 2.50 × 500 million))/1,500 million). The rights issue will also have the effect of significantly reducing the level of gearing in XRG which will lower the shareholders' required return and hence the cost of equity. Whether this increases the share price above the TERP or below it is hard to establish. Theoretically if we were to value the equity of XRG (and therefore the share price) using the dividend valuation model then within the model there would be a reduced dividend per share but also a reduced cost of equity – the effects of which cancel each other out to a certain extent, leaving shareholders with lower risk matched by lower returns.

- With a rights issue the dividend per share will obviously be reduced but as long as the shareholders have taken up their rights then their absolute level of dividend will actually be improved as a result of lower finance costs given that the payout ratio remains the same. In addition, earnings will remain proportionately the same for shareholders providing they take up their rights.

Evaluation from debt providers' perspective

- Providers of new secured debt might be disappointed to lose the business if financing is with rights (depending on how the debt was to be raised), but this is of little consequence to anybody. Advisers might be happy with a rights issue as the cost of a rights issue is likely to be greater than for an issue of new debt.

- If present lenders consider the current gearing level to be uncomfortably high, they are likely to prefer financing strategy 2 as this results in a significant reduction in gearing and hence in credit worthiness.

Tutorial note – extracted from the Examiner's "Post Exam Guide"

Part (a) of the question was very well attempted and many candidates got full marks for this part of the question. A sizeable minority however were unable to construct a simple P&L or a statement of equity and debt. This is a major weakness at this stage of the qualification.

Part (b) of the question presented few problems to the well prepared candidate.

37 PPT (MAR 13 EXAM)

Key answer tips – extracted from the Examiner's "Post Exam Guide"

Part (a)

Begin by ungearing proxy company TT's equity beta to obtain an ungeared/asset beta to apply to PPT. Re-gear this beta using PPT's gearing to obtain a geared equity beta for PPT.

Use the CAPM formula to obtain a cost of equity for PPT.

Calculate a post-tax cost of debt for PPT by deducting taxation from the pre-tax figure.

Calculate PPT's WACC using the cost of equity and post-tax cost of debt calculated above.

Part (b)

Consider each of the three mini requirements in turn.

Item 1: Start by explaining the distinction between systematic and unsystematic risk.

Item 2: Explain all components of the CAPM formula, not just beta.

Item 3: Don't forget to explain the relationship between the components rather than simply focussing on the individual components in isolation.

Part (c)

Consider the benefits and limitations of using the WACC calculated in part (a), starting with the limitations of the theories involved. Also consider whether PPT is a suitable proxy company to use. Thirdly, consider whether the same discount rate should be used for all projects regardless of business risk and impact on capital structure. Apply answers to the scenario, noting that R&D projects are likely to be much more risky than manufacturing projects.

(a) 1 First ungear β:

$$\beta_u = \beta_g \left[\frac{V_E}{V_E + V_D[1-t]} \right] + \beta_d \left[\frac{V_D[1-t]}{V_E + V_D[1-t]} \right]$$

βd is zero

So TT and PPT's β_u is 1.8771 $\quad = 2.4 \times \dfrac{7}{7 + 3 \times (1 - 0.35)}$

2 Next regear β:

$$\beta_g = \beta_u + [\beta_u - \beta_d] \frac{V_D[1-t]}{V_E}$$

So PPT's β_g is 2.6905 $\quad = 1.8771 + 1.8771 \times \dfrac{4 \times (1 - 0.35)}{6}$

3 Use CAPM to calculate ke $\quad k_e = R_f + [R_m - R_f]\beta$

So PPT ke is 11.76% $\quad = 1\% + 2.6905 \times 4\%$

4 Finally, calculate WACC for PPT using $WACC = k_e \left[\dfrac{V_E}{V_E + V_D} \right] + k_d[1-t]\left[\dfrac{V_D}{V_E + V_D} \right]$

So PPT's WACC is 7.84% $\quad = 0.1176 \times \left[\dfrac{6}{6+4} \right] + 0.03 \times (1 - 0.35) \times \left[\dfrac{4}{6+4} \right]$

(b) **The difference between systematic and unsystematic risk**

CAPM assumes that there are two types of risk affecting a company:

- Unsystematic risk (or specific) is the risk of the company's cash flows being affected by factors specific to the company and the industry in which it operates such as strikes, R&D successes, systems failures, etc. Unsystematic risk can be eliminated by diversification, that is, by investors holding well diversified portfolios of investments.

- Systematic risk (or market) is the risk of the company's cash flows being affected to some extent by general macro-economic factors such as tax rates, unemployment or interest rates, factors which affect all companies to some degree. In the case of PPT, systematic risk will include economic conditions that might affect levels of spending on luxury items such as PPT's luxury skin care products. Systematic risk cannot be diversified away through holding a diversified portfolio.

The components of the CAPM formula

The components of the formula are:

- Rj or Ke

- Rf

- beta

- Rm

Rj or Ke is the return required from the company by equity investors.

Rf, the risk free rate of return, is the rate of return achieved on a risk free investment. This rate is typically taken to be the central bank rate or the yield on government paper such as treasury bills in the USA, on the assumption that depositing funds with the government is risk free.

Beta is a measure of systematic risk in relation to the market. The market has a beta of '1'. A company which has a greater exposure to systematic risk than the market as a whole will have an equity beta greater than '1' and a company with lower exposure to systematic risk will have an equity beta of between '0' and '1'. The equity beta for TT is 2.4. This means that TT (and therefore by inference PPT) has a higher exposure to systematic risk (i.e. macro-economic factors) than the market as a whole.

Rm is the rate of return that investors demand for investing in shares. That is, it is the average return expected to be generated across all shares in the market.

CAPM formula:

Rj (return required by investors for security j) = Rf (risk free return) + beta x (Rm (market return) – Rf)

The relationship between the components

The CAPM provides a measure of an investor's required return for investment in a particular company based upon that's company's relationship to the market as a whole (i.e.: it's beta) using a risk free return as a starting point.

The CAPM is based on the assumption that a diversified investor will have diversified away unsystematic risk and will therefore only be interested in a company's systematic risk when determining the required return for investing in that company. That is, the investor will only be interested in the extent to which the company is affected to a greater of lesser extent than the market as a whole in the face of changes in general macro-economic factors, as shown by the beta.

(c) **Benefits and drawbacks of using a WACC derived in part (a) in investment appraisal**

The benefits of using WACC calculated using CAPM include:

- WACC takes into account the return required by both equity and debt investors when evaluating the returns from new investments.

- The WACC derived from CAPM takes systematic risk into account and therefore, where this WACC is used in investment appraisal, ensures that positive NPV projects provide returns commensurate with the level of systematic risk the company faces.

- CAPM provides a standard, recognised theoretical approach for deriving a company's WACC which can be used for both listed and unlisted companies due to widely available published data on company betas.

However, WACC based on CAPM assumes that the average investor has successfully diversified away all unsystematic risk, but this may not be the case in practice.

In addition, a WACC based on a proxy company's beta may not be appropriate for PPT if the proxy company does not have the same business risk as PPT or if investors in PPT require higher returns than the investors in TT due to the possibly higher risks associated with PPT being a private company.

There are also potential problems in making decisions about projects that will occur in the future based on historic data. For example:

- Past business risks and financial risks may not be indicative of risk profiles in the future.

- The risk free rate may not be constant over time.

- The market risk premium may also vary over time (but is likely to be more stable than market returns themselves).

In addition, it is unlikely to be appropriate for PPT to use the same discount rate when evaluating all projects. PPT's WACC can only be used if the project under consideration has:

- The same business risk as PPT.

- Will not change PPT's capital structure in the long term.

It can be assumed that projects proposed by the R&D department will be much more risky than projects within the manufacturing department. If the R&D department is investigating and carrying out clinical trials of a new product, there is a risk that that product will never actually be sold due to unacceptable side effects. It will be necessary to adjust the discount rate to allow for added risk.

Tutorial note – extracted from the Examiner's "Post Exam Guide"

Part (a) was generally handled well. The most common errors here were:

- *Ungearing but not regearing (or using the alternative MM adjusted cost of capital formula)*

- *Ungearing using PPT's gearing.*

- *Applying CAPM directly using TT's unadjusted beta.*

- *Ungearing, regearing, applying CAPM and then applying the alternative MM formula.*

- *Ungearing, regearing, applying CAPM and then labelling the answer as WACC rather than cost of equity.*

- *Omitting to apply the tax rate to the cost of debt in the WACC computation.*

- *Getting one or both of the ungearing and regearing formulae upside down.*

Note that it was equally acceptable to use the alternative MM adjusted cost of capital formula in part (a).

> *The main issue with part (b) was some significant degree of confusion over the meaning of the components of CAPM. Very few candidates addressed the final part of the question by explaining the underlying relationship between the different components.*
>
> *Part (c) was generally answered well. The main omission was to discuss the appropriateness of a single discount rate for all projects. There were clear hints in the question that the company in question had two quite different business activities – production and research and development. It is therefore highly unlikely that a single discount rate would be appropriate for all projects.*

38   PPP (MAY 13 EXAM)

Key answer tips – extracted from the Examiner's "Post Exam Guide"

In (a), candidates should reperform the calculation of the implied interest rate in the lease to prove that it is 4%. An annuity approach is faster than a 'sum-of-digits' approach in this instance due to the long 15 year time period involved. However, either approach would be acceptable.

In (b) (i), review the lease versus buy computation, line by line, looking for data lines that should not be there at all in the first instance and listing these. Then go back over the other data lines, looking for errors in the figures provided, and provide a second list of these data lines. Identifying the data lines by their line number is sufficient in part (b)(i).

In (b) (ii), explain how each of the items in your second list above could be corrected. This can be addressed either with a narrative answer or by showing how the relevant figure(s) could be corrected accompanied by a brief explanation of the change made.

In part (c), identify the key issues involved in the lease versus buy evaluation and ultimate decision in the context of PPP and then consider the implications of each in turn.

(a)   Proof that the rate implicit in the lease is 4%:

Cost of machine/annual lease rental payment = Z\$ 500,000/Z\$ 45,000 = 11.11

Looking 11.11 up in annuity tables under '15 years' gives an implied interest rate of 4%.

(b)   (i)   Data lines that should not have been included in the evaluation:

Line 3: Maintenance costs of Z\$ 18,000 a year should not be shown under the 'buy' option unless they are also shown under the 'lease' option and therefore cancel out. As they are the same under both the lease and borrow/buy strategies, they can be omitted altogether. Maintenance costs are of no significance to the decision on whether to lease or buy in this instance. Similarly, no tax relief on maintenance should be shown. ·

Line 5: Tax relief on the lease payments should not be included – the tax relief available is based on the sum of the accounting depreciation and implied interest.

Line 6: Accounting depreciation should not be included, only tax relief on accounting depreciation.

Line 8: Bank interest is taken into account through the discount rate and should not be shown here.

Examiner's note:

The line numbers were sufficient to obtain full marks here. The additional explanations above have been provided for teaching purposes only.

Data lines containing an error

Line 2

Line 9

Line 10

Line 12

Line 13

(ii)   Data lines containing an error (any four listed below):

Line 2: Tax relief on initial investment should be shown in column '2014' since tax is payable one year in arrears.

Line 9: Figures in line 9 are incorrect only because they are derived from line 12 which contains an error.

Line 10: The evaluation is based on after tax cash flows and so, for consistency, an after tax discount rate should be used. That is, discount factors should be based on the after tax cost of debt of 3.5% (= 5% × (1 − 0.3)).

Line 12: The opening balance on the implied loan under the lease should be Z$ 500,000 rather than Z$ 350,000 since the cost of the machine is Z$ 500,000.

Line 13: The implied interest should be calculated on the revised opening loan balance. In addition, the implied interest should be ADDED to the opening balance rather than SUBTRACTED from it since the interest due in each period increases the amount borrowed.

Examiner's note:

A corrected evaluation is included below for teaching purposes only.

Line	30 June:	2013	2014	2015	2016
	BUY				
1	Initial investment	500.0			
2	Tax relief on initial investment		(150.0)		
	VERSUS LEASE				
4	Lease payment		(45.0)	(45.0)	(45.0)
7	Tax relief on accounting depreciation (30% tax rate)			10.0	10.0
9	Tax relief on implied interest (30% tax rate)			6.0	5.7
	Net cash flow	500.0	(195.0)	(29.0)	(29.3)
10	Discount factor (3.5% discount rate)	1.0	0.966	0.934	0.902
	Present value for first three years	500.0	(188.4)	(27.1)	(26.4)

Workings:

(W1) **Accounting depreciation**

11	Machine costs Z\$ 500,000 and is depreciated over 15 years. (33.3 = 500/15)		33.3	33.3	33.3

(W2) **Implied interest in the lease**

Line		2013	2014	2015	2016
12	Opening balance (now Z\$ 500,000)		500.0	475.0	449.0
13	Less implied interest on lease (now added)		20.0	19.0	18.0
14	Less lease payment		(45.0)	(45.0)	(45.0)
	Closing balance		475.0	449.0	422.0

(c)   The final NPV result of the evaluation over a 15 year period will provide an important indication of which approach is likely to be the cheapest. At first sight, the lease appears to be cheaper as it has an attractive implied interest rate of 4% against the interest rate on borrowings of 5%. However, the purchase route allows accelerated capital allowances and this favours the bank borrowings. Although not expected in a candidate's answer, it is interesting to note that, if extended for the full 15 year period, the evaluation would prove that the bank borrowings are marginally cheaper than the lease, despite the 'headline' interest figures indicating the opposite position.

A key issue in the evaluation of the two alternatives is the reliability and completeness of the inputs used. Would there be additional costs under either option not shown here, for example, is the purchase cost realistic and have transport and set up costs been taken into account? Would the machine have a residual value at the end of the 15 year period and continue to be of value to the business after that time? If so, would the lessor be willing to sell the machine to PPP for a negligible sum?

Another important issue is the degree of flexibility that each option provides. Is there a risk that the company will not require the use of this equipment for the full 15 year period? How certain is it that the company will continue operating in this business for the next 15 years? And, if some flexibility is required, is that greater under the buy or the lease option? For example, is there a break clause in the lease and what is the likelihood of being able to find a buyer for the equipment and at what price?

Are there any other obligations under either the loan or lease that are not mentioned here? E.g., are there any covenants on the debt or security levied?

Indeed, could the cost of the loan be reduced by offering security?

Note that the cost of maintenance and the predictability of the cost of finance are identical under both options and so these are not issues of interest in this context.

Tutorial note – extracted from the Examiner's "Post Exam Guide"

This was a popular question but very poorly answered. It was popular possibly because on first reading candidates thought it much easier than it actually was.

Part (a)

Few candidates understood what was required in this part of the question and many did not even attempt an answer. It was much better answered in some overseas centres than in home centres.

Part (b)

Many candidates did not understand the instruction "identify" and discussed the nature of the error at length. A common failing was to confuse lines that should not have been included in the question and those that contained errors.

Many did not identify the line numbers as required by the question and it was clear that most answers were guesses.

Part (c)

This part of the question was also very poorly answered and many candidates did not understand that the only difference between the vendors was that one had offered to structure the deal as a finance lease rather than an outright purchase. It was also common for candidates to ignore the information that fixed rate borrowings are available and so ask "where would PPP get the money from" if it did not take out the finance lease.

Candidates tended to focus their advice on gearing and cash flow issues, which are largely irrelevant except for the benefit of the 100% FYA with the buy option. Many discussed how to account for lease vs buy decisions and irrelevant "off balance sheet" issues.

---

39   BBB (MAY 13 EXAM)

Key answer tips – extracted from the Examiner's "Post Exam Guide"

In part (a)(i), point out the inverse relationship between WACC and entity value and support that position by reference to the numerical approach to calculating an entity value using a discounted cash flow (DCF) approach.

In part (a)(ii), calculate both the market value of debt and of equity for BBB from the price data provided and use these results to calculate gearing. Then use the same results to calculate WACC, being careful to use the post-tax rate of debt.

In part (a)(iii), use Modigliani and Miller's formula 'Kadj = Keu (1 – tL)' to calculate the ungeared cost of equity (Keu) using the WACC calculated in (a) (ii) as Kadj and the values of debt and equity calculated in (a)(ii) to derive L, where L = debt/(debt + equity). Then reapply the formula to calculate Kadj at a gearing level of 60%, using the value of Keu calculated earlier.

In part (b), identify the key issues and then evaluate each in turn.

(a)   (i)   The entity value can be calculated by discounting future after tax cash flows (before financing costs or dividends) using the WACC as the discount factor.

Entity value is therefore inversely related to WACC.

(ii)   BBB's current entity value is:

Equity: 150 million × B$12.83   = B$1,925 million

Debt: B$300 million + 1.05 × B$500 million   = B$825 million

Total entity value: B$2,750 million (= B$1,925 million + B$825 million)

BBB's current gearing level is:

B$825 million/B$2750 million × 100% = 30.00%

And BBB's current WACC is:

$$WACC = k_e \left[\frac{V_E}{V_E + V_D} \right] + k_d [1-t] \left[\frac{V_D}{V_E + V_D} \right]$$

So, WACC = 8% × 70% + 5% (1 – 0.33) × 30% = 6.6%

(iii)   **Step 1:** Calculate Keu.

Kadj = Keu (1 – tL) where L = debt/(debt + equity)

So, currently,   6.6% = Keu × (1 – (0.33 × 30%))

So Keu = 7.33%

Step 2: Use the ungeared cost of equity to calculate WACC at 60% gearing

Kadj = Keu (1 – tL)

So kadj = 7.33% × (1 – (33% × 60%)) = 5.88%

According to Modigliani and Miller theories (with tax), WACC would reduce from 6.6% to 5.88% if gearing were to increase from the current level of 30% to a new level of 60%. This is a downwards movement in WACC of 72 percentage points which is equivalent to an overall reduction of 10.9%.

(b)   The theories of gearing all point to the benefit of increasing gearing up to a certain sustainable level. This is demonstrated in part (a) (iii) where under MM it shows that an increase of gearing to 60% generates a reduction in WACC (under MM this is wholly due to the tax shield available on the debt). However, in reality there are significant risks arising from high levels of gearing in a real life situation, many of which are not taken into account by either MM or the traditional theory of capital structure. These practical considerations tend to point towards a lower optimum gearing level than that predicted in theory.

One important consideration is that economic and market conditions are continually under flux. So what might be ideal today may prove to be too risky tomorrow. The recommended 60% gearing has been based on historical data that may not be a good indication of the future. Indeed, the very nature of BBB's business means that conditions are changing all the time and BBB's revenue and cost streams are highly sensitive to changes in many external factors such as changes in interest rates, house prices, planning regulations, building regulations, unemployment levels etc. For example, an increase in interest rates could lead to both increased cost of servicing floating rate borrowings and also reduced demand for housing due to the rise in the cost of mortgages for prospective house purchasers. A fall in property prices could similarly be very detrimental to BBB's results, reducing profit margins and, more importantly, reducing demand for new houses.

Another important consideration is that BBB requires considerable up-front finance in order to purchase and develop land and properties before being able to sell new homes. Access to new bank finance and the ability to issue new bonds into the capital markets is heavily dependent on the perceived financial strength of the company by prospective investors and rating agencies. Indeed, a high credit rating could be essential to ensure a successful bond issue.

BBB's borrowings may also carry debt covenants that need to be honoured and it is much easier to keep within debt covenants at lower levels of gearing.

Significant gearing headroom is advisable to ensure that BBB can continue operating even in extreme adverse economic conditions.

This is a classic example of the trade-off between risk and reward. BBB may be able to improve shareholder returns to a certain degree by increasing gearing, but it is far more important to shareholders that the company has sufficient financial strength to be able to continue in business even in the face of unforeseen economic and business downturns at a future date. The potential increase in returns from increasing gearing to 60% is not worthwhile in view of the additional risk of future financial distress and reduced business or financial manoeuvrability that is likely to result from such a move.

Tutorial note – extracted from the Examiner's "Post Exam Guide"

This question was answered satisfactorily on the whole although few correctly answered or even attempted part (a)(iii).

Part (a)(i)

Many candidates could explain the inverse relationship between WACC and entity value although many defined the terms without explaining the relationship. Rather fewer candidates then went on to explain how WACC affected NPV. Candidates in overseas centres tended to write lengthy discussions about the effect of gearing on value, which was not required.

Part (a)(ii)

The calculations of WACC were generally done very well. The most common error was not calculating the bond as B$525 million. There were also a variety of errors in the costs of debt to be used in the WACC; many adjusted the 5% assuming it was the coupon rate. The scenario explains it is the yield, or return. No adjustment other than for tax was necessary. Many candidates failed to recognise that an equity beta of an all-equity financed company is an ungeared beta and therefore needs to be geared for CCC.

Part (a)(iii)

Few candidates understood which MM formula to use, and if they did, they confused the geared and ungeared costs. The majority of candidates who attempted this question ignored this part completely.

Part (b)

Many answers focussed on generalities of capital structure theory and said very little about the context, i.e. recognising that this is a construction company which requires substantial up-front finance.

40 FF (SEPT 13 EXAM)

Key answer tips – extracted from the Examiner's "Post Exam Guide" (note that the comments regarding WORD and/or EXCEL only relate to the COMPUTER BASED papers in March and September each year)

In part (a), firstly calculate closing working capital balances. This information, together with the data provided on opening balances, can then be used to adjust sales and purchases forecasts onto a cash basis. A cash forecast can then be built up, starting with sales receipts and purchase payments and adding other cash items to derive a figure for the net cash movement in the period.

Although not required in the question, note that it is a good idea to add in the opening cash balance and calculate a closing cash balance at this point as a cursory glance at requirement (b) reveals that this information will prove useful later on in the question.

In part (b), it is probably simplest to use EXCEL to 'copy and paste' the original cash forecast three times. Each of these copied versions can then be amended to reflect the change in circumstances outlined in each of the three scenarios provided in the question. Add the opening cash balance in order to derive the closing cash balance or borrowing requirement at the end of the period under each scenario. Now evaluate your results, comparing the relative size of the borrowing requirement under each scenario

In part (c), consider how the potential increased borrowing requirement could be met, either by changes to the management of working capital or by arranging additional short term loans, back-up bank facilities or a paper issuance programme. Finally, consider any changes that should be considered in respect of long term financial strategy in order to ensure that the company has sufficient liquidity to meet its needs in the long term.

(a)

Forecast for year ended 30 June 2014:	F$ million	
Sales revenue	725.00	
Purchases	(370.00)	Note that purchases are equivalent to COGS since inventory is unchanged
Other costs	(325.00)	
Add back: Depreciation	40.00	
Less: Capex	(30.00)	
Less: Dividend	(20.00)	
Add: Accounts receivable at start	37.20	
Less: Accounts receivable at end	(35.75)	= F$ 725 m × 30% × 60/365
Less: Accounts payable at start	(124.90)	
Add: Accounts payable at end	121.64	= F$ 370 m × 120/365
	———	
Net cash inflow	18.19	
Add opening balance	50.00	
	———	
Forecast closing balance	68.19	
	———	

(b)

	Scenario 1 (F$ million)	Scenario 2 (F$ million)	Scenario 3 (F$ million)
Sales revenue	630.00	630.00	630.00
Purchases	(321.00)	(321.00)	(321.00)
Other costs	(325.00)	(325.00)	(325.00)
Add back: Depreciation	40.00	40.00	40.00
Less: Capex	(30.00)	(30.00)	(30.00)
Less: Dividend	(20.00)	(20.00)	(20.00)
Add: AR at start	37.20	37.20	37.20
Less: AR at end	(31.07)	(51.78)	(31.07)
Add: Inventory at start	42.00	42.00	42.00
Less: Inventory at end	(42.00)	(42.00)	(42.00)
Less: AP at start	(124.90)	(124.90)	(124.90)
Add: AP at end	105.53	105.53	0.00
Net cash outflow	(39.24)	(59.95)	(144.77)
Add opening balance	50.00	50.00	50.00
Forecast closing balance	10.76	(9.95)	(94.77)

The largest impact on liquidity is the potential withdrawal of credit by suppliers (negative impact of F$ 105.53 million (= 94.77 million + 10.76 million)), the difference between the outcome of scenarios 1 and 3. The second largest effect is the deterioration in sales which, together with a reduction in purchases has a negative impact on liquidity of F$ 57.43 million (= 68.19 million – 10.76 million) in scenario 1.

In both scenarios 2 and 3, FF requires additional funding. In Scenario 3, new borrowings of at least F$ 95 million would be required. This is clearly a very large sum to find, especially given FF's very low profit margin (30/725 = 4% before dividends in the year ended 30 June 2014). Even in 'best case' scenario 1, FF's cash resources are severally diminished and back-up borrowing facilities would be required to provide reassurance that future cash needs could be met.

(c) **The management of working capital**

Inventory

- It may not be possible for FF to reduce inventory since this could create a risk of product shortages and consequential loss of sales.

- Products could be ordered in store and then delivered to the customer directly from the manufacturer rather than held by FF in storage. However, FF would then be reliant on speedy delivery by the manufacture, something that would be outside its control.

Accounts receivable

- FF might attempt to apply credit control procedures on a stricter basis. However, there is a risk that such a policy could lead to a loss of sales, especially given the current poor market conditions.

Accounts payable

- At present, it should be a higher priority for FF to maintain good relationships with suppliers rather than seek to extend credit terms.

Financing working capital and other short term liquidity requirements

- Greater borrowing headroom is required in order to cope with uncertain future cash flows

- FF should attempt to negotiate back-up bank facilities that can be drawn down as required. These might include a revolving credit facility (RCF) (committed finance) or overdraft facility (uncommitted, so less reliable than RCF) to enable it to meet short term cash needs.

Working capital could be used to support financing. For example:

- Use factoring to gain access to funds tied up in accounts receivable.

- Borrow against inventory. (Banks may be more willing to lend and at a lower interest rate where assets are used as security since such borrowings may make lesser demands on a bank's capital requirements.)

- Negotiate the use of consignment stock. Attempt to arrange with suppliers that they would only be paid for the goods on display once they had been sold. However, this is unlikely to prove successful given FF's current financial weakness.

Releasing cash elsewhere in the business

- FF could consider delaying other payments, for example, refurbishment of stores or other capital expenditure programmes.

- The dividend forecast to be paid on 20 June 2014 could be altered. Either no dividend could be paid or it could be deferred, reduced, or paid in a non-cash form such as a scrip dividend.

Long term financial strategy

Over the longer term, it is important that the company manages the business in a profitable manner. Ultimately, profits turn into cash and the company can only survive if it has a business strategy that creates profit and value. We can see from a further analysis of scenarios 1 to 3 that a fall sales and purchases as modelled in these scenarios creates an accounting loss:

	Scenarios 1 to 3 (F$ million)
Sales revenue	630.00
Purchases	(321.00)
Other costs	(325.00)
Accounting loss	(16.00)

This position is clearly unsustainable in the longer term and changes would be needed to reduce other costs and/or increase the gross profit margin.

FF should continually monitor and update a medium to long term cash forecasts to give early warning of future liquidity demands and enable appropriate changes to be made to financial and business strategy to ensure that liquidity demands can be met.

Tutorial note – extracted from the Examiner's "Post Exam Guide"

There was a wide divergence of marks awarded in this question. It was surprising how much variation there was in the answers to the relatively simple calculations in parts (a) and (b), indeed a significant number of candidates scored full marks whilst others only three of four marks out the thirteen marks available for calculations.

In part (a) common errors included:

- *Ignoring working capital altogether.*

- *Calculating closing accounts receivable and accounts payable balances but then failing to adjust for them in the cash flow workings.*

- *Including either only cash sales or credit sales within the cash flow statement.*

- *Deducting the deprecation charge from cash flow rather than adding it back.*

- *Forgetting to adjust for the dividend and/or capital expenditure.*

Note that monthly analysis was not required here.

In part (b) common errors included:

- *Failing to adjust the revenue and purchases across all three scenarios.*

- *Not re-calculating closing accounts receivable and accounts payable balances appropriately.*

- *Not showing the impact on the borrowing requirement (which is what the requirement asked for).*

- *Not providing any evaluation commentary. It was clear from the requirement that only seven marks were available for calculations.*

Generally, answers to part (c) were poor. The majority of candidates wrote fairly brief answers, often little more than a series of bullet points. Of the three sections requiring comment the management of working capital was the best answered, although some candidates did suggest that FF should expand payables days even further, which in the context of this scenario is clearly not achievable. The element on long term financial strategy was least well answered, with many candidates advising on long term finance rather than long term financial strategy. Indeed, most candidates failed to identify that the key long term strategic issue was that FF was no longer trading profitably. It was apparent that many candidates are not utilising the scenario information, but instead relying on pre-prepared generic answers on the subject matter. Such an approach is not acceptable at strategic level.

41 RR (SEPT 13 EXAM)

Key answer tips – extracted from the Examiner's "Post Exam Guide" (note that the comments regarding WORD and/or EXCEL only relate to the COMPUTER BASED papers in March and September each year)

Part (a) requires the calculation of the Theoretical Ex-Rights Price. The simplest way to arrive at the correct answer is to draw up a table with a column for number of shares, share price and total value. The first row in the table can be completed by copying information across from the question concerning the current position. Information on the value of the project can then be added to the final 'value' column. Then add the number of shares being issued under the rights issue, together with the price of those shares. Total each column and use the totals to derive the missing figure for the resultant share price post rights issue.

There are a number of acceptable approaches to answering part (b)(i).

Standard IRR approach:

Firstly schedule the cash flows arising from the production of product X. Note that you are already given the NPV at a discount rate of 10%, so just one more NPV result is required in order to derive the IRR by interpolation. In the answers we have used a discount rate of 12%. There is no value in repeating the NPV at 10% here. Note that it is not possible to obtain the IRR by applying the EXCEL IRR function in the normal manner here since a perpetuity is involved. The EXCEL IRR function is applied to pre-discounted cash flows and these continue indefinitely into the future.

Alternative approach to proving the IRR:

Show that the NPV is zero at 11.3% and, hence, that 11.3% is, indeed, the IRR. Calculate the NPV using EXCEL and the perpetuity formula.

In part (b)(ii), apply the yield-adjusted TERP formula using 11.3% as 'Y_{new}', being the effective yield on the project, and 10% as 'Y_{old}', being the current WACC of the company.

In part (c), address each of the issues raised in the requirement in turn, beginning by outlining the efficient market hypothesis and its relevance in this scenario. Conclude by considering broader business and risk factors that can be expected to influence the share price in this scenario.

(a) Issue price is (100% - 30%) × USD 4.80 = USD 3.36 per share

$$\text{TERP} = \frac{1}{N+1}[(N \times \text{cum rights price}) + \text{issue price}]$$

+ NPV or project/number of shares after the rights issue

$$= \frac{1}{6}[(5 \times 4.80) + 3.36] + 44.6/(750 + 150)$$

$$= 4.56 + 0.05$$

$$= \text{USD } 4.61 \text{ per share}$$

(b) (i) NPV at a discount rate of 10% is USD 44.6 million (as given in the question)

Now calculate the NPV at, say, a discount rate of 12%:

Time	0	1	2	3	4	5	6	7+
Cash inflows		260.0	275.0	305.0	340.0	350.0		
Cash outflows		−250.0	−250.0	−250.0	−250.0	−250.0		
NCF		10.0	25.0	55.0	90.0	100.0		
Tax at 30%		−3.0	−7.5	−16.5	−27.0	−30.0		
After tax CF		7.0	17.5	38.5	63.0	70.0	70.0	391.2(W1)
Capex	−500							
Tax relief on capex		37.5	37.5	37.5	37.5			
Total cash flows	−500	44.5	55.0	76.0	100.5	70.0	70.0	391.2
Discount factor	1	0.893	0.797	0.712	0.636	0.567	0.507	0.507
PV	−500	39.7	43.8	54.1	63.9	39.7	35.5	198.3

NPV = − USD 25.0 million

So IRR = 10% + 2% × 44.6/(44.6 + 25.0) = 11.3%

Workings

(W1) 391.2 = 70 × 0.95/(0.12 + 0.05)

(ii) Yield-adjusted TERP =

$$\frac{1}{N+1} \text{[(N × cum rights price) + issue price × (Ynew/Yold)]}$$

= 1/6 [(5 × 4.8) + (3.36 × 11.3/10.0)]

= 1/6 [24 + 3.7968]

= USD 4.6328 per share

(c) Under the semi-strong form of the efficient market hypothesis, share prices reflect not only historical share price information and other historical information about a company, but also respond immediately to current publicly-available information about the company.

Assuming a semi-strong form, the market can be expected to react straight away to the news of the rights issue and product launch. Only under the strong form of efficient market would the share price already have begun to take the news into account.

There are two conflicting forces at work here.

- Firstly, the rights issue will push the share price down to take the discount into account. Ignoring the project, the TERP will be USD 4.56 (being, ((USD 4.80 × 5) + USD 3.36)/6). This represents a fall in the share price purely as a result of the new shares being issued at a discount. However, whilst the share price can be expected to fall to USD 4.56 post rights issue before taking the project into account, this would not result in a fall in overall shareholder wealth since it only reflects the impact of the discount on the right issue.

- Secondly, the perceived future benefit from the launch of product X is likely to have a positive influence on the post rights issue share price as this will potentially increase overall shareholder wealth.

Based on our calculations above we can see that the project-adjusted TERP is higher that the non-project adjusted TERP, reflecting the increase in shareholder wealth arising from the positive NPV generated by the project. Whether the share price ends up higher or lower than the project-adjusted TERP following the announcement will depend on how the market reacts to the announcement.

Market reaction will largely depend on reaction to the product launch and the rights issue:

- Product launch. Market reaction will depend on investors' confidence that product X will meet company expectations. For example, their perception of the riskiness of the project. With a WACC of 10% and a project IRR of 11.3%, even a 1.3% risk premium built into the discount rate would mean that the project would cease to be financially beneficial.

- Rights issue. Market reaction will also depend on the readiness of shareholders to subscribe to a rights issue. Investors will only be willing to increase their investment and hence exposure to RR if they both have sufficient funds available and have sufficient confidence in the future of RR and /or product X to be willing to purchase additional shares in RR under the rights issue.

The two TERP calculations should produce the same result in this case. There may be slight differences due to:

- Roundings in the calculation (as we were only working to one decimal place).

- Difference in the Mathematical approach. However, note that if growth had been assumed to be zero and we had been valuing a simple perpetuity, the methods would have given exactly the same result.

If choosing between them, the result in (a) would be considered to be slightly more accurate as it takes into account the profile of the project cash flows in more detail.

Tutorial note – extracted from the Examiner's "Post Exam Guide"

In part (a) most candidates could successfully calculate the TERP without adjusting for the NPV of the project. A significant minority were also then able to take account of the NPV of the project as well.

Part (b)(i) required candidates to demonstrate that the IRR of the project was 11.3%. This could be achieved by either discounting relevant cash flows at 11.3% to arrive at an NPV of zero, or by calculating the NPV at a discount rate other than 10% and then calculating the IRR by interpolation. It should be noted that many candidates did actually apply the IRR interpolation formula correctly, which is encouraging as this has been an issue in previous exam diets.

Common errors included:

- *Miscalculating the relief on tax writing down allowances – either applying reducing balance rather than straight line, or using the incorrect number of years.*

- *Treating the relief on tax writing down allowances as an outflow rather than an inflow.*

- Using 10% as a discount rate (the NPV at 10% was already given and therefore a different discount rate should have been used).

- Miscalculation of the declining perpetuity often by forgetting to apply the negative growth rate to the cash flow or by forgetting to adjust the discount rate for the negative growth. However, it should be noted that a good number of candidates did actually deal with the declining perpetuity correctly.

- Not calculating the IRR after working out the NPV of the project.

Part (b)(ii) was usually answered correctly, where attempted.

Answers to part (c) were mixed. Most candidates seemed well prepared to discuss the EMH and often went into great lengths to define each of its states, which in this instance was not required in any depth. Many were able to make the connection between the state of the market and how the share price would react. However, very few candidates identified that there were two forces at play impacting the share price (being the discount on the rights issue and the positive NPV of the project), as shown by the TERP results. Most candidates were able to identify at least one or two 'other relevant factors' such as investor /market expectations.

INVESTMENT DECISIONS AND POJECT CONTROL I – ACQUISITIONS AND MERGERS

42   AB PLC AND YZ PLC *Walk in the footsteps of a top tutor*

Top tutor tips

This is a question that requires knowledge of valuation of firms using P/E ratios and the dividend valuation model in a takeover context. It also requires discussion of the factors that investors should consider in accepting or rejecting a bid.

Not required: Discussion of anti-bid defences. Discussion of sources of costs savings and post-merger integration problems, etc. Don't waste time writing about things which are not specifically asked for.

(a)   **Evaluation: supporting information**

Top tutor tips

Do not forget to adjust for tax in working out EPS and share price.

Do not use the average (of year's high and low) prices in your evaluation – this is very misleading and simplistic, quite apart from ignoring most of the information provided.

	AB plc	YX plc	Combined
PBT (£m)	126.60	112.50	
PAT @ 30% (£m)	88.62	78.75	167.37
EPS in pence	35.45	43.75	
P:E ratio pre-bid	11:1	7:1	
Share price pre-bid (p)	390	306	
Market Value (£m)	974.80	551.30	1,526.10
No. of new shares (W 1)	250m	150m	400m
Ownership of new enterprise	62.5%	37.5%	100%
Value to original owners* (£m)	953.80	572.3	1,526.10
Post-announcement share price (p) (W2)	382	318	

*Assuming no synergies

Workings

(W1) Pre-bid number of shares in YZ = 180 million. The 5 for 6 offer terms means issuing (180m × 5/6) = 150 new shares in AB.

(W2) AB: £953.8/250m = 382p

YZ: £572.3/150m = 318p

Comment

Ignoring cost saving potential and synergies, the post-bid prices of 382p and 318p for AB and YX respectively suggest a fall in AB's share price of 8p and a 12p increase for YZ, threatening a wealth transfer from YZ's owners. Indeed, AB's share price has already fallen to reflect this presumably to (90% × 390p) = 351p, which seems overdone. Conversely, YZ's share price has risen by 14%, presumably to (1.14 × 306p) = 349p, which values YZ above the cash offer of 345p.

The bid motivation is presumably synergies that would improve the post-bid performance of the expanded entity. This is suggested by AB pitching the cash bid above the market price, a premium of (345p – 306p) = 39p (13%).

The central question is really what price can be expected post-bid? The analysis above incorporates a weighted average P/E ratio, but if synergies are priced in and assumed to materialise quickly, then AB's higher P/E ratio, or something approaching it, might be applied. For example, using the full 11:1 P/E ratio implies a market value of (11 × £167.37m) = £1,841m, corresponding to 460p per share in combined entry. This is a valuation premium of 21% for the whole enterprise.

On this basis, AB's owners, holding 250 million shares, would enjoy increased wealth of (460p – 390p) = 70p per share, some £175m in total, an 18% increase.

The former shareholders of YZ, holding 5/6 of their previous number of shares, would see an increase in share price to (460p – 306p) × 5/6 = 383p, a 25% increase. Their wealth would be (150 million × 460p) = £690 million, an increase of some £140 million over the pre-bid market value.

Of the total gains, (£1,841m – £1,526m) = £315m, about 55% would accrue to AB's owners and 45% to YZ's shareholders.

The dividend growth model could be used to value the shares in both firms.

Top tutor tips

To find the dividend per share, multiply the percentage dividend yield by the share price. Do not apply the percentages to the PATs – they are not pay-out ratios.

Using pre-bid values, AB's DPS = (2.4% × 390p) = 9.36p, and YZ's is (3.1% × 306) = 9.49p.

$$\text{Value of AB's shares} = \frac{9.36p(1.04)}{(k_e - g)} = \frac{9.73p}{(13\% - 4\%)} = 108p$$

$$\text{Value of YZ's shares} = \frac{9.49p(1.04)}{(k_e - g)} = \frac{9.87p}{(11\% - 4\%)} = 141p$$

Clearly, these values, well below the market prices, suggest that neither firm is valued purely for its current dividend-paying capacity. In support of this, using the EPS for each firm (35.45p for AB and 43.75p for YZ), which assumes all earnings are paid out as dividends, the valuations increase to 409p and 650p respectively, suggesting that the market slightly undervalues AB, but significantly undervalues YZ. This again makes AB's 345p cash bid look unattractive to YX.

(b) **Whether to accept the bid? If so, cash or shares?**

Top tutor tips

Ensure that you make use of the available figures. A report format is not required.

Factors to consider:

- Valuations of such firms in 'people industries' are very difficult, and thus all figures are suspect. The most valuable assets have legs, and could easily walk away.

- The bid is weighted in favour of AB's shareholders (not surprisingly). How high would AB be prepared to bid, thus transferring more of the gains to YZ?

- To what extent does the market expect AB to exploit synergies? The market value pre-bid (306p) is well below the value based on YZ's earnings stream. Maybe the market is sceptical about the ability of YZ's managers to achieve the 4% growth rate. This is borne out by the 4 point gap in the two firm's P/E ratios.

- YZ's share price is only just above the year's low of 285p – the bid looks opportunistic at a time of temporary weakness in YZ's market rating. No other competing firm sells at such a low P/E ratio. This sort of discrepancy often suggests management difficulties, e.g. the actual or threatened resignation of key staff.

- If YZ really is undervalued, what is the likelihood of another bidder entering the fray? WX enjoys a high market rating (P/E ratio of 16:1) that might support an all-share offer.

Cash vs. shares

Top tutor tips

Beware of double-counting here – some points in favour of shares will be points against cash.

- Using the post-announcement price the two offers are worth:

  Cash: (6 × 345) = 2,070p

  Paper: (5 × 382) = 1,910p

  Hence, the cash offer is marginally superior at present.

- The cash offer is certain, whereas the value of the share alternative will fluctuate both during the bid process and thereafter. Accepting shares will expose us to a stock-market downturn before the bid is completed.

- Some investors accepting cash may be liable for capital gains tax, although there are certain allowances available.

- Taking cash prevents participation in any future improvements in management performance.

- Taking shares means sharing in the substantial costs of the takeover, both of the bid process and during the post-merger integration phase.

- Taking shares is a gamble on improvements in operating performance.

- The future situation regarding dividend policy is uncertain – AB pays out a lower dividend per share than YZ, although this might improve along with higher earnings. Not all investors are dividend seekers.

(c)   **Recommendations**

Top tutor tips

There is no right answer here – any reasoned, balanced argument will fit.

It is difficult to offer 'blanket' advice relevant to all investors. The decision is essentially a choice between a certain cash sum and a variable paper investment. However, the key issues are:

- This is the best opportunity to 'sell out' that we have had for some time.

- But it undervalues the prospective future gains should AB utilise YZ's assets as effectively as its own.

- The market rating of AB is not impressive, suggesting some doubts about the ability of its management.

- The tabled terms may be a 'sighting shot' – many bids are revised upwards as defending managers resist the bid and/or as competing bids emerge.

- Even if the bid fails, AB is able to make a new bid after 12 months. Meanwhile, YZ is 'in play' and another bidder could well emerge. The danger is that a White Knight bidder may protect the positions of the existing managers who have performed so badly recently.

On balance, we should urge the existing managers to hold out for better terms, and then accept. This would avoid exposure to the risks inherent in waiting for AB's management to turn YZ around.

43   TAKEOVER BID (MAY 07 EXAM)

Key answer tips

Part (a) is bookwork and thus straightforward if learnt in advance.

With part (b) it is essential that your answer is related to the specific scenario given.

Part (c) is easier if you consider both entities before and after the merger.

(a)   **Role of competition authorities**

There is a general belief that increased competition leads to lower prices of goods and services, higher quality and more choice for consumers.

The main role of competition authorities, such as the Competition Directorate in Country Y, is thus to protect the public interest by prohibiting or placing conditions on mergers or acquisitions that might result in a substantial lessening of competition in an industry. Once a merger has been authorised, the Competition Directorate would continue to monitor the situation to ensure that imposed conditions are followed and that competition is still operating fairly.

As well as considering the degree of competition, the Competition Directorate would look at the wider issue of whether or not a merger was in the public interest. For example, a foreign acquisition of a domestic weapons manufacturer may be blocked on national security grounds.

(b)   **Potential problems of the merger**

Merging management structures

Potential problem	How they could be minimised
• Q could lose key staff from Z once consideration is paid. Retaining senior staff is often key to a successful merger or acquisition (Drucker).	• It is stated that a condition of the bid would be the retention of the current management team. This could be through an earn-out arrangement, for example. • Beyond the earn-out period, staff could be encouraged to stay through the use of share options, attractive salaries and by giving key staff from Z senior positions in the new business.

Potential problem	How they could be minimised
• The two firms have head offices in different parts of the country. Q's building has spare space but is far from the country's capital, so relocating Z's team may be problematic. On the other hand, relocating Q's staff to the capital would result in an empty building.	• It is important to integrate the management teams in one location. Senior staff from both firms should be interviewed to assess their reaction to relocation so the cheapest option can be adopted.

Systems

Potential problem	How they could be minimised
• At present Q and Z have very different and seemingly incompatible IT systems – Q's is bespoke but out of date and inflexible while Z's is basic and relies on individual capabilities.	• There is little point migrating Z's systems to match Q's when Q's really need upgrading anyway. In the short term the two systems should be maintained. • Going forwards the firm should investigate a new system for both entities. In particular ERP-driven redesign of processes using generic software from a vendor such as SAP or Oracle is recommended.

(c)   **Choice of capital structure**

There are two main theories of capital gearing:

- The traditional theory argues that there is an optimal gearing level that balances the benefits of cheap debt with the extra gearing risk to shareholders.

- Modigliani and Miller (MM) argued that, in the absence of taxation, capital structure did not affect wealth but with corporation tax firms should gear up as much as possible. However, when bankruptcy risk and limits on debt capacity are incorporated into the MM model, it too results in the conclusion that an optimal gearing level exists.

This can be applied to the proposed merger as follows:

- Q has low levels of debt and is probably at a point below optimal gearing. The value of Q could thus be increased by taking its debt levels closer to its debt capacity, taking advantage of the tax benefits of cheap debt.

- Z on other hand has a high level of borrowing, possibly beyond its optimal gearing level. As a result it is paying excessively high interest rates on some of its debt. Z would benefit from a reduction in gearing.

- The merger would thus benefit both entities as it would help both move closer to optimal gearing. However, it would still be advisable to repay Z's expensive debt and take out new loans via Q to reduce costs.

Another factor to consider is how the takeover will be financed. Should Q decide to raise further debt finance, then this would also have to be included in a discussion of optimal gearing.

44 GG (MAY 07 EXAM)

Key answer tips

This is a demanding question where you have to be careful not to get bogged down and overrun your time allocation.

In part (b)(i) there are a number of different ways growth can be calculated and incorporated so it is essential that you explain your approach. In part (b)(ii) your discussion should incorporate both the assumptions and implications of your calculations.

Part (c) is more straightforward. The key here is to relate your comments to the scenario as much as possible.

(a) **Cost of equity for BB**

Step 1: De-gear proxy industry beta.

$$\beta_u = \frac{E}{E+D(1-t)}\beta_g = \frac{4}{4+1(0.7)}1.4 = \frac{4}{4.7}1.4 = 1.1915$$

Step 2: Re-gear for BB.

$$\beta_g = \beta_u (1 + (1-t)\frac{D}{E}) = 1.1915 \times (1 + \frac{1(0.7)}{2.5}) = 1.525$$

Step 3: Use CAPM equation.

Required return = $R_f + \beta_g(R_m - R_f)$ = 3% + 1.525 × (8% − 3%)= 10.63%

(b)   (i)   **Valuation of BB**

P/E ratio approach: MV = P/E × Earnings

	Pre-synergy Earnings = $1m	Post-synergy Earnings = $1.1m
P/E ratio = 13 (Industry proxy)	MV = 13 × 1 = **$13m**	MV = 13 × 1.1 = **$14.3m**
P/E ratio = 11 (Predator HH)	MV = 11 × 1 = **$11m**	MV = 11 × 1.1 = **$12.1m**
P/E ratio = 14 (GG)	MV = 14 × 1 = **$14m**	MV = 14 × 1.1 = **$15.4m**

Dividend Valuation Model: $MV = \dfrac{d_1}{k_e - g}$

K_e = 10.63% per (a)

Assuming a payout ratio of 50%, growth is estimated to be g = 7%.

However, the lower payout ratio of 40% should result in higher growth than this. One way of estimating this is to use the 'g = r × b' model. With b = 0.5, g = 7%, suggesting that b = 14%.

Thus with b = 0.6, g = 14 × 0.6 = 8.4%. An acceptable alternative would be simply to use 7% again with the 40% payout ratio, but recognise that this would undervalue the business.

	Pre-synergy Earnings = $1m	Post-synergy Earnings = $1.1m
Payout ratio 50% g = 7%	$\dfrac{1 \times 50\% \times 1.07}{0.1063 - 0.07}$ = **$14.7m**	$\dfrac{1.1 \times 50\% \times 1.07}{0.1063 - 0.07}$ = **$16.2m**
Payout ratio 40% g = 8.4%	$\dfrac{1 \times 40\% \times 1.084}{0.1063 - 0.084}$ = **$19.4m**	$\dfrac{1.1 \times 40\% \times 1.084}{0.1063 - 0.084}$ = **$21.4m**
Payout ratio 40% g = 7%	$\dfrac{1 \times 40\% \times 1.07}{0.1063 - 0.07}$ = **$11.8m**	$\dfrac{1.1 \times 40\% \times 1.07}{0.1063 - 0.07}$ = **$13.0m**

Asset valuations

There is not enough information to use an asset-based approach.

(ii)   **Comments**

Earnings calculations

From GG's point of view it could be argued that BB is currently contributing $14 million to GG's value (i.e. GG's P/E ratio applied to pre-synergy earnings of $1 million) and that it would thus be unlikely to accept an offer below this.

However, it would be more accurate to value BB separately from GG, in which case the industry proxy P/E should be used provided the proxy has a similar risk and growth profile to BB. The relatively low P/E of 13, despite BB having higher growth forecasts to GG, would indicate that either telecommunications is deemed to be much more risky that engineering or that the proxy has lower growth expectations than BB. If the proxy is a good match, then GG should be advised that any offer over $13 million is worth considering.

From HH's perspective a P/E of 13 (industry) applied to post-synergy earnings of 1.1 would give an upper limit on the bid price of $14.3 million. However, they may be cautious as there may be negative boot-strapping given that HH's P/E is significantly lower at 11.

DVM approach

Central to the above DVM calculations are the assumptions about reinvestment rates and the resulting growth. Assuming GG can maintain the current payout ratios and growth, the DVM model would suggest that GG should hold out for offers in excess of $14.7 million.

However, if HH can only maintain the growth of 7% despite a lower payout ratio of 40%, then BB may only be worth $13 million to them, even with synergy. If HH can maintain the return on new investment at that currently earned in BB, then the lower payout should result in higher growth and a potential value to HH nearer to $21 million. Clearly the valuations are very sensitive to the growth estimates used.

Market expectations

Based on the possible sale, GG has seen its share price increase by 15% over the last two months to $8.

- This would suggest that the price two months ago was $8 ÷ 115% = $6.96.

- Given earnings growth of 6% p.a., the share price would have been expected to rise by 1% over the two-month period anyway to give a price of 6.96 × 1.01 = $7.03.

- The difference between this and $8 must be due to the bid, i.e. 97¢ per share.

- In total this equates to 4 million shares × 0.97 = $3.88 million.

The problem is then splitting this between the premium the market expects HH to pay for BB and the increase in value of the rest of GG due to greater focus, etc. However, it would not be unreasonable to suggest that a substantial premium is expected, say in excess of $2 million.

Other considerations

A fair price for BB would have to incorporate the following factors:

- How many other companies are interested in buying BB and how strong is the strategic argument for acquisition? Competition would obviously increase the price.

- How important is BB to HH's future plans?

Advice

HH should start with an offer around the 'proxy market value' of $13 million. This is likely to be rejected so HH should then increase its bid. However, it is unwise to factor the bulk of the synergy into the bid price, so HH would be advised to keep any subsequent bids to below $14 million.

Tutorial note

Part (c) could have been answered even if you struggled with the numbers in this question. Always look for the easy marks in a question and try to get those first.

(c) **Divestment**

The potential benefits and drawbacks of the divestment are as follows:

Benefits	Drawbacks
• Divestment should allow the management of GG to focus on core activities, thus increasing shareholder value.	• GG would lose any synergy that exists between BB and the rest of the company. While the two businesses are very distinct there will still be some economies of scale.
• If BB is sold at a premium to what it currently contributes to GG's value, then divestment should increase shareholder value. The recent rise in the share price would suggest that this is how the markets view the disposal.	• GG would lose a high growth part of its business (BB's 7% v GG's 6%), thus reducing GG's future growth potential.
• The cash can be invested elsewhere.	• There would be a reduced diversification of risk, although the shareholders of GG are probably city institutions that will be well-diversified.
	• It is important that funds generated are reinvested. Failure to find suitable projects, for example, could make GG more exposed to a hostile takeover.

45   SB PLC (NOV 08 EXAM)

Key answer tips

It is important in this question to comment on the methods of valuation as you also present your calculations. In general, the marks for calculation and discussion in valuation questions will be approximately equal.

(a)   **Net asset valuation**

At the most recent balance sheet date, the value of SB's assets was £22,595,000. On a per share basis, the value is £4.52.

This asset based valuation is unlikely to be useful as we try to assess the true value of the business. Asset based valuations take no account of the value of intangible assets and intellectual property. In a firm like SB, these values are likely to be high since the firm operates in a low capital intensive industry.

The only benefit of an asset based valuation is that it gives us an absolute minimum figure (i.e. the lowest value that the business should ever be sold for).

Price Earnings valuation

The current level of profit after tax is £20,188,000

There are three different P/E ratios quoted, giving the following range of values:

P/E ratio	Total value (£m)	Value per share (£)
9	181.7	36.33
12	242.3	48.45
25	504.7	100.94

The P/E method is the simplest of all the earnings based valuation methods. However, it is reliant on estimating the P/E ratio and the earnings (Profit after Tax) figures accurately.

In this case, there is considerable doubt as to what an appropriate P/E ratio might be – the calculations presented show a huge range in forecast values. It is also questionable whether using P/E ratios from similar quoted firms is appropriate when valuing unquoted companies.

Also, although SB's current earnings are £20.2m, it is not certain that this level of earnings will be sustainable in the future given the high level of risk in the industry. A reduction in future earnings would have a negative impact on the values calculated.

Dividend valuation model

SB has never paid a dividend and there is no suggestion that this dividend policy will be changed. Thus we cannot use the dividend valuation model in this case.

Discounted cash flow method

£000	t_1	t_2	t_3
Revenue	52,250	62,700	75,240
Operating profit (40%)	20,900	25,080	30,096
Tax (28%)	(5,852)	(7,022)	(8,427)
Net profit/cashflow	15,048	18,058	21,669
DF @ 12%	0.893	0.797	0.712
Present values	13,438	14,392	15,428
NPV (€)	43,258 + perpetuity from t_4 onwards		

$$\text{Value of perpetuity} = \frac{(21,669 \times 1.06)}{0.12 - 0.06} \times 0.712 = 272,567$$

Tutorial note

This formula for the value of a delayed, growing perpetuity is important. It is commonly tested in valuation questions.

Therefore total value = 43,258 + 272,567 = £315.8m

This corresponds to £63.16 per share.

Theoretically, the discounted cash flow method is the best valuation method. The present value of future cashflows links directly to shareholder wealth and hence the value of the business.

However, the method is reliant on the accuracy of the forecasts of future cashflows, and the estimate of an appropriate discount rate.

It is very difficult to estimate the future cashflows of SB with any certainty, given the risky nature of the new Caribbean opportunities. Also, there is considerable doubt whether SB's cashflows will continue to grow at the same rate into perpetuity.

Also, the given discount rate of 12% seems very low when considering the potential risks facing SB in the future.

Summary of valuation figures

Method	Total value (£m)	Share value (£)
Net assets	22.6	4.52
P/E (range)	181.7 – 504.7	36.33 – 100.94
DCF	315.8	63.16

Recommendation

As explained above, the net asset valuation is not relevant in the context of a trade sale or IPO.

Similarly the range of figures generated by the P/E method suggests that that method is unreliable in this case – it is difficult to know whether SB is more similar to the quoted companies at the upper or the lower end of the spectrum.

Therefore, I suggest that the figure given by the DCF method of approximately £63 per share should be used as a starting point.

In a trade sale, this valuation will be subject to negotiation with the buyer.

For an IPO, it will be important to assess the likely demand for the shares at this price before going ahead with the offer.

(b) **Advantages of trade sale**

SB has already been approached by some interested parties. This means that a trade sale might be very easy to organise compared with an IPO.

In a trade sale, the administrative burden (including costs) is much less than with a flotation.

In a trade sale, the value can be decided between the two parties and will not be driven by the general market factors which affect the valuation of stock market shares.

The directors would relinquish control of the business through a trade sale. Whether this an advantage or a disadvantage will depend on their objectives. This is arguably the key issue as they try to decide between the two alternatives.

Advantages of flotation

A flotation will improve the standing of the company, leading to higher valuation of shares.

The founding directors may retain control of the business by offering a minority of the entity's shares to the market.

An IPO now will give the company access to more funding opportunities in the future. This may well be important if SB wants to undertake the new Caribbean projects.

46 LP (MAY 09 EXAM)

Key answer tips

It should have been easy enough to see in part (a) that the current offer was undervaluing the target based on current share prices. Any suggestion of a revised offer which valued MQ at market value AND incorporated a premium to encourage MQ shareholders to sell would have scored credit here.

After proposing your own offer terms in part (a) it was then important to follow your own numbers through the rest of the question, and you would have scored full marks even if your answer differed from the given "model" answer.

(a)   The terms of the bid are 2 LP shares for 1 MQ share.

Looking at today's share prices, the market appears to be expecting a substantially increased bid; 2 LP shares are worth 610 pence (2 × 305 pence) whereas 1 MQ share is worth 680 pence. On this ratio the bid could not possibly succeed.

To make sure that LP is valuing MQ at its current market value, the value of the offer needs to be 680 pence × 130m shares = £884m in total. Given the current LP share price of 305 pence, this amounts to £884m / £3.05 = 289.8m shares in LP.

An exchange of 289.8m LP shares for the 130m MQ shares represents a ratio of 289.8m to 130m or 2.23 to 1.

However, if the terms of the offer were to be exactly 2.23 LP shares for every 1 share in MQ, there would be no incentive for the MQ shareholders to sell (financially, they'd be indifferent between keeping their existing shares and exchanging them for LP shares).

In order to encourage MQ's shareholders to sell, a premium would have to be offered.

Hence, an offer of (say) 2.5 LP shares for every 1 share in MQ would probably be needed to encourage the MQ shareholders to sell.

However, there are some other key points to consider:

- The bid is taking place in a dynamic market and there are other, external influences that might affect share prices.

- Over the last month the share price of LP has fallen, while that of MQ has increased. This is not untypical in bid situations and reflects uncertainty of the market of the likely success of LP's bid and increased interest in the shares of the target. Studies have shown that in hostile bid situations bidders typically pay too much to acquire their target.

- The share prices of the two entities will react to any revised bid based on market perceptions of the benefits to be gained by the shareholders of the two entities. If the market thinks LP is paying too much, its own share price will fall, thus making the terms less attractive to MQ.

- Evidence has shown that in a hostile bid it is usually the target entity's shareholders who obtain all the gains from a merger.

(b)   (i)   **Advantages and disadvantages of cash alternative**

The advantages of offering cash as an alternative to a share exchange are:

- The amount of the offer is more certain, so can be more easily understood by the target shareholders.

- The target company's shareholders are paid off, so the company no longer has to pay dividends to them in the future.

- There is no dilution of control in the bidding company.

The disadvantages are:

- Cash has to be raised, most probably by the issue of a long-term debt instrument so gearing increases.

- There might also be taxation implications for individual shareholders, although as the offer is optional, this should not be a problem.

- It is necessary to recognise that as some of both LP's and MQ's existing debt matures within the next three to four years, refinancing needs to be considered. LP will, of course, obtain MQ's cash balances post-merger, but the cost of the acquisition process is likely to be high and will require a considerable amount of cash-generating capacity in the short-term. Also, the cash available at the balance sheet date (six months' ago) might not be available now.

Calculation of cash required

A bid of 2.5 for 1 implies a price per MQ share of 762.5 pence and a total value of the bid of £991.25 million (130 million shares × 762.5 pence).

Assuming 60% of MQ's shareholders accept a cash offer, approximately £595 million is required in cash.

The combined cash at bank balances of £355 million could be used, leaving £240 million to be raised in new debt.

Effect on gearing

This is difficult to do without more information and it is almost impossible to forecast the value of the equity post-merger. If the combined entity increases the amount of debt in its capital structure, which is likely if a large proportion of MQ's shareholders opt for a cash alternative, then the gearing ratio will rise.

The effect on the cost of equity capital could be estimated by making a number of assumptions, for example, the cost of new debt. It is likely that any new debt will carry a higher rate of interest because of this increased risk.

Ignoring this, and assuming debt is quoted at par, gearing can be estimated as follows:

Current gearing:

$D/D+E$ = $350/(350 + 1,464)$ = 19.3%

Approximate gearing for enlarged group if a full share exchange

$D/D+E$ = $455/[455 + (1,464 + 991.25)]$ = 15.6%

If £240m is raised for the cash alternative, this would increase gearing to:

$D/D+E$ = $695/[695 + (1,464 + 396)]$ = 27.2%

Tutorial note

Clear workings were important here. Gearing can be measured in several different ways, so it was important to show which formula you were using.

(ii) **How the cash alternative might be financed**

A rights issue is a possibility but this would take considerable time to organise and in the circumstances here is very unlikely.

The most likely form of finance is a long-term debt instrument.

Secured debt with a maturity of 10 to 15 years would be the most obvious, but alternatives that could be considered and that have cost advantages are convertible debt or debt with warrants.

The key feature of these types of debt finance is that they tend to offer lower rates of interest because of the opportunity of buying into the entity's equity "cheaply" at some future date. Debt with warrants also has the advantage that additional money will be raised at some time in the future, subject of course to the holders exercising their warrants. Convertible debt does not raise additional money, but has the advantage of being self-liquidating if all holders convert into equity on or before the final maturity date.

47   RV (MAY 09 EXAM) *Walk in the footsteps of a top tutor*

Top tutor tips

Part (a) covered business valuation, but in a different way from in previous papers – the Modigliani and Miller theory is tested much less frequently than many of the other valuation methods. However, MM's formula for the valuation of a geared entity is presented on the exam formula sheet, so it was always going to be tested one day. This emphasises how important it is to have a good grasp of the full syllabus in order to be successful at this level.

Part (b) was interesting, in that it looked at valuation in the context of a small unlisted entity. Due to the lack of available information, and the lack of scrutiny applied to unlisted entities, the principles of valuation are quite different from those relating to listed companies.

(a)   (i)   **Calculations of the value of RV**

Using DVM

Dividend in 20X8 = £10m × 0.7 × 0.25 = £1.75m

If no growth in dividends or earnings is expected if the entity does not borrow and invest, the value of the entity and of equity is a simple perpetuity:

Ve = D_1/0.12 = £175/0.12 = £14.58m or 72.9 pence per share

Using MM

Vug firm   =   post tax earnings before interest payments in perpetuity, assuming 6% growth

=   (£10m × 0.95 × 0.7) × 1.06/(0.12 − 0.06)

=   £117.48m

Then, Vg = Vug + the value of the tax shield on debt (Vts):

	£million
Vug	117.48
Plus Vts £20m × 30%	6.00
Total Vg	123.48
Less value of debt (assume par)	20.00
Value of equity	103.48
Value per share = £103.48 million/20 million =	517 pence

(ii)   **Assumptions and limitations of DVM and MM**

The DVM is more appropriate for valuing a small parcel of shares than an entire entity but still suffers from some simplistic assumptions, mainly that dividends are the only determinant of value although the earnings model could be used instead.

Modigliani and Miller's theory might be suitable for valuing the entire entity, although it has serious flaws in a real world environment. These are primarily caused by the fact that MM's theory assumes perfect markets and rational investors so real world market imperfections such as transaction costs and irrational shareholder behaviour cause a problem.

More appropriate methods of valuation would be:

- a PE ratio approach. The earnings per share could be multiplied by an industry average PE ratio to give an estimate of share value. However, there is no guarantee that the industry PE ratio would be appropriate to the circumstances of RV as a private entity.

- an NPV approach. Forecast cash flows more accurately by project or product line and discount these at a rate that reflects the specific risk of the different cash flow streams.

Tutorial note

The discursive points in part (b) are not related to the calculations in part (a), so you could have started with part (b) if you felt it was easier. As long as you label your questions clearly in your answer book, the marker will give you credit for all the work you present, irrespective of which order you put it in.

(b)   **Advice to directors**

Value of small parcels of shares vs entire entity

As noted above, the use of the DVM is useful for valuing a small parcel of shares as individual shareholders look at the value of their income stream.

An alternative method might simply be to take the asset value. Certainly small shareholders would be able to understand this method better than the DVM.

In terms of valuing the entity, the influence of dividends on the value of a private entity such as RV is rather different from those that influence a public listed entity as rather fewer people are scrutinising the actions and pronouncements of the entity and the "signalling" mechanism is irrelevant.

Therefore, a theoretical model such as the DVM may be of very limited value here. In a large listed entity, the value of the entity is often quite different than the sum of the value of small parcels of shares because the rationale for selling an entire entity is different from the rationale and motivation to sell of individual shareholders.

If the owners/managers wish to sell the entire entity they would have to put together a significant amount of additional information, looking at the present value of the cash flows from their investments and also taking into account issues such as:

- P/E ratios of similar entities that are listed

- Economic prospects for the industry

- Likely buyers.

How and to whom small shareholdings might be sold.

The most obvious buyer would be the entity, in a share repurchase scheme. Other possibilities are:

- The venture capital trust might be willing to buy additional shares if the trust deed allows this, especially if a fairly low valuation is agreed.

- Other existing shareholders.

- Customers/suppliers who might be interested in a stake in RV.

Note that flotation would not be an option here, since the entity is too small for a flotation.

The sale would be effected by a fairly straightforward share transfer on payment of the agreed price per share. The key issue is the valuation.

48 XK (MAY 10 EXAM)

Key answer tips

Read the requirement to part (a) carefully: don't simply identify stakeholders, but make sure you consider the effect of the new arrangement on them.

(a) **The effect on stakeholders**

The main stakeholders to consider will be the shareholders of XK, the directors and employees of the subsidiary and the creditors of both entities.

XK's shareholders

Shareholders will have bought shares in XK recognizing and understanding its policies in respect of risk and return. Approximately 6% of the earnings are provided by subsidiary Y and removing this might impact the risk profile and earning capacity and, hence, the value of XK.

Directors and employees of XK

This group of stakeholders is unlikely to be affected to any great extent, other than by the overall impact on the level of earnings, although some services provided to the subsidiary by head office will no longer be required. This might involve a small number of redundancies unless they can be transferred to the subsidiary on divestment.

Directors and other employees of subsidiary Y

Executive directors appear willing to take the risk of the proposed management buyout as they are collectively prepared to find US$5 million of the equity required. Non-director employees might be adversely affected. The divested subsidiary's directors might take the opportunity to review current personnel and employment terms and conditions, which could involve redundancy and/or reduced pay. In the long-term, the new entity could provide increased employment if it adopts an aggressive growth strategy but in the short-term there could be redundancies.

Creditors (suppliers) and bankers

XK's bankers are unlikely to be affected as the bonds are secured on XK's non-current assets. The lenders would only be concerned if the sale of Company Y made it less likely that the bonds would be fully secured. The scenario says the subsidiary's non-current assets are valued at US$220 million in the accounts. Removing this amount from group non-current assets still leaves US$2,030 million which comfortably covers the secured debt of US$1,000 million.

The current ratio of XK, at the last balance sheet date, is 1.65:1 (current assets/current liabilities = 700/425 = 1.65) so trade creditors seem well protected but this is getting close to the externally imposed overdraft condition of 1.5:1.

Some suppliers could be affected if the purchasing policy for Company Y is currently controlled by the parent. This responsibility will pass to the newly independent company and it is possible there will be some changes to terms of trade.

Customers

The customers of Company Y, the divested subsidiary, might notice some changes to terms and conditions. As an independent company, Company Y might lose some customers as it will no longer benefit from joint marketing initiated by XK. This possible loss of earnings will affect other groups of stakeholders rather than the customers themselves.

Other

Other groups that could possibly be affected are government and local communities. It is hard to see from the information available how either group will be significantly affected one way or another. The national and local governments will of course have an interest in ensuring employment is maintained.

In summary, the main winners are likely to be the executive directors in the buyout team. The main losers, possibly, will be some of XK's current employees and, also possibly, XK's suppliers.

(b) **The economic and market factors affecting the negotiations**

The decision to divest Company Y could have been influenced by the recession of the last two years as the household electrical goods sector was not immune to its effects. This might affect XK's bargaining position.

The main economic factors that might impact on negotiations are interest rates, stock market movement/sentiment, alternative investment opportunities, and regulatory controls.

Interest rates and inflation

- A change in interest rates is likely to have a major impact on the divested subsidiary's future cash flows and the cost of capital. An increase in interest rates can be expected to lead to a reduction in discretionary expenditure on household electrical goods. It will also increase the discount rates used in NPV calculations which will have the effect of decreasing the value of the subsidiary. Both of these factors could be used by the buyout team to argue that the buyout price should be reduced.

- Increased inflation will undermine confidence in the economy, making it harder to assess future cash flows and again will cause the buyout team to claim a lower valuation for the subsidiary.

Stock market movement/sentiment

- Shareholders have not yet been informed or consulted so their reaction is not known. However, it is very difficult for this type of negotiation to remain confidential and the market is almost certain to have obtained some "insider" information. The share price has risen 5% over the past 3 months which might imply the market is at least not opposed to the planned divestment. Subsequent movements in the share price will depend on what the market had been expecting.

- Once details of the divestment are known, the share price can be expected to rise further since the company is disposing of only 6% of earnings at a price equivalent to 10% of the market value (= 325/3281). On the other hand, it does make a positive contribution to group earnings and this will be lost to current shareholders.

- We have not been given any information about the risk profile of Y. Only if it is more risky than XK will the risk of XK reduce with the sale of Y.

Alternative investment opportunities

Assuming a sale is agreed at or near the valuation of US$325 million, XK will have a large cash balance to invest. It could pay off some of its debt. However, the group is not overly indebted – using the book value of debt as an approximation of market value, gearing is only 23% excluding overdraft (23% = 1,000/(1,000 + 3,281)) and 26% including overdraft (26% = (1,000 + 150)/(1,000 + 150 + 3,281)) – and this would not be a good use of funds. The group should evaluate alternatives before agreeing to divest what is a profitable subsidiary.

Regulatory controls

There are unlikely to be any issues that would concern the competition authorities.

(c) **Advantages and disadvantages of the proposed buyout structure**

Venture capital

The main advantage of a venture capital investor (VC) is that this investor shares in the risk – in fact takes most of the risk and only ranks ahead of the buyout team of executive directors. The VC may or may not require a dividend but will require substantial returns for the risk it is taking. In the scenario here the VC has stated it requires all earnings to be re-invested. The consequence of reinvesting all earnings is that capital growth is encouraged. The return required appears high but this is typical of this type of investor. If we assume the NPV of the subsidiary is its initial market capitalisation the implied P/E ratio is 10.6, (US$325m divided by US$30.6m earnings (where 30.6m = 6% × 510m)) which does not seem excessive.

However, there would need to be significant growth in the business to enable the VC to realise 25% per annum return. With debt of US$198 million, earnings would be reduced to approximately US$21.7 million (see W1) which represents a return of less than 18% (see W3) to the VC, even before providing any return to the management buyout team of executive Directors. The VC would only be prepared to invest in the business if it believes in the new management's ability to 'transform' the business and achieve rapid growth.

Workings

		US$ million
(W1)	Previous year's earnings	30.6
	Less interest after tax relief of 6% × 198 × (1 – 0.25)	(8.91)
	Profit after tax and interest	21.69

(W2)	Venture capitalist contribution	
	Price	325
	Less Director's contribution	(5)
	Less Investment bank	(198)
	Balance from VC	122

(W3) 17.8% = 21.7/122

The main disadvantages of using venture capitalist finance is that, if the ultimate exit route is by Initial Public Offering (IPO), the majority of the returns will go to the venture capitalists. However, the buyout team has limited choice.

Buyout team of executive directors

The executive directors will be at the bottom of the pile in terms of returns on their investment. As we have calculated above, they need to realise substantial growth and 'transform' the business in order to satisfy the VC and therefore also provide themselves with some return on their investment.

Investment bank

Financing a proportion of the buyout from an investment bank allows equity investors to retain a greater share of the business but there is a high cost in terms of interest payments that will impact on earnings and affect the overall risk of the business. The value of the subsidiary is likely to be lower with the involvement of this type of finance because of the interest payments and the increased cost of equity.

There are however some serious concerns about the amount of borrowing from this bank.

1   The debt of US$198 million is only just covered by the estimated value of the non-current assets. This leaves little spare debt capacity and explains the high interest rate relative to current market rates for secured borrowings.

2 If earnings are maintained at around US$30.6 million in the first year of operations then the interest cover is just about adequate at 3.1 times (W4). However, the figures here are based on many assumptions that might not be accurate.

3 The earnings need to be adequate to allow an accumulation of cash to repay the US$198 million secured loan (principal) at the end of the 5 years. Unless the new entity can grow its earnings substantially over the next 5 years this will not be possible.

(W4) Profit before interest and tax attributable to Y is:

$6\% \times (510/(1 - 0.25) + 7.5\% \times 1,150) = 46.0$ million

(assuming interest on overdraft is also 7.5%)

Interest payable by Y is:

$7.5\% \times 198$ million $= 14.9$ million

Interest cover $= 3.1$ times $= 46.0/14.9$

Summary

The key points to emerge are that:

1 The divestment appears to have few "losers" among the stakeholders and the market appears to be reacting favourably to "insider" information about the divestment.

2 There are no major external threats that would seriously de-rail negotiations.

Alternative financing structures

The most serious concerns are the methods of financing. The interest payments to the investment bank are very high and leave little or no room for accumulating cash from earnings to repay the principal of the debt and fund future growth. The venture capital entity will certainly not receive its required growth of 25% if 61% of the purchase consideration is via an investment bank.

The recommendation is that the financing of the buyout is reconsidered. The buyout team could consider one or more of the following options:

- Negotiate a staged payment to XK – if XK has no immediate need of the funds this could be attractive to both parties.

- Discuss the venture capital entity taking a larger share of the business.

- Look for alternative providers of debt or re-negotiate with the investment bank to provide, say, debt with warrants rather than straight debt although this will dilute the equity in the longer term and might not be acceptable to the venture capital entity.

49 ADS (NOV 10 EXAM)

Key answer tips – extracted from the Examiner's "Post Exam Guide"

Part (a)

Introduce your answer by recognising the similarities between the Modigliani & Miller (MM) and traditional approaches. Then discuss how they differ. Up to 3 graphs should be provided to accompany your discussion; one of the traditional model, one of MM without taxes and one of MM with taxes. It is important to remember to label the axes on your graphs and clearly indicate which graph is which. Conclude with a discussion of the limitations of MM to real world situations.

Part (b)(i)

Calculate the value of equity by dividing the forecast earnings of ADS by the cost of equity minus expected growth rate.

Part (b)(ii)

Calculate:

- The value of equity assuming Vg = Vug +TB

- The cost of equity using MM's formula with taxes, as shown in the formulae sheet

- The WACC using the cost of equity just calculated.

Part (c)

Explain the impact of taxes on lowering the cost of capital and that when cost of capital decreases the value of the company will increase. Advise the directors why the apparent fall in the value of equity is not of long term concern when new finance is raised by debt.

(a) **How MM differs from the traditional model**

Under both the MM models and the traditional model, the cost of equity increases as the level of gearing increases. This is because the introduction of debt brings financial risk, which will cause the earnings available to the equity shareholders to become more volatile as interest has to be paid before dividends. The equity shareholders will therefore require higher returns in order to compensate for the increase in financial risk, which pushes the cost of equity up.

Debt is assumed to be a cheaper source of finance than equity, as it ranks above equity for both the distribution of earnings and on liquidation and therefore carries less risk for the investor.

The traditional view of gearing is that WACC will be lowest at a level of gearing that represents an "optimal" capital structure. At this optimum WACC will be minimised, which will therefore maximise the value of the firm (assuming earnings to be independent of the capital structure). The relationship between the k_e, k_d and WACC under the traditional theory is shown in diagram 1.

Under MM's assumptions, firms identical in all respects apart from capital structure (allowing for size), should have the same value. Value is determined by a stream of operating cash flows and the degree of business risk attaching to these, regardless of how the cash flows are shared out between different classes of investor. Under MM, and excluding taxes, WACC remains the same –as gearing increases the impact of the increasing K_e is exactly offset by the lower k_d as shown in diagram 2. Note from the diagram that at very high levels of gearing MM believed that the k_e would fall as equity risk-takers come into the market, although this would be compensated for by an increase in the k_d resulting for the increased risk perceived by debt investors.

However, this ignores the fact that, generally, interest on debt is a tax-deductible expense and the issue costs of debt are normally lower than those for equity. This tax benefit implies K_e will rise and WACC will fall, as shown in diagram 3.

Diagram 1

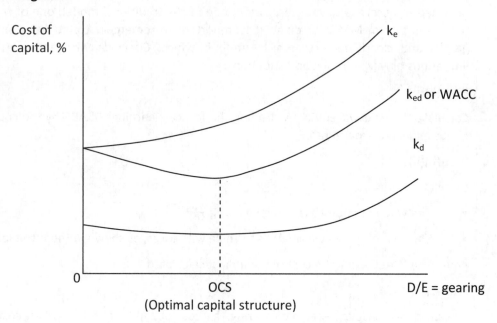

Figure 4.1 Traditional theory of gearing
Note: k_e = cost of equity; k_d = cost of debt; ke_d = WACC

Diagram 2

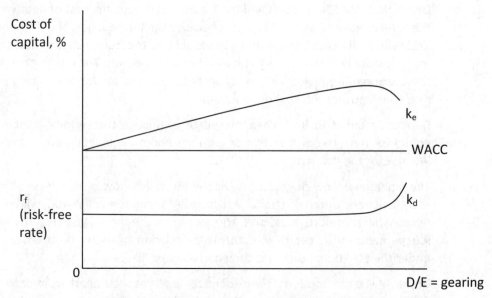

Figure 4.3 MM's gearing propositions without tax

Diagram 3

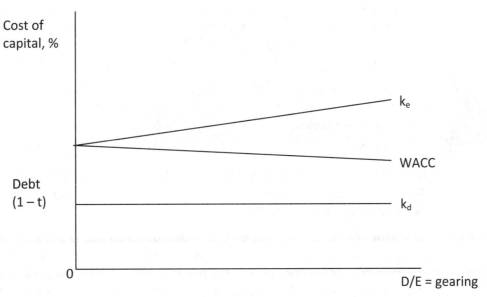

Figure 4.4 MM's gearing propositions with tax

Limitations to "real world" applications

The limitations to "real world" applications are:

- Cost of capital is not likely to remain constant.

- MM assume personal and corporate leverage are equivalent, this is unlikely to be true as companies even of medium size are likely to have a better credit rating than most individual investors.

- Very high levels of gearing carry considerable dangers of corporate collapse. MM's later model allowed for this but the main limitation still maintain.

- Assumes zero transaction costs.

(b) (i) **Assume equity finance**

$$V_u = \frac{127.1}{0.09 - 0.04} = A\$2,542m$$

(ii) **Assume bond finance**

Value of equity

$V_g = V_{ug} + TB$

$V_g = A\$2,542m + (A\$250m \times 25\%) = A\$2,605m$

Value of equity = A\$2,605m − A\$250m = A\$2,355m

Cost of equity

$$k_{eg} = k_{eug} + \left[(1-t)\frac{D}{E}(k_{eu} - k_d) \right]$$

$$= 9 + \left[(0.75 \times \frac{250}{2,355}) \times (9-5) \right]$$

$= 9 + 0.32 = 9.32$

That is, $k_e = 9.32\%$

WACC

$$WACC_g = \left[k_{eg} \times \frac{E}{D+E} \right] + \left[k_d(1-t)\frac{D}{D+E} \right]$$

$$= \left[9.32 \times \frac{2,355}{2,605} \right] + \left[5(0.75) \times \frac{250}{2,605} \right]$$

$$= 8.43\% + 0.36\%$$

$$= 8.79\%$$

(c) Under MM theory with taxes, introducing debt finance reduces the cost of capital. This is supported by the calculations in part (b). It can be seen that the WACC has decreased from 9.00% to 8.79%.

When the cost of capital decreases, the value of the company will increase as there is an inverse relationship between cost of capital and company value. Indeed, we can see from the calculations in part (b) that the value of the company as a whole has increased from A$2,542 million to A$2,605 million. This is an increase of A$63 million which represents the PV of the tax shield on the new debt.

When looking at the value of equity however, it appears to fall from A$2,542 million to A$2,355 million – a fall of A$187 million. So why is the value of equity lower if ADS issues the undated bond rather than raising new capital using equity? The reason is that the shareholders will contribute A$250 million of equity capital if the stores are financed by equity but will not need to contribute any funds if the stores are financed by debt. Overall shareholder wealth has therefore increased when the cash contribution is taken into account.

Scenario	Value of equity A$ million	Shareholder wealth A$ million
Equity finance	2,542	2,542 – 250 = 2,292
Debt finance	2,355	2,355

From the table we can see that if equity is used the total value of the equity will be A$2,542 million, however to get this shareholders will need to spend A$250 million – hence overall shareholder wealth will be A$2,292 million. However, if debt is used the shareholders would not need to use any of their existing wealth and the value of their equity will be A$2,355 million. The difference in wealth is A$63 million which represents the tax benefit from debt – all of this benefit going to the shareholders.

Therefore, under MM's model with corporate tax, the fall in the value of equity should not be of concern to the Directors since overall shareholder wealth has increased by the value of the tax shield.

In 'real life', the traditional view is more likely to hold. That is, the impact of additional debt on the WACC will depend on the current level of gearing. WACC will follow a "U" shape and, once the bottom of the curve has been passed, any increase in gearing is likely to create an increase in the cost of capital (due to the increased risk to the investors) and therefore a decrease in the value of the net assets of the company. Under certain circumstances, especially at high levels of gearing, it is therefore possible that shareholder wealth could decrease, but this is only likely to happen at exceptionally high levels of gearing.

Tutorial note – extracted from the Examiner's "Post Exam Guide"

This question tended to be answered very well indeed, or very poorly. Some overseas centres provided very good answers to part (a) in particular. Few candidates gained more than token marks for the MM graphs, which were generally very poorly reproduced e.g. showing curves going in the wrong direction and not labelling (or mis-labelling) the axes.

Some candidates discussed MM's theory of dividend-irrelevancy instead of gearing.

Answers to (b)(i) frequently simply multiplied the share price by number of shares in issue rather than using the DCF approach as required.

Part (b)(ii) required the use of MM's model with taxes. Many candidates attempted valuation of ADS's equity using a variety of other methods. On the 'own answer' principle, most candidates gained marks for the WACC calculation.

Part (c) was particularly poorly attempted and most candidates failed to address the question asked.

50 WW (MAY 11 EXAM)

Key answer tips – extracted from the Examiner's "Post Exam Guide"

Part (a)

- Calculate XX's existing cost of equity using CAPM.

- Adjust XX's cost of debt for tax and then use this cost of debt, together with the cost of equity calculated above, to calculate XX's WACC.

- Ungear and regear YY's beta.

- Calculate an adjusted cost of equity based on this adjusted beta and using CAPM.

- Recalculate a WACC using this adjusted cost of equity.

Part(b)(i)

Present a range of values, starting with the asset figures provided in the question. Then use the earning valuation model to calculate the value of the division based on each WACC calculated in part (a) above.

Part (b)(ii)

Discuss the validity of each valuation method in turn

Part (b)(iii)

Conclude by advising an appropriate purchase price.

(a)   (i)   **XX's cost of equity**

$k_e = R_f + [R_m - R_f]\beta$

$= 5\% + 6\% \times 1.5$

$= 14.0\%$

(ii)   **XX's WACC**

$$WACC = k_e\left(\frac{V_E}{V_E + V_D}\right) + k_d[1-t]\left(\frac{V_D}{V_E + V_D}\right)$$

$= 14.0\% \times 60\% + 6\% (1 - 0.30) \times 40\%$

$= 10.08\%$

(iii)   **WW's Specialist division based on proxy YY, adjusted for XX's gearing**

For YY:

$$\beta_x = \beta_g \times \left(\frac{V_E}{V_E + V_D[1-t]}\right)$$

$= 0.8 \times 75/(75 + 25 \times 0.7)$

$= 0.65$

Regear for XX:

$$\beta_g = \beta_u + [\beta_u - \beta_d]\frac{V_D[1-t]}{V_E}$$

$= 0.65 + 0.65 \times 40(1 - 0.3)/60$

$= 0.95$

$k_e = R_f + [R_m - R_f]\beta$

$= 5\% + 6\% \times 0.95$

$= 10.7\%$

Calculate WACC for the Specialist Division:

$$WACC = k_e\left(\frac{V_E}{V_E + V_D}\right) + k_d[1-t]\left(\frac{V_D}{V_E + V_D}\right)$$

$= 10.7\% \times 60\% + 6\% (1 - 0.30) \times 40\%$

$= 6.42\% + 1.68\%$

$= 8.1\%$

(b) (i) A range of values for the Specialist division based upon the valuation methods suggested by Directors A, B and C is shown below:

Method	Result	Workings
Director A: Net assets	A$ 15 million book value A$ 20 million replacement value	Figures given in question
Director B: Cash flow basis using XX's WACC	A$ 27.8 million	Discount the division's cash flows using XX's WACC of 10.08% and a growth rate of 1%: A$2.5m(1.01)/(0.1008 − 0.01) = A$27.8m
Director C: DCF using a WACC based on proxy YY	A$ 35.6 million	Discount the division's cash flows using a WACC of 8.1% and a growth rate of 1%: A$2.5m (1.01)/(0.081 − 0.01) = A$35.6m

(ii) Points for discussion:

Director A

- Net assets are not appropriate – these are only used in break-up situations whereas XX is acquiring the business as a going concern.

- Net asset values would be expected to undervalue the division because they do not take intangible assets and goodwill into account

Director B

- Director B has suggested using the operating cash flows of the business (adjusted for tax) discounted at XX's existing WACC.

- As a valuation methodology, this approach will value the whole of the business before taking into account the way that it is funded. This is an appropriate basis on which to value the Specialist Division as it does not have its own debt, as long as an appropriate WACC is used.

- Although XX's WACC reflects the capital structure of XX, it does not reflect the business risk of the Specialist Division which is not the same as the business risk of XX. A WACC can be obtained that reflects the business risk of the division by using the ungeared beta of the proxy company, YY.

Director C

- Business risk can be taken into account by basing the WACC calculation on YY's beta. This beta can then be ungeared and regeared to take into account the risk profile and capital structure of XX and used to calculate both a cost of equity and a WACC for XX to use in valuing WW's Specialist division. This gives a significantly higher valuation, reflecting the lower risk of YY than XX. The validity of this result is backed up by comparing the likely underlying risk of both businesses. YY has more reliable repeat business from publishing specialist in-house company journals whereas XX is in the more risky book publishing business. This explains the higher beta value for XX.

Director D

- The earnings valuation method requires figures for both earnings and cost of equity.

- However, neither of these figures are available for the Specialist Division as it is not a separate subsidiary company with its own capital structure, share price and dividend history.

- Estimates may be possible if more information were available about the capital structure of WW and an appropriate allocation of capital and interest costs across divisions. It would also be possible to use the capital structure of YY in the evaluation of the interest cost.

- Note that the earnings valuation method only provides the value of equity. So the value of debt would need to be added to the final result to obtain an estimate of the value of the assets being acquired by XX.

(iii) **Advice on price**

It could be argued that each of the valuations calculated above has some degree of validity and that XX should start by offering a value near the bottom of the range as an initial bargaining position.

It is likely that XX would regard the proposal put forward by Director C as having the greatest validity in this instance as this is based on pre-debt cash flows and XX is not acquiring any debt attached to the Division. This gives a value of A$35.6 million. Indeed, XX may even be prepared to pay more for the business if it believes that it is possible to achieve growth in excess of the current projected growth rate of 1%. However, this price is at the top of the range of valuations and XX should open negotiations at a lower level, especially as WW may be working on different figures and may not have uplifted the valuation to reflect the lower perceived riskiness of the Specialist Division when compared with other parts of the business.

In conclusion, I would recommend a starting bid of around A$28 million (which is the valuation of the cash flows discounted at XX's own WACC) and negotiate from that starting point up to a maximum price of A$35 million, a valuation that reflects the lower risk profile of the Specialist Division than that of XX.

Tutorial note – extracted from the Examiner's "Post Exam Guide"

Parts (a) and b(i) were very well answered on the whole. Answers to part b(ii) were often too brief and failed to recognise the key issues.

51   MMM RECRUITMENT (SEPT 11 EXAM)

Key answer tips – extracted from the Examiner's "Post Exam Guide"

Several different approaches are possible here. However, a successful approach should always focus on a comparison of shareholder value both before and after the takeover.

The first step is to calculate the value of the combined entity before the takeover.

The second step is to calculate the value of the combined entity after the takeover, including synergistic benefits in part (a) only. For the share exchange, the combined value should be split between the two groups of shareholders in proportion to their post-merger holdings. For the cash bid, the post-takeover value to the acquirer is the value of the combined entity minus the cash offer itself and the post-takeover value for the shareholders of the target company is simply the cash offer itself.

This approach can be repeated in part (b)(i). The only change is the beginning of the second step where synergistic benefits can be ignored.

The answer to part (b)(ii) should identify key issues such as careful planning and the integration and retention of key personnel. These key areas should then each be explored in greater depth.

(a)   Calculation of financial benefit to the shareholders of MMM and JJJ assuming synergistic benefits are realised.

	BEFORE			AFTER SHARE OFFER		AFTER CASH OFFER	
	Number of shares (million)	Price per share ($)	Total value ($ million)	Number of shares (million)	Total value ($ million)	Number of shares (million)	Total value ($ million)
MMM	30	6.90	207.0	30	209.4 ($6.98 per share)	30	211.7 ($7.06 per share)
JJJ	5	12.84	64.2	10	69.8 ($6.98 per share)	Cash	67.5
	Synergies		8.0				
Total			279.2	40	279.2		279.2

Workings

MMM's market cap is: $207.0 million = 30m shares × $6.90 per share

JJJ's market cap is: $64.2 million = 5m × $12.84 per share

$209.4 million = 30/40 × $279.2 million

The cash offer is worth $67.5m (= 5m × $13.50 per share)

$211.7 million = $279.2 million – cash offer of $67.5 million

The above table shows that the bid offer is advantageous to both JJJ and MMM shareholders assuming that synergistic benefits are realised.

MMM shareholders can expect to make a higher financial gain under the cash offer than under the share offer. Under the cash offer, the share price is expected to increase from $6.90 to $7.06, a gain of $0.16 per share and $4.7 million in total. Under the share offer, a lower rise in the share price is expected, from $6.90 to $6.98 per share, a total of $2.4 million.

JJJ shareholders can expect to benefit from an immediate and certain financial gain of $3.3 million ($67.5 million – $64.2 million) under the cash offer. They need to weigh this up against a theoretical gain of $5.6 million ($69.8 million – $64.2 million) from the share offer. However the share offer carries greater risk for the shareholders of JJJ because they are exposed to the risk of a fall in the share price of MMM if the market fails to respond to the merger favourably and/or the potential synergistic benefits are not realised. They are also accepting a shareholding in a company with lower growth prospects than JJJ and lower growth in value could wipe out any short term gains.

The value of JJJ assumes a growth rate of 9% which is considerably higher than MMM's growth rate of 6%. It is important that MMM's management is able to manage business activities acquired from JJJ efficiently in order to protect the higher growth rate associated with these activities. If JJJ's activities are simply merged into MMM's business structure, there is a danger of the growth rate associated with JJJ's business area dropping to something closer to MMM's previous growth rate of 6%. That would clearly have a serious impact on shareholder value.

The cash offer has the advantage of protecting the proportionate ownership of the current shareholders of MMM. After the share offer there would be 40 million shares on issue, including 10 million held by the previous shareholders of JJJ.

However, the cash offer has the problem of accessing the required funds. $67.50 million is a material value to raise for a company that has a market capitalisation of just $207 million. MMM would need to consider the impact on gearing levels and earnings per share of the new borrowings. The share offer also has cash flow implications in paying future dividends on a larger number of shares. This could have an even greater call on cash over time but has a delayed impact on cash flow.

(b) (i) Assuming no synergistic benefits, the combined entity would be worth $8 million less at $271.2 million.

	BEFORE			AFTER SHARE OFFER		AFTER CASH OFFER	
	Number of shares (million)	*Price per share ($)*	*Total value ($ million)*	*Number of shares (million)*	*Total value ($ million)*	*Number of shares (million)*	*Total value ($ million)*
MMM	30	6.90	207.0	30	203.4 ($6.78 per share)	30	203.7 ($6.79 per share)
JJJ	5	12.84	64.2	10	67.8 ($6.78 per share)	Cash	67.5
Total			271.2	40	271.2		271.2

If synergistic benefits fail to be realised, the takeover would ONLY be beneficial to JJJ's shareholders.

MMM's shareholders can expect to see a fall in share price under both the share offer and the cash offer (in the order of $3.6 million for the share offer and $ 3.3 million for the cash bid). The acquisition will therefore only be attractive to MMM's shareholders if additional benefits can be realised such as the synergistic benefits arising from improved IT/IS systems or enhanced future growth throughout the business.

JJJs shareholders would expect to benefit from an immediate and certain financial gain of $3.3 million ($67.5 million − $64.2 million) under the cash offer and a higher theoretical gain of $3.6 million ($67.8 million − $64.2 million) under the share offer. However, the share offer carries greater risk for the shareholders of JJJ because they are exposed to the risk of a fall in the share price of MMM if the market fails to respond to the merger favourably and are also accepting a shareholding in a company with lower growth prospects than JJJ.

(ii) The realisation of synergistic benefits will depend upon a smooth and efficient integration process. Key issues to discuss:

- Careful planning – detailed timetable, allocated responsibilities, interim targets.

- Retention of key personnel (programmers and operators) – possibly by offering enhanced packages and by keeping these personnel fully informed.

- Building good relationships between staff transferring from JJJ to MMM.

- Training of key personnel on how to operate the system.

- Parallel running of the systems and possible test data before going live.

- Looking at post completion audit reports of any such projects that have happened before to see if any lessons can be learnt.

- Proper management control via regular meetings and involvement of key personnel throughout.

Tutorial note – extracted from the Examiner's "Post Exam Guide"

Most candidates were able to calculate the current market value of each company and the value of the cash offer to the target company's shareholders. However, many candidates then made the mistake of assuming that the acquirer company's share price would remain unchanged following the takeover and therefore subsequent calculations produced invalid results.

A tabular approach to these computations appeared to help candidates adopt a more logical approach and achieve more reliable results.

In part (b)(ii), there was a marked tendency to wander off course when addressing the final part of the question. For example, some answers focussed on how best to assess the extent of potential synergistic benefits rather than how to ensure the successful implementation of the system changes required in order to realise potential synergistic benefits. The question also asked for specific application to the scenario provided. A list of all possible implementation controls without any application to the scenario provided was therefore also unlikely to achieve a pass in this section.

52   YY GROUP (SEPT 11 EXAM)

Key answer tips – extracted from the Examiner's "Post Exam Guide"

The suggested approach in this case is simply to consider the issues raised by each Director in turn, starting with Mr A, the Managing Director of TS, being careful to ensure that all relevant angles are covered in each case.

Briefing notes

For use in: TS Management Team meeting

Date prepared: 1 October 20X1

Prepared by: X, independent advisor to the management team of TS

Subject: Possible MBO

(a)   **Mr. A – Managing Director of TS**

Mr A is concerned that the directors of YY will not see the benefit to them of an MBO and hence would firstly like to identify how the MBO management team would increase the returns of the business and secondly how to convince the Board of YY to accept an MBO rather than a trade sale. A balance is required here between making YY an attractive offer but without revealing forecast bullish returns that could result in a higher price and greater interest from other interested parties.

Greater returns are likely to be achieved by the management of TS under an MBO for the following reasons:

1   The managers and employees of TS understand the telecommunications industry probably better than the YY board. They can identify their own objectives and long term strategy which do not have to be subject to review and possible censure by a holding company that views it as "peripheral".

2   There is likely to be more flexibility in day to day decision making as top management and decision makers will only have one company on which to focus.

3   The TS cost base is likely to be lower as there will no longer be any centrally administered management charges. However, it is possible that some economies of scale could be lost as a result of no longer being part of a larger group.

4   If the managers and employees own 20% of the company with the eventual possibility of owning a greater percentage they have greater personal motivation to succeed.

In respect of an MBO versus a trade sale, the main benefits to YY are that the administrative costs of the MBO would be borne by the management of TS and valuable management time would not be taken up in finding a suitable trade purchaser. Also, the managers of TS are aware of its financial strengths and weaknesses which might allow a speedier agreement on the sale price.

(b) **Ms B – Financial Manager of TS**

Ms B is concerned about the involvement of a venture capital company and wishes to identify alternative methods of finance.

The advantages and disadvantages of venture capital finance can be summarised as follows:

Advantages

- The main advantage of a venture capitalist is that this type of investor shares in the risk – in fact takes most of the risk – and has money readily available.

- VC's can also provide valuable support and advice to the management team (especially in the early days and in the run up to any potential IPO in the future) on matters such as dealing with banks and markets.

Disadvantages

- VC's always require a high annual return on their investment – often in the region of 25% per annum. The management of TS therefore needs to be confident in their forecasts of the future to ensure that the VC's returns can be met.

- VCs will always look for an exit route which will, typically, be to sell their shares on the market either via a placing or offer for sale (which would involve an IPO) or to another venture capital entity. If the exit route is by IPO, the majority of the returns will almost certainly go to the venture capitalist.

- Valuing shares for an IPO in, say, 5 years' time is difficult and the issue could be frustrated by market factors beyond the control of either the VC or TS.

- Control would be surrendered as here the VC would own up to 80% of the company. Decision making could therefore become problematic.

If TS performs well, the manager/employee shareholders might be able to buy back their shares via an earn-out basis. This method allows the venture capitalist to sell shares back to the owners on the basis of the entity achieving certain levels of returns, often on an annual basis.

The only realistic alternatives are:

1   An investment bank. Such a company is unlikely to provide 80% of the finance. Even if it did, the servicing costs would be prohibitive.

2   Ask YY to continue to own a shareholding. This would, in effect, mean YY acting as a venture capitalist. If YY wishes to divest the subsidiary it is unlikely to want to continue to own a substantial stake. However, if YY has no immediate investment opportunity readily available, as implied by the FD, then it might be willing to consider a phased sale.

3   A combination of methods of finance. This might be difficult, costly and time consuming to arrange.

(c)   **Mr C – Marketing Manager of TS**

Mr C is concerned with the valuation of TS at $1,000 million. In answer to his specific concerns:

The FD's valuation is based on YY's P/E ratio as Ms B has explained and will have been applied to TS's earnings. The market capitalisation of YY based on the latest financial information is $16,380 million (525 million shares at $31.20 per share). Therefore, YY's P/E ratio is 13 (market capitalisation of $ 16,380 million divided by earnings of $1,260 million). On this basis TS's value is therefore $975 million (earnings of $75 million multiplied by 13).

The book value of TS's net assets is $735 million as at 31 August 20X1. This represents approximately 9% of YY's total net assets compared with only 6% of its total earnings. However, as a manufacturing company TS will have a relatively high level of tangible assets which might explain the differential. In addition, TS may have a different gearing ratio to YY. Even so, this value has little relevance (because by definition it is based upon the statement of financial position which excludes important intangible assets such as brand strength and goodwill) except in specific circumstances such as a liquidation or break up of the subsidiary. Neither of these situations applies here as YY wish to divest the entire subsidiary and it is a going concern.

In addition, the net assets figure is given after deducting borrowings. If these are intra-group borrowings, these need to be added back to the net assets figure to obtain the aggregate figure that YY needs to raise by the disposal of TS. However, if the borrowings are from external sources and are to be assigned to the new owner, they do not need to be added back when arriving at a valuation of the equity for sale.

In terms of alternative valuations we could consider using a different P/E ratio. TS is in an unrelated business to YY and its shares are unlisted so a P/E of 13 might not be accurate. In the case of an unlisted entity, a P/E ratio that is representative of similar quoted entities might be used as a starting point for arriving at an estimated market value. If we use the telecommunications industry average P/E of 15 given in the scenario, TS would have an even higher value of $1,125 million (earnings of $75 million multiplied by 15). Again it could be argued that this P/E is not appropriate as TS manufactures telecoms equipment which is only one part of the telecoms industry as a whole. In addition, TS's gearing ratio may not be typical of the industry as a whole as it is a wholly owned subsidiary.

In terms of alternative methods TS should undertake a valuation of its business using discounted cash flows. This involves discounting net cash flows as far into the future as reasonably possible at a discount rate that reflects the risk of the operation. Determining an appropriate discount rate can be a difficult process but TS should be able to obtain an approximation using a similar company's data. As TS is a wholly owned subsidiary, a WACC based on pre-interest free cash flows may be more appropriate than the cost of equity applied to post-interest free cash flows post-interest. It may be possible to obtain a suitable WACC from a proxy company in the same business as YY. The bid company is likely to use its own WACC when valuing TS.

Tutorial note – extracted from the Examiner's "Post Exam Guide"

It was not uncommon for answers to parts (a) and (b) to fail to focus on the question set.

In part (a) it would appear that some candidates overlooked the fact that the Director in question worked for TS rather than YY and was therefore interested in seeing how the current management of TS could move TS forward after an MBO rather than criticising past performance by that same management team.

In part (b), a standard list of all possible sources of finance (rights issue, bond etc) is of little relevance in the context of an MBO.

In part (c), several candidates struggled to work out how the $1 billion valuation had been obtained. Note that this is a straightforward application of YY's P/E ratio to TS's earnings figure. Also note that a comparison of YY and TS's earnings per share is of no interest as TS is a division of YY and therefore has an arbitrary number of shares in issue.

53   TNG (MAR 13 EXAM)

Key answer tips – extracted from the Examiner's "Post Exam Guide" (note that the comments regarding WORD and/or EXCEL only relate to the COMPUTER BASED papers in March and September each year)

Part (a)

When calculating a DCF value start by listing all relevant cash flows under appropriate time periods and grouped by currency.

Next calculate future exchange rates and convert foreign currency cash flows at these rates.

Then discount the net cash flow in each period at L&P's WACC of 10%. Use the EXCEL NPV formula to save time for the first 3 years. Use an annuity formula for the remaining time period.

Part (b)

Consider all categories of intangible assets which are likely to be of particular importance for a business such as L&P.

Explain the rationale behind CIV, first the comparison to industry returns and, second, the assumption that such value spread continues in perpetuity, hence discounting the value spread at L&P's cost of capital.

Part (c)

Consider the assumptions made and basis used to produce each valuation and consider how these might affect the validity of the answers. Compare and contrast your findings for the two valuation methods.

(a)   **Calculation of DCF valuation for L&P in EUR as at 1 April 2013**

	EUR m 0	EUR m 1	EUR m 2	EUR m 3
Net operating CF in USD million		120.00	132.00	145.20
Exchange rate (based on spot of 1.3000, increasing by 1% a year)		1.3130	1.3261	1.3394
Net USD operating cash flows in EUR m		91.39	99.54	108.41
EUR operating cash flows		(40.00)	(44.00)	(48.40)
Net operating cash flows		51.39	55.54	60.01
Tax at 30%		(15.42)	(16.66)	(18.00)
After tax ongoing investment cash flows		(5.00)	(5.25)	(5.51)
New machinery	(30.00)			
Tax depreciation allowances		3.00	3.00	3.00
Net cash flows	(30.00)	33.98	36.63	39.50
Discount factor at 10%	1.000	0.909	0.826	0.751
Present value	(30.00)	30.89	30.26	29.66

NPV to the end of year 3   EUR 60.81 million

PV of cash flows year 4 onwards using the constant growth version of the DVM:

	EUR million
Year 3 FCF (i.e.: NOCF excluding tax depreciation allowances) =	36.50
Value of perpetuity = ((EUR 36.50 million × 1.05)/ (0.10 − 0.05))*0.751 =	575.64

So, using the discounted cash flow approach, the net present value of L&P as at 1 April 2013 is EUR 636.45 million (= EUR 60.81m + EUR 575.64m).

(b)   **Types of intangible asset likely to be held by L&P**

Intangible assets, or intellectual capital encompasses goodwill, brands and other intellectual capital such as human resources (e.g. staff knowledge), intellectual assets (e.g. codified knowledge) and intellectual property (e.g. patents).

L&P offers maintenance and support services for the equipment supplied by other TNG subsidiaries. The most important intangible assets are therefore likely to be the collective skills, experience and knowledge of employees engaged in highly specialised maintenance work.

Any agreement between TNG and L&P for TNG to automatically refer customers to L&P for support services may also be an intangible asset that does not form part of L&P's tangible assets.

The reputation of L&P for service quality is also an important intangible asset.

Rationale behind the CIV method of valuing intangible assets

The Calculated Intangible Value (CIV) method of company valuation has been developed to estimate the value of a company's intellectual property (in other words the value of the intangible assets that do not appear in a company's statement of financial position). Therefore it is an advance on the basic asset valuation.

The CIV method is based on a comparison of the total return that the company is producing against the return that would be expected based on industry average returns on tangible assets. Any additional return is assumed to be return on intangible assets.

This additional return is assumed to continue in perpetuity and converted into a present day value for intangibles by discounting at the company's cost of capital. The value of intangible assets thus calculated is then added to the value of the tangible assets of the business to generate a total value.

(c) **Comparison of the validity of the DCF and CIV valuations of L&P for the purpose of establishing an appropriate asking price for the sale of L&P**

DCF valuations are generally considered to be the most appropriate method of valuation as they are based on the actual forecast cash flows of the business, discounted at the subsidiary's cost of capital. DCF valuations therefore look forward into the future based on best estimates of future outcomes.

In contrast, CIV is an adaption of the asset valuation method. It suffers from many of the same drawbacks as the basic asset valuation method when valuing a going concern. For example, it does not allow for growth in cash flows and does not recognise the time value of money. It also has as its base profit rather than cash flow and incorporates a perpetuity formula which lacks precision. The CIV method is also limited by the fact that it is based on an industry average return which might not be representative of L & P.

The DCF valuation also has drawbacks due to its reliance on estimates of future outcomes. For example, the result relies heavily on forecast cash flows in perpetuity from year 4 onwards and it would seem unlikely that a growth rate of 5% is sustainable in perpetuity. The DCF valuation is therefore likely to overvalue L & P. In addition, the forecast cash flows rely heavily on forecast exchange rates and oil prices that affect oil companies' spending on consultancy and other services and so may prove to be quite different from that forecast. The DCF result also depends on the use of an appropriate cost of capital for the subsidiary company when taking into account the time value of money. No information is given about how the subsidiary's cost of capital has been estimated.

Indeed, the DCF valuation method gives a result that is more than double the value given by the CIV method. The most appropriate asking price for the sale of L&P is likely to fall somewhere in-between.

Tutorial note – extracted from the Examiner's "Post Exam Guide"

The discounted cash flows (DCF) valuation in part (a) was generally done at least satisfactorily.

Common errors were:

- *Incorrect calculation of future exchange rates.*

- *Omitting tax depreciation (or including the allowance before calculating tax but then omitting to reverse the data).*

- *Omitting tax on profits.*

- *Ignoring on-going investment, not inflating it or only including it for a single time period.*

- *Poor attempts at the perpetuity (often simply dividing the year 3 cash flow by 10%).*

- *Using TNG's discount rate of 14% rather than L&P's rate of 10%.*

Part (b) was generally answered well and most candidates managed to consider at least two types of intangible assets and apply these in the context of L&P. The section about CIV was less well handled even though a full calculation of CIV was presented in the question.

Some confusion about the rationale behind the CIV valuation was often carried over into part (c), where a significant number of candidates incorrectly stated that DCF valuations excluded the value of intangibles (that is, the income earned from the use of intangibles).

54   NN (MAY 13 EXAM)

Key answer tips – extracted from the Examiner's "Post Exam Guide"

Part (a)(i) requires a straightforward DCF perpetuity valuation based on estimated free cash flows. Central overheads therefore need to be added back before carrying out the DCF valuation.

Part (a)(ii) should start with the calculation of the increase in market capitalisation for each company involved in the deal based on the observed change in share prices following the announcement of the deal.   These values should then be compared with the DCF valuations calculated in (a)(i) and to the agreed price and differences identified and explained.

Part (b) should consider each of the three issues raised by Mr Q in turn, taking into account the results in part (a) where relevant.

(a)   (i)   **Viewpoint of NN:** N4 made a loss in the last financial year ended 31 March 2013.

Adding back central overhead costs of USD 21 million, N4 made a cash based loss of USD 20 million.

At a WACC of 8%, and assuming that this level of loss continues into perpetuity, this gives N4 a negative value of USD 250 million.

Workings: USD 250 million = USD 20 million/8%

Viewpoint of QQ:

N4 is expected to achieve free cash flow of USD 22 million per annum into perpetuity and at QQ's real WACC of 6% this gives a positive value of USD 366.7 million (= 22 million/0.06).

(ii)

	Asking price	Value of deal to either NN or QQ	Increase in market capitalisation following the announcement of the proposed sale
NN	USD 150 million	USD 400 million	USD 360 million
		Workings: *250m + 150m asking price*	*Workings:* *6,000 m × 0.06 = 360 m*
QQ	USD 150 million	USD 216.7 million	USD 413 million
		Workings: *366.7m − 150m*	*Workings:* *1,800 m × 15.53 × 1.5%/1.015 = 413 m*

For NN, we can see that the increase in market capitalisation is very close but just slightly less than NN's own estimate of the value of the deal to the shareholders.

For QQ, the market is considerably more enthusiastic about the deal than QQ's own estimates reveal. This is to be expected since QQ has used conservative estimates of free cash flow and hence has produced a 'worst case' valuation of the deal, ensuring that even based on cautiously low performance estimates, the deal would still be considered to be worthwhile pursuing. QQ is purchasing N4 for its potential earning capacity rather than its historic performance. By making certain changes such as lowering costs and improving marketing, QQ can hope to turn around N4's performance and generate positive returns.

(b)   **How is it possible that the share price of both QQ and NN increased on the day that the offer is announced?**

Firstly, the speed of reaction. This is due to the efficient market hypothesis (EMH) which states that, in theory, in a perfect market, the market value of a listed company should be a fair reflection of all the information which is known about that company. The markets have reacted strongly on the day that the offer was made public which indicates that the stock exchange is semi-strong form efficient.

Secondly, the way the market has reacted. The increase in both companies' share prices, shows that the acquisition appears to have been favourably received by both sets of shareholders, leading to increased demand for shares and a rise in share prices.

NN's shareholders clearly benefit by disposing of N4 since N4 was loss making and took up management attention that can now be wholly focused on the core brands, leading to an increase in shareholder value which is reflected in the rise in the share price.

QQ's shareholders benefit by achieving both economies of scale and increased revenue streams by managing N4 as part of its current portfolio of products, N4 being a good 'fit' for QQ's current business. However, this assumes that the estimated annual free cash flow of USD 22 million is realistic. Indeed, the market believes that this figure is conservative, as shown by the increase in the share price.

How can QQ expect to generate higher profits from N4 than NN was able to?

QQ already focuses on low cost, high volume sales. N4 is therefore a better 'fit' within its current structure and it should be able to achieve economies of scale. If QQ can use current customer contacts and the current marketing team to sell the use of the N4 brand name, this will further reduce the central costs per brand.

QQ already has market presence and staff expertise in handling low-price brands. QQ will therefore be in a better position to successfully market N4 within its current customer base.

What courses of action are open to QQ if it fails to generate sufficient returns from N4?

If QQ fails to generate sufficient profit from N4 to justify retaining the brand, it could dispose of N4.

The most likely way of achieving this would be to find an interested buyer, in the same way as QQ is now responding to information released by NN earlier indicating its interest in selling N4. It is, however, unlikely that QQ would succeed in recovering the sum paid for N4 originally, as the expected profit from the brand will be lower than before.

Alternatively, the management of the brand may be interested in purchasing the brand name themselves under the umbrella of a management buyout. The brand managers may consider that they can increase the profitability of the brand if they are given a freer hand in developing and marketing the brand in a more aggressive manner than QQ may have allowed.

Tutorial note – extracted from the Examiner's "Post Exam Guide"

This was the least popular of the optional questions, in home and overseas centres. Performance on the whole was satisfactory, especially if the candidate understood the correct approach to Part (a).

Part (a)

The answers were often all or nothing; candidates could either calculate the correct figures or not at all. Very few candidates understood that, for NN, the overheads had to be added back. A common error was to value NN and QQ using USD22 million.

In part (a)(ii) the weaker candidates either discussed little other than the EMH or simply noted that the share prices had risen because the market identified them as good strategies. A better answer would have focussed on why these two companies valued the deal differently.

Part (b)

This part of the question was answered quite well by most candidates who attempted the question and their answer here often converted a potential fail into a pass.

INVESTMENT DECISIONS AND PROJECT CONTROL II – PROJECT APPRAISAL

55   CTC TECHNOLOGY COLLEGE (MAY 05 EXAM)

(a)   We need to calculate the incremental costs and benefits of running the ITC course rather than the old ITS course.

Let x = the additional number of students who would do an ITC course rather than the 150 doing an ITS course.

(This means that there are $150 + x$ total students doing the ITC course. Assume for now that x is less than 50 so that we don't need the additional member of staff.)

Time	Item	Cash flow	Discount factor at 8%	Present value
		€		€
0	Cancelled sale of computers (20 × €100)	(2,000)		
0	Computer upgrade	(15,000)	1.0	(47,000)
0	Staff training	(30,000)		
0–3	Student fees	360 x		
0–3	Additional benefit	20 x	3.577	1,144.64 x
0–3	Books & consumables	(60 x)		
1–4	Direct costs (2,000 – 1,000)	(1,000)	3.312	(3,312)
				1,144.64 x – 50,312

Tutorial note

Some students might be put off by the use of algebra in this question, but notice that most of the marks would have been gained for dealing with standard NPV problems (e.g. the value of the €1,000 direct costs annuity, the opportunity costing issue on the cancelled sale of computers). Even if you are not particularly mathematically minded, there are plenty of easy marks here.

The breakeven additional number of students is found where:

$$1{,}144.64x = 50{,}312$$

so $\quad$ x = 43.95, say 44 students

We conclude that, for × being less than 50, the breakeven point for the decision is where the new course has 150 + 44 = 194 students. This means that the new ITC course is worthwhile if there are between 194 and 199 students.

If 200 or more students enrol, then the additional member of staff is required, costing €10,000 p.a. If again we let x = the additional number of students doing the ITC course, we now have a breakeven value for × given where:

$$1{,}144.65x = 50{,}312 + (3.577 \times 10{,}000)$$

$$x = 75.2, \text{ rounded up to } 76$$

Thus, if 200 or more students enrol, we need at least 150 + 76 = 226 students before we should run the new ITC course rather than the old ITS course.

Conclusion

The above calculations have shown that, if the number of enrolments on the ITC course is between 194 and 199, or is 226 students or above, then it is worthwhile switching from the ITS course. In practice it seems unlikely that the number of students over a four year period will remain in such a narrow band as 194 to 199, so this possibility should be rejected.

In planning whether to switch to the ITC course, the college should use 226 students as the minimum annual enrolment for the switch to be worthwhile on financial grounds.

(b) (i) The costs and revenues of the project should be monitored and controlled as follows:

- appoint a single individual with responsibility for the project. They should have authority to take decisions as required, as the project proceeds

- hold regular meetings (e.g. monthly) with all interested parties present to review the development of the project

- use these meetings to monitor the actual costs and revenues against budgeted costs and revenues. Overruns in costs and shortfalls in revenues should be addressed immediately

- set up expenditure authorisation levels so that minor items can be authorised by the project leader, larger items by a nominated manager, and very large items of expenditure must be authorised by the whole management board

- adjust the budgeted levels of costs and revenues, if necessary, to reflect actual market conditions at the time.

(ii)   The options available are:

- cancel the course immediately

- extend the enrolment deadline and market the course intensively

- run the course for one year only

- carry on regardless.

The 150 students who have enrolled will not be pleased if their course is cancelled for two weeks before it is due to start. The good reputation of the college will be damaged, and the poor publicity attracted may dissuade other students from enrolling on other courses.

The enrolment deadline could be extended a further week, coupled with multiple marketing initiatives. The price cannot be dropped without offering the same price cut to the existing students, but other ideas could be tried, e.g. heavy advertising within the college, mailshots to past and present student lists, vouchers to those introducing new students that offer money off the price of books, etc.

It seems premature to decide now to cancel years 2 to 4 of the ITC course. The market research indicated that there was demand for the ITC course, so it is likely that student numbers in years to 4 will be greater than in year 1, once the quality of the course is disseminated throughout the market.

Carrying on regardless is not stupid, since the course is anticipated as being profitable in future years.

The best approach is likely to be extension of the enrolment deadline, intensive short-term marketing, and deferral of any decision to cancel the course either now or in the future. The market research indicated a rosy future for the ITC course, so it would be wrong to cancel it before it has been given a chance.

56   RST (MAY 06 EXAM)

Key answer tips

This was a rare but straightforward question on capital rationing.

In part (a) ensure that you use the net outflow at time 1.

(a)   (i)   Based on NPV, the projects would be ranked in the order C, B, A, E, D (W1).

The $30m available at time 1 would thus enable the firm to undertake C, B and A, giving a total NPV of $12.9m.

(ii)   Using a profitability index based on NPV/$ net investment at time 1, the ranking becomes C, D, E, B, A (W2).

The best way to invest is thus to undertake C, D, E and B, giving a NPV of $15.22m.

Trial and error confirms that C, D, E, B is the optimal investment as it yields the highest NPV.

Workings

(W1) **Project NPV ($m)**   *Ranking*

A: NPV $= -9$ -16×0.870 $+4 \times 1/0.15$ $= 3.747$ 3

B: NPV $= -10$ -10×0.870 $+4 \times (1/0.15 - 0.870)$ $= 4.487$ 2

C: NPV $= -10$ -12×0.870 $+5 \times 5.019$ $= 4.655$ 1

D: NPV $= -8$ -5×0.870 $+6 \times (4.160 - 1.626)$ $= 2.854$ 5

E: NPV $= -9$ -8×0.870 $+2 \times 3.352 + 5 \times (5.847 - 3.352)$ $= 3.219$ 4

(W2) **Profitability index = NPV per $ invested at t_1**

	A	B	C	D	E
NPV ($m)	3.747	4.487	4.655	2.854	3.219
Net outflow at t_1 ($m)	16–4=12	10	12–5=7	5	8–2=6
NPV/$ at t_1	0.31	0.45	0.67	0.57	0.54
Ranking	5	4	1	2	3

(b)   (i)   Capital rationing techniques based on NPV are suspect in the case of RST due to the following:

- The NPV technique is appropriate for businesses where the organisation's primary goal is the maximisation of shareholder wealth. The situation with public bodies such as RST is more complex:

    – RST will have multiple objectives including enhancing the quality of life of citizens through healthcare projects and achieving value for money with public funds. The former of these is very difficult to quantify in financial terms.

    – RST will have multiple stakeholder groups with a more even balance of power rather than the dominant group of shareholders for companies.

However, it could be argued that most firms experience soft capital rationing due to internal budgetary constraints and can usually borrow more if they wish to. With RST the (external) government will not allow them further funds so capital rationing is perhaps more of an issue for such organisations.

(ii) The other analyses RST should undertake are as follows:

- *Sensitivity analysis* – analysis of key variables could reveal a different solution.

- *Jobs created* – the government will be seeking to reduce unemployment and may prefer RST to accept projects that generate more jobs even if they have lower NPV.

- *Environmental impact* – cutting down a wood to build a new hospital, for example, may be rejected on environmental grounds.

- *Quality of life* – RST should analyse how many people will be affected by each project and the extent to which their quality of life is improved. A project may have a low NPV because it offers affordable services to help poorer people. Such a project should be commended not rejected.

These are obviously difficult to quantify but that should not prevent RST looking at them.

57   GHI (MAY 06 EXAM)

Key answer tips

Part (a) is a standard question on APV. As always a methodical approach is essential. Part (b) is less conventional and you have to draw extensively on previous studies to answer it well.

(a) **APV calculation**

Step 1: Calculate the base-case discount rate.

To get a base-case discount rate, GHI's cost of equity needs to be 'degeared' using the M&M equation:

$$k_{eg} = k_{eu} + (k_{eu} - k_d) V_D(1 - t)/V_E$$

$$0.107 = k_{eu} + (k_{eu} - 0.05) 40(1 - 0.35)/60$$

$$0.1287 = 1.4333 k_{eu}$$

$$k_{eu} = 0.08976...\text{or } 9\%$$

Step 2: Calculate the base-case present value.

	0	1	2	3	4	5
Cash flow (£000)	(10,000)	5,000	5,000	4,000	3,000	3,000
UK tax @ 25%	–	(1,250)	(1,250)	(1,000)	(750)	(750)
Net UK cash flow	(10,000)	3,750	3,750	3,000	2,250	2,250
Exchange rate (£1= €...)	1.600	1.552	1.505	1.460	1.416	1.374
Euro flows (€000)	(16,000)	5,820	5,644	4,380	3,186	3,092
Additional tax (×10/75)	–	(776)	(755)	(584)	(425)	(412)
Net cash flow (€000)	(16,000)	5,044	4,889	3,796	2,761	2,680
Discount factor @ 9%	1	0.917	0.842	0.772	0.708	0.650
Present value (€000)	(16,000)	4,625	4,117	2,931	1,955	1,742

Base-case present value   (630)

Step 3: Calculate the present value of financing side effects.

To calculate the present value of financing side effects the pre-tax risk free cost of debt, here 5%, should be used.

(**Note:** With issue costs GHI will have to raise more than €16m. However, the question does state that the loan will be for €16m, so this figure has been used.)

Narrative	CF (€000)	Timing	DF @ 5%	PV
Issue costs (16m × 2% × 0.65)	(208)	0	1	(208)
Tax relief on interest (16m × 5% × 35%)	280	1–5	4.329	1,212
Overall PV of financing side effects				**1,004**

Step 4: Calculate the adjusted present value.

	€000
Base case NPV	(630)
PV of financing side effects	1,004
APV	374

These figures would suggest that the project viewed in isolation is not worthwhile but with this method of finance is worth undertaking.

Key questions

- Is the finance dependent on this particular project e.g. a development loan?

- Are there any better projects available that are not currently being undertaken because of capital rationing?

- Further sensitivity analysis is needed given the marginal result.

Limitations of APV

- Finding a suitable base-case cost of equity is subjective and may not fully reflect project risks.

- Estimating all of the financing costs can be difficult, especially when incorporating changes to debt capacity.

(b) The function of the project committee of GHI would be as follows:

(i) **Determining customer requirements**

- Full market research in the UK to assess UK customer requirements. This will involve a blend of desk research (e.g. reviewing business monitors and consumer reports) and filed research (e.g. commission new research of target customer groups).

- In-depth consideration of key differentiating factors in the UK telephone industry and how important they are to different customer groups – e.g. design features (e.g. camera, video, music, size, ease of use).

Product design

- To enable a successful market entry product positioning is vital. The committee must decide how to blend the above factors to position itself relative to incumbent firms.

(ii) **Control of implementation**

As always control should involve the following steps:

(1) Prepare plans and set targets.

(2) Implement plans – a test market or trial would be advisable before undertaking a national launch.

(3) Evaluate performance – details of sales, market share, customer profiles, etc should be collected on a regular basis and compared to budget.

(4) Feedback – deviations for budget (for both the trial and national launch) should be investigated and appropriate action taken. The committee should also carry out a post-completion review.

58 CD FURNITURE MANUFACTURER (NOV 06 EXAM)

Key answer tips

This is a relatively straightforward question on investment appraisal. In part (i) you need to ensure that you have incorporated inflation into all cash flows and have used PPP to estimate forward rates. In part (iii) ensure you discuss a wide range of non-financial issues in contrast with the conclusions of the calculations.

(a) **NPV**

	0	1	2	3
Investment ($m)	(25.00)			
$ Receipts (inflated at 4% p.a.)		2.70	4.11	4.61
Exchange rate (W1)	1.600	1.616	1.632	1.648
$ flows converted into £	(15.63)	1.67	2.52	2.80
Additional £ receipts (inflated at 3% p.a.)		3.81	4.46	5.03
Net cash flow (£m)	(15.63)	5.48	6.98	7.83
Discount factor @ 9%	1	0.917	0.842	0.772
Present value (£m)	(15.63)	5.03	5.88	6.04

Net present value   **1.32**

Note: The investigation costs are sunk and hence ignored.

(W1) Forward exchange rates, using Purchasing Power Parity

1 + forward rate = spot × (1+US inflation)/(1+UK inflation)

t=1 1 + forward rate = 1.6 × 1.04/1.03 = 1.616

t=2 1 + forward rate = 1.616 × 1.04/1.03 = 1.632

t=3 1 + forward rate = 1.632 × 1.04/1.03 = 1.648

IRR

Using 15% as a second guess:

	0	1	2	3
Net cash flow (£m)	(15.63)	5.48	6.98	7.83
Discount factor @ 15%	1	0.870	0.756	0.658
Present value (£m)	(15.63)	4.77	5.28	5.15

Net present value   **(0.43)**

IRR = A + N_a (B − A)/(N_a − N_b) = 0.09 + 1.32 × (0.15 − 0.09)/(1.32+0.43) = 13.5%

MIRR

Terminal value of receipts at t=3 if reinvested at the cost of capital is given by:

$5.48 \times 1.09^2 + 6.98 \times 1.09 + 7.83 = 21.95$

MIRR is found by solving

3 year discount factor @MIRR × 21.95 =15.63

3 year discount factor @MIRR =15.63 ÷ 21.95 = 0.712

From the tables the MIRR is 12%.

(b) **MIRR**

The MIRR has the following advantages as a method of investment appraisal.

Advantages:

- The MIRR, as a percentage rather than an absolute value, is more easily understandable than NPV.

- The MIRR avoids the possibility of multiple rates of return, as is possible with the IRR i.e. the MIRR will be a unique figure.

- The MIRR takes account of the possibility that the reinvestment rate might be different from the IRR.

- Rankings under the MIRR are usually consistent with those calculated under the NPV criterion.

(c) **Summary**

	Alternative 1	Alternative 2
NPV (£m) @ 9%	1.45	1.32
IRR	10.5%	13.5%
MIRR	13.2%	12.0%

Tutorial note

Presenting a summary table like this is a good way of gathering your thoughts before embarking upon the comparison of the two projects.

Assuming that the discount rate of 9% is correct, alternative 1 should be chosen as it has the higher NPV and thus should increase shareholder value by the greater amount.

However, should there be some uncertainty over the discount rate, then alternative 2 may be preferred as it has a higher break-even cost of capital, or IRR.

Other issues to consider include the following:

- *Competition* – by reducing quality CD is effectively moving market segments. It needs to investigate whether the mid-market sector is more competitive than the high quality sector.

- *Brand names* – should the new lower quality products be marketed under a different brand name to avoid compromising CD's reputation or should the CD name be used to enhance the perceived quality of the new ranges?

- *Risk* – other than a calculation of IRR, there has been little analysis of the respective risks of the two alternatives. Sensitivity and other detailed analysis should be carried out before any decision is made.

- Alternative 2 is also likely to result in lower operating gearing than alternative 1.

- *Impact on employees* – skills in high quality manufacturing will be less demanded by CD if the changes are made. This could result in redundancies and/or a drop in staff motivation.

- *Environmental issues* – CD needs to ensure that woods used under alternative 2 are from sustainable sources. The pollution implications of alternative 1 should also be considered.

- *Impact on other customers* – to date CD has only had discussions with one major customer. Other customers may be concerned that the quality of existing ranges will be compromised by the changes envisaged.

59   UVW (NOV 07 EXAM)

Key answer tips

In part (a) there are a number of different ways of interpreting the information so it is vital that you state your assumptions and show clear workings.

Part (b) is tricky and would have presented problems for many students due to a lack of knowledge. The key is to consider each aspect of working capital management.

(a)   (i)   **NPV without using certainty equivalents**

	t_0	t_1	t_2	t_3
Capital investment in Asia ($m)	(100)			
Operating costs in Asia ($m)		(70.0)	(65.0)	(60.0)
Exchange rate (W1)	20	20.77	21.57	22.40
Equivalent £m cash flows	(5.000)	(3.370)	(3.013)	(2.679)
Equipment purchased in UK for Asian project	(2.000)			
UK operation costs avoided		1.500	4.500	4.750
Net cost/benefit of Asian operation (£m)	(7.000)	(1.870)	1.487	2.071
Discount factors @ 10%	1	0.909	0.826	3.599(W2)
Present values (£m)	(7.000)	(1.700)	1.228	7.453

NPV   **(0.019)**

Given the NPV is negative, the project should be rejected. However, given the marginal nature of the result, sensitivity analysis should be undertaken and estimates revisited before a decision is made.

Notes:

- The feasibility study is a sunk cost and so excluded from the above figures

- Regarding the costs associated with the two senior managers we are not told whether any additional staff will be recruited to perform their UK roles while they are in Asia. Presumably this would be the case and the relevant cash flow would be the difference between these amounts. Alternatively, if not replaced, it could be argued that their salaries are not relevant as they would have been paid anyway. However, travel and accommodation costs certainly would be relevant, so there would be a problem splitting the cost. Furthermore it is not clear whether costs have been included in the "comparable costs of UK operations". For simplicity it is assumed here that the full £250,000 is incremental and has been included correctly where relevant in the figures in the question.

Workings

(W1) Future exchange rates using interest rate parity theory ("IRP"):

Tutorial note

A common mistake is applying the parity formula the wrong way up. If the spot and forward rates are quoted as US$/£ then the US interest rate comes first (as the numerator) and the UK rate appears as the denominator.

$$\text{'Forward rate US\$/\pounds} = \text{Spot US\$/\pounds} \times \frac{1 + \text{nominal US interest rate}}{1 + \text{nominal UK interest rate}},$$

- Year 1 exchange rate $= 20 \times \dfrac{1.08}{1.04} = 20.77$

- Year 2 exchange rate $= 20.77 \times \dfrac{1.08}{1.04} = 21.57$

- Year 3 exchange rate $= 21.57 \times \dfrac{1.08}{1.04} = 22.40$

(W2)

- Year 3 savings are said to continue until year 8.

- Discount factor = 8 year annuity factor − 2 year annuity factor = 5.335 − 1.736 = 3.599

NPV using certainty equivalents (£m)	t_0	t_1	t_2	t_{3-8}
Net cost/benefit per above	(7.000)	(1.870)	1.487	2.071
Certainty equivalent % of base	1	0.80	0.75	0.70
Certainty equivalent CFs	(7.000)	(1.496)	1.115	1.450
Discount factors @ 3% (risk free rate)	1	0.971	0.943	7.020–1.913
Present values	(7.000)	(1.453)	1.051	7.405
Revised NPV	**+0.003**			

The NPV is now marginally positive, now suggesting that the project should be accepted.

(ii)   **Internal factors to consider**

- A key issue here is the measurement and treatment of risk. Using a risk-adjusted discount rate and certainty equivalents are two distinct techniques. The Finance manager would have obtained a substantial negative NPV if he had applied certainty equivalents to the cash flows and then used the 10% risk-adjusted discount rate, in effect adjusting for risk twice (see W3). The company should also undertake sensitive analysis to investigate risk further.

- It is vital that the new Asian manufacturing facility can match or surpass the quality levels currently achieved in the UK. If this is not possible then customers may be lost.

- Given that UVW operates a just-in-time system it is also critical that it establishes good relations with Asian suppliers and gains the required staff flexibility to ensure that delays do not occur.

- The net impact on distribution costs will need to be considered by analysing the geographical spread of customers.

- Asian working practices may be different from those in the UK, so it is necessary that UVW has or acquires the expertise and experience required to set up an Asian manufacturing base.

- What will happen to the roles currently performed by the two senior managers who will be seconded to Asia? Will their current roles be eliminated or will additional staff be required to replace them?

- Will spare production capacity exist and are redundancies planned in the UK as production switches to Asia? Such plans would have to be handled sensitively.

Tutorial note

You were not expected to perform the following calculation in the exam. It is done here for illustrative purposes.

NPV using certainty equivalents (£m)	t_0	t_1	t_2	t_{3-8}
Certainty equivalent CFs per above	(7.000)	(1.496)	1.115	1.450
Discount factors @ 10%	1	0.909	0.826	3.599
Present values	(7.000)	(1.360)	0.921	5.219
Revised NPV	**(2.220)**			

(b) The arguments for and against centralising working capital management are as follows:

Arguments in favour of managing working capital in Asia

- Better relationships can be established with local customers, resulting in quicker payment terms and hence a reduced cost of receivables

- Local managers may have a better understanding and information regarding local suppliers and production issues, so may be better placed to determine and manage inventory levels of raw materials.

Arguments in favour of centralising working capital management in the UK

- Global credit policies and checks can be applied to customers giving greater control.

- Centralising working capital makes it easier to assess exchange risk exposure (after netting) and implement appropriate hedging.

- Cash budgeting is easier as all aspects of working capital can be controlled more efficiently. This should result in lower amounts needed to be borrowed or invested short term.

- There are likely to be more options for short term borrowing and lending in London than available locally.

- A centralised function will benefit from economies of scale, avoiding duplication of roles. For example, they will be able to afford to pay staff with greater expertise, resulting in greater efficiencies.

60   CM LIMITED (MAY 08 EXAM) *Walk in the footsteps of a top tutor*

Top tutor tips

NPV is a very commonly tested topic so this question should have been expected.

Similarly, part (b) on non-financial factors is a very common follow-up to an NPV analysis.

To help with this sort of question, learn some generic points from the text book, but then try to adapt the points to make them specific to the given scenario.

Be aware in part (a) that NPV is a cash based method, whereas ROI is an accounting measure, so there are different treatments of several input factors.

(a)   (i)   **Accounting rate of return (ARR) = Average annual profit after tax**

                                          Average Investment

Profit	Investment 1 (£000)	Investment 2 (A$000)
PBT – year 1	(23)	73
PBT – year 2	25	193
PBT – year 3	108	354
Total PBT	110	620
Tax (25%/10%)	(28)	(62)
Total Profit After Tax	82	558
Average Annual Profit After Tax $(\div 3)$	27	186

Investment	Investment 1 (£000)	Investment 2 (A$000)
Initial investment	1,100	2,900
Scrap proceeds	300	NIL
Average Investment Value	700	1,450

Investment 1 ARR $= \dfrac{27}{700} \times 100\% = 3.9\%$

Investment 2 ARR $= \dfrac{186}{1450} \times 100\% = 12.8\%$

(ii)   **NPV Investment 1**

£000	t_0	t_1	t_2	t_3
Revenue		375	450	575
Costs		(131)	(158)	(201)
		244	292	374
Tax (25%)		(61)	(73)	(94)
Capital investment/residual value	(1,100)			300
Tax relief on Capital Allowances (W1)	110	66	40	(16)
	(990)	249	259	564
Discount factors @ 11% (W3)	1	0.901	0.812	0.731
Present values	(990)	224	210	412
NPV (£000)	**(114)**			

NPV Investment 2

A$000	t_0	t_1	t_2	t_3
Revenue		1,300	1,450	1,650
Costs		(260)	(290)	(330)
		1,040	1,160	1,320
Tax (10%)		(104)	(116)	(132)
Capital investment	(2,900)			
Tax relief on Capital Allowances (W2)	290			
Net A$ cashflow (A$000)	(2,610)	936	1,044	1,188
Exchange rate (A$/£) (W4)	2.0000	1.9100	1.8241	1.7420
Net £ cashflow (£000)	(1,305)	490	572	682
Discount factors @ 11% (W3)	1	0.901	0.812	0.731
Present values	(1,305)	441	464	499

NPV (£000)   99

Workings

(W1) Tax relief on capital allowances – Investment 1

Time		£000	Tax relief (25%)	Timing of tax relief
t_0	Investment	1,100		
t_0	Claim Capital Allowance (40%)	(440)	110	t_0
		660		
t_1	Claim Capital Allowance	(264)	66	t_1
		396		
t_2	Claim Capital Allowance	(158)	40	t_2
		238		
t_3	Sales proceeds	300		
		62		
t_3	Balancing Charge	62	(16)	t_3

(W2) Tax relief on capital allowances – Investment 2

Time		A$000	Tax relief (10%)	Timing of tax relief
t_0	Investment	2,900		
t_0	Claim Capital Allowance	(2,900)	290	t_0
		–		

(W3) **Discount rate**

$$(1+m) = (1+r)(1+i) = 1.08 \times 1.0275$$

$$m = 0.1097, \text{ which rounds to 11\%}$$

(W4) **Exchange rates**

Time	£	A\$	
t_0	1	2.0000	given
t_1	1	1.9100	× 95.5% (£ weakens by 4.5% p.a.)
t_2	1	1.8241	
t_3	1	1.7420	

(b) **Results of financial analysis**

Based on the ARR method of project appraisal, neither of the investments should be accepted, since both ARRs are lower than CM's target of 15%.

Based on the NPV calculations, Investment 2 should be accepted since it has a positive NPV.

This analysis seems to conflict, but the NPV method is generally considered to be theoretically superior since it gives the absolute gain (or loss) to shareholders if the project is undertaken.

Thus, the financial analysis would lead us to prefer Investment 2.

Non-financial factors

Before a final decision can be made on whether to accept Investment 2, CM's management should also consider the following non-financial factors:

- Investment 2 is based in Asia, a new market for CM. The managers will need to be aware of local customs and cultures if undertaking this investment.

- The political risk in the Asian country will have to be analysed carefully. Is the government encouraging, or hostile, to foreign investors?

- The financial analysis has assumed that Asian cashflows will be immediately remitted back to the UK. There may be maximum limits on remittances which prevent this from happening.

- It will be very difficult to manage an Asian operation from the UK. Therefore experienced local managers may have to be recruited, or managers might have to be redeployed from the UK. This might cause problems for the existing UK operations.

61   DOMINIQUE (NOV 09 EXAM)

Key answer tips

This question contained a mass of information regarding foreign currency denominated cash flows. Try not to be overwhelmed by the level of detail. A logical, systematic approach will ensure that you score most of the marks in a question like this i.e. set up a proforma for the cashflows and enter them systematically, remembering to account for the tax impact where necessary.

Leave time for part (b). There were plenty of easy marks here for students who managed their time carefully.

(a)

Forecast A	1/1/X0 T$m	31/12/X0 T$m	31/12/X1 T$m	31/12/X2 T$m	31/12/X3 T$m	31/12/X4 T$m
Initial investment	(150)					40
Logistics planning (0.38 × 2.1145)	(0.8)					
T$ operating cashflows		45.0	54.0	64.8	68.7	72.8
Tax 20% in country T		(9.0)	(10.8)	(13.0)	(13.7)	(14.6)
Tax depn allowances (W3)		6.0	4.8	3.8	3.1	4.3
Net remitted to country D	(150.8)	42.0	48.0	55.6	58.1	102.5
Tax 5% in country D (W1)		(2.1)	(2.4)	(2.8)	(2.9)	(3.1)
Net cashflow in T$	(150.8)	39.9	45.6	52.8	55.2	99.4
DF 12%	1	0.893	0.797	0.712	0.636	0.567
PV	(150.8)	35.6	36.3	37.6	35.1	56.4

NPV = 50.2/2.1145 = **D$23.7 million**

Forecast B	1/1/X0 T$m	31/12/X0 T$m	31/12/X1 T$m	31/12/X2 T$m	31/12/X3 T$m	31/12/X4 T$m
Net cashflow in T$ (as above)	(150.8)	39.9	45.6	52.8	55.2	99.4
Exchange rate (W2)	2.1145	2.2287	2.3490	2.4759	2.6096	2.7505
Net cashflow in D$	(71.3)	17.9	19.4	21.3	21.2	36.1
DF 12%	1	0.893	0.797	0.712	0.636	0.567
PV	(71.3)	16.0	15.5	15.2	13.5	20.5

NPV = **D$9.4 million**

Workings

(W1) Tax at 5% excludes initial and residual value investment cash flows

i.e. 3.1 = 5% × (72.8 – 14.6+4.3)

So the impact of the T$ depreciating against the D$ by 5.4% a year rather than staying constant at the spot rate of 2.1145 is a reduction in the NPV of the project from D$ 23.7 million to D$ 9.4 million, a reduction of over 60%.

(W2) Future exchange rates

Date	Rate	Workings
1/1/X0	2.1145	
20X0	2.2287	(2.1145 × 1.054) etc
20X1	2.3490	
20X2	2.4759	
20X3	2.6096	
20X4	2.7505	

(W3) Tax depreciation allowances

Year	T$	Tax allowance	Tax impact at 20%
	150.0		
20X0	(30.0)	30.0	6.0
	120.0		
20X1	(24.0)	24.0	4.8
	96.0		
20X2	(19.2)	19.2	3.8
	76.8		
20X3	(15.4)	15.4	3.1
	61.4		
	(40.0)	residual value	
20X4	21.4	21.4	4.3

Advice on whether to proceed

The project shows a strong positive NPV under both exchange rate scenarios.

If it considers Forecast B to be a 'worst case scenario', Dominique can be confident in proceeding with the project. Indeed, this is a highly conservative assessment as it only covers a 5 year time horizon and assumes a low residual value. Taking a longer term view or assuming a higher residual value can be expected to result in a significantly higher NPV result.

The project would appear to fit in well with its already wide geographical spread of business.

Conclusion: Dominique should be advised to proceed with the project.

(b) The Dominique group has a significant exposure to movements in both exchange rates and tax rates because of its wide geographical spread of businesses and continued expansion into new territories.

Higher tax rates will directly reduce the profitability of the Dominique group.

Exchange rates will impact in several ways:

- *translation risk* – subsidiary carrying values will fluctuate as exchange rates change.

- *transaction risk and economic risk* – exchange gains or losses may arise on purchases and sales in foreign currency.

- *financing risk* – the cost of servicing foreign currency debt will fluctuate as exchange rates change.

Exchange rates impact on:

- net investment values of subsidiaries

- value of repatriated profits via dividends (dividend planning and hedging of predictable future dividend streams to protect against a relative rise in the value of the D$)

- cost of servicing foreign currency debt

- cost of goods imported in a different currency to that where the goods are to be sold

Impact on financial strategy:

In order to address the impact of tax and exchange rate changes, the Dominique group should:

- structure funding in tax efficient manner.

- limit withholding tax by appropriate corporate structure.

- generally aim to generate higher earnings in lower tax regimes.

- keep informed of government plans and policies and ensure there is sufficient mark-up and profit in any new country to reduce the risk of losses if tax rates were to increase.

- match currency of funding to net investment currency to reduce exposure to exchange rate movements.

- try and ensure that interest streams are matched by dividend or interest streams in the same currency.

- use hedging instruments to fix currency rates on predictable cash flows.

62   MR (SEPT 10 EXAM)

Key answer tips

This was a very standard investment appraisal question, using the three most commonly tested investment appraisal methods; NPV, IRR and MIRR.

Show all your workings in a neat table, so that the marker can easily follow your answer through. Even if you make minor mistakes along the way, a good layout will ensure that you receive most of the available marks.

(a)   (i)   **Net Present Value**

US$m	1/1/X1	31/12/X1	31/12/X2	31/12/X3
Operating cashflows		14	17	22
Tax (25%)		(3.5)	(4.25)	(5.50)
Investment – NCA	(30)			
Residual value – NCA				3
Working capital investment	(16)			16
Tax relief on depreciation		2.25	2.25	2.25
(US$30m × 90% × ⅓ × 25%)				
Total cashflow	(46)	12.75	15	37.75
DF at 9%	1	0.917	0.842	0.772
PV	(46.0)	11.7	12.6	29.1
NPV	**US$7.4m**			

Note: The consultants' investigation cost has been ignored since MR is committed to paying it whether or not the project goes ahead.

Internal Rate of Return

Discount the above cashflows at a higher discount rate, say 20%

US$m	1/1/X1	31/12/X1	31/12/X2	31/12/X3
Total cashflow	(46)	12.75	15	37.75
DF at 20%	1	0.833	0.694	0.579
PV	(46.0)	10.6	10.4	21.9
NPV	**US$(3.1m)**			

$$\text{Hence IRR} = 9\% + \frac{7.4}{7.4+3.1}(20\% - 9\%) = 16.8\%$$

Modified Internal Rate of Return

Project outflow is US$46m 1/1/X1

Project inflows in the following three years need to be compounded up to terminal value:

i.e. $37.75 + (15 \times 1.09) + (12.75 \times 1.09^2) = \text{US}\$69.25\text{m}$

Hence $69.25 \times DF_3$ @ MIRR = 46

So, DF_3 @ MIRR = 46/69.25 = 0.664

From tables it can be seen that MIRR is approximately 15% (where the 3 year discount factor is 0.658).

(ii)　**Advantages and limitations of MIRR**

The best method of appraising investments in theory is the NPV method, since it gives the absolute gain in wealth for the shareholders if a project is undertaken.

However, it is easier for non-financially minded decision makers to understand the concept of a percentage measure, which is why IRR and MIRR are sometimes used as investment appraisal methods instead of NPV. Unfortunately, neither of these two methods give the absolute gain in shareholder wealth if a project is undertaken, so neither of them relate directly to the overriding objective of financial management.

If using a percentage measure (IRR or MIRR) to appraise an investment, it is important to interpret the result properly.

An advantage of MIRR is that it does actually measure the percentage return generated by a project over its life. It can therefore easily be compared with the firm's cost of capital to decide whether the project is worthwhile.

IRR, on the other hand, is not a measure of the actual return from a project, but instead is a measure of a breakeven discount rate i.e. a discount rate which would give a zero NPV. IRR is therefore more difficult to interpret than MIRR.

The other key advantage to MIRR over IRR is that MIRR is always a unique figure for each project, whereas a single project can have several IRRs (or none at all). This again makes IRR more difficult to interpret.

(b)　**Impact on MR's financial objectives**

MR has two financial objectives:

1　to earn a return on shareholders' funds of 11% per annum

2　to keep the gearing ratio below 35%

Return on shareholders' funds of 11% per annum

If the project is undertaken, it will generate a positive NPV and an MIRR of 15% per annum. As explained above, the MIRR measures the actual return from a project, so we can see that the objective of an 11% shareholder return will be achieved on this project.

It is not clear what returns are being made on the other activities undertaken by MR. The heavy discounting seen in the last year will have affected overall returns adversely. However, it seems that if this new project goes ahead, the objective is more likely to be met overall.

Gearing

MR's current gearing level is US$350m/(US$350m + US$760m) = 31.5%

If the new project goes ahead, MR will increase its borrowing by US$23m (50% of the initial investment cost). At the same time, the value of equity will increase by the NPV of the project (US$7.4m from part (a) above).

Therefore, the new gearing level will be:

350 + 23/(350 + 23 + 760 + 7.4) = 32.7%

which is still below the ceiling set out in the objective.

Conclusion

If the project is undertaken, it appears that it is likely to enable MR to achieve its objectives.

63   PEI (NOV 10 EXAM)

Key answer tips – extracted from the Examiner's "Post Exam Guide"

Part (a)

Discount the cash flows and calculate an NPV for each project. Projects A and B should be discounted at 8% and project C at 9% to reflect the additional risk. For project B note there is a residual value. For project C, calculate exchange rates to convert the operating cash flows into GBP sterling from A$.

Profitability indices should be calculated for each project by dividing the NPV by the initial investment.

Part (a)(ii) requires recognition that capital is limited to £25 million. It is therefore useful to rank the projects in order of NPV and profitability index (PI) and then look at the combination of any two projects. The discussion should focus on which combination gives the highest NPV and PI without breaking the investment limit. Some discussion should be provided about the limitations of PI when all projects are not of equal duration and risk. Finish your answer with advice on which projects to accept.

Part (b)

Explain that the alternative method involves working with A$ cash flows and an A$ discount rate. Then calculate the A$ discount rate.

Part (c)

Discuss key *financial* factors.

(a)   (i)   Exchange rates for project C (A$ weakening against GBP by 1.5% per annum)

1 Jan 20X1	2.00
End 20X1	2.03
End 20X2	2.06
End 20X3	2.09
End 20X4	2.12
End 20X5	2.15

Calculations of NPV and PI for each project

PROJECT A	GBP Million	DF @8%	DCF GBP Million	
Initial Investment	−15.50	1.000	−15.50	
Net Operating Cash Inflows	1.75	12.500	21.88	
Residual Value	0.00		0.00	
			⎯⎯⎯	
NPV			6.38	
PI			41.1%	(6.38/15.50 × 100)

PROJECT B	GBP Million	DF @8%	DCF GBP Million	
Initial Investment	−10.20	1.000	−10.20	
Net Operating Cash Inflows Yr 1	1.15	0.926	1.06	
Net Operating Cash Inflows Yrs 2–7	3.10	4.280	13.27	
Residual Value	2.50	0.583	1.46	
			⎯⎯⎯	
NPV			5.59	
PI			54.8%	(5.59/10.20 × 100)

PROJECT C	£GBP Million	DF @9%	DCF GBP Million	
Initial Investment	−9.50	1.000	−9.50	
Net Operating Cash Inflow 20X1	4.58	0.917	4.20	
Net Operating Cash Inflow 20X2	4.51	0.842	3.80	
Net Operating Cash Inflow 20X3	4.45	0.772	3.43	
Net Operating Cash Inflow 20X4	4.39	0.708	3.11	
Net Operating Cash Inflow 20X5	4.33	0.650	2.81	
Residual Value	0	0.650	0	
			⎯⎯⎯	
NPV			7.85	
PI			82.6%	(7.85/9.50 × 100)

(ii) The profitability index (PI) shown above is the NPV expressed as a percentage of the initial investment, this is the "net" method. The GPV or "gross" method would be equally acceptable, where the PI is the NPV expressed as a percentage of the sum of the NPV and the initial investment. PI is most appropriate when projects are divisible. However, it is technically acceptable to apply the profitability index alongside other analysis when determining the best combination of non-divisible projects in a capital rationing situation. Although PI may lead to an incorrect ranking, it still provides useful information. Indeed, in many cases a PI analysis will identify the optimum combination of projects.

As all three projects cannot be undertaken given the entity's capital expenditure limit of GBP 25 million, it is necessary to look at combinations of any two projects.

Summary of rankings

Project	Initial Investment GBP million	NPV GBP million	PI %	Rank using NPV	Rank using PI
A	15.50	6.38	41.2	2	3
B	10.20	5.59	54.8	3	2
C	9.50	7.85	82.6	1	1
A+C	25.00	14.23	56.9	1	2
B+C	19.70	13.44	68.2	2	1

The combination of projects A&C gives the highest NPV, B&C has the highest ranking using PI, and is well within the company's investment limit, leaving just over GBP5 million to invest elsewhere.

A&B breaches the limit of capital available. This combination also ranks last so PEI might not wish to even consider sourcing the additional GBP700,000 required to make both investments (although the combination has a positive NPV and in theory is worth investment if money can be raised and there are no other limitations).

PI should only really be used if the projects being considered are of equal duration and equal risk.

Here we are comparing A + C with B + C. Both combinations include Project C so we are really only interested in comparing the duration and risk of Projects A and B. Project B has the advantage of being both of shorter duration than Project A but the same risk and so we can be fairly confident that the top ranking PI combination of B + C is superior to the highest ranking NPV combination of A + C assuming that we can make constructive use of the unused capital.

Conclusion: The best investment appears to be a combination of Projects B and C.

(b) The alternative method involves working with A$ cash flows and an A$ discount rate. The expected movements in the A$/GBP exchange rate are taken into account in the adjusted discount rate. The A$NPV result is then converted into GBP at the spot rate.

In this case, we would adjust the GBP discount rate of 9% to take account of the anticipated 1.5% per annum strengthening of GBP(weakening A$). That is, the A$ discount rate is 1.09 × 1.015 = 1.106 or 10.6% per annum.

(c) Key factors to consider include:

Foreign exchange exposure arising on Project C.

- Availability of suitable finance. PEI has cash available but this might not be the most appropriate type of finance in a foreign investment. Borrowing in A$, if available, would provide a natural hedge by matching (to a greater or lesser extent) income streams with interest payments and A$ denominated assets with liabilities.

- Risk appetite of shareholders. This is a private company and the profile of shareholdings is not known but it is likely that at least some of the shareholders are also directors or employees of the company.

- Political risks – the foreign country in which Project C will be invested is not specified but investment in any foreign jurisdiction carries some risk.

- Tax implications – these might have been accounted for in the net operating cash flows but PEI needs to assess the impact of differential tax rates and/or whether a double taxation treaty exists between the two countries.

- Appropriateness of the discount rate – no indication was given as to how the 9% was determined.

Tutorial note – extracted from the Examiner's "Post Exam Guide"

Part (a) was very well answered by most candidates who attempted this question. Common errors were:

- *Ignoring Residual Value in Project B*

- *Getting the exchange rates the wrong way round in Project C*

- *Not calculating profitability indexes (PIs)*

Part (b) was frequently ignored or misunderstood. The requirement for a calculation of the A$ discount rate should have been the clue as to what approach was required.

In Part (c) many answers discussed all types of key factors whereas the question required a focus on financial factors.

---

64   GOH (MAR 11 EXAM)

Key answer tips – extracted from the Examiner's "Post Exam Guide" (note that the comments regarding WORD and/or EXCEL only relate to the COMPUTER BASED papers in March and September each year)

In part (a)(i) candidates should calculate the post-tax cost of debt and the WACC for JKL. In part (a)(ii) candidates should identify the key differences between public and private sector organisations and address each in turn and also examine other issues such as whether JKL's WACC or, indeed, a commercial WACC of any type, would be appropriate for GOH in this scenario.

In part (b)(i) candidates should calculate the NPV of the proposed project by first identifying all the components of the investment appraisal and the timing of the cash flows. These should then be discounted at the rate of 4%.

In part (b)(ii) candidates should identify the key issues GOH needs to take into account before a decision is taken and advise on each one in turn.

(a) (i)   JKL's pre-tax cost of debt is estimated as: $5.79\% = 5.5\% \times 100/95$

As a private sector organisation, JKL will be subject to taxation and therefore it is necessary to calculate a post tax cost of debt: $5.79\% \times 0.7 = 4.05\%$

Note that this is an estimation only – a yield to maturity calculation would take into account the discount of 5% on the price. However, no information is provided about the maturity of the bonds other than that they are 'long dated' and therefore the annual effect of the discount is likely to be insignificant and has been ignored for the purposes of arriving at this estimate.

JKL's WACC is calculated as:

Type of security	Market Value G$ million	Rate of return %	Proportion of total %	Weighted return %
Equity	318.50	9.00	77.03	6.93
Long term debt	95.00	4.05	22.97	0.93
Total	413.50			7.86

(that is, approximately 8%)

(ii)   A private sector organisation is likely to have very different financial and non-financial objectives than a public sector organisation.

A private sector organisation will focus on maximising shareholder wealth by maximising profits. Shareholder wealth can be measured by the return that shareholders receive from their investment, represented partly by the dividend received each year and partly by the capital gain from the increase in the value of the shares over that period. The value of the shares should increase when the entity is expected to make additional profits that will be paid out as dividends or reinvested for future growth. The focus will be on financial targets. Shareholders expect higher returns than lenders in order to compensate for the greater risks that they take.

A public sector organisation will usually have a greater focus on non-financial objectives such as:

- value for money
- social benefits (including education and health)
- environmental benefits (of growing concern)

within pre-determined financial budgets.

A lower discount rate is appropriate for a public sector organisation such as GOH because it is not necessary to make the large returns that shareholders expect in a private sector organisation. The 4% rate is often set to reflect 'time preference', that is, the preference of society as a whole to receive goods and services sooner rather than later.

Inputs are also different. A public sector organisation measures returns and benefits of a project in a non-financial nature (such as improvements in public health) and so it is appropriate to include estimates of these non-financial benefits in an appraisal exercise.

In addition, the funding structure of JKL and GOH are completely different. JKL's WACC will reflect both the high returns demanded by equity holders and also the cost of debt whereas GOH will effectively only be funded by debt. The debt itself will be at different rates. Debt investors in JKL will expect a higher return then investors in government debt in order to reflect the credit risk involved in investing in JKL.

Based on the above, using the WACC of JKL as a discount rate for GOH's project appraisal is not appropriate.

(b) (i)

Year	0	1	2	3	4 – 15	15
	G$ million	G$ million	G$ million	G$ million	G$ million	G$ million
Initial investment	(950.00)					150.00
Land	(250.00)					600.00
Net future benefits		90.00	110.00	120.00	130.00	
DF at 4% (Gohland rate)	1.000	0.962	0.925	0.889	9.385 × 0.889	0.555
Total DCF	(1,200.00)	86.58	101.75	106.68	1,084.62	416.25

Total NPV of G$595.88 million

(ii) On the basis of the return on investment the project should clearly go ahead.

However, a number of important factors need to be taken into account before a final decision can be reached. These include:

- Sensitivity analysis to ascertain the critical variables.
- In particular, the social benefits of the health centre should be considered in depth. These appear to have been factored into the cash inflows in terms of "perceived social benefits" of inflows but these are extremely difficult to quantify unless the Gohland government has some established basis of quantification (as in the UK's NHS).

- The relationship of the investment to GOH's objectives should be examined.

- This is a very long term investment that has obvious follow on expenditure in 15 years time. In this case, 15 years might not be long enough for the evaluation.

- The availability of government funding both for the initial investment and the on-going running costs of the centre.

- Prioritising the use of government funds – what would they be used for if not used for the health centre – where is the greatest need.

- Alternative strategic approaches could be examined such as:

  - co-operating with other government agencies

  - co-locating or sharing health facilities with other agencies

  - engaging the voluntary sector

  - transferring service provision to another body

  - provision of the service by the private sector

  - refurbishing existing facilities rather than building new

  - changing location or scale

Tutorial note – extracted from the Examiner's "Post Exam Guide

This question had the highest average marks of any question in this exam, largely as a result of the WACC calculation and investment appraisal calculation.

Understanding of the relevance of JKL's WACC to GOH was less well answered and highlighted a lack of understanding of the different business and financial risks faced by JKL and GOH.

There were some good answers to part (b)(ii) which helped lift the average mark.

Common errors included:

- *Incorrect calculation of the cost of debt – omitting either the tax adjustment or the pricing adjustment. Note that a yield to maturity calculation was not necessary as the debt is long dated and so the yield should approximate to the coupon.*

- *Incorrect use of the nominal value of debt rather than the market value in the calculation of WACC.*

- *Incorrect deduction of tax in the investment appraisal as GOH is a government owned organisation.*

- *Omitting the value of the land in the investment appraisal.*

- *Error in the annuity factor calculation. Note that in EXCEL it is quick and easy to work with a large number of years and feedback from markers indicated that there were generally fewer errors where candidates itemised every year rather than calculated an annuity factor in this instance.*

65   CIP MANUFACTURING (SEPT 11 EXAM)

Key answer tips – extracted from the Examiner's "Post Exam Guide"

Part (a)(i) requires a basic NPV evaluation of the project. A tabular layout should be used.

In part (a)(ii), it is firstly necessary to ungear and then regear PPP's equity beta to obtain a risk-adjusted WACC for use in the NPV evaluation. Alternatively, the M&M adjusted WACC formula can be applied directly to the proxy company's ungeared cost of equity. The original NPV calculation can then be repeated using this adjusted WACC.

Part (a)(iii) requires an APV calculation. Firstly, a base case NPV should be obtained using the ungeared cost of equity for PPP as the discount rate. Separate calculations are then required of the present value of the after tax interest saving provided by the subsidised borrowing and of the tax relief obtained on the interest payment under both borrowings. In each case, the pre-tax cost of debt should be used as the discount rate. These items can then be added to the base case NPV, together with the issue costs, to obtain the APV result.

The answer to part (b) should consider the pros and cons of each of the three approaches used in part (a) and then the appropriateness of each one in turn. These issues can then be drawn together to provide an overall conclusion on the financial viability of the project in answer to part (c).

(a)   (i)   **NPV of project at CIP's existing WACC of 10%**

Year	Cash Flow EUR	Discount Factor @ 10%	PV EUR
0	(6,500,000)	1	(6,500,000)
1	750,000	0.909	681,750
2	950,000	0.826	784,700
3	1,400,000	0.751	1,051,400
4–6	2,100,000	2.487 × 0.751 = 1.868	3,922,800

NPV: (59,350)

(ii)   **NPV of project at a risk adjusted WACC**

To establish the risk adjusted discount rate firstly, it is necessary to establish an appropriate beta for the project. PPP has been identified as an appropriate proxy and has an equity beta of 1.95. This firstly needs to be de-geared and then re-geared to give an equity beta that reflects the business risk of the project and the existing financial risk of CIP.

De-gear

$$\beta_u = \beta_g \left(\frac{V_E}{V_E + V_D[1-t]} \right)$$

So, $\beta_u = 1.95 \times (4/(1(0.7) + 4)) = 1.66$

Re-gear

$$\beta_g = \beta_u + [\beta_u - \beta_d]\ \frac{V_D[1-t]}{V_E}$$

So, β_g = 1.66 + 1.66 × ((1 × 0.7)/3) = 2.05

$k_e = R_f + [R_m - R_f]\beta$

So, k_e = 4% + (9% - 4%) × 2.05 = 14.25%

$$WACC = k_e\left(\frac{V_E}{V_E + V_D}\right) + k_d[1-t]\left(\frac{V_D}{V_E + V_D}\right)$$

So, WACC = 14.25% × (3/4) +6% × (0.7) × (1/4) = 10.69% + 1.05% = 11.74%, therefore use 12%

Alternative approach using formula $K_{adj} = k_{eu}\ [1 - tL]$

$k_{eu} = R_f + [R_m - R_f]\ \beta_u$

So, k_{eu} = 4% + (9% - 4%) × 1.66 = 12.30%

$K_{adj} = k_{eu}\ [1 - tL]$

So, K_{adj} = 12.30% × [1 − (0.3 × (1/4))] = 11.38%, therefore it would be acceptable to use 11% as the discount rate

NPV calculation at a discount rate of 12%

Year	Cash Flow EUR	Discount Factor @ 12%	PV EUR
0	(6,500,000)	1	(6,500,000)
1	750,000	0.893	669,750
2	950,000	0.797	757,150
3	1,400,000	0.712	996,800
4–6	2,100,000	2.402 × 0.712 = 1.710	3,591,000
			NPV: (485,300)

(iii) **APV of project at a base-case discount rate of Keu**

Base–case discount rate

Under APV to discount the project cash flows we need a discount rate that assumes that the project is fully funded by equity. Therefore the discount rate should be the cost of equity for an all equity financed company. To establish this we need an asset beta appropriate to the project, which we have already calculated above as 1.66. This then needs to be applied to the CAPM formula to establish the ungeared cost of equity.

$k_{eu} = R_f + [R_m - R_f]\ \beta_u$

So, k_{eu} = 4% + (9% − 4%) × 1.66 = 12.30%

We will round this to the nearest whole number − therefore a rate of 12% should be applied to the cash flows to establish the base case. Given that this is the same discount rate as above the base case NPV is therefore negative at EUR (485,300).

Financing side effects

The financing side effects need to be discounted at a rate that reflects the systematic risk of the cash flows. It is normally assumed that this will be the pre-tax cost of debt, which in this instance is 6%.

PV of tax relief on loan interest

Subsidised loan   EUR 6,500,000 × 40% × 1% × 0.3 × 4.917 =   EUR 38,353

Bank loan   EUR 6,500,000 × 20% × 6% × 0.3 × 4.917 =   EUR 115,058

Giving a total of EUR 153,411

PV of subsidy: Interest saving

EUR 6,500,000 × 40% × [(0.06 − 0.01)(1 − 0.3)] × 4.917   = EUR 447,447

Issue costs

EUR 6,500,000 × 60% × 0.01 = EUR 39,000

APV can now be calculated as:

	EUR
Base case NPV	(485,300)
PV of tax relief on loan interest	153,411
PV of subsidy	447,447
Issue costs	(39,000)
APV	76,558

(b)   The results of the calculations in part (a) are:

		EUR 000	Decision
(i)	NPV at CIP's existing WACC	(59)	Reject
(ii)	NPV at a risk-adjusted WACC	(485)	Reject
(iii)	APV	77	Accept

Based on considering only the financial benefits, the project would be rejected under the two NPV methods but accepted under the APV method. Therefore before making a recommendation we need to consider the appropriateness of each of the methods in turn.

NPV at existing WACC

The company's existing WACC is not appropriate here as both the business risk and financial gearing of the project are different from those of the company itself prior to the project.

The proposed project carries a higher level of risk than CIP's current business activities. In addition, the benefit to the company of the subsidy on the government borrowing and access to higher levels of debt (leading to higher tax relief) is project-specific have not been taken into account.

NPV at risk adjusted WACC

The risk adjusted WACC is superior to the existing WACC in that it provides an adjustment to reflect the business risk specific to the project. A proxy company's beta is used for this purpose.

However, this method does not solve the financing issues identified previously in the discussion of the use of the existing WACC.

APV

APV can be used in situations where a project has special financing features such as providing access to subsidised financing or where the financing structure of the project is more relevant to the project appraisal than the financing structure of the company itself (e.g. where the project represents a new area of business for the company where a different capital structure is appropriate).

For CIP, the APV approach has the advantage of taking into account:

- The NPV of the subsidy on the government borrowing (net of issue costs).

- Greater tax benefit due to the higher level of debt funding supported by the project.

By using the ungeared cost of equity derived from the proxy company, APV is correctly based on the project risk rather than CIP's current business risk.

(c) **Advise on whether to proceed with the project**

Based on APV we should accept this project.

We should, however, recognise that this decision relies on the underlying assumptions of APV analysis, including the important assumption that it is appropriate to use the actual gearing level for the project where different projects support different levels of debt, as appears to be the case here.

Tutorial note – extracted from the Examiner's "Post Exam Guide"

A number of candidates incorrectly included interest cash flows in the NPV computations. Note that it would have been acceptable here to include cash flows equivalent to the post tax value of the subsidy but that no other interest cash flows were given credit.

Very few candidates were able to successfully complete the APV calculation. Common errors included:

- *Omitting the base case NPV*

- *Calculating the base case NPV using WACC rather than ungeared cost of equity*

- *Only including a single year of interest saving*

- *Omitting to discount the cash flows*

- *Omitting one or more of the elements required in the APV calculation*

Note that a tabulated approach to the APV calculation, incorporating the subsidy and tax relief elements into the base case NPV, was equally valid and produced exactly the same final result.

Candidates' understanding of the information provided by the APV calculation also tended to be quite poor.

---

66   CMEC (NOV 11 EXAM)

Key answer tips – extracted from the Examiner's "Post Exam Guide"

Part (a)

Preliminary calculations:

* Forward exchange rates A$/GBP for 3 years

* Working capital movements noting the incremental nature of the cash flows

Calculate the NPV in GBP terms using the two methods required in the question.

Part (b)

Recognise that the reason they should be the same is due to interest rate parity and explain the key principles behind this theory.

Part (c)

* Identify the key additional risks involved in foreign investments

* Advise how the project evaluation could be adapted to take these risks into account

Part (d)

* Recognise and discuss areas of similarity between previous UK projects and proposed foreign investment e.g. need for trial run, appointment of project team, budget costs

* Identify and discuss the differences between PCA for previous projects and the proposed investment e.g. location of proposed project and role of local management.

(a)   (i)   **Calculation of NPV based on GBP discount rate**

Year ended 31 December		2012	2013	2014
Time	0	1	2	3
Net operating cash flow (A$m)		200.00	250.00	350.00
Investment – stores (A$m)	(415.00)			450.00
Investment – refurb (A$m)	(170.00)			
Investment in working capital (A$m)	(150.00)	(15.00)	(16.50)	181.50
A$ cash flows	(735.00)	185.00	233.50	981.50
Exchange rate	1.300	1.370	1.444	1.522
GBP remitted cash flows	(565.38)	135.04	161.70	644.88
Additional UK costs (GBP)		(14.00)	(14.00)	(14.00)
Net GBP cash flows	(565.38)	121.04	147.70	630.88
Discount factor at 10%	1.000	0.909	0.826	0.751
Present value (GBP)	(565.38)	110.03	122.00	473.79
NPV	GBP	140.4	million	

Exchange rates workings

Date	Spot	Workings
01-Jan-12	1.300	
31-Dec-12	1.370	=1.300 × 1.075/1.02)
31-Dec-13	1.444	=1.370 × 1.075/1.02)
31-Dec-14	1.522	=1.444 × 1.075/1.02)

Working capital workings

	Balance	Movement
01-Jan-12	150.0	150.0
31-Dec-12	165.0	15.0
31-Dec-13	181.5	16.5
31-Dec-14	–	(181.5)

(ii) **Calculation of NPV based on A\$ discount rate**

Calculation of A\$ discount rate

$$\frac{(1 + \text{A\$ discount rate})}{(1 + \text{GBP discount rate})} = \frac{(1 + \text{A\$ interest rate})}{(1 + \text{GBP interest rate})}$$

So, 1 + A\$ discount rate = 1.10 × 1.075/1.02

= 1.1593

So use A\$ discount rate of 16%

Alternative approach:

$$1 + \text{A\$ discount rate} = \frac{\text{future spot rate}}{\text{current spot rate}} \times (1 + \text{GBP discount rate})$$

$$= \frac{1.300 \times 1.075/1.02}{1.300} \times 1.10$$

= 1.1593

So use A\$ discount rate of 16%

Discounting A\$ cash flows at A\$ discount rate of 16%

Year ended 31 December		2012	2013	2014
Time	0	1	2	3
	A\$m	A\$m	A\$m	A\$m
A\$ cash flows	(735.00)	185.00	233.50	981.50
UK CF translated into A\$		(19.18)	(20.22)	(21.30)
Total A\$ cash flows	(735.00)	165.82	213.28	960.20
Discount factor at 16%	1.000	0.862	0.743	0.641
Present value	(735.00)	142.93	158.47	615.49

NPV in A\$	A\$		181.89 million
Translate at spot of GBP/A\$	1.3000		
giving a GBP value of:	GBP		139.93 million

(b)   The reason why the two calculations for NPV are almost the same (and indeed had a discount rate and discount factors been used to an accuracy of five decimal places, the answers would have been exactly the same) is because of the interest rate parity theory upon which the predictions of exchange rate are based.

Interest rate parity states that there is a relationship between foreign exchange rates and money markets. Other things being equal the currency with the higher interest rate will be at a discount in the forward market against the currency with the lower interest rate.

In terms of the approaches adopted in (a) both use interest rate parity, but in different ways. The first approach uses it to adjust future exchange rates and the second uses it to adjust the discount rate. Because both are based on the same theory, ultimately they give the same answer.

(c)   The additional risks involved in foreign investment include:

- Exchange rate sensitivities.

- Less certainty over costs and revenues due to lack of familiarity with the market.

- Uncertainty over management time and cost involved in overseeing the development and subsequent operations.

These can be taken into account using:

- Sensitivity analysis (of exchange rates and property values after 3 years and other individual costs and revenues).

- Certainty equivalents (applied to net operating cash flows to allow for lower returns).

- Using a risk-adjusted discount factor in the npv analysis, based on an assessment of additional risk and an analysis of the beta of businesses in the same sector.

- Assessing alternative possible outcomes by applying probability of outcome to different scenarios.

(d)   Lessons learnt from previous UK projects could be useful to a certain extent. The basic implementation framework for UK projects can be applied to foreign projects but foreign investments have many additional complications which need careful monitoring and control.

Similar items include:

- Trial run.

- Project team.

- Budget control.

However, the whole structure of the project team may need to be different. Decisions will need to be taken on, for example:

- The location of the project team(s).

- Role of local management in the implementation.

New items that will need to be added to the project team's agenda will include:

- Regulatory risk (working within a new regulatory regime e.g. different employment law and health and safety regulations).

- Human resource issues (employees in Asia may be used to different working arrangements).

- Control over foreign travel and accommodation costs.

Tutorial note – extracted from the Examiner's "Post Exam Guide"

This question was the most popular of the optional questions and generally answered well by those who attempted it, especially the calculations for part (a). Common errors in this part of the question were:

- *Ignoring the incremental nature of working capital cash flows.*

- *Timing differences, for example showing working capital as starting in year 1 rather than year 0.*

- *Calculating the A\$ as appreciating against sterling rather than depreciating.*

- *Incorrect application of forex rates.*

- *Providing all the calculations twice instead of recognising that up to a point the calculations for (a)(i) and (a)(ii) are the same. This is not an error as such but wastes time.*

Part (b) was often ignored. Most who attempted it did not understand that the question required explanation of the theory of interest rate parity. Some did recognise this but were unable to offer sensible explanations of what the theory entailed.

In part (c) candidates tended to discuss risks in general or, if they did recognise the additional risks such as forex or political risks, they failed to suggest how the project evaluation should be adapted.

Part (d) was often a discussion of all aspects of PCAs and did not recognise the context of the question.

---

67   RST (MAR 12 EXAM)

(a)   (i)   **Validity of using a proxy company and CAPM to arrive at a discount rate**

There may be issues relating to the use of a proxy company as it may not be directly comparable with RST in terms of the nature of its business and business risk. In addition, it is not certain that the cost of equity used to calculate the WACC has been adjusted to reflect RST's financial risk.

The use of the CAPM in modern financial markets is questionable given the model's simplifying assumptions. A beta is also more difficult to obtain and assess for a private company such as RST. However, on the positive side, this approach might be better than using rough and ready adjustments to the basic cost of capital.

Validity of using NPV

Using NPV in project analysis is theoretically sound and is a refinement on the analysis of the cash flows themselves as it takes into account the time value of money and the riskiness of the project. Higher risk projects can be discounted at a higher, risk-adjusted discount rate. As long as the cost of capital is appropriate and the cash flows have been accurately predicted a positive NPV means that the project will generate wealth for the shareholders in excess of the returns that they require.

(ii)   **Validity of conclusion reached by the finance manager that RST should proceed with the investment in Perth**

The finance manager appears to have based his decision to proceed with the investment on the fact that the overall expected NPV is positive, arrived at by applying probabilities to a number of different possible outcomes. This is not sufficient data on which to make a decision when it is for a one-off project of this nature.

It is not appropriate to accept the project solely on the basis of the AUD 21.6 million expected NPV. Indeed this NPV is not actually achievable and hence is fairly meaningless in this context.

Instead the finance manager should consider each of the outcomes separately and then consider the risk appetite of the Board. In this instance, there is an 80% chance of making a positive NPV and only a 20% chance of making a negative NPV. Ultimately, whether the project is acceptable will depend upon the Board's attitude to accepting a 20% risk that shareholder value will fall. Therefore before making the decision to proceed it is important that the Board are aware of this risk and carefully considers further information such as sensitivity analysis and other qualitative factors.

(b)   **Impact of real options on the investment decision**

There are three different forms of real options that need to be considered when making investment decisions. These are – the abandonment option, the follow-on option and the wait option.

The abandonment option

If, once a project is undertaken, it can be abandoned for very little cost then knowing this at the outset (when a decision is being made about proceeding with a project) has a value. Therefore, when evaluating a project, the value of any abandonment option should be included with the NPV of the project itself.

The ability to abandon a project is particularly valuable where there is significant uncertainty surrounding the results of a project. In our example we are told that there are three possible outcomes, one of which has a negative result. If the project is undertaken, but once commenced it is found that the worst case scenario is valid, then RST would like to be able to abandon the project. Therefore knowing upfront that it could be abandoned has value in the decision, because further losses can be eliminated by taking the abandonment option.

The follow-on option

Many projects, once undertaken can lead to further projects or opportunities. If such opportunities exist then there is an argument that they should be considered and valued whilst making the initial decision. In this situation it might be the case that even though a project on its own has a negative NPV, by including the follow on projects (which only arise as a result of doing the main project) that it is worthwhile.

In the context of RST, opening up in Perth may, for example, provide new contacts at major groups of companies that have offices elsewhere in Australia and hence lead on to additional work or the development of another office in another Australian city or in another country altogether.

The wait option

This is the option to be able to wait and see how the market develops before commencement of the project. This is particularly important where there is significant uncertainty in the forecasts such as in the case of RST. The option to be able to wait for a period of time to see whether the worst case scenario materialises could have significant value as potentially it would stop RST taking on a negative NPV project. However, it could also lead to loss of opportunity altogether if competitor companies set up in Perth in the meantime. Therefore the wait option may have very little value to RST.

(c)   **Response to comments from Director S**

Using a lower cost of capital such as the cost of debt would only be expected to increase the NPVs of the project if gearing is currently lower that the 'optimum' gearing based on the relationship between WACC and gearing for RST. Regardless of this issue, however, it is not appropriate to use the cost of the debt as a discount rate in project appraisal. This is because the project needs to be viewed in the context of the company as a whole and needs to satisfy the required returns of all of the providers of capital to the business not just to the debt providers. This is why the discount rate should normally be the weighted average cost of capital adjusted for the specific business risk of the project.

The concern over gearing is a valid concern because as gearing increases so does the return required by the equity providers and hence the cost of equity also increases. This is particularly the case where gearing is already relatively high. In the case of RST we know that it is heavily reliant on debt and therefore it is likely that any further increase in gearing will have a significant impact on WACC.

Interest payments might well be lower for USD debt than for AUD debt, especially in the early years. However, expectations theory predicts that , over the longer term, any benefit from lower interest costs would be offset by an equivalent movement in the USD/AUD exchange rate, thereby eliminating any such benefit.

However, exchange rates rarely move as predicted by such theories and so the use of USD debt in the absence of any other USD cash flows arising in the business that might provide a natural offset, will produce potential very large currency risk. RST would be exposed to:

- Transaction risk on converting interest cash flows and the final capital repayment.

- Economic risk if competitor companies do not carry similar currency risks.

- Translation risk on accounting for the borrowing at reporting dates.

In conclusion, if the USD were to strengthen against the AUD, RST could be exposed to significant and unnecessary currency exposures and such an arrangement should be avoided.

Tutorial note – extracted from the Examiner's "Post Exam Guide"

The answers to part (a) were often too brief and did not consider all aspects required. Some candidates focused only on one aspect at length (e.g.: the use of a proxy company to adjust the cost of equity) which obviously then limited the number of marks that could be awarded. Areas that were often not mentioned included the limitations of CAPM and the apparent lack of adjustment for financial risk. The evaluation of using expected values was also generally poorly answered as many candidates failed to recognise that using EV in this situation was not a valid approach given that it was a one-off project. However, there were some excellent answers in this section as well.

There were also some excellent answers to part (b) but on the whole, the standard of answers was disappointing. Some candidates clearly had no idea about the meaning of the term "real options" and wasted time discussing general factors to be considered when making an investment decision. Others managed to name the three types of real option and made an attempt at linking them to the scenario but, disappointingly, failed to comment on how the options could be factored into the initial investment decision.

In terms of part (c), the increased gearing risk and foreign currency debt comments were well dealt with. However the use of the cost of debt as a discount rate was not well answered and often ignored altogether.

68   PP (MAY 12 EXAM)

Key answer tips – extracted from the Examiner's "Post Exam Guide"

Part (a)(i)

Calculate NPV of the proposed IT project

Show NPV as a loss

Part (a)(ii)

Calculate additional cash flow requirement using the annuity factor for 4 years at 12% and "grossing" up at 52%.

Part (b)(i)

Discuss appropriateness of the DCF approach to this specific situation.

Note key point that obtaining a discount rate is especially difficult.

Part (b)(ii)

Provide advice on financial and strategic factors PP should consider before deciding whether to proceed.

(a) (i) **DCF of project cash flows excluding possible new business:**

Year	0	1–4
	USD000	USD000
Initial investment	(600.0)	
Maintenance costs		(50.0)
One off redundancy costs	(200.0)	
Annual staff cost saving		100.0
Net Cash flow	(800.0)	50.0
DF at 12%	1.000	3.037
Present value	(800.0)	151.9
NPV before new business CF	(648.1)	

(ii) In order to break even, the PV of the net cash flows from the new business must be equal to USD 648.1k. Assuming that the benefit is spread evenly over the 4 years, we can use a four year annuity factor to estimate the annual cash flows required from new business.

A PV of USD 648.1k is equivalent to an annual net cash inflow of USD 213.4k a year for four years.

(Workings: USD 213.4k = USD 648.1k/3.037 where 3.037 = AF(4, 12%))

In this case, given that the new business is expected to generate a net cash inflows of 52% of new cash inflows, additional annual net cash inflows of USD 213.4k represent additional cash inflows of USD 410.4k a year. *(Workings: USD 410.4k = USD 213.4k/52%).*

Conclusion: the amount of additional revenue required to break even is USD 410.4k a year.

(b) (i) **Use of conventional DCF approach**

Benefits:

A conventional DCF approach is attractive in that it ensures that all projects are assessed on a similar basis. It can also help avoid the dangers of subjective judgment that is inevitable when 'softer' criteria are used in terms of qualitative benefits such as 'improved information'.

Drawbacks:

However, unlike most other types of project, the costs and benefits of IT projects are both tangible and intangible and it can be almost impossible to assign meaningful and valid figures to intangible costs and benefits. In addition, the risks involved in IT projects are difficult to ascertain and so it is not easy to arrive at an appropriate discount rate for use in the evaluation.

Some adjustment for risk is needed in the analysis. One approach would be to adjust the discount rate used in the DCF calculation to reflect the specific risk of such an IT project. An alternative approach would be to calculate the DCF by applying probabilities to different possible outcomes for new business and establishing an expected value. Sensitivity analysis could also be used to analyse the impact on the DCF result of changes in key input variables.

(ii) Fit with business operational and strategic plans

It is important to understand how the IT project fits within the overall strategic plans for the partnership and also how it contributes to meeting targets at the operational level.

IT systems should be treated as a strategic resource like other capital investments. If this particular investment is required as part of the strategic plans of the business, the question is not whether to go ahead but whether this particular system is the one that best meets the partnership's needs (that is, a qualitative judgment) in the most cost effective manner (that is, a quantitative judgment).

Similarly, the IT investment may be an essential part of an operational plan and therefore there is little choice about whether or not to go ahead with the project. All that can be done is to fine tune it and choose the best system and system development/purchase approach.

Reputation and competitive position

PP will clearly be more likely to be successful in generating new business if it has a good reputation in the market place, therefore analysis of market position is important. This is particularly important if PP faces strong competition from businesses operating in the same market.

State of the industry and economic conditions in general

The current state of the economy in which PP operates is also relevant, therefore this should also be considered. The partnership will only be successful in generating new business if the market is sufficiently buoyant and there is new business available.

Staffing issues

PP needs to be confident that it has staff in place who have the necessary skills and/or experience to be able to successfully operate the new system. Suitable training should be arranged if required.

Conclusion

In conclusion, analysis is required of the needs of the business, both at strategic and operational level, and whether or not the proposed IT system meets those needs. DCF analysis may therefore be of secondary importance if the project is essential to the successful development of the underlying business. Further analysis and market surveys may also be useful in pinning down likely new business levels more accurately. Finally, staffing issues need to be considered to ensure that staff have adequate skills and training required to both maintain and use the new system.

Tutorial note – extracted from the Examiner's "Post Exam Guide"

Part (a)

Most candidates could adequately attempt the NPV calculation for part (a)(i) but few could answer fully the break even value required in part (a)(ii). Common errors or omissions that prevented higher marks were:

- *In part (a)(i) including cash flows from the new business – the question says to ignore them.*

- *Incorrect timing – there were many variations on this type of error, such as showing the redundancy payments in year 1 instead of year 0 or maintenance costs starting in year 0 instead of year 1.*

- *In part (a)(ii) many candidates could correctly calculate annual net cash flow although some simply divided by 4 rather than by the 4 year annuity factor. The majority of candidates stopped there and did not then uplift the net cash flow by 52% to get the (gross) annual cash inflow.*

Part (b)(i)

This was surprisingly poorly answered. Many candidates failed to recognise the difficulty of identifying intangible benefits and determining an appropriate discount rate.

Part (b)(ii)

The part of the question was generally well answered. A common failing was to discuss shareholders and/or dividend policy – the question deals with a partnership and so such issues are not relevant here.

69 WIDGET (SEPT 12 EXAM)

Key answer tips – extracted from the Examiner's "Post Exam Guide"

In answering the first part of this question, candidates should firstly calculate the payback period and profitability index for each of the 4 projects and then rank the projects on each of the bases requested. The second part of the question then requires an explanation of the strengths and weaknesses of each of these prioritisation methods in the situation of capital rationing with non-divisible projects. Answers here should focus on capital rationing rather than just discussing the overall strengths and weaknesses of each method.

The third part of the question asks for the optimum combination of projects in this situation of non-divisible projects. A trial and error approach of different combinations of projects should be used – selecting the combination with the highest overall NPV.

> The final element of the question asks for explanation of how the optimal combination might be impacted if soft capital rationing applied and if capital rationing applied in future years. In terms of the soft capital rationing candidates should identify that potentially all projects could be undertaken if the funds could be found because they are all worthwhile. Other possible combinations of projects and the additional amount of funding needed should be identified and commented upon. In the future capital rationing situation candidates should identify that the payback of projects becomes more important, although without more sophisticated techniques assessing which projects to choose would be difficult.

(a) (i) **Base data – workings (all figures are in F$ million)**

Project	Year 0	PV of cash flows Year 1+	NPV	PI	Annual cash flows	Term (Years)	Payback (Years)
A	−100	135	35	35%	151.2	1	0.7
B	−150	250	100	67%	82.3	4	1.8
C	−300	410	110	37%	242.6	2	1.2
D	−350	510	160	46%	124.0	6	2.8

Ranking of individual projects according to:

Project	NPV	PI	Payback
A	(4)	(4)	(1)
B	(3)	(1)	(3)
C	(2)	(3)	(2)
D	(1)	(2)	(4)

(ii) NPV gives an indication of the increase in shareholders' funds as a result of investing in each project. However, if capital is limited, it is also important to look at how much of the limited capital resource is required by each project when deciding which projects to invest in.

The profitability index is most appropriate when choosing between projects that are divisible but is less reliable when projects are non-divisible. However, it can also be helpful when ranking non-divisible projects. Indeed, it often indicates the 'optimum' combination and, if not, a combination of projects that is very close to the optimum combination. However, in this case it has not identified the optimal combination of projects and, indeed, the simpler approach of ranking by NPV result has produced a better result.

Payback places a greater emphasis on the timing of the cash flows. It therefore gives project A the highest priority because the initial investment is paid back within the year. This is very useful information for multi-period scenario situations as it indicates that the funds can be reinvested in new projects in the following year. If there are even more lucrative projects planned next year, this could be an important advantage. However, this is not so useful if we are only concerned with immediate capital restrictions in the current year. Uncertainty as to the realisation of cash flows generally increases with time, so the payback can also give a helpful indication of the riskiness of the project. A project with a low payback will often carry lower risk and therefore be more attractive.

However, all three methods have major drawbacks in practice. In the majority of cases, a capital rationing decision is much more complicated than purely the choice of projects indicated by such measures as NPV, PI or payback. For example:

- If capital rationing applies in the current year, it will almost certainly also apply in subsequent years. A multi-period model is therefore required.

- The projects are unlikely to have the same other characteristics. For example, some may provide follow on opportunities and others may be of more strategic significance than others.

- Some projects may be 'once only' opportunities and need to be pursued in the current year whereas it may be possible to delay others to the following year.

In conclusion, none of the three methods listed is likely to provide the best solution in isolation. Each contributes some useful information that can be used in the decision making process, but each only provides 'part of the picture'.

(b) **(i)** **Combination of projects based on rankings of individual projects and subject to $700m initial investment**

	Combination F$ million	Initial investment F$ million	NPV F$ million
NPV	D C	650	270
PI	B D	500	260
Payback	A C B	550	245
BEST	**A B D**	**600**	**295**

Conclusion: The optimal combination is provided by projects A, B and D. This leaves F$ 100 million unspent.

(ii) **Soft versus hard capital rationing**

Soft capital rationing is where the restriction is internally imposed by the company for budgetary purposes and, for example, to allocate capital investment provision between different operating units. The limits are targets only and can be adjusted according to circumstances. Hard capital rationing is where the restriction cannot be moved where, for example, capital is limited by covenant restrictions on borrowings.

If WIDGET were to apply soft capital rationing, it is likely to prefer to undertake the projects with the highest PIs if it were possible to increase the limit on the total value of the initial investment from F$700 million to F$800 million.

That is, carry out projects B, C and D at a total initial investment of F$800 million and a much higher NPV of F$370 million. This compares to an NPV of F$295 million in part (b)(i). The NPV has increased by F$75 million (F$ 370 million – F$295 million), an increase of 25%, as a result of increasing the capital investment by just 14% (F$100 million/F$700 million).

Indeed, it would be of benefit to shareholders to undertake all 4 projects if there funding is available to cover all 4.

Capital rationing in the following year

The optimal combination of projects is likely to be quite different when assumptions are added regarding capital rationing in the following year.

Indeed, Project A becomes much more attractive since it provides a payback of less than one year and so the capital is available for re-investment again in the second year. Assuming that this amount can be added to the F$700 million new capital available in a year's time, this would greatly enhance WIDGET's investment capability at that time.

Where multi-period capital rationing is involved, an alternative technique such as linear programming is required. However, this is outside the scope of the F3 syllabus.

Tutorial note – extracted from the Examiner's "Post Exam Guide"

This was the least well answered question (on this exam paper) with an overall average mark significantly below 12.5, perhaps indicating that for many candidates this was a last chance choice.

Part (a)(i):

This was very well answered on the whole with many candidates scoring full marks. The most common error was miscalculation of the profitability index (often with calculations completely missing out the investment), showing a lack of knowledge in this area.

Part (a)(ii):

Most candidates answered this requirement very poorly, with answers that simply listed the strengths and weaknesses of each of the three methods as means of investment appraisal in general, rather than as means of prioritising projects in the context of capital rationing. Those candidates who did not relate their comments to capital rationing scored very few marks for this part of the question, even though sometimes they had written at length about, for example, the strengths and weaknesses of NPV in the context of investment appraisal. This is not the only occasion in this exam where a number of candidates appear to have ignored the question set and answered the question that they wanted to see.

Part (b)(i):

Some candidates ignored this part of the question, although many did recognise that in the context of non-divisible projects that an NPV approach was the most appropriate. Many candidates simply suggested projects C and D (being those ranked 1 and 2), rather than applying a trial and error approach to ascertain the combination of projects which maximised NPV and therefore shareholder wealth.

Part (b)(ii):

This part of the question was generally not well answered. Most candidates were able to define 'soft' and 'hard' capital rationing but then failed to comment upon how soft capital rationing would impact the optimum combination. It was encouraging, however, that some candidates did understand that if additional resources could be found that the overall NPV could be significantly increased for relatively little extra investment. Indeed some candidates did quantify this and scored well as a result. The element regarding capital rationing in future years was not well answered and, indeed, often left out altogether.

---

70 APT (NOV 12 EXAM)

Key answer tips – extracted from the Examiner's "Post Exam Guide"

Part (a)(i)

Recognise that the components of a DCF/NPV evaluation include capital flows as well as operating cash flows then discount each year's net cash flows at the 11% discount rate for that year. Realise that, as DCFs for years 3, 4 and 5 are constant, it is quicker to use annuity factors rather than annual discount factors for these years. Finally, sum the annual DCFs to arrive at the NPV.

Part (a)(ii)

Calculate the project's adjusted discount rate using the information of the "proxy" company, YYY. This takes four steps: (1) ungear YYY's beta, (2) regear the ungeared beta for the project's capital structure (note: the question requires the use of the project's capital structure rather than that APT's capital structure), (3) calculate cost of equity using this re-geared beta in the CAPM formula, and (4) calculate WACC using the cost of equity from step 3 and the cost of debt, remembering to adjust this for tax relief.

The NPV can now be recalculated using the revised WACC. Note that it is not necessary to write out all the cash flows again, you can begin from the total cash flow line calculated in part (a) as all you are changing is the discount rate.

Part (b)

The adjusted present value is calculated by adding together the "base case" NPV and the side effects of financing, which here are the present value of the tax relief obtained on the loan raised to finance 50% of the project.

Part (c)

Advise the company on each of the three valuation methods used. Your answer should have three sub headings; one for each of the methods. Under each sub heading explain very briefly what that method means then proceed to discuss the advantages and disadvantages in general terms then as they relate to APT. Include in your answer the potential difficulties of each method, for example obtaining accurate costs or a suitable discount rate to apply to the side effects of financing in the APV calculation.

(a) (i) **Calculation of project NPV using current WACC:**

Year	0	1	2	3–5	5
	EURm	EURm	EURm	EURm	EURm
Investment	(500)				
Residual value					170
Net operating cash flows		70	100	115	
Total cash flows	(500)	70	100	115	170
Discount factor at 11%	1	0.901	0.812	1.983 (W1)	0.593
DCFs	(500.0)	63.1	81.2	228.0	100.8
NPV	(26.9)				

(W1) Annuity factor for years 3-5 is 1.983 = 3.696 – 1.713

(ii) **Calculation of project NPV using risk adjusted discount rate:**

First calculate the project specific adjusted discount rate

Step 1 – Ungear YYY's beta of 1.3

$$\beta_u = \beta_g \left[\frac{V_e}{V_e + V_d(1-t)} \right] + \beta_d \left[\frac{V_d(1-t)}{V_e + V_d(1-t)} \right] =$$

$$1.3 \left[\frac{660}{660 + 250(1-t)} \right] + 0.2 \left[\frac{250(1-t)}{660 + 250(1-t)} \right]$$

= (1.3 × 0.7857) + (0.2 × 0.2143) = 1.0214 + 0.0429 = 1.064 (where 1–t = 1– 0.28)

Step 2 – Regear for different project capital structure

$\beta_u = 1.064$ (as in Step 1)

$$\beta_g = \beta_u + \left[\beta_u - \beta_d \right] \frac{V_d(1-t)}{V_e}$$

$$= 1.064 + \left[(1.064 - 0.2) \times \frac{250(1-t)}{250} \right] = 1.064 + \left[0.864 \times \frac{250(1-t)}{250} \right] = 1.686$$

Step 3 – Calculate the cost of equity using the risk adjusted beta

$K_e = R_f + \beta(R_m - R_f)$ = 4.5 + 1.686 (9.5 – 4.5) = 12.93%

Step 4 – Calculate the risk adjusted WACC

Cost of debt is 7% (1 – .28) = 5.04%

WACC is therefore

(EUR 250 million/EUR 500 million) × 12.93% + (EUR 250 million/EUR 500 million) × 5.04%

= 8.985% (say 9%)

Secondly, reperform the NPV calculation using the revised WACC

NPV using risk adjusted WACC

Year	0	1	2	3–5	5
	EURm	EURm	EURm	EURm	EURm
Total cash flows	(500)	70	100	115	170
Discount factor at 9%	1	0.917	0.842	2.131 (W1)	0.650
DCFs	(500.0)	64.2	84.2	245.1	110.5
NPV	4.0				

(W1) Annuity factor for years 3–5 is 2.131 = 3.89 – 1.759

(b)   **Adjusted present value approach:**

Using beta of an ungeared company, (1.064), the discount rate to use for the base case NPV is

4.5% + 1.064(9.5% − 4.5%) = 9.82%, say 10%

Year	0	1	2	3–5	5
	EURm	EURm	EURm	EURm	EURm
Total cash flows	(500)	70	100	115	170
Discount factor at 10%	1	0.909	0.826	2.055 (W1)	0.621
DCFs	500.0	63.6	82.6	236.3	105.6
NPV	(11.9)				

Workings

(W1)   Annuity factor for years 3–5 is 2.055 = 3.791 − 1.736

Base case NPV	(11.9)
PV of tax relief	20.1 (W2)
	———
APV	8.2

(W2)   Tax relief per annum calculated as: EUR 250 million × 7% × 28% = EUR 4.9 million, so PV of 5 years = EUR4.9 million × 4.1 (the 5 year annuity factor for 7%) = EUR 20.1 million.

(c)   **Advice on appropriateness of each valuation method:**

Current WACC

The main advantage of the current WACC is that it is easily calculated from information currently available. However, it is only appropriate if:

1   The new project is the same risk as the company's existing business.

2   The project will not alter the long term gearing of the company.

3   There are no project-specific financing issues, such as a subsidised loan or one-off higher interest cost on the project loan, that create additional benefits or costs that need to be taken into account in the project appraisal.

In the given scenario, we are told that the project carries a different level of risk from the underlying business (item 1 above) and so we can be confident that the current WACC is not appropriate without adjusting for risk. Also, in relation to item 2 above, the project does change the company's debt ratio significantly; from 20.8% to 34.5% (EUR 500 million/EUR 1,450 million ignoring the NPV of the project itself). The scenario does not mention whether APT has a "target" gearing. As it is a manufacturing company 34% might not be excessive but this is not a long term increase as the project is only for 5 years. The current WACC is therefore clearly inappropriate given the differences between the project and the company's existing profile.

Risk-adjusted WACC

The use of an adjusted WACC can be achieved by "ungearing" a proxy company's beta (YYY's) to strip out the element of financial risk that applies to the proxy and "regearing" using the capital structure of the project.

The use of a risk adjusted WACC satisfies the first objection (item 1) to using WACC above, because by adjusting the beta of a proxy company we are able to correctly identify the return required for the business risk of the project (that is assuming that the proxy company used is reasonable).

The risk adjusted WACC approach also attempts to take into account that the gearing of the company (and therefore financial risk) might change as a result of the project by using the project gearing ratio rather than the company's existing gearing. However, ideally we would like to be able to adjust for the post investment gearing position of the company as a whole rather than the project in isolation, however, in order to adjust for the post investment gearing of the company we would need to know the NPV of the project itself (because this will obviously increase the equity value), which we can't establish without a post investment WACC. Therefore, there is a cyclical problem here in that without knowing the NPV of the project we can't establish the post investment gearing position and the ultimate level of financial risk that the project will generate. This is where APV is useful because it allows the financial risk generated by the project to be dealt with separately (see below). APV is also a useful tool where there are specific project-related financing issues that also need to be taken into account.

Adjusted present value

This method calculates a "base case" NPV using a discount rate based on the ungeared beta appropriate for the project's level of business risk and adjusts for the side effects of financing.

The APV method is most appropriate in the following circumstances:

- When it permanently changes the level of gearing of a company.
- When the project involves unusual financing costs such as a subsidised loan
- It significantly changes the company's debt capacity.
- If a number of project-specific financing options are to be considered

The main benefits of this method are that

- It should provide a more accurate assessment of the real worth of the project to the company.
- It can deal more transparently with the side effects of financing.
- The base case NPV stays the same even if assumptions about capital structure change, therefore fewer recalculations are required.

The main disadvantage might be in determining the costs involved and a suitable discount rate, for example the rate to use to discount the side effects of finance.

In this case, the APV result provides a useful measure of the value of the project based on the finance suggested rather than on the company's WACC. However, if the long term capital structure of the company is unlikely to change and the WACC represents that target, it is unlikely that APV should be used as the primary measure when deciding whether or not to proceed with the project. The argument being that, for example, the use of a higher proportion of debt to finance this project restricts the company's ability to raise further debt in the future without first raising more equity or retaining more earnings –i.e.: in the long term the level of gearing will stay the same and therefore it is only this long term gearing level that we should be concerned with. In these circumstances perhaps the most appropriate approach would be to use a proxy company to establish a beta reflecting the correct business risk but then regear and calculate WACC on the basis of the long term gearing ratio for the company (rather than the gearing of the project as in the risk adjusted WACC).

And, if indeed the capital structure is likely to change as a result of the project, this would have implications not only for this project but for all other projects that the company is involved with and so there are wider ramifications than shown by the APV result for this project in isolation. A marginal cost of capital approach might then be more appropriate.

Tutorial note – extracted from the Examiner's "Post Exam Guide"

This question was generally more popular, and better answered, in non-UK centres than in UK centres. Almost all candidates could calculate the basic NPV required in part (a)(i), although a minority included interest payments. Part (a)(ii) required a CAPM approach and most candidates made a reasonable attempt at applying the formulae given in the exam paper to the numbers used in the question. Unfortunately many did not read the question properly and misunderstood the instructions about gearing, which were very clear.

Part (b), which required calculation of the APV, was generally poorly attempted and most candidates either did not attempt it or did not understand what was being asked. The question was quite clearly worded and this failure was probably due to lack of preparation of the topic before the exam.

There was often a lack in depth in the answers to part (c) and many answers were confused and haphazard in their approach.

Section 5

SPECIMEN PAPER QUESTIONS

We are grateful to CIMA for their kind permission to reproduce their specimen papers. They are © Chartered Institute of Management Accountants.

SECTION A – 50 MARKS

(*Note:* **The indicative time for answering this section is 90 minutes.**)

Answer this question

1   **PRE-SEEN CASE MATERIAL**

Background

Power Utilities (PU) is located in a democratic Asian country. Just over 12 months ago, the former nationalised Electricity Generating Corporation (EGC) was privatised and became PU. EGC was established as a nationalised industry many years ago. Its home government at that time had determined that the provision of the utility services of electricity generation production should be managed by boards that were accountable directly to Government. In theory, nationalised industries should be run efficiently, on behalf of the public, without the need to provide any form of risk related return to the funding providers. In other words, EGC, along with other nationalised industries was a non-profit making organisation. This, the Government claimed at the time, would enable prices charged to the final consumer to be kept low.

Privatisation of EGC

The Prime Minister first announced three years ago that the Government intended to pursue the privatisation of the nationalised industries within the country. The first priority was to be the privatisation of the power generating utilities and EGC was selected as the first nationalised industry to be privatised. The main purpose of this strategy was to encourage public subscription for share capital. In addition, the Government's intention was that PU should take a full and active part in commercial activities such as raising capital and earning higher revenue by increasing its share of the power generation and supply market by achieving growth either organically or through making acquisitions. This, of course, also meant that PU was exposed to commercial pressures itself, including satisfying the requirements of shareholders and becoming a potential target for take-over. The major shareholder, with a 51% share, would be the Government. However, the Minister of Energy has recently stated that the Government intends to reduce its shareholding in PU over time after the privatisation takes place.

Industry structure

PU operates 12 coal-fired power stations across the country and transmits electricity through an integrated national grid system which it manages and controls. It is organised into three regions, Northern, Eastern and Western. Each region generates electricity which is sold to 10 private sector electricity distribution companies which are PU's customers.

The three PU regions transmit the electricity they generate into the national grid system. A shortage of electricity generation in one region can be made up by taking from the national grid. This is particularly important when there is a national emergency, such as exceptional weather conditions.

The nationalised utility industries, including the former EGC, were set up in a monopolistic position. As such, no other providers of these particular services were permitted to enter the market within the country. Therefore, when EGC was privatised and became PU it remained the sole generator of electricity in the country. The electricity generating facilities, in the form of the 12 coal-fired power stations, were all built over 15 years ago and some date back to before EGC came into being.

The 10 private sector distribution companies are the suppliers of electricity to final users including households and industry within the country, and are not under the management or control of PU. They are completely independent companies owned by shareholders.

The 10 private sector distribution companies serve a variety of users of electricity. Some, such as AB, mainly serve domestic users whereas others, such as DP, only supply electricity to a few industrial clients. In fact, DP has a limited portfolio of industrial customers and 3 major clients, an industrial conglomerate, a local administrative authority and a supermarket chain. DP finds these clients costly to service.

Structure of PU

The structure of PU is that it has a Board of Directors headed by an independent Chairman and a separate Managing Director. The Chairman of PU was nominated by the Government at the time the announcement that EGC was to be privatised was made. His background is that he is a former Chairman of an industrial conglomerate within the country. There was no previous Chairman of EGC which was managed by a Management Board, headed by the Managing Director. The former EGC Managing Director retired on privatisation and a new Managing Director was appointed.

The structure of PU comprises a hierarchy of many levels of management authority. In addition to the Chairman and Managing Director, the Board consists of the Directors of each of the Northern, Eastern and Western regions, a Technical Director, the Company Secretary and the Finance Director. All of these except the Chairman are the Executive Directors of PU. The Government also appointed seven Non Executive Directors to PU's Board. With the exception of the Company Secretary and Finance Director, all the Executive Directors are qualified electrical engineers. The Chairman and Managing Director of PU have worked hard to overcome some of the inertia which was an attitude that some staff had developed within the former EGC. PU is now operating efficiently as a private sector company. There have been many staff changes at a middle management level within the organisation.

Within the structure of PU's headquarters, there are five support functions; engineering, finance (which includes PU's Internal Audit department), corporate treasury, human resource management (HRM) and administration, each with its own chief officers, apart from HRM. Two Senior HRM Officers and Chief Administrative Officer report to the Company Secretary. The Chief Accountant and Corporate Treasurer each report to the Finance Director. These functions, except Internal Audit, are replicated in each region, each with its own regional officers and support staff. Internal Audit is an organisation wide function and is based at PU headquarters.

Regional Directors of EGC

The Regional Directors all studied in the field of electrical engineering at the country's leading university and have worked together for a long time. Although they did not all attend the university at the same time, they have a strong belief in the quality of their education. After graduation from university, each of the Regional Directors started work at EGC in a junior capacity and then subsequently gained professional electrical engineering qualifications. They believe that the experience of working up through the ranks of EGC has enabled them to have a clear understanding of EGC's culture and the technical aspects of the industry as a whole. Each of the Regional Managers has recognised the changed environment that PU now operates within, compared with the former EGC, and they are now working hard to help PU achieve success as a private sector electricity generator. The Regional Directors are well regarded by both the Chairman and Managing Director, both in terms of their technical skill and managerial competence.

Governance of EGC

Previously, the Managing Director of the Management Board of EGC reported to senior civil servants in the Ministry of Energy. There were no shareholders and ownership of the Corporation rested entirely with the Government. That has now changed. The Government holds 51% of the shares in PU and the Board of Directors is responsible to the shareholders but, inevitably, the Chairman has close links directly with the Minister of Energy, who represents the major shareholder.

The Board meetings are held regularly, normally weekly, and are properly conducted with full minutes being taken. In addition, there is a Remuneration Committee, an Audit Committee and an Appointments Committee, all in accordance with best practice. The model which has been used is the Combined Code on Corporate Governance which applies to companies which have full listing status on the London Stock Exchange. Although PU is not listed on the London Stock Exchange, the principles of the Combined Code were considered by the Government to be appropriate to be applied with regard to the corporate governance of the company.

Currently, PU does not have an effective Executive Information System and this has recently been raised at a Board meeting by one of the non-executive directors because he believes this inhibits the function of the Board and consequently is disadvantageous to the governance of PU.

Remuneration of Executive Directors

In order to provide a financial incentive, the Remuneration Committee of PU has agreed that the Executive Directors be entitled to performance related pay, based on a bonus scheme, in addition to their fixed salary and health benefits.

Capital market

PU exists in a country which has a well developed capital market relating both to equity and loan stock funding. There are well established international institutions which are able to provide funds and corporate entities are free to issue their own loan stock in accordance with internationally recognised principles. PU is listed on the country's main stock exchange.

Strategic opportunity

The Board of PU is considering the possibility of vertical integration into electricity supply and has begun preliminary discussion with DP's Chairman with a view to making an offer for DP. PU's Board is attracted by DP's strong reputation for customer service but is aware, through press comment, that DP has received an increase in complaints regarding its service to customers over the last year. When the former EGC was a nationalised business, break-downs were categorised by the Government as "urgent", when there was a danger to life, and "non-urgent" which was all others. Both the former EGC and DP had a very high success rate in meeting the government's requirements that a service engineer should attend the urgent break-down within 60 minutes. DP's record over this last year in attending urgent break-downs has deteriorated seriously and if PU takes DP over, this situation would need to improve.

Energy consumption within the country and Government drive for increased efficiency and concern for the environment

Energy consumption has doubled in the country over the last 10 years. As PU continues to use coal-fired power stations, it now consumes most of the coal mined within the country.

The Minister of Energy has indicated to the Chairman of PU that the Government wishes to encourage more efficient methods of energy production. This includes the need to reduce production costs. The Government has limited resources for capital investment in energy production and wishes to be sure that future energy production facilities are more efficient and effective than at present.

The Minister of Energy has also expressed the Government's wish to see a reduction in harmful emissions from the country's power stations. (The term harmful emissions in this context, refers to pollution coming out of electricity generating power stations which damage the environment.)

One of PU's non-executive directors is aware that another Asian country is a market leader in coal gasification which is a fuel technology that could be used to replace coal for power generation. In the coal gasification process, coal is mixed with oxygen and water vapour under pressure, normally underground, and then pumped to the surface where the gas can be used in power stations. The process significantly reduces carbon dioxide emissions although it is not widely used at present and not on any significant commercial scale.

Another alternative to coal fired power stations being actively considered by PU's Board is the construction of a dam to generate hydro-electric power. The Board is mindful of the likely adverse response of the public living and working in the area where the dam would be built.

In response to the Government's wishes, PU has established environmental objectives relating to improved efficiency in energy production and reducing harmful emissions such as greenhouse gases. PU has also established an ethical code. Included within the code are sections relating to recycling and reduction in harmful emissions as well as to terms and conditions of employment.

Introduction of commercial accounting practices at EGC

The first financial statements have been produced for PU for 2008. Extracts from the Statement of Financial Position from this are shown in Appendix A. Within these financial statements, some of EGC's loans were "notionally" converted by the Government into ordinary shares. Interest is payable on the Government loans as shown in the statement of financial position. Reserves is a sum which was vested in EGC when it was first nationalised. This represents the initial capital stock valued on a historical cost basis from the former electricity generating organisations which became consolidated into EGC when it was first nationalised.

Being previously a nationalised industry and effectively this being the first "commercially based" financial statements, there are no retained earnings brought forward into 2008.

APPENDIX A

EXTRACTS FROM THE PRO FORMA FINANCIAL STATEMENTS OF THE ELECTRICITY

GENERATING CORPORATION

Statement of financial position as at 31 December 2008

	P$ million
ASSETS	
Non-current assets	15,837
Current assets	
Inventories	1,529
Receivables	2,679
Cash and Cash equivalents	133
	4,341
Total assets	20,178
EQUITY AND LIABILITIES	
Equity	
Share capital	5,525
Reserves	1,231
Total equity	6,756
Non-current liabilities	
Government loans	9,560
Current liabilities	
Payables	3,862
Total liabilities	13,422
Total equity and liabilities	20,178

END OF PRE-SEEN MATERIAL

UNSEEN CASE MATERIAL

Background

Assume today is 20 May 2009.

Power Utilities (PU) is located in an Asian country. It is planning to diversify its business activities by moving away from total reliance on coal fired power stations and building a hydroelectric power station to produce electricity using natural resources. A dam would need to be constructed to create a reservoir of water above the dam. Electricity would be generated by releasing water from the upper reservoir through the dam. Modern hydroelectric power stations can be very responsive to consumer demand and it is expected that the power station would be able to generate up to 100 megawatts of electricity within 60 seconds of the need arising.

Hydroelectric power stations do not directly produce harmful emissions such as carbon dioxide. However, some carbon dioxide will be produced during the construction phase. There is also a potential source of harmful greenhouse gases in the form of methane gas from decaying plant matter in flooded areas.

Public opinion on the project has been very mixed and there is a significant risk of opposition to the project from local people. Their housing and farming businesses will be seriously affected by the proposed development which will require flooding of local land to construct the dam.

Corporate objectives

Corporate objectives in line with a recent government drive include:

- Improved efficiency of energy production

- Reduction in harmful emissions such as greenhouse gases.

Financial objectives include maintaining group gearing (debt:debt plus equity) below 40% based on market values.

Hydroelectric power station project

Initial research has shown that a major river in the south of the country may be suitable for use in this project.

Extensive engineering and environmental studies have already begun to assess the viability of the project. These are expected to cost US$15,000,000 in total, payable in three equal instalments at the end of the calendar years 2008, 2009 and 2010. The payment for 2008 has already been made. PU is committed to pay the 2009 instalment but a clause in the contract would enable it to cancel the payment due in 2010 if it decides to withdraw from the project and future viability studies before the end of 2009.

Construction costs will be payable in US$. Other project costs and all project revenue will be in PU's functional currency, P$.

Construction and operating cash flows for the project are as follows:

	Year(s)	US$ million	P$ million
Construction costs	3 and 4	60 payment each year	–
Pre-tax net operating cash flows	5 to 24	–	150 receipt each year

Additional information:

- Time 0 is 1 January 2010;

- Cash flows should be assumed to arise at the end of each year;

- Business tax is 30% and is payable a year in arrears; also note that the government has announced plans to reduce the tax rate to 10% from 1 January 2014 on "clean" energy schemes such as this one (and would therefore only affect the tax position of the operating cash flows); however, this still needs to be approved by parliament and there is a risk that approval will not be obtained;

- Tax depreciation allowances of 100% can be claimed on construction costs but no tax relief is available on the cost of the engineering and environmental studies;

- The assets of the project have no residual value;

- Exchange rate as at today, 20 May 2009, is US$/P$6.3958 (that is, US$1 = P$6.3958). Some economic forecasters expect this exchange rate to remain constant over the period of the project but other forecasts predict that the US$ will strengthen against the P$ by 5% each year;

- PU normally uses a cost of capital net of tax of 10% to assess investments of this type.

Financial information for PU

Extracts from the latest available financial statements for PU are provided in the pre-seen material. The ordinary share capital consists of P$1 shares and the current share price on 20 May 2009 is P$2.80. The long term government borrowings shown in the statement of financial position are floating rate loans and the amount borrowed is unchanged since 31 December 2008

Financing the project

Two alternative financing schemes are being considered which would each raise the equivalent of US$130 million on 1 January 2012. These are:

(i)   A five-year P$ loan at a fixed interest rate of 5% per annum;

(ii) A subsidised loan denominated in US$ from an international organisation that promotes "clean energy" schemes. There would not be any interest payments but US$145 million would be repayable at the end of the five year term.

Required:

(a) Calculate the NPV of the project as at 1 January 2010 for each of the two different exchange rate forecasts and the two tax rates. **(14 marks)**

(b) Write a report to the Directors of PU in which you, as Finance Director, address each of the following issues:

    (i) Explain your results in part (a) and explain and evaluate other relevant factors that need to be taken into account when deciding whether or not to undertake the project. Conclude by advising PU how to proceed; **(15 marks)**

    (ii) Explain and evaluate the costs and risks arising from the use of foreign currency borrowings as proposed by financing scheme (ii) and advise PU on the most appropriate financing structure for the project.

    Up to 7 marks are available for calculations **(11 marks)**

In the event, the Board of Directors of PU decided to go ahead with the project and it has now been operational for six years. The Board has, however, now decided to dispose of the hydroelectric power station. To assist with these plans, a new entity, PP, has been formed and the plant and its operations have been transferred to PP.

(c) Discuss why PU might wish to dispose of the hydroelectric power station and advise the Directors of PU on alternative methods for achieving the divestment.

(10 marks)

(Total: 50 marks)

SECTION B – 50 MARKS

(*Note:* The indicative time for answering this section is 90 minutes.)

Answer TWO of the THREE questions – 25 marks each

2   AB is a large retailing organisation with revenue in the last financial year exceeding €1 billion. Its head office is in a country in the euro zone and its shares are listed on a major European stock exchange. Over the last few years AB has opened several new stores in a number of European capital cities, not all of them in the euro zone. AB is planning to allow all of its stores to accept the world's major currencies as cash payment for its goods and this will require a major upgrade of its points of sale (POS) system to handle multiple currencies and increased volumes of transactions

AB has already carried out a replacement investment appraisal exercise and has evaluated appropriate systems. It is now in the process of placing an order with a large information technology entity for the supply, installation and maintenance of a new POS system. The acquisition of the system will include the provision of hardware and software. Routine servicing and software upgrading will be arranged separately and does not affect the investment appraisal decision.

AB is considering the following alternative methods of acquiring and financing the new POS system:

Alternative 1

- Pay the whole capital cost of €25 million on 1 January 2010, funded by bank borrowings. This cost includes the initial installation of the POS system.

- The system will have no resale value outside AB

Alternative 2

- Enter into a finance lease with the system supplier. AB will pay a fixed amount of €7.0 million each year in advance, commencing 1 January 2010, for four years.

- At the end of four years, ownership of the system will pass to AB without further payment.

Other information

- AB can borrow for a period of four years at a pre-tax fixed interest rate of 7% a year. The entity's cost of equity is currently 12%.

- AB is liable to corporate tax at a marginal rate of 30% which is settled at the end of the year in which it arises..

- AB accounts for depreciation on a straight-line basis at the end of each year

- Under Alternative 1, tax depreciation allowances on the full capital cost are available in equal instalments over the first four years of operation.

- Under Alternative 2, both the accounting depreciation and the interest element of the finance lease payments are tax deductible.

- Once a decision on the payment method has been made and the new system is installed, AB will commission a post completion audit (PCA).

Required:

(a) (i) Calculate which payment method is expected to be cheaper for AB and recommend which should be chosen based solely on the present value of the two alternatives as at 1 January 2010 **(10 marks)**

(ii) Explain the reasons for your choice of discount factor in the present value calculations. **(3 marks)**

(iii) Discuss other factors that AB should consider before deciding on the method of financing the acquisition of the system **(3 marks)**

(b) Advise the Directors of AB on the following:

- The main purpose and content of a post completion audit (PCA).

- The limitations of a PCA to AB in the context of the POS system. **(9 marks)**

Note: A report format is not required in this question **(Total: 25 marks)**

3   CD is a privately-owned entity based in Country X, which is a popular holiday destination. Its principal business is the manufacture and sale of a wide variety of items for the tourist market, mainly souvenirs, gifts and beachwear. CD manufactures approximately 80% of the goods it sells. The remaining 20% is purchased from other countries in a number of different currencies. CD owns and operates 5 retail stores in Country X but also sells its products on a wholesale basis to other local retail outlets.

Although CD is privately owned, it has revenue and assets equivalent in amount to some entities that are listed on smaller stock markets (such as the UK's Alternative Investment Market (AIM)). It is controlled by family shareholders but also has a number of non-family shareholders, such as employees and trade associates. It has no intention of seeking a listing at the present time although some of the family shareholders have often expressed a wish to buy out the smaller investors.

CD has been largely unaffected by the recent world recession and has increased its sales volume and profits each year for the past 5 years. The directors think this is because it provides value for money; providing high quality goods that are competitively priced at the lower end of its market. Future growth is expected to be modest as the directors and shareholders do not wish to adopt strategies that they think might involve substantial increase in risks, for example by moving the manufacturing base to another country where labour rates are lower. Some of the smaller shareholders disagree with this strategy and would prefer higher growth even if it involves greater risk.

The entity is financed 80% by equity and 20% by debt (based on book values). The debt is a mixture of bonds secured on assets and unsecured overdraft. The interest rate on the secured bonds is fixed at 7% and the overdraft rate is currently 8%, which compares to a relatively recent historic rate as high as 13%. The bonds are due to be repaid in 5 years' time. Inflation in CD's country is near zero at the present time and interest rates are expected to fall.

CD's treasury department is centralised at the head office and its key responsibilities include arranging sufficient long and short term financing for the group and hedging foreign exchange exposures. The Treasurer is investigating the opportunities for and consequences of refinancing.

CD's sole financial objective is to increase dividends each year. It has no non-financial objective. This financial objective and the lack of non-financial objectives are shortly to be subject to review and discussion by the board. The new Finance Director believes maximisation of shareholder wealth should be the sole objective, but the other directors do not agree and think that new objectives should be considered, including target profit after tax and return on investment.

Required:

(a) **Discuss the role of the treasury department when determining financing or re-financing strategies in the context of the economic environment described in the scenario and explain how these might impact on the determination of corporate objectives.** **(15 marks)**

(b) **Evaluate the appropriateness of CD's current objective and of the two new objectives being considered. Discuss alternative objectives that might be appropriate for CD and conclude with a recommendation.** **(10 marks)**

(Total: 25 marks)

4 EF is a distributor for branded beverages throughout the world. It is based in the UK but has offices throughout Europe, South America and the Caribbean. Its shares are listed on the UK's Alternative Investment Market (AIM) and are currently quoted at 180 pence per share

Extracts from EF's forecast financial statements are given below.

Extracts from the (forecast) statement of profit or loss for the year ended 31 December 2009

	£000
Revenue	45,000
Purchase costs and expenses	38,250
Interest on long term debt	450
Profit before tax	6,300
Income tax expense (at 28%)	1,764
Note: Dividends declared	1,814

EF – Statement of financial position as at 31 December 2009

	£000
ASSETS	
Non-current assets	14,731
Current assets	
Inventories	5,250
Trade receivables	13,500
Cash and bank balances	348
	19,098
Total assets	33,829

EQUITY AND LIABILITIES

Equity

Share capital (ordinary shares of 25 pence)	4,204
Retained earnings	16,210
Total equity	**20,414**

Non-current liabilities

(Secured bonds, 9% 2015)	5,000
Current liabilities	
Trade payables	8,415
Total liabilities	**13,415**
Total equity and liabilities	**33,829**

You have obtained the following additional information:

1   Revenue and purchases & expenses are expected to increase by an average of 4% each year for the financial years ending 31 December 2010 and 2011.

2   EF expects to continue to be liable for tax at the rate of 28 per cent. Assume tax is paid or refunded the year in which the liability arises.

3   The ratios of *trade receivables to sales* and *trade payables to purchase costs and expenses* will remain the same for the next two years. The value of inventories is likely to remain at 2009 levels for 2010 and 2011.

4   The non-current assets in the statement of financial position at 31 December 2009 are land and buildings, which are not depreciated in the company's books. Tax depreciation allowances on the buildings may be ignored. All other assets used by the company are currently procured on operating leases.

5   The company intends to purchase early in 2010 a fleet of vehicles (trucks and vans). These vehicles are additional to the vehicles currently operated by EF. The vehicles will be provided to all its UK and overseas bases but will be purchased in the UK. The cost of these vehicles will be £5,000,000. The cost will be depreciated on a straight line basis over 10 years. The company charges a full year's depreciation in the first year of purchase of its assets. Tax depreciation allowances are available at 25% reducing balance on this expenditure. Assume the vehicles have a zero residual value at the end of ten years.

6   Dividends will be increased by 5% each year on the 2009 base. Assume they are paid in the year they are declared.

EF plans to finance the purchase of the vehicles (identified in note 6) from its cash balances and an overdraft. The entity's agreed overdraft facility is currently £1 million.

The company's main financial objectives are to earn a post-tax return on the closing book value of shareholders' funds of 20% per annum and a year on year increase in earnings of 8%

Assumption regarding overdraft interest

It should be assumed that overdraft interest that might have been incurred during 2009 is included in expenses (that is, you are not expected to calculate overdraft interest for 2010 and 2011).

Required:

Assume you are a consultant working for EF

(a) Construct a forecast statement of profit or loss, including dividends and retentions for the years ended 31 December 2010 and 2011. **(6 marks)**

(b) Construct a cash flow forecast for each of the years 2010 and 2011. Discuss, briefly, how the company might finance any cash deficit. **(9 marks)**

(c) Using your results in (a) and (b) above, evaluate whether EF is likely to meet its stated objectives. As part of your evaluation, discuss whether the assumption regarding overdraft interest is reasonable and explain how a more accurate calculation of overdraft interest could be obtained. **(10 marks)**

(Total: 25 marks)

Section 6

ANSWERS TO SPECIMEN PAPER QUESTIONS

We are grateful to CIMA for their kind permission to reproduce their specimen papers. They are © Chartered Institute of Management Accountants.

1 POWER UTILITIES (SPECIMEN EXAM)

(a) **Appendix A**

1 **Assume constant exchange rate**

Project years	1	3	4	5	5 to 24	6 to 25
Calendar years (31 December)	2010	2012	2013	2014	from 2014 for 20 years	from 2015 for 20 years
	US$m	US$m	US$m	US$m	US$m	US$m
Final payment for engineering/environmental	(5.0)	–	–	–	–	–
Initial investment	–	(60.0)	(60.0)		–	–
US$ cashflows	(5.0)	(60.0)	(60.0)	–	–	–
FX rate (P$ per US$)	6.3958	6.3958	6.3958			
	P$m	P$m	P$m	P$m	P$m	P$m
P$ equivalent of US$ cashflows	(32.0)	(383.7)	(383.7)	–	–	–
Tax relief on initial investment			115.1 W1	115.1		
Operating net cash inflows in P$	–	–	–		150.0	–
Less tax at 30%	–	–	–	–	–	(45.0)
Net total cashflows expressed in P$	(32.0)	(383.7)	(268.6)	115.1	150.0	(45.0)
Discount factor at 10.0%	0.909	0.751	0.683	0.621	5.815 W2	5.287 W3
PV	(29.1)	(288.2)	(183.5)	71.5	872.3	(237.9)
Total NPV in P$ millions:	**205.1**					

Workings

(W1) 115.1 = 383.7 × 30%

(W2) 5.815 = 8.514 × 0.683

(W3) 5.287 = 8.514 × 0.621

2   **Assume that the US$ will strengthen against the P$ by 5% each year**

	P$m	P$m	P$m	P$m	P$m	P$m
Project years	1	3	4	5	5 to 24	6 to 25
Calendar years (31 December)	2010	2012	2013		from 2014 for 20 years	from 2015 for 20 years
P$ equivalent of US$ cashflows (above)	(5.0)	(60.0)	(60.0)	–		
FX rate reflecting 5% increase in US$ value	6.9206	7.6300	8.0115	–		
Adjusted US$ cash flows expressed in P$	(34.6)	(457.8)	(480.7)	–		
Tax relief on initial investment			137.3			
P$ cash flows (from above)	–	–	–	150.0	(45.0)	
Total cashflows expressed in P$	(34.6)	(457.8)	(343.4)	150.0		
Discount factor at 10.0% (from above)	0.909	0.751	0.683	5.815		
PV		(31.5)	(343.8)	89.5	872.3	(237.9)

Total NPV in P$ millions: **114.1**

In both cases:

Saving if tax rate dropped to 10% is P$ 158.6 million where 158.6 = 237.9 × (30 − 10)/30

So result in 1 above becomes P$363.7m (= 205.1 + 158.6)

and result in 2 above becomes P$272.7m (= 114.1 + 158.6)

(W4) **Exchange rates**

Assuming the US$ strengthens against the P$ by 5% a year, future rates are:

Date	Year	FX Rate	Workings		
01 January 2010	0	6.5911	6.3958 1.05^(225/365)	where 225 days is:	
31 December 2010	1	6.9206	6.5911 × 1.05	May	11
31 December 2011	2	7.2667	6.9206 × 1.05	Jun	30
31 December 2012	3	7.6300	7.2667 × 1.05	Jul	31
31 December 2013	4	8.0115	7.6300 × 1.05	Aug	31
31 December 2014	5	8.4121	8.0115 × 1.05	Sep	30

(b) **To:**   The Directors of PU

From: Finance Director

Date: Today's date

Subject: Hydroelectric power station project – project appraisal

Introduction

The purpose of this report is to present the findings of recent exercises to evaluate:

- the likely financial contribution of the proposed project and examine other relevant factors that might affect the decision on whether or not to undertake the project; and

- suitable financing structures to fund the project.

Investment appraisal

Financial appraisal based on project cash flows.

A full financial appraisal has been undertaken based on the present value of future cash flows arising from the project. There are several important uncertainties surrounding the project. In particular:

- a large proportion of US$ costs are involved which could vary in P$ terms, and

- it is possible that the tax rate for such projects may fall from 30% to 10% from 2014

The investment appraisal model was therefore run for each combination of these base assumptions. Summary results are given below.

Summary of results – NPV as at 1 January 2010 of forecast project cash flows:

	Tax rate 30%	Tax rate 10%
Constant exchange rate	P$205.1 million	P$363.7 million
US$ strengthening by 5% per annum	P$114.1 million	P$272.7 million

Full results of the exercise are attached at Appendix A.

Other relevant factors to take into consideration

Impact of movement in exchange rate

If the US$ were to strengthen against the P$ by 5% a year, the NPV of the project would fall by approximately P$90 million under both tax rate scenarios. For example, assuming a tax rate of 30%, the NPV of the project falls to P$114.1 million from P$205.1 million once the strengthening of the US$ has been taken into account.

This is a very large exchange rate risk and could be hedged by the use of short-term hedging instruments such as forward contracts. These forward exchange rates can then be used in the investment appraisal of the project and a revised NPV result obtained based on the hedge cash flows.

Forward contracts cannot be cancelled, so they should only be entered into if and when a firm decision has been taken to proceed with the project.

Impact of tax rates

The results in part (a) show that a fall in the tax rate in 2014 from 30% to 10% would result in a large increase in the NPV of the project from P$205.1 million to P$363.7 million, assuming a constant US$/P$ exchange rate.

A real option open to PU is to delay the project until a decision has been made on the future tax rate. In the meantime, the entity should lobby the government to try and influence the decision in its favour.

Reliability of base data

The investment appraisal exercise has been based on best estimates. Changes to the estimates could occur as a result of changes in underlying data such as:

- construction costs

- market demand/prices for electricity that would impact on operating revenues

- accuracy of estimates of maintenance costs

- possible delays due to local objection to the scheme and how that might impact on costs and viability of the project

- accuracy of estimates of relocation costs for people who are living or working on land that will be flooded as a result of the construction of the dam.

Sensitivity analysis would be useful to examine the impact of changes in the underlying data on the financial appraisal.

Suitability of the discount rate

The discount rate should be reviewed to see if:

- it meets the underlying risk expectations of the project

- it needs to be adjusted to reflect a change in capital structure of PU as a result of

- proceeding with the project.

The project is not large enough to change the capital structure of the entity and so this is not a relevant issue here.

However, the project is moving the entity into a completely new and untested area of business and the discount rate may therefore need to be adjusted upwards to reflect the higher risks arising from this project.

Results of the environmental studies exercise

The environmental studies investigation is still on-going. Although it is considered highly unlikely that the project will be cancelled at this stage, final approval to proceed can only be made once the full results of the studies are known.

Impact on corporate and financial objectives

Financial objective: Gearing

Gearing is currently 38% (based on market values at 20 May 2009) against a maximum gearing target of 40%.

The project is so small in size in relation to the entity as a whole that it would not be expected to have a major impact on gearing levels. However, the size of the borrowing is still sufficient to push the gearing level just above the maximum gearing target of 40%. The new gearing level is estimated as 40.4%, an increase of approximately 2% from the current level of 38.2%.

Workings:

Current Gearing:

Equity	P$15,470 million	(= 5,525 million × P$2.80)
Debt	P$9,560 million	
So, current gearing is	38.2%	(= 9,560/(9,560 + 15,470))

New gearing after taking into account the project and the following additional assumptions:

- tax rate of 30%

- an increase of 5% a year in the value of the US$ against the P$

- a share price that has already moved to reflect the increase in shareholder value as represented by the NPV of the project.

So new figures for equity and debt are:

- Equity P$15,584 million (= 5,525 million × P$2.80 + P$114.4 million (the project NPV)

- Debt P$10,552 million (= P$9,560 million + P$992 (see workings W1))

So the new gearing level is: 40.4% (= 10,552/(10,552 + 15,584))

(W1) US$130 million × 7.6300 = P$992 million

Other corporate objectives

The new power station is unlikely to improve efficiency rates of energy production but it would make a major contribution to reducing harmful emissions such as greenhouse gases when generating electricity. It is inevitable that some harmful emissions will be emitted during the construction process and there may also be some carbon dioxide emitted from decomposing vegetable matter that is flooded as part of the project. Overall, however, the hydroelectric power station would be expected to generate only a very small proportion of the harmful emissions that would have been generated by a coal fired power station with a similar output.

Conclusion – whether or not to undertake the project

It is recommended that PU should:

- wait for the full results of the environmental studies exercise before reaching a decision

- recalculate the investment appraisal using forward exchange rates

- perform a sensitivity analysis to determine the results under a "worst case scenario" and determine the probability of the project showing a loss if some of the key assumptions are changed;

If a decision is taken to proceed with the project, all US$ cash flows should be hedged using forward contracts to fix the exchange rate on these cash flows.

Overall recommendation: Only proceed with the project if satisfactory outcomes are obtained from all the above research and if the revised figures for the project using forward exchange rates still show a profit, even under a "worst case" scenario.

Financing structure

A significant exchange rate risk would arise in respect of US$ borrowings as proposed in financing structure (ii). At a constant exchange rate, the US$ borrowings are very attractive and have a significantly lower cost than the P$ borrowings. However, if the US$ were to strengthen by 5% a year against the P$, the US$ borrowings becomes comparatively more expensive.

The cash flows arising under the US$ borrowings and the effective cost of the borrowings (on a yield to maturity basis) under each exchange rate scenario are shown below:

US$ loan assuming a constant exchange rate

Year	Cash flow US$ million	Exchange rate	Cash flow Local $ million	DF @ 3%	PV @ 3%	DF @ 2%	PV @ 2%
0	−130.0	6.3958	−831.5	1	−831.5	1	−831.5
5	145.0	6.3958	927.4	0.863	800.3	0.906	840.2
					−31.2		8.7

YTM by interpolation: 2.2% = 2% + 1% × 8.7/(8.7 + 31.2)

US$ loan assuming the US$ strengthens against the local $ by 5% a year

Year	Cash flow US$ million	Exchange rate	Cash flow Local $ million	DF @ 6%	PV @ 6%	DF @ 8%	PV @ 8%
0	−130.0	7.2667	−944.7	1	−944.7	1	−944.7
5	145.0	9.2744	1344.8	0.747	1004.6	0.681	915.8
					59.9		−28.9

YTM by interpolation: 7.3% = 6% + 2% × 59.9/(59.9 +28.9)

Workings

(W1) 7.2667 is the exchange rate on 1 January 2012 (see workings W4 in part (a))

(W2) 9.2744 = 7.2667 × 1.05^5

Ignoring any investment income on funds that are not needed in the first year, and assuming exchange rates stay constant, the US$ borrowings have an effective cost of 2.2% but this rises to an effective cost of 7.3% if the US$ were to strengthen against the P$ by 5% a year. This compares with a known cost of 5% under alternative financing structure (i).

If such a high risk is unacceptable, US$ borrowings should only be considered if it is possible to guarantee the exchange rate for the interest and capital repayments used to service the borrowings. This may be possible to arrange by using hedging instruments such as forward contracts or a cross currency swap.

Note that there is no US$ income that could be used to set off against US$ payments to service the borrowings.

Recommendation

Exchange rate risk arising on the borrowings could be effectively eliminated if PU were to enter into a cross currency swap contract to fix the exchange rate on the US$ borrowings. Calculations should be performed of the cost of debt for the hedged borrowings and this should be compared to the cost of the P$ borrowings. The calculations should also be adjusted to take account of any investment income that could be earned before the funds are required in the project. The cheapest method should then be chosen.

(c)   **Possible reasons for disposing of the hydroelectric power station**

There are a number of possible reasons why PU might wish to dispose of the hydroelectric power station.

The most likely reason is one of strategic planning:

- to refocus the business on coal fired power stations and concentrate on the main area of management expertise – the hydroelectric power station may not have proved to be a good fit of business alongside the coal fired power stations

- to raise funds for use in moving into new business areas such as developing new power stations using alternative fuels

- to lower cost of capital by disposing of a high risk business.

PU may also have encountered problems in running the hydroelectric power station such as a failure to manage it efficiently or realise its full profit potential. There may be a potential buyer who has the expertise to run the hydroelectric power station more efficiently.

PU itself may have suffered a fall in business and need to raise cash by selling the hydroelectric power station.

Methods for achieving the divestment

1   *Sell-off*

In a sell-off, PP would be sold to another entity, usually in return for cash. This is most likely to be achieved by setting up PP as a separate subsidiary entity and selling the entire entity as a going concern. Shares in the acquirer would be of no interest to PU if its objective is to move out of this area of business and use the cash raised for other purposes.

2   *Spin-off*

In a spin-off, PP would be constructed so that it is owned by the same shareholders as PU. This is normally known as a demerger. A spin-off can lead to a clearer management structure as management of PP can concentrate solely on that business without reference back to PU.

3   *Management buyout*

A management buyout is where the business is purchased by members of the management team, generally in association with a financing institution.

2   AB

(a)   (i)   The discount rate to be used in this type of evaluation is the after-tax cost of debt, which is 7% × (1 − 0.3 = 4.9%) say 5%.

Alternative 1 – Evaluation of 'borrow and buy'

Year	0	1 to 4
	€million	€million
Purchase cost	(25)	
Tax relief on tax depreciation allowances (W1)		1.875
	———	———
DF @5%	1.000	3.546
DCF	(25)	6.649
	———	———
Present value	(18.4)	

(W1) €1.875 million = 30% × €25 million/4

Alternative 2 – Evaluation of the finance lease

Base data

	€million	
Lease payments in advance	7.0 pa	Total payments: 4 × 7 = €28 million
Cost of leased asset	25	but use £18m in the calculations because the first lease payment is made in advance and should be deducted from the cost
Finance charge	3	= 28 − 25
Number of interest periods	3	Ignore the final period as there is no interest element

Examiner's note

As the question does not specify which method to use to allocate implicit interest between years, either the actuarial method or the sum of digits method would be acceptable. Both are shown here as a guide to students.

Method 1 – Actuarial method

Firstly, calculate the implied interest rate using IRR:

The annuity factor for the interest can be found by dividing the cost of the asset by the annual lease payment.

We will use a net cost of €18 million and 3 interest periods.

So three year annuity factor = 18/7.0 = 2.5714

This approximates to an interest rate of 8% (which has a three year annuity factor of 2.577).

Examiner's note

If there is no exact match, use interpolation to find the implied interest rate.

Actuarial method – interest allocation (and proof of interest allocation)

Accounting year	1	2	3
	€million	€million	€million
Opening balance	18.0	12.44	6.44
Interest (add)	1.44 (= 8% × 18.0)	1.00 (= 8% × 12.44)	0.52 (= 8% × 6.44)
Repayment (lease rental)	(7.0)	(7.0)	(7.0)
Closing balance	12.44	6.44	(0.04)

Actuarial method – present value calculation of finance lease

Time	0	1	2	3	4
	€million	€million	€million	€million	€million
Calculation of tax shield based on accounting figures:					
Depreciation	0	(6.25)	(6.25)	(6.25)	(6.25)
Implicit interest	0	(1.44)	(1.00)	(0.52)	0
Total eligible for tax relief	0	(7.69)	(7.25)	(6.77)	(6.25)
Cash flows:					
Tax relief at 30%	0	2.31	2.18	2.03	1.87
Finance lease	(7.0)	(7.0)	(7.0)	(7.0)	0
Total cash flows	(7.0)	(4.69)	(4.82)	(4.97)	1.87
DF @5%	1.000	0.952	0.907	0.864	0.823
DCF	(7.0)	(4.46)	(4.37)	(4.29)	1.54
Present value	(18.6)				

Method 2 – sum of digits

Base the sum of digits calculation on three interest periods as before.

The sum of digits is 6.   **Workings:** $6 = n(n+1)/2 = 3 \times (3+1)/2$

So the interest in the first period is 3m × 3/6 and in the 2nd period is 3m × 2/6 etc.

Sum of digits – interest allocation (and proof of interest allocation)

Accounting Year	1	2	3
	€million	€million	€million
Opening balance	18.0	12.5	6.5
Interest (add)	1.5 (= 3m × 3/6)	1.0 (= 3m × 2/6)	0.5 (= 3m × 1/6)
Repayment (lease rental)	(7.0)	(7.0)	(7.0)
Closing balance	12.5	6.5	0.0

Sum of digits – present value calculation of finance lease

Time	0	1	2	3	4
	€million	€million	€million	€million	€million
Calculation of tax shield based on accounting figures:					
Depreciation	0	(6.25)	(6.25)	(6.25)	(6.25)
Implicit interest	0	(1.5)	(1.0)	(0.5)	0
Total eligible for tax relief	0	(7.75)	(7.25)	(6.75)	(6.25)
Cash flows:					
Tax relief at 30%	0	2.33	2.17	2.03	1.87
Finance lease	(7.0)	(7.0)	(7.0)	(7.0)	0
Total cash flows	(7.0)	(4.67)	(4.83)	(4.97)	1.87
DF @5%	1.000	0.952	0.907	0.864	0.823
DCF	(7.0)	(4.45)	(4.38)	(4.29)	1.54
Present value	(18.6)				

(Which gives the same result as that obtained using the actuarial method.)

On the basis of the present value analysis, there is a marginal benefit from choosing alternative 1, giving a relatively small saving of approximately €200,000. However, this is small in relation to the size of the project and other factors may have a greater impact on the choice of financing structure.

(ii)   The two main possible discount rates to consider are:

- The cost of capital to the entity (which has presumably been used to evaluate the decision to acquire the POS) or

- The cost of the next best alternative means of finance (here, bank borrowings).

The discount rate that should be used in financing decisions is the opportunity cost. Finance leases are considered a direct substitute for borrowing, the opportunity cost of leasing is the after-tax cost of borrowing.

(iii) • Consideration must be given as to how or when the borrowings are to be repaid if alternative 1 is chosen.

• Tax benefits appear to have a significant influence on the decision; a sensitivity analysis should be carried out to determine the impact on the decision if tax rates or regulations change.

(b) The main purpose of a PCA:

A post-completion audit (PCA) can be defined as "an objective and independent appraisal of all phases of the capital expenditure process as it relates to a specific project". The main purposes include: project control; improving the investment process; and assisting the assessment of performance of future projects.

A major requirement of a PCA is that the objectives of the investment project must be clear and an adequate investment proposal should have been prepared. The objectives should also be stated, wherever possible, in terms that are measurable. If these have not been done before the POS system was acquired then a PCA is not possible.

The PCA should provide a source of information that will help future management decision making and should include an assessment of the reasons for any variance from the expected performance, cost and time outcomes. This should improve project control and governance and enable changes to be introduced to put the project back on track in a timely manner.

The key factors of importance of a PCA to AB:

• It enables a check to be made on whether the performance of the system corresponds with the expected results. If this is not the case, the reasons should be sought. This could form the basis for improvements in development of the system.

• It generates information, which allows an appraisal to be made of the managers who took the decision to upgrade the system. Managers will therefore tend to arrive at more realistic estimates of the advantages and disadvantages of the proposed investments.

• It can provide for better project planning in the future. If, in the evaluation, it is found that the planning of the investment programme was poor, provision can be made to ensure that it is better for future acquisitions.

The limitations of a PCA to AB in the context of the POS system:

• Sufficient resources are often not allocated to the task of completing PCAs so often are not undertaken.

• They can be time consuming and costly to complete.

• They are sometimes seen as tools for apportioning blame, so even where undertaken the lessons are often not disseminated and are not then embedded in future projects. If undertaken by the managers of the project, they may claim credit for all that went well and blame external factors for everything that did not.

3   CD

(a)   The scenario in this question concerns a privately owned entity based in a holiday destination. Inflation is near zero and interest rates are expected to fall. The treasury department needs to decide how to deal with the challenges and opportunities the specific set of circumstances provide and evaluate the impact on the entity's capital structure.

Finance theory suggests that entities should use a certain amount of debt in their capital structure to lower the cost of capital. Debt is cheaper than equity because interest payments (usually) attract tax relief and expected returns are lower. This is because interest is (usually) secured and providers of debt do not participate in profits. Here we have a mixture of secured and unsecured debt, but the entity appears sound and of high credit worthiness so should be able to borrow at comparatively favourable rates.

This might even be an argument in favour of increasing gearing which will provide the ability to undertake a share buyback, as seems to be the desire of the major, family shareholders.

The opposite argument is that in a period of low and falling interest rates, fixed rate debt becomes a burden. Some of the reasons are as follows:

- The real value of debt is not being eroded when there is low or no inflation, so one of the benefits of debt disappears.

- If growth is expected to be modest, debt interest may have to be paid out of static (or even falling) profits, lowering returns to shareholders.

- Although nominal interest rates may fall, they never become negative, so the real cost of borrowing increases.

Raising equity is safer if profits are falling as dividends do not have to be paid and the shareholders do not get their money back in a liquidation. However, raising new equity in a private entity is more difficult than in a public entity and this method of raising new capital raises many additional issues such as whether to plan for a public listing or a rights issue and how to value the shares.

In theory (according to Modigliani and Miller), the mix of debt and equity does not affect the value of the entity, other than the value of the tax shield, but it does have an effect on the attribution of profits to three groups of stakeholders: lenders, government and owners (shareholders).

The main issue for the treasury department to decide is what combination of dividend policy and capital structure is likely to maximise the present value of cash flows to shareholders. This is where the financing strategies adopted contribute to the determination of the objectives of the entity.

The treasury department needs to specifically:

- Look at the terms of existing borrowing to see if refinancing at lower rates is feasible, recognising any possible penalties for early retirement of loans.

- Discuss with the major shareholders the possibility (or even probability) that returns are likely to be lower; the lower the rate of interest, the lower the cost of capital and therefore the lower the returns that can be expected.

(b) Theory supports the Finance Director, suggesting that maximisation of shareholder wealth is the only true objective of the entity but this is now considered an extreme view. Many entities now establish objectives that aim to maximise shareholder wealth while recognising constraints, legally enforceable or voluntary, imposed by society. A major problem with this objective in the circumstances of CD is that this is a private entity that does not have a quoted share price. Shareholder wealth, as traditionally valued, is difficult to determine.

In addition, although dividend levels may have no direct impact on shareholder wealth, there may well be private family shareholders who rely on a steady and predictable dividend stream from entity CD.

Looking only at dividends as an objective has its limitations, for example dividends could increase while earnings fall. The dividend ratio therefore needs to be considered alongside dividend payout. Other objectives mentioned such as profitability as measured by returns after tax and return on investment have some advantages. For example they are well understood measures and recognised guidelines are available in the form of International Accounting Standards. Also, shareholders expect and understand profitability.

Disadvantages of accounting-based measures include:

- They are historic and backward-looking

- They can be subject to manipulation

- A variety of accounting policies are available – even within Accounting Standards

- Tax can be affected by factors outside the control of managers

- They do not take account of non-financial objectives.

Recommendation

Maximisation of shareholder wealth, using the theoretical definition, is difficult to apply in the circumstances of CD. However, it would be worth introducing an objective that incorporates earnings growth as well as dividend growth.

A range of objectives could be considered, such as risk-related returns to investors, but again this is more difficult with a private entity than one with a share listing.

The entity needs to consult its shareholders and, possibly, consider using a balanced scorecard approach to determine a range of objectives appropriate for an entity such as CD.

4   EF

(a)   Forecast statements of profit or loss for the years ended 31 December

	2009	*2010*	*2011*
	£000	*£000*	*£000*
Revenue	45,000	46,800	48,672
Purchase costs and expenses	(38,250)	(39,780)	(41,371)
Depreciation	0	(500)	(500)
Profit before finance costs	6,750	6,520	6,801
Less: Interest on long term debt	(450)	(450)	(450)
Profit before tax	6,300	6,070	6,351
Tax @ 28% (see note)	(1,764)	(1,490)	(1,656)
Profit after tax (earnings)	4,536	4,580	4,695
Dividends declared and paid	(1,814)	(1,905)	(2,000)
Retained earnings for year	2,722	2,675	2,695

Examiner's note

The question did not require candidates to show the figures for 2009, they are shown here in italics for convenience.

Tax depreciation allowances:

Cost of vehicles	5,000
2010 WDA @ 25%	(1,250)
Written Down Value	3,750
2011 WDA @ 25%	(938)
Written Down Value	2,812

Note: Tax is calculated on profit before tax and depreciation less capital allowances:

2010 (6,070 + 500 − 1,250) × 28% = 1,490

2011 (6,351 + 500 − 938) × 28% = 1,656

Examiner's note

It was not intended that candidates should consider the impact of deferred taxation in their answer here. Credit was available for those who did so.

(b) **Cash flow forecasts for 2010 and 2011**

Calculations of cash receivable and cash payable:

	2010	2011
	£000	£000
Revenue	46,800	48,672
O/B trade receivables	13,500	14,040
C/B trade receivables at 30%	(14,040)	(14,602)
(13,500/45,000 × 100)		
Cash receivable	46,260	48,110
Costs and expenses	39,780	41,371
O/B trade payables	8,415	8,752
C/B trade payables (at 22% of costs and expenses	(8,752)	(9,102)
= 8,415/38,250 × 100)		
Cash payable	39,443	41,021

Cash flow forecasts

	2010		2011	
	£000		£000	
Cash received from sales		46,260		48,110
Costs and expenses	39,443		41,021	
Vehicles	5,000		0	
Tax	1,490		1,656	
Dividends	1,905		2,000	
Interest	450		450	
Total outflows		(48,288)		(45,127)
Net cash flows		(2,028)		2,983
Opening cash balance		348		(1,680)
Closing cash balance		(1,680)		1,303

An alternative, equally acceptable, approach to presenting the cash flow forecasts is as follows. Note that IAS7 allows for some discretion in the presentation format of cash flow statements. The question here required a forecast rather than a published statement and any sensible format gained credit.

	2010 £000	2011 £000
Operations		
Profit before financing costs	6,520	6,801
Add back depreciation	500	500
Change in receivables	(540)	(562)
Change in payables	337	350
Subtotal	6,617	7,089
Interest paid	(450)	(450)
Taxation	(1,490)	(1,656)
Net cash flows from operations	4,877	4,983
Investments		
New vehicles	(5,000)	0
Financing		
Dividends paid	(1,905)	(2,000)
Total net cash flows	(2,028)	2,983
Opening cash balance	348	(1,680)
Closing cash balance	(1,680)	1,303

There is need to finance a cash shortfall of £1,680,000 by the end of 2010. Of course, if the vehicles are bought early in 2010, there may well be a requirement to finance a much greater cash shortfall earlier in the year. There is insufficient information in the question to comment further on this. By the end of 2011 there is a positive cash balance of £1,303,000 by just over half way through the year (if cash flows are spread more or less evenly throughout the year). If sales increase as forecast the cash balance is likely to become positive earlier.

As the shortfall is caused by the purchase of new assets, there should be no problem increasing the overdraft limit given the size of the entity and the relatively short period of time this facility is needed. Other possibilities include supplier credit or short-term leasing.

It could be argued that as these are long term assets they should be funded by long-term finance but the amount is relatively small compared to the value of the entity.

A problem that needs to be addressed is the disparity between the ratio of trade receivables to sales and trade payable to purchase costs & expenses. The former is 30% and the latter 22%. However a breakdown between cost of sales and operating expenses is necessary to analyse the problem further.

(c)   **Key aspects and implications**

Preliminary calculations:

	2009	2010	2011
	£000	£000	£000
Total equity:			
Share capital	4,204	4,204	4,204
Retained earnings	16,210	18,885	21,580
Total equity	20,414	23,089	25,784
Return on shareholders' funds	22.2%	19.8%	18.2%
EPS – pence	27.0	27.2	27.9
% increase	–	0.7	2.6
DPS – pence	10.8	11.3	11.9

Return on shareholders' funds

EF met this objective in 2009 but narrowly falls short in 2010 and the ratio declines even further in 2011. The new assets might begin to contribute to an improvement but they are clearly replacement assets for an existing facility and as such are unlikely to have a significant impact.

The management of working capital needs to be addressed as noted above.

Investment and financing:

No investment appraisal appears to have been carried out for the purchase of the new assets. This should be done before the investment is made, even though the entity appears more than capable of funding the purchase.

Increase in earnings:

The increase in earnings is well below EF's target for 2010 and 2011 but is moving in the right direction. The main impact in 2010 was the sudden increase in depreciation (although there was a tax benefit as tax depreciation allowances were higher than book depreciation). EF needs to examine its costs and expenses as these are increasing in line with sales. There might be scope for reducing costs by reviewing its suppliers and/or terms of trade, and possible elimination of some expenses.

Dividends:

DPS are growing at 5% as per the scenario. If earnings increase in the future at the target rate of 8% then this implies EF will build up its retained earnings for future investment (assuming finance is available). The entity should perhaps review its dividend policy in the light of investment opportunities.

Key assumption regarding overdraft interest:

The removal of the simplifying assumption regarding overdraft interest can be expected to have a significant effect on forecast cash flows after tax. Indeed, the increase in earnings that is observed above is so small that an increase in overdraft interest in 2010 could reduce earnings to the point at which earnings actually decline in 2010 from 2009 levels.

I would advise the compilation of a more accurate calculation of overdraft interest (or deposit interest if there is a positive cash balance) and the associated tax benefit (or tax expense). This would involve identifying the timing of large items such as tax and dividend cash flows in order to calculate an average cash balance for each year. An estimate of overdraft interest or deposit interest could then be calculated based on that average cash balance and an assumed average overdraft or deposit rate. Note that any overdraft or deposit interest and associated tax cash flows will affect the closing cash balance for the year and therefore also impact on average cash balance and interest and tax cash flows in the following year.

DO NOT OPEN THIS QUESTION PAPER UNTIL YOU ARE TOLD TO DO SO.

Financial Pillar

F3 – Financial Strategy

21 November 2013 – Thursday Morning Session

Instructions to candidates

You are allowed three hours to answer this question paper.
You are allowed 20 minutes reading time **before the examination begins** during which you should read the question paper and, if you wish, highlight and/or make notes on the question paper. However, you will **not** be allowed, **under any circumstances**, to open the answer book and start writing or use your calculator during this reading time.
You are strongly advised to carefully read ALL the question requirements before attempting the question concerned (that is all parts and/or sub-questions).
ALL answers must be written in the answer book. Answers written on the question paper will **not** be submitted for marking.
You should show all workings as marks are available for the method you use.
The pre-seen case study material is included in this question paper on pages 2 to 6. The unseen case study material, specific to this examination, is provided on pages 8 and 9.
Answer the compulsory question in Section A on page 11. This page is detachable for ease of reference.
Answer TWO of the three questions in Section B on pages 14 to 19.
Maths tables and formulae are provided on pages 21 to 25.
The list of verbs as published in the syllabus is given for reference on page 27.
Write your candidate number, the paper number and examination subject title in the spaces provided on the front of the answer book. Also write your contact ID and name in the space provided in the right hand margin and seal to close.
Tick the appropriate boxes on the front of the answer book to indicate which questions you have answered.

F3 – Financial Strategy

TURN OVER

Pre-seen case study

Introduction
The Games is an international multi-sport event that is held within a region of the world every four years. It attracts competitors from 10 different countries within the region and is held at a different time from the Olympic Games. The Games are held in each of the countries within the region in turn. The next Games are scheduled to take place in Country C in October 2015. There are 25 sports included within the Games ranging from archery through to weightlifting. The Games were first held in 1979 and this is the first time that Country C has hosted them.

Games Co-ordinating Committee (GCC)
The Games Co-ordinating Committee was established to set out the framework within which the individual country organisations should work in delivering the Games. Membership of the GCC is drawn from all the countries within the region which take part in the Games. Its aim is to promote the Games throughout the region of the world in which the Games take place. It is also responsible for setting out the mission under which the Games are established in each country.

Mission of the GCC
The mission of the GCC is to:

- Encourage and promote ethical competition in sport;
- Encourage and co-operate with public and private organisations in the preparation for and staging of the Games;
- Achieve high levels of sustainability for the infrastructure of the Games and the environment in which they take place;
- Promote sport and healthy lifestyles amongst young people;
- Promote the Games' values of excellence, unity and achievement.

The mission of the GCC is untouchable in the sense that all who are involved in the Games, in whatever role, must adopt and promote it.

Organisation of the Games within Country C
In 2010, the Parliament in Country C passed an Act creating GAMESCO, a company limited by guarantee to organise and deliver the Games on time and within budget. GAMESCO also has responsibility for disposal of assets after the Games and selling any surplus land which is not retained for sporting purposes.

The Minister of Sport in Country C and the elected Mayor of the city in which the Games are due to take place are the only two shareholders of GAMESCO. Governance of the Games is carried out entirely by GAMESCO. In carrying out this role, it co-ordinates the activities of all people and organisations engaged in preparing for and operating the Games and it is responsible for the subsequent liquidation of all the Games' assets.

The Government of Country C believes that the Games will provide a major boost to Country C by providing commercial opportunities for enterprises such as hotels and retail outlets and enabling the re-generation of the current dilapidated land on which the Games will take place. It is expected that the prosperity of Country C and, in particular, the whole area in which the Games will take place, will increase.

Mission, Vision and Values of GAMESCO

The Board of GAMESCO is committed to meeting the mission of the GCC. It has established its own mission and values as follows:

Mission:
"To deliver the Games successfully on time and on budget in accordance with the expectations of our stakeholders and in accordance with the mission of the GCC."

GAMESCO is responsible for preparing, operating and winding up the Games, all within its budget. Country C's Government provided capital to GAMESCO for building work to proceed. However, Country C's Government is clear that it does not intend to support the Games beyond the funding it has already invested. This places a large responsibility on GAMESCO to ensure that its overall expenditure does not exceed the revenue it generates from its activities and the government grants it has received.

Values:
"GAMESCO will work tirelessly towards achieving the mission set out by the GCC. In striving to achieve the GCC's mission, GAMESCO will act fairly and responsibly with all its stakeholders, in particular its employees and partners, in order to generate trust and transparency."

GAMESCO's organisational structure
GAMESCO has a Board of Directors comprising: Chairman, Chief Executive, Directors for Finance, Sponsorship, Operations, Marketing, Commercial Activities, Estates, Communications, Human Resources, Information Systems, Venues, Athletes' Services, a representative from each of the Minister of Sport and the Mayor, a sports representative drawn from each of the sporting activities which will be competed in during the Games and a representative of the GCC.

GAMESCO's financial structure and budget
Country C's currency is C$. GAMESCO's financial structure is different from most commercial organisations. Under the Act of Parliament which set the company up, a provision was made that GAMESCO would not be subject to corporate tax.

Revenue is generated by a mixture of government grants, sponsorships, ticket sales for the Games, rental of accommodation and broadcasting and other commercial fees. All capital works relating to the Games themselves, such as the athletics stadium, the cycling velodrome, the gymnastics arena and the swimming pool, are funded by government grants. However, construction of buildings for commercial activities such as cafes and restaurants is funded by the commercial organisations themselves and is not the responsibility of GAMESCO. The budget for the expected final cost of the Games is shown at Appendix 1.

Project management
An overarching supervisory consortium of experts in project management has been engaged by GAMESCO as an outsourced service. The role of the consortium is to prepare and monitor construction work on the whole of the Games Park site. The Games Park site will accommodate such buildings as the athletics stadium, the cycling velodrome, the gymnastics arena and the swimming pool. In addition, the consortium will ensure that utilities are installed, plans for construction works are approved, construction work progresses according to schedule and that contractors are able to access the site when building work takes place.

GAMESCO employs independent project management teams with project managers responsible for each major building construction on-site. These project managers report directly to the consortium on the progress of the construction project for which they are responsible. An Information Systems Project Manager has been appointed by GAMESCO, whose role is to co-ordinate the provision of information systems on the site and to liaise with all the project managers on their information systems requirements for the construction projects for which they are responsible.

A project management team has also been established to market the Games. All GAMESCO's marketing staff, with the exception of the Marketing Director, are attached to this project team.

Service provision
Professional architects, engineers and building companies are all engaged in developing the Games Park. In addition, land on which buildings will be erected must be clear of pollution. Utility services, such as water and electricity supplies to all venues involved with the Games are in the process of being provided.

On the Games Park site itself, there will be a number of fast-food outlets, cafes and restaurants as well as ice cream parlours, sweet stores and souvenir shops. Hygiene facilities, such as toilets, will need to be provided. All of these will remain on-site for the duration of the Games and will be demolished afterwards. Some parks and gardens will be constructed within the Games Park. The parks and gardens will not be demolished but remain as amenities for the local population after the Games have finished.

Security for the Games will be tight. It is proposed that GAMESCO will engage a highly reputable security services contractor to provide security at all the Games' venues, around the perimeter as well as within the grounds of the Games Park. It will be essential for the security contractor to engage sufficient staff to carry out this very large security service.

Staffing
While GAMESCO does employ its own staff, the majority of people working on-site are contractors. At present most of the activity being undertaken on-site is construction work. GAMESCO does employ its own Human Resource Management, Information Technology support and accounting staff.

Senior staff and project managers are contracted for the duration of the Games and in some cases beyond. They are paid at a competitive rate. However, most staff are employed on temporary contracts on a month-to-month basis and generally receive relatively low pay compared with unskilled labour in Country C which has a high level of unemployment.

When the Games begin, it is expected that most ancillary staff on-site, who will direct spectators to venues and facilities, will be volunteers. Many of these volunteers will take annual leave from their places of work in order to carry out this task.

Sponsorship
A major source of revenue for GAMESCO is sponsorship deals with major business organisations and this is therefore crucial to the successful staging of the Games. Sponsors are required to provide a guarantee of a minimum payment of C$ 1 million to GAMESCO. For this, sponsors become official partners of the Games and acquire marketing rights. This enables sponsors to build their brands and customer relationships, increase their revenue and enhance their own commercial reputation. Sponsorship can be divided into two types, direct and indirect.

Direct sponsorship - gold sponsorship
There are two levels of direct sponsorship, gold and silver. Gold is the highest level of sponsorship and gives sponsors major marketing rights. Gold sponsors are drawn from businesses such as electronic equipment suppliers, soft drink manufacturers and fast-food chains which can provide products and services to support the staging of the Games, in addition to providing a financial contribution. Gold sponsors are also expected to promote the Games by engaging in the development of sporting events across the region of the world in which the Games take place. For this, gold sponsors are entitled to use the Games logo on their products and services.

Gold sponsors are required to engage in a range of activities to support the mission of GCC at the Games. See page 2 for details of the mission of the Games.

Direct sponsorship - silver sponsorship
Silver sponsors are only required to make a financial contribution to the staging of the Games. However, they too, are able to use the Games logo.

Indirect sponsorship
A form of indirect sponsorship which takes place when the Games are in progress is hospitality. Hospitality sponsorship relates to large businesses hiring facilities on-site in the Games Park to entertain their own customers and clients while the Games are in progress. These facilities mainly consist of hospitality rooms and boxes. The hospitality rooms and boxes in prestige venues, such as the athletics stadium, the cycling velodrome, the gymnastics arena and the swimming pool, will command a higher price on days when popular Games events are being held and also when medals are being awarded.

Brand Leases
One significant area of revenue generation is the opportunity for GAMESCO to lease its brand to all organisations engaged in supplying products and services to the Games. It is a condition for all goods and service suppliers that they must display the Games brand in all the venues in which they operate and in doing this, they incur a leasing charge which is directly payable to GAMESCO. In addition, any other organisation wishing to use the Games brand must also pay a leasing charge to GAMESCO for permission to do so.

Marketing

GAMESCO has carried out considerable press and television advertising and intends to increase this as the Games draw closer in order to stimulate public enthusiasm and ticket sales. Television rights to broadcast the Games have been agreed and GAMESCO has invested in stocks of merchandise which it has distributed to retailers around Country C.

Games Village

The athletes will be accommodated in the Games Village which is located in the Games Park. The Games Village will consist of several purpose built blocks of accommodation which provide hotel services in respect of individual bedrooms with en-suite toilet and shower facilities. The Games Village will also have its own catering and laundry facilities, using locally contracted staff. The daily cleaning of the rooms will also be contracted out to a local company.

The Games Village will provide a regular bus shuttle service for the use of athletes to and from the city centre in which the Games are being held and also to and from the airport.

After the Games, the Games Village will be converted into apartments to house local people.

Drug testing and medical facilities

A specific building will be constructed to enable appropriately qualified experts to carry out internationally approved drugs tests on athletes. The drug testing facility will be located close to the medical centre which will be specifically built for treating the athletes. If any spectator requires medical attention beyond basic first-aid, he or she will be taken to the nearest hospital as will any athlete if he or she requires treatment which cannot be provided at the medical centre. After the Games have finished, it is expected that the medical centre will be converted into a health clinic which will provide services to local residents.

Business opportunities and legacy

Much has been made in Country C about the huge opportunities for local businesses and the legacy of the Games. There is a range of contracts and work being done or still to be undertaken by businesses in Country C. These include construction, land regeneration, the provision of utility supplies and catering facilities before and during the Games. After the Games have finished, there will still be much work particularly for construction companies in reinstating land and undertaking buildings alteration work.

Construction works including hotels and shopping facilities are now planned to be built on derelict land and all will be within easy reach of the Games Park. The hotels and shopping facilities are particularly attractive to developers as it is expected that the regeneration of the land, parks, gardens and sports facilities which remain after the Games will attract visitors and tourists.

A major legacy is that many new homes and amenities will become available after the Games. For example, the athletes' accommodation in the Games Village will replace much sub-standard accommodation in which many local people are currently housed. The Government thinks that the Games, which will be televised across the region and in other parts of the world, will showcase the country in general, attracting visitors and businesses not just for the duration of the Games but afterwards as well.

In addition to the economic benefits, the Government hopes that the Games will inspire the public in Country C to take more physical exercise which it anticipates will bring health benefits to the population. Some of the facilities which will be constructed for the Games, such as the cycling velodrome, the gymnastics arena and the swimming pool, will become available for public use after the Games, enhancing the amenities for the local population.

Budget for the delivery of the Games

C$ million

Preparation of the Site and Infrastructure

Power and utilities	550
Preparatory construction work	370
Structural work including access roads	760
Landscaping	250
Other preparation and infrastructural works	185
Total preparation of site and infrastructure	**2,115**

Venues

Athletics stadium	500
Swimming pool	260
Cycling velodrome	50
Gymnastics arena	45
Venues operations control centre	20
Other Games Park venues	100
Total venues	**975**

Transport

Transport capital projects	300
Transport operating costs	350
Total transport	**650**

Games Park Operations and Security

Games Park Operations	220
Security for Games Park construction	240
Security during Games	70
Insurance	80
Total Games Park Operations and Security	**610**

Games Village and Media Centre

Games Village construction	750
Media Centre construction	300
Total Games Village and Media Centre	**1,050**

Total expected final cost before contingency	**5,400**
Contingency	540
Total expected final cost	**5,940**

End of Pre-seen Material

The unseen material begins on page 8

This page is blank

TURN OVER

SECTION A – 50 MARKS

[You are advised to spend no longer than 90 minutes on this question.]

ANSWER THIS QUESTION. THE QUESTION REQUIREMENTS ARE ON PAGE 11, WHICH IS DETACHABLE FOR EASE OF REFERENCE

Question One

Unseen case material

CC's Gold Sponsorship Project

CC, a fast-food chain, is considering becoming a Gold Sponsor for the Games and thereby being allowed to build and operate a fast-food outlet in a prominent position in the Games Park during the Games.

The Games are expected to draw spectators from many countries and CC hopes that operating a fast-food outlet, together with becoming a Gold Sponsor, would promote CC's brand name both within Country C and in other countries. Currently, all CC's fast-food outlets are located within Country C but CC wishes to expand beyond Country C.

Linking the brand name with the promotion of sporting activities and healthy lifestyles may also help improve the public image of fast-food products. Such products are often considered to be unhealthy.

Gold Sponsorship Application

Applying to become a gold sponsor would involve completing an official application pack, including full details of how the applicant company would support the mission of GCC. In particular, how it would:

- Achieve high levels of sustainability for the infrastructure of the Games and the environment in which they take place;
- Promote sport and healthy lifestyles amongst young people;
- Promote the Games' values of excellence, unity and achievement.

As part of its application to become a Gold Sponsor, CC hopes to be able to state that it would re-use 75% of the materials used in the construction and operation of the fast-food outlet. Materials such as timber and light bulbs would be re-used in other CC fast-food outlets after the Games. Used cooking oils would be incorporated into a new blended biofuel product.

CC would promote sport and healthy lifestyles by offering 'healthy eating' items on its Games Park menu and by providing sports coaching in volleyball skills throughout Country C.

CC's fast-food outlet in the Games Park would be staffed by top performing employees from current outlets. These employees would also be given tickets to attend the Games in their leisure time.

Financial data for the Gold Sponsorship Project

Sponsorship costs would comprise:

- Gold Sponsorship of C$ 1 million, payable on 31 October 2014.
- Cost of providing sports coaching in volleyball skills, estimated to be C$ 240,000 in total, payable in 4 equal annual instalments beginning 31 October 2014.

Forecast construction costs:

Cost of construction	C$ 4,000,000 on 31 October 2014
Cost of fixtures and fittings	C$ 500,000 on 31 October 2014
Ovens, dish-washers and other equipment (which would be imported from Country K)	K$ 2,100,000 on 31 October 2015

Forecast operating cash flows:

- On average, 200 customers are expected to be served every hour, 10 hours a day, 7 days a week for 4 weeks during the Games. Average spend per customer is expected to be C$ 12.
- Operating costs during the Games are estimated to be C$ 330,000 in total.

Additional information:

- CC's financial year end is 31 October.
- Corporate income tax is charged at 40% on taxable profits and is settled a year in arrears.
- The Gold Sponsorship payment of C$ 1 million would be treated as a prepayment and released to profit or loss on 31 October 2015, with 100% tax deduction at that time. The cost of providing coaching in volleyball skills would be deductible for tax purposes as incurred.
- Ovens, dish-washers and other equipment would be imported from Country K, invoiced in K$.
- The C$/K$ spot rate on 31 October 2013 is C$/K$ 2.7000 (that is, C$ 1 = K$ 2.7000). The C$ is expected to appreciate against the K$ by 2% a year.
- All construction costs would attract 100% tax depreciation allowances in the year the expenditure is incurred and CC has sufficient taxable profits to benefit from any tax relief on capital expenditure.
- The residual value of the outlet and contents on 31 October 2015 is expected to be C$ 1 million. This figure includes the value of re-usable materials. However, it does not take into account the cost of dismantling and cleaning the site, including the disposal cost of materials that cannot be re-used, which is estimated to be C$ 200,000.
- In discounted cash flow analysis, treat operating cash flows as arising on 31 October 2015.

Financial data for CC

Summary data from CC's forecast statement of financial position as at 31 October 2013 (C$ millions):

Ordinary shares (50 cents nominal)	57
Share premium account	38
Retained earnings	60
7.2% Preference shares (irredeemable, $1.00 nominal)	30
Bank borrowing for repayment 31 October 2016	90
Total equity and borrowings	275

Additional information:

- Preference shares are trading at C$ 0.95 each on 31 October 2013.
- Floating rate interest is payable on the bank borrowing at interbank rates plus 2%. Current interbank rates are 6%.
- CC's share price is C$ 2.33 cum dividend on 31 October 2013, including a dividend of C$ 0.15 per share.
- Dividends have increased at an average compound growth rate of 13.4% over the past five years.
- In the year ended 31 October 2013, operating profit is C$ 35 million and profit after tax is C$ 24 million.

Choice of new funding

CC needs to borrow approximately C$ 10 million on 31 October 2014 for a ten year period to finance this project. Some directors have learned that several companies in Country C have borrowed from local banks in US$ rather than in C$ in order to take advantage of the lower US$ interest rate. Country C has successfully pegged the C$ against the US$ in the last three years.

The following two alternative funding structures are therefore being considered, both for a 10 year term starting 31 October 2014:

- C$ 10 million bank borrowing; annual interest rate: 6.0%.
- US$ 15 million bank borrowing; annual interest rate: 3.0%.

Market information on 31 October 2013:

Spot:	US$/C$ 0.6500	Interest rates (all maturities):	C$	6.0% per annum
That is, US$ 1 = C$ 0.6500			US$	3.0% per annum

The requirement for question one is on page 11

This page is blank

Required:

Write a report addressed to the board of CC in which you, as Chief Financial Officer (CFO) of CC:

(a) **Evaluate** the key challenges at the conceptual stage of CC's Gold Sponsorship Project AND how best to address them.

(9 marks)

(b) (i) **Calculate:**
- CC's cost of ordinary equity, using the dividend valuation model.
- CC's weighted average cost of capital (WACC).

(7 marks)

(ii) **Calculate** the net present value (NPV) of the forecast cash flows for the Gold Sponsorship Project as at 31 October 2013 using the WACC calculated in part (b)(i).

(12 marks)

(iii) **Advise** on the key factors to be considered when deciding whether to proceed with the Gold Sponsorship Project.

(9 marks)

(c) (i) **Calculate:**
- The expected US$/C$ spot rate on 31 October 2024 based on interest rates on 31 October 2013.
- The C$ cost of repaying the US$ 15 million borrowing on 31 October 2024 based on the exchange rate calculated above.

(4 marks)

(ii) **Evaluate** the two alternative funding methods being considered, concluding with a recommendation.
No further calculations are required in part (c)(ii).

(6 marks)

Additional marks available for structure and presentation:

(3 marks)

(Total for Question One = 50 marks)

(Total for Section A = 50 marks)

End of Section A

Section B begins on page 14

TURN OVER

This page is blank

This page is blank

SECTION B – 50 MARKS

[You are advised to spend no longer than 45 minutes on each question in this section.]

ANSWER *TWO* OF THE THREE QUESTIONS

Question Two

ABC is a listed company based in Country A in Asia and has the A$ as its functional currency. ABC is the parent company for the ABC Group. ABC is wholly equity financed and has a financial year end of 31 October.

ABC designs and produces computer equipment for sale via its own retail outlets which are operated by ABC in Country A and by wholly owned subsidiary companies in other countries. The business was started 10 years ago by two entrepreneurs. It grew rapidly and ABC was floated on Country A's stock market via an initial public offering (IPO) just over three years ago, on 31 October 2010. The IPO issue price was A$ 3.63 per share. 1,000 million ordinary shares were issued as part of the IPO and no additional shares have been issued since that date.

Share price history for ABC:

Date	Share price (A$)
31 October 2010	3.63
31 October 2011	4.80
31 October 2012	8.07
31 October 2013	6.03

The ABC group has continued to grow rapidly since the flotation of ABC. It has successfully launched an innovative and highly successful new product each year. However, sales growth was lower in the last 12 months than in previous years and this led to a fall in the share price.

ABC's directors have so far been reluctant to return any cash to shareholders in case it was needed in the business. No dividends were paid in the three years following the IPO. However, in the past 6 months, the directors have been under increasing pressure from major institutional shareholders to pay out cash to shareholders and have finally decided to do so. The initial plan is to return A$ 900 million to shareholders via a share repurchase programme. The institutional shareholders have not yet been informed. A public announcement will be given once a decision has been made on how to finance the programme.

Two alternative schemes are being considered to finance the A$ 900 million required for the share repurchase programme. In each case, A$ 450 million would be financed by using cash already held by ABC in Country A. The remaining A$ 450 million would be financed by either of the following schemes:

Scheme 1:
Raise A$ 450 million by issuing a 5% 15 year bond.

Scheme 2:
Repatriate sufficient cash from foreign subsidiaries to provide a further A$ 450 million, net of tax.

Additional relevant financial data for ABC:

- A\$ 1,500 million of cash and liquid investments is held by the ABC group. Of this, only A\$ 500 million is held by ABC. The remaining A\$ 1,000 million is held by foreign subsidiaries and would be subject to tax if paid to ABC.
- ABC pays corporate income tax at 30% on taxable profits.
- The tax rate for foreign subsidiaries is 20% and double tax treaties exist between Country A and the countries in which the foreign subsidiaries are located. A further 10% tax is payable by ABC on funds paid to ABC by foreign subsidiaries.
- ABC has a weighted average cost of capital of 8%.

Required:

(a)   (i)   **Calculate** the compound average growth in ABC's share price from 31 October 2010 to 31 October 2013.

(2 marks)

(ii)   **Explain** why ABC's share price has risen significantly over that period of time even though the company has not paid any dividends.

(5 marks)

(b)   **Discuss** the arguments for and against ABC returning a substantial amount of cash to shareholders at this time.

(8 marks)

(c)   **Evaluate** the financial benefits and drawbacks to ABC of adopting Scheme 1 rather than Scheme 2 to finance the share repurchase scheme.
Up to 6 marks are available for calculations.

(10 marks)

(Total for Question Two = 25 marks)

A REPORT FORMAT IS NOT REQUIRED FOR THIS QUESTION

TURN OVER

Question Three

Company BR is a listed company based in South America which manufactures sports equipment. Its functional currency is SA$.

SA$ 30 million has been set aside for upgrading production lines in 2014 and the company is reviewing four possible projects: Projects A, B, C and D.

The four projects are divisible but each can be undertaken no more than once. The projects are independent of each other and each has a four year life. It is unusual for BR to have so many highly profitable projects to choose from.

Normally, the company uses net present value (NPV) analysis in investment appraisal. However the Chairman has asked the Finance Director to also consider internal rate of return (IRR) and modified internal rate of return (MIRR) for the current investment decision so that he can understand what, if any, additional information such analysis could provide. The company uses its weighted average cost of capital of 8% in all investment appraisal decisions, whatever the risk profile of the project.

Project A cash flows

Post tax project cash flows (SA$ million)	Time 0	Year 1	Year 2	Year 3	Year 4
Initial investment	(7.0)				
Operating cash inflows		2.0	2.5	3.0	4.0

Investment appraisal analysis for all four projects

Project	NPV (SA$ million)	MIRR	IRR	Initial investment on 1 January 2014 (SA$ million)
A	2.3	?	20%	7
B	8.1	20%	38%	15
C	7.7	24%	28%	10
D	8.4	18%	19%	20

Ignore taxation.

MIRR formula

$$\text{MIRR} = \left(\frac{\text{terminal value of cash inflows}}{\text{present value of cash outflows}} \right)^{\left(\frac{1}{n}\right)} - 1$$

(a) **Explain** the extent to which analysis of NPV, IRR and MIRR is useful in the context of capital rationing involving:
- Mutually exclusive projects.
- Divisible projects.

(6 marks)

(b) (i) **Calculate** Project A's MIRR.
Note: You should show all workings as marks are available for the method you use.

(5 marks)

(ii) **Advise** which combination of projects is expected to maximise shareholder return within the capital constraint of SA$ 30 million. Your answer should include project rankings by BOTH MIRR and profitability index.

(4 marks)

(iii) **Advise** THREE key factors that might affect BR's choice of projects, explaining what adjustments to the original analysis might be needed in each case.

(10 marks)

(Total for Question Three = 25 marks)

A REPORT FORMAT IS NOT REQUIRED FOR THIS QUESTION

TURN OVER

Question Four

Country T and Country V are separated by sea but linked by a rail tunnel. They have different currencies (T\$ and V\$ respectively) but are part of the same Trade Group which promotes free trade between its members and has authority over membership countries in matters relating to competition.

TNL is a public listed company, based in Country T, which owns and operates the rail link between Country T and Country V.   Trains that travel through the tunnel carry passengers, cars and other vehicles such as trucks.

TNL was first listed on 1 June 2004 by offer for sale of 100 million ordinary shares to the public at a price of T\$ 3.70. Today, 21 November 2013, the share price is just T\$ 2.95. The fall in the share price since 2004 is largely the result of disappointing growth and market concerns about TNL's ability to renegotiate bank borrowings that are shortly due for repayment. The ordinary shares are held by a large number of individual shareholders as well as by large institutions and pension funds. The number of shares in issue remains unchanged since 2004.

Debt funding is in the form of bank borrowings from a consortium of 10 banks to a total principal value of T\$ 190 million. The borrowings were taken out on 1 June 2004 and have a 10 year term. New borrowings are currently being negotiated to finance the repayment of the original borrowings on 1 June 2014.

There is strong price competition between TNL and two independent ferry companies, TT and VV which are based in Countries T and V respectively. Prices are generally low for travel by ferry since ferries are less convenient as they operate less frequently and have longer journey times than the rail tunnel link.   TT has incurred losses in the past two years.

The board of TNL has approached ferry company TT with a view to acquiring it. The directors of TT are opposed to the bid and have referred the bid to the regional competition authorities of both Country T and the Trade Group.

(a) (i) **Discuss** the possible reasons why TNL may wish to acquire TT.

(5 marks)

(ii) **Explain:**
- Why the competition authorities in Country T and in the Trade Group might be concerned about the proposed acquisition.
- The possible actions that the competition authorities could take and the implications of these for TNL.

(6 marks)

(b) **Advise** TNL on:

(i) The factors that the banks are likely to consider when deciding whether or not to renew the loans made to TNL.

(8 marks)

(ii) Other appropriate sources of finance that should be considered.

(6 marks)

(Total for Question Four = 25 marks)

A REPORT FORMAT IS NOT REQUIRED FOR THIS QUESTION

(Total for Section B = 50 marks)

End of Question Paper

Maths tables and formulae are on pages 21 to 25

This page is blank

MATHS TABLES AND FORMULAE

Present value table
Present value of 1.00 unit of currency, that is $(1 + r)^{-n}$ where r = interest rate; n = number of periods until payment or receipt.

Periods (n)	Interest rates (r)									
	1%	2%	3%	4%	5%	6%	7%	8%	9%	10%
1	0.990	0.980	0.971	0.962	0.952	0.943	0.935	0.926	0.917	0.909
2	0.980	0.961	0.943	0.925	0.907	0.890	0.873	0.857	0.842	0.826
3	0.971	0.942	0.915	0.889	0.864	0.840	0.816	0.794	0.772	0.751
4	0.961	0.924	0.888	0.855	0.823	0.792	0.763	0.735	0.708	0.683
5	0.951	0.906	0.863	0.822	0.784	0.747	0.713	0.681	0.650	0.621
6	0.942	0.888	0.837	0.790	0.746	0.705	0.666	0.630	0.596	0.564
7	0.933	0.871	0.813	0.760	0.711	0.665	0.623	0.583	0.547	0.513
8	0.923	0.853	0.789	0.731	0.677	0.627	0.582	0.540	0.502	0.467
9	0.914	0.837	0.766	0.703	0.645	0.592	0.544	0.500	0.460	0.424
10	0.905	0.820	0.744	0.676	0.614	0.558	0.508	0.463	0.422	0.386
11	0.896	0.804	0.722	0.650	0.585	0.527	0.475	0.429	0.388	0.350
12	0.887	0.788	0.701	0.625	0.557	0.497	0.444	0.397	0.356	0.319
13	0.879	0.773	0.681	0.601	0.530	0.469	0.415	0.368	0.326	0.290
14	0.870	0.758	0.661	0.577	0.505	0.442	0.388	0.340	0.299	0.263
15	0.861	0.743	0.642	0.555	0.481	0.417	0.362	0.315	0.275	0.239
16	0.853	0.728	0.623	0.534	0.458	0.394	0.339	0.292	0.252	0.218
17	0.844	0.714	0.605	0.513	0.436	0.371	0.317	0.270	0.231	0.198
18	0.836	0.700	0.587	0.494	0.416	0.350	0.296	0.250	0.212	0.180
19	0.828	0.686	0.570	0.475	0.396	0.331	0.277	0.232	0.194	0.164
20	0.820	0.673	0.554	0.456	0.377	0.312	0.258	0.215	0.178	0.149

Periods (n)	Interest rates (r)									
	11%	12%	13%	14%	15%	16%	17%	18%	19%	20%
1	0.901	0.893	0.885	0.877	0.870	0.862	0.855	0.847	0.840	0.833
2	0.812	0.797	0.783	0.769	0.756	0.743	0.731	0.718	0.706	0.694
3	0.731	0.712	0.693	0.675	0.658	0.641	0.624	0.609	0.593	0.579
4	0.659	0.636	0.613	0.592	0.572	0.552	0.534	0.516	0.499	0.482
5	0.593	0.567	0.543	0.519	0.497	0.476	0.456	0.437	0.419	0.402
6	0.535	0.507	0.480	0.456	0.432	0.410	0.390	0.370	0.352	0.335
7	0.482	0.452	0.425	0.400	0.376	0.354	0.333	0.314	0.296	0.279
8	0.434	0.404	0.376	0.351	0.327	0.305	0.285	0.266	0.249	0.233
9	0.391	0.361	0.333	0.308	0.284	0.263	0.243	0.225	0.209	0.194
10	0.352	0.322	0.295	0.270	0.247	0.227	0.208	0.191	0.176	0.162
11	0.317	0.287	0.261	0.237	0.215	0.195	0.178	0.162	0.148	0.135
12	0.286	0.257	0.231	0.208	0.187	0.168	0.152	0.137	0.124	0.112
13	0.258	0.229	0.204	0.182	0.163	0.145	0.130	0.116	0.104	0.093
14	0.232	0.205	0.181	0.160	0.141	0.125	0.111	0.099	0.088	0.078
15	0.209	0.183	0.160	0.140	0.123	0.108	0.095	0.084	0.079	0.065
16	0.188	0.163	0.141	0.123	0.107	0.093	0.081	0.071	0.062	0.054
17	0.170	0.146	0.125	0.108	0.093	0.080	0.069	0.060	0.052	0.045
18	0.153	0.130	0.111	0.095	0.081	0.069	0.059	0.051	0.044	0.038
19	0.138	0.116	0.098	0.083	0.070	0.060	0.051	0.043	0.037	0.031
20	0.124	0.104	0.087	0.073	0.061	0.051	0.043	0.037	0.031	0.026

Cumulative present value of 1.00 unit of currency per annum

Receivable or Payable at the end of each year for n years $\left[\dfrac{1-(1+r)^{-n}}{r}\right]$

Periods (n)	Interest rates (r)									
	1%	2%	3%	4%	5%	6%	7%	8%	9%	10%
1	0.990	0.980	0.971	0.962	0.952	0.943	0.935	0.926	0.917	0.909
2	1.970	1.942	1.913	1.886	1.859	1.833	1.808	1.783	1.759	1.736
3	2.941	2.884	2.829	2.775	2.723	2.673	2.624	2.577	2.531	2.487
4	3.902	3.808	3.717	3.630	3.546	3.465	3.387	3.312	3.240	3.170
5	4.853	4.713	4.580	4.452	4.329	4.212	4.100	3.993	3.890	3.791
6	5.795	5.601	5.417	5.242	5.076	4.917	4.767	4.623	4.486	4.355
7	6.728	6.472	6.230	6.002	5.786	5.582	5.389	5.206	5.033	4.868
8	7.652	7.325	7.020	6.733	6.463	6.210	5.971	5.747	5.535	5.335
9	8.566	8.162	7.786	7.435	7.108	6.802	6.515	6.247	5.995	5.759
10	9.471	8.983	8.530	8.111	7.722	7.360	7.024	6.710	6.418	6.145
11	10.368	9.787	9.253	8.760	8.306	7.887	7.499	7.139	6.805	6.495
12	11.255	10.575	9.954	9.385	8.863	8.384	7.943	7.536	7.161	6.814
13	12.134	11.348	10.635	9.986	9.394	8.853	8.358	7.904	7.487	7.103
14	13.004	12.106	11.296	10.563	9.899	9.295	8.745	8.244	7.786	7.367
15	13.865	12.849	11.938	11.118	10.380	9.712	9.108	8.559	8.061	7.606
16	14.718	13.578	12.561	11.652	10.838	10.106	9.447	8.851	8.313	7.824
17	15.562	14.292	13.166	12.166	11.274	10.477	9.763	9.122	8.544	8.022
18	16.398	14.992	13.754	12.659	11.690	10.828	10.059	9.372	8.756	8.201
19	17.226	15.679	14.324	13.134	12.085	11.158	10.336	9.604	8.950	8.365
20	18.046	16.351	14.878	13.590	12.462	11.470	10.594	9.818	9.129	8.514

Periods (n)	Interest rates (r)									
	11%	12%	13%	14%	15%	16%	17%	18%	19%	20%
1	0.901	0.893	0.885	0.877	0.870	0.862	0.855	0.847	0.840	0.833
2	1.713	1.690	1.668	1.647	1.626	1.605	1.585	1.566	1.547	1.528
3	2.444	2.402	2.361	2.322	2.283	2.246	2.210	2.174	2.140	2.106
4	3.102	3.037	2.974	2.914	2.855	2.798	2.743	2.690	2.639	2.589
5	3.696	3.605	3.517	3.433	3.352	3.274	3.199	3.127	3.058	2.991
6	4.231	4.111	3.998	3.889	3.784	3.685	3.589	3.498	3.410	3.326
7	4.712	4.564	4.423	4.288	4.160	4.039	3.922	3.812	3.706	3.605
8	5.146	4.968	4.799	4.639	4.487	4.344	4.207	4.078	3.954	3.837
9	5.537	5.328	5.132	4.946	4.772	4.607	4.451	4.303	4.163	4.031
10	5.889	5.650	5.426	5.216	5.019	4.833	4.659	4.494	4.339	4.192
11	6.207	5.938	5.687	5.453	5.234	5.029	4.836	4.656	4.486	4.327
12	6.492	6.194	5.918	5.660	5.421	5.197	4.988	4.793	4.611	4.439
13	6.750	6.424	6.122	5.842	5.583	5.342	5.118	4.910	4.715	4.533
14	6.982	6.628	6.302	6.002	5.724	5.468	5.229	5.008	4.802	4.611
15	7.191	6.811	6.462	6.142	5.847	5.575	5.324	5.092	4.876	4.675
16	7.379	6.974	6.604	6.265	5.954	5.668	5.405	5.162	4.938	4.730
17	7.549	7.120	6.729	6.373	6.047	5.749	5.475	5.222	4.990	4.775
18	7.702	7.250	6.840	6.467	6.128	5.818	5.534	5.273	5.033	4.812
19	7.839	7.366	6.938	6.550	6.198	5.877	5.584	5.316	5.070	4.843
20	7.963	7.469	7.025	6.623	6.259	5.929	5.628	5.353	5.101	4.870

FORMULAE

Valuation models

(i) Irredeemable preference shares, paying a constant annual dividend, d, in perpetuity, where P_0 is the ex-div value:

$$P_0 = \frac{d}{k_{pref}}$$

(ii) Ordinary (equity) shares, paying a constant annual dividend, d, in perpetuity, where P_0 is the ex-div value:

$$P_0 = \frac{d}{k_e}$$

(iii) Ordinary (equity) shares, paying an annual dividend, d, growing in perpetuity at a constant rate, g, where P_0 is the ex-div value:

$$P_0 = \frac{d_1}{k_e - g} \quad \text{or} \quad P_0 = \frac{d_0[1 + g]}{k_e - g}$$

(iv) Irredeemable bonds, paying annual after-tax interest, $i\,[1 - t]$, in perpetuity, where P_0 is the ex-interest value:

$$P_0 = \frac{i[1 - t]}{k_{dnet}}$$

or, without tax:

$$P_0 = \frac{i}{k_d}$$

(v) Total value of the geared entity, V_g (based on MM):

$$V_g = V_u + TB$$

(vi) Future value of S, of a sum X, invested for n periods, compounded at $r\%$ interest:

$$S = X[1 + r]^n$$

(vii) Present value of 1·00 payable or receivable in n years, discounted at $r\%$ per annum:

$$PV = \frac{1}{[1 + r]^n}$$

(viii) Present value of an annuity of 1·00 per annum, receivable or payable for n years, commencing in one year, discounted at $r\%$ per annum:

$$PV = \frac{1}{r}\left[1 - \frac{1}{[1 + r]^n}\right]$$

(ix) Present value of 1·00 per annum, payable or receivable in perpetuity, commencing in one year, discounted at $r\%$ per annum:

$$PV = \frac{1}{r}$$

(x) Present value of 1·00 per annum, receivable or payable, commencing in one year, growing in perpetuity at a constant rate of $g\%$ per annum, discounted at $r\%$ per annum:

$$PV = \frac{1}{r - g}$$

Cost of capital

(i) Cost of irredeemable preference shares, paying an annual dividend, d, in perpetuity, and having a current ex-div price P_0:

$$k_{\text{pref}} = \frac{d}{P_0}$$

(ii) Cost of irredeemable bonds, paying annual net interest, $i[1-t]$, and having a current ex-interest price P_0:

$$k_{d\,\text{net}} = \frac{i[1-t]}{P_0}$$

(iii) Cost of ordinary (equity) shares, paying an annual dividend, d, in perpetuity, and having a current ex-div price P_0:

$$k_e = \frac{d}{P_0}$$

(iv) Cost of ordinary (equity) shares, having a current ex-div price, P_0, having just paid a dividend, d_0, with the dividend growing in perpetuity by a constant $g\%$ per annum:

$$k_e = \frac{d_1}{P_0} + g \quad \text{or} \quad k_e = \frac{d_0[1+g]}{P_0} + g$$

(v) Cost of ordinary (equity) shares, using the CAPM:

$$k_e = R_f + [R_m - R_f]\beta$$

(vi) Cost of ordinary (equity) share capital in a geared entity :

$$k_{eg} = k_{eu} + [k_{eu} - k_d]\frac{V_D\,[1-t]}{V_E}$$

(vii) Weighted average cost of capital, k_0 or WACC

$$WACC = k_e\left[\frac{V_E}{V_E + V_D}\right] + k_d\,[1-t]\left[\frac{V_D}{V_E + V_D}\right]$$

(viii) Adjusted cost of capital (MM formula):

$$K_{adj} = k_{eu}\,[1 - tL] \qquad \text{or} \qquad r^* = r[1 - T^*L]$$

(ix) Ungear β:

$$\beta_u = \beta_g\left[\frac{V_E}{V_E + V_D[1-t]}\right] + \beta_d\left[\frac{V_D\,[1-t]}{V_E + V_D[1-t]}\right]$$

(x) Regear β:

$$\beta_g = \beta_u + [\beta_u - \beta_d]\frac{V_D\,[1-t]}{V_E}$$

(xi) Adjusted discount rate to use in international capital budgeting (International Fisher effect)

$$\frac{1 + \text{annual discount rate B\$}}{1 + \text{annual discount rate A\$}} = \frac{\text{Future spot rate A\$/B\$ in 12 months' time}}{\text{Spot rate A\$/B\$}}$$

where A\$/B\$ is the number of B\$ to each A\$

Other formulae

(i) Expectations theory:

$$\text{Future spot rate A\$/B\$} = \text{Spot rate A\$/B\$} \times \frac{1 + \text{nominal country B interest rate}}{1 + \text{nominal country A interest rate}}$$

where:

A\$/B\$ is the number of B\$ to each A\$, and

A\$ is the currency of country A and B\$ is the currency of country B

(ii) Purchasing power parity (law of one price):

$$\text{Future spot rate A\$B\$} = \text{Spot rate A\$/B\$} \times \frac{1 + \text{country B inflation rate}}{1 + \text{country A inflation rate}}$$

(iii) Link between nominal (money) and real interest rates:

$$[1 + \text{nominal (money) rate}] = [1 + \text{real interest rate}][1 + \text{inflation rate}]$$

(iv) Equivalent annual cost:

$$\text{Equivalent annual cost} = \frac{PV \text{ of costs over } n \text{ years}}{n \text{ year annuity factor}}$$

(v) Theoretical ex-rights price:

$$\text{TERP} = \frac{1}{N + 1} \; [(N \times \text{cum rights price}) + \text{issue price}]$$

(vi) Value of a right:

$$\frac{\text{Theoretical ex rights price} - \text{issue price}}{N}$$

where N = number of rights required to buy one share.

This page is blank

LIST OF VERBS USED IN THE QUESTION REQUIREMENTS

A list of the learning objectives and verbs that appear in the syllabus and in the question requirements for

each question in this paper.

It is important that you answer the question according to the definition of the verb.

LEARNING OBJECTIVE	VERBS USED	DEFINITION
Level 1 - KNOWLEDGE		
What you are expected to know.	List	Make a list of
	State	Express, fully or clearly, the details/facts of
	Define	Give the exact meaning of
Level 2 - COMPREHENSION		
What you are expected to understand.	Describe	Communicate the key features
	Distinguish	Highlight the differences between
	Explain	Make clear or intelligible/State the meaning or purpose of
	Identify	Recognise, establish or select after consideration
	Illustrate	Use an example to describe or explain something
Level 3 - APPLICATION		
How you are expected to apply your knowledge.	Apply	Put to practical use
	Calculate/compute	Ascertain or reckon mathematically
	Demonstrate	Prove with certainty or to exhibit by practical means
	Prepare	Make or get ready for use
	Reconcile	Make or prove consistent/compatible
	Solve	Find an answer to
	Tabulate	Arrange in a table
Level 4 - ANALYSIS		
How are you expected to analyse the detail of what you have learned.	Analyse	Examine in detail the structure of
	Categorise	Place into a defined class or division
	Compare and contrast	Show the similarities and/or differences between
	Construct	Build up or compile
	Discuss	Examine in detail by argument
	Interpret	Translate into intelligible or familiar terms
	Prioritise	Place in order of priority or sequence for action
	Produce	Create or bring into existence
Level 5 - EVALUATION		
How are you expected to use your learning to evaluate, make decisions or recommendations.	Advise	Counsel, inform or notify
	Evaluate	Appraise or assess the value of
	Recommend	Advise on a course of action

Financial Pillar

Strategic Level Paper

F3 – Financial Strategy

November 2013

Thursday Morning Session

Strategic Level Paper

F3 – Financial Strategy

November 2013 examination

Examiner's Answers

Question One

Rationale

Question One tests the ability to evaluate an unusual type of project that has greater non-financial than financial benefits. A net present value calculation is required, but the negative result obtained needs to be understood and interpreted within the wider objectives of the investment. The question also tests the ability to analyse and document the implementation challenges, including environmental challenges, which this project presents. Finally, candidates are required to choose between two alternative financing structures, taking into account their distinct risk and cost profiles.

Question One tests syllabus areas A2(c), B1(c)&(d), C1(a),(b),(c).

Suggested Approach

In Part (a), candidates should take time initially to identify key issues. This may involve re-reading the relevant sections in the pre-seen relating to sponsorship and the mission of the umbrella organisation to identify the issues that are key to the company's success in its application to become a gold sponsor.

In Part (b)(i), use the dividend valuation model to calculate the cost of equity, using the share price and growth rate provided in the question. Then calculate the WACC, remembering to calculate the cost and market value of the preference shares using the current share price rather than nominal value. Remember to adjust the cost of bank borrowings for tax but not the cost of preference shares.

In Part (b)(ii), it is best to use a columnar approach with the dates or time periods at the top. Analyse the data provided and insert relevant cash flows into the table drawn. Remember to delay tax by one year since it is settled a year in arrears. Do not include interest costs as a cash flow, this is taken into consideration in the discount factor.

Part (b)(iii) is the place to discuss your results from (b)(ii) and show an understanding of the wider issues involved in the decision as to whether or not to proceed with the project. Concentrate on the key issues first (such as non-financial benefits) and then briefly cover all other relevant factors, considering each in turn.

In part (c)(i), two calculations are required, related to the proposed foreign currency borrowing. The first is a simple compounding exercise for 11 years (the project is for 10 years and starts in one year's time, so we are looking at a total of 11 years here). The exchange rate in 11 years' time can then be used to calculate the C$ cost of repaying the US$ principal at that point in time.

The results from (c)(i) can be used in part (c)(ii) to evaluate the two proposed funding methods. The evaluation should focus on potential cost savings versus additional risk inherent in the foreign currency borrowing.

REPORT

To: The Board of Directors of CC
From: Mr X, Chief Financial Officer (CFO)
Date: 21 November 2013

Purpose of the report

The purpose of this report is to present an evaluation of the proposed bid to become a Gold Sponsor at the forthcoming Games to be held in October 2015. The report will consider expected key challenges in respect of the implementation of the project and how these can best be addressed. The report will also evaluate and summarise the benefits, costs and risks of the project and how best to finance the project.

(a)

This project presents new and unique challenges. It is 'breaking new ground' in more ways than one, involving new, temporary construction design and a focus on sustainability and re-use of materials used in construction. In addition, the ultimate objective of the project is brand promotion both within Country C and in other countries rather than an operating profit.

Challenges at conceptual stage include:

Meeting CC's own objectives in terms of building brand strength.
Challenge: The ultimate aim of the project is to promote the brand and it would be easy to lose sight of this amongst all the other challenges involved in this project.

Response: Promotional opportunities should be taken full advantage of at every stage.

Meeting Gold sponsorship requirements.
Challenge: The conceptual stage will require alignment of plans with the GCC's objectives in terms of promoting sport, healthy lifestyles and sustainability of infrastructure and environment required in order to be eligible for consideration as a Gold sponsor. These involve a new direction and new activities for CC.

Response: A high calibre project management team is required to coordinate such a complex and important project. External experts should be consulted and involved in the planning stage and beyond in areas that are outside the experience and expertise of the team.

Complexity and feasibility

Challenge:

Many new areas are involved, including:
- new building techniques and high sustainability levels
- high level of re-use of materials
- new "healthier" food menu
- promoting sport (e.g. volley ball training)

Response:

A number of different sub-project teams are required, each focussing on a different aspect. Each part will need a separate project team to focus on particular issues.

For example:
- One project team should focus on the re-use of materials. Detailed plans will be needed as to where each component will be reused. Components will need to be tracked from purchase to re-use.
- Another project team should focus on the operation of the outlet and organise careful research and testing into a suitable new menu.

Ensuring success/dealing with risk

Challenge:

There are a number of potential risks involved in the project.

For example:
- There could be a backlash in the press about the association of fast food with a sporting event.
- A major challenge could be providing adequate cover and training at existing outlets for those staff who were transferred temporarily to the games.

Response:
- Attention to public relations aspects of the project plus careful planning and pre-testing. E.g. pre-testing the new menu to ensure that it is well received while at the same time not alienating customers who would prefer CC's more traditional products.
- Securing additional temporary staff at other outlets and giving them appropriate training.

Breaking new ground and the use of experts

Challenge:

Many changes are required to the standard business plan for an outlet. Some involve completely new areas of business). Feasibility is an issue here. For example, how confident are the team that used cooking oils can, indeed, be redeployed successfully as proposed?

Response: Careful preparation and testing of new ideas is required. Expert advice and involvement should be sought wherever necessary.

(b) (i)

Under dividend valuation model (DVM):

$K_e = D_o (1 + g) / P_o + g$ so, $K_e = 0.15 \times (1 + 0.134) / (2.33 - 0.15) + 0.134 = 0.212$

That is, $\underline{K_e = 21.2\%}$

WACC calculation:

Finance source	Cost %	Market value C$ million	Cost x market value C$ million
Equity - ords	21.2% (from above)	248.5 (= 114millionx(2.33–0.15))	52.7 (= 21.2% x 248.5)
Equity - prefs	7.6% (7.2 / 0.95)	28.5 (= 0.95 x 30)	2.2(= 7.6% x 28.5)
Bank borrowings	4.8% = (6%+ 2%) x (1–40%)	90.0	4.3 (= 4.8% x 90.0)
Total		367.0	59.2

So WACC = C$ 59.2 million / C$ 367.0 million x 100% = 16%

(b) (ii)

Project NPV (in C$'000), 31 October:

	2014	2015	2016	2017	2018	Workings
Operating costs		(330)				
Revenue		672				672=200x10x7x4x12
		342				
Tax at 40%			(137)			Year delay
Gold sponsorship	(1,000)					
Tax relief on gold sponsorship			400			
Sports programme	(60)	(60)	(60)	(60)		
Tax relief on sports programme		24	24	24	24	Year delay
Net operating cash flow	(1,060)	306	227	(36)	24	
Construction	(4,000)					
Fixtures and fittings	(500)					
Equipment		(748)				748 = 2,100/2.8091 where 2.8091=2.7000 x 1.02^2
Residual value		800				800 = 1000 – 200
Tax impact (year delay)		1,800	(21)			21=40%x(800–748) 1800=40%(4000+500)
Cash flow	(5,560)	2,158	206	(36)	24	
DF at 16%	0.862	0.743	0.641	0.552	0.476	
PV	(4,793)	1,603	132	(20)	11	

NPV: Loss of C$ 3.1 million

(b) (iii)

The reliability of the WACC used in (b)(ii) should be considered. The WACC used may not be a true reflection of the WACC of the company; the cost of equity figure is particularly suspect, being based on a seemingly unrealistic growth rate of 13.4% projected into perpetuity. The growth rate was based on just five years' of historical dividends which may not reflect future outcomes. The cost of equity figure appears to be unusually high. Alternative calculation methods are needed to verify this figure. For example, using the capital asset pricing model to derive a cost of equity from CC's equity beta.

In addition, the project may have a different risk profile to the company as a whole, adding yet more doubt on the suitability of the discount rate used in the project investment appraisal.

However, it should also be noted that the WACC is largely irrelevant. The short term nature of the project and the extent to which the initial investment exceeds cumulative net cash inflows anticipated throughout the life of the project, means that the NPV result can be expected to show a loss of approximately C$ 3 million regardless of the discount rate used.

A loss of C$ 3 million directly impacts on shareholder wealth. This, is a material loss. It equates to 10% of the C$ 35 million operating profit and 12.5% of the C$ 24 million profit after tax last year. Whether or not the project is worthwhile will therefore depend almost exclusively on the intangible benefits arising from the project.

The decision hangs largely on the value of intangible benefits – that is, increased brand recognition both at home and abroad and the ability to successfully launch new stores. Much more research is required in this area.

Funding needs to be considered. How is this loss to be financed?

Another major factor that needs to be taken into account is the reliability of the forecast data used in the analysis. For example, how confident are the planners that the goods to be reused will actually be in a sufficiently good condition to enable them to be reused? What is the sensitivity of the NPV results to changes in customer numbers?

(c) (i)

Forecast US$/C$ spot rates in 11 years' time:
US$/C$ 0.8914 = 0.6500 x (1.06/1.03)^11
Hence US$ 15 million would cost C$ 13.37 million to repay (where 13.37 = 15 x 0.8914).
Note that this is considerably greater than today's value of C$ 9.75 million (where 9.75 = 15 x 0.6500).

(c) (ii)

US$ borrowings appear cheap because of the lower interest cost. If the currency peg between US$ and C$ holds for the 10 year period, US$ borrowings would therefore prove to be less expensive than C$ borrowings. However, the history of currency pegs shows that they are very unlikely to last 10 years without re-adjustment. The differential in interest rates is likely to force a realignment of the peg. As calculated in (c)(i), if the currency peg was realigned in line with the interest differential, it would cost CC C$ 13.37 million to repay a US$ borrowing, compared to only C$10 million for a C$ borrowing. Such additional cost would eliminate the interest saving from denominating the borrowing in US$.

US$/C$ spot in 10 years' time cannot be predicted with any certainty. Borrowing in US$ creates significant exchange rate risk and is not advisable.

If hedged, any benefit from lower US$ interest rates would be eliminated by the forward points. Under interest rate parity, the forward points reflect the interest differential between the two currencies.

Recommendation
It is recommended that CC source the bank borrowings in C$ rather than US$ in order to avoid the large currency exposure that US$ borrowings would create. Any expected saving in interest by using 'cheaper' US$ borrowings is likely to be offset by currency movements and so CC cannot be confident of achieving any cost saving. Indeed, there is a risk that the US$ borrowings could cost significantly more overall than C$ borrowings if exchange rates were to move unfavourably during the 10 year term.

Question Two

(a) (i)

The compound average annual growth over the 3 year period is 18.4% ,
(where 18.4% = (((6.03 − 3.63)/3.63) + 1))^(1/3) − 1).
Alternative approach: (6.03/3.63)^(1/3) = 1.184. That is, compound growth of 18.4% a year.

(a) (ii)

A successful company such as ABC increases in value because it generates profits which are reinvested and accumulates cash or assets which are then used to generate future profits.

The company's value can be calculated as the present value of expected future free cash flows. A company's share price is therefore a reflection of the market's expectation of its future earnings ability.

If a company pays zero or very low dividends when it is making significant profits and generating growth (as is the case for ABC) then this is likely to mean that the company is reinvesting the cash generated rather than paying it out as dividends. This reinvestment creates growth in the company which then increases the earnings potential, which in turn increases the share price.

ABC is wholly equity owned, so the value of one of its shares is simply the value of ABC divided by the number of shares in issue. As the value of the company increases, so does the share price.

(b)

Arguments in favour of returning cash to shareholders:
- It rewards shareholders for remaining faithful to the company even after the share price dropped and discourages others from selling their shares, thereby protecting the share price from falling further.
- If immediate investment opportunities are not available and the cash is truly surplus to requirements, the shareholders might be able to make higher returns by investing the cash elsewhere and therefore shareholder wealth is maximised by returning surplus cash.
- ABC is still highly profitable and cash generative so the cash would be quickly replenished.
- Reduces vulnerability to a hostile takeover. Companies with a significant surplus cash can be attractive takeover targets because the acquiring company can extract the cash on acquisition and use it for its own purposes. For example, to help finance the acquisition.

Arguments in favour of retaining cash in the company:
- It enhances the company's ability to respond promptly to any new investment opportunities.
- Surplus cash is important to ensure continued liquidity in times of economic downturn.
- Repatriating the cash from foreign subsidiaries would necessitate paying more tax. It might also impact on the subsidiaries' abilities to invest themselves in new projects.
- The market may interpret the repatriation of cash to shareholders as a sign of weakness and poor growth prospects – that the company cannot find strong projects to invest in.

(c)

Impact on shareholder wealth
One advantage of Scheme 1 is that company value would be expected to increase due to the more efficient capital structure. Modigliani and Miller calculate the benefit to be approximately equal to the value of the tax shield on the bond. That is, A$ 58 million (where A$ 58 million = A$ 450 million x 5% x 30% x 8.559, where 8.559 is AF(15 years, 8%)).

In contrast, under Scheme 2 shareholder value would be expected to be lost due to the additional tax due. This is a loss of approximately A$ 50 million (where A$ 50 million = (A$ 450 million) / 0.9 x 10%).

The aggregate benefit to the value of ABC of Scheme 1 in comparison to Scheme 2 can therefore be estimated to be approximately A$ 108 million (where A$ 108 million = A$ 50 million + A$ 58 million).

Impact on gearing

There is a slight increase in gearing under Scheme 1 from 0% to 8% (D/D+E). This should have very little impact as it is so small. There would be a small increase in shareholder risk accompanied by slightly higher returns which balance this effect.

Assuming the share price moves in line with the financial benefit of the tax shield on debt:
- Gearing before the share repurchase programme:
    - Debt = 0, Equity = A$ 6,030m (= A$ 6.03 x 1000m), so Gearing (D/D+E) = 0%
- Gearing change under Scheme 1:
    - Debt = A$ 450m, Equity = A$ 5,188 (= A$ 6,030m – A$ 900m + A$ 58m (the tax shield)), so Gearing (D/D+E) = 8.0% (= A$ 450/(A$ 450 + A$ 5,188))
- Gearing unchanged at 0% under Scheme 2

Impact on liquidity risk

Retaining group cash reserves (as in Scheme 1), may increase ABC's ability to take advantage of future investment opportunities. However, the borrowings created in Scheme 1 will need to be repaid on maturity. If ABC is confident that it will generate large net operating cash inflows, this would not be a problem. However, even if insufficient funds are generated, ABC could use group cash as a back-up and repatriate cash as necessary to service the borrowings.

Question Three

Suggested Approach

It would be helpful to begin part (a) with a definition and description of the basis of the result provided by each of NPV, IRR and MIRR. This will then give a good base from which to examine how each type of result might be useful in the two given scenarios. Look at one scenario in full before moving onto the next in order to avoid confusion.

In part (b)(i), calculate the project's MIRR. There are two main ways of approaching this. Method 1: Calculate the future value of each cash flow at time 4, that is, the terminal value, using the project discount rate of 8%. Next, divide this into the value of the original investment and use annuity tables to look up the implied annual return of the project in the '4 year' column of the present value table. Alternatively, Method 2: Calculate the terminal value as before. Then calculate the average compound annual return implied by the growth in value between the original investment and the terminal value. That is, take the square root to the power of 4 of the terminal value divided by the original investment. Then subtract '1' to obtain the average compound annual return.

In part (b)(ii), first calculate a profitability index (PI) for each project by dividing the NPV result by the original investment. Then use the PI as the basis for prioritising the projects, giving priority to projects with the highest PI.

In part (b)(iii), first identify three key issues, such as taking the risk profile of each project, softening the capital rationing constraint or multi-period analysis to take future years into account. Secondly, explain how to adjust the capital rationing analysis to take each into account.

(a)

	NPV	IRR	MIRR
Suitability for mutually exclusive projects	Where projects are mutually exclusive the project with the greatest NPV should be selected, as ultimately this will have the greatest impact on shareholder wealth.	Where projects are mutually exclusive IRR would select that project with the highest IRR. However, because IRR ignores the size of the investment this might not actually be the project which increases shareholder wealth the most.	MIRR uses a superior reinvestment assumption to IRR and therefore gives a more realistic view of the return of the project. However, MIRR is still a percentage measure and therefore ignores the size of the investment where mutually exclusive projects are concerned.
Suitability for capital rationing (divisible projects)	In a capital rationing situation selecting on the basis of NPV alone will not give an optimum decision because it does not take into account the size of the initial investment required in the context of the capital available. However this can be easily modified by calculating the profitability index (PI) for each project which gives the NPV per SA$ invested. Projects can then be ranked on this basis.	Because of the reinvestment assumption in IRR and the fact that it does not take into account the size of the investment, IRR should not be used in capital rationing situations.	MIRR will in fact give the same project ranking as PI in a capital rationing situation.

(b) (i)

Future value (Terminal value) of cash inflows (workings in SA$ millions):

Time	Cash flow	Factor	TV
1	2.0	$(1.08)^3$	2.52
2	2.5	$(1.08)^2$	2.92
3	3.0	1.08	3.24
4	4.0	1	4.00
			12.68

Method 1:

Look up 0.5521 in present value table (where 0.5521 = (7/12.68), to give a result of 16%

Method 2:
Calculate the implied average compound growth rate over 4 years
That is, MIRR = $(12.68/7)^{(1/4)}$ -1 = 0.16, that is 16%.

(b) (ii)

Rankings by MIRR and PI are as follows:

	MIRR	Ranking	PI (workings in SA$ millions)	Ranking
A	16%	4	0.33 (= 2.3/7)	4
B	20%	2	0.54 (= 8.1/15)	2
C	24%	1	0.77 (= 7.7/10)	1
D	18%	3	0.42 (= 8.4/20)	3

Since the projects are divisible, we know that projects can be ranked according to their MIRR.

To maximise increase in shareholder wealth, invest in Projects C, B and 5/20 of project D (in order to keep within the overall capital constraint of SA$ 30 million).

(b) (iii)

Reliability of forecast cash flows:
- The reliability of the forecasts should be reviewed in conjunction with a risk assessment of each project.

Different project risk profiles:
- Apply a risk-adjusted discount factor by increasing the discount rate used to evaluate each project in line with the perceived risk of that project.
- Certainty equivalents. Apply a certainty equivalent to all cash flows, reducing the expected cash inflows to reflect the level of uncertainty surrounding those inflows.
- Apply probabilities to different outcomes (decision tree approach). Consider more than one possible cash outcome in each year and apply probabilities to the occurrence of each, adding up to 100% for each year.

Soft rather than hard capital rationing
- 'Soften' the SA$ 30 million capital constraint– this would encourage greater investment as there are, unusually, so many highly profitable projects to choose from this year.
- Illustrate answer by showing calculations of the additional NPV that could be obtained by increasing capital invested by incremental amounts such as SA$ 5 million and SA$ 10 million.

Capital rationing constraints in future years
- Use of linear programming techniques.
- This is likely to favour projects with greater cash inflows in earlier years, as indicated by a greater difference between MIRR and IRR (as for Projects A and B) since the funds generated could be used in another project sooner, increasing NPV generated for the same capital input when taking more than one year into account.

Question Four

(a) (i)

TNL may wish to acquire TT in order to:

- Gain economies of scale/synergistic benefits. For example, TNL and TT could share the same booking internet site and/or combine some head office and administrative functions.
- Increase market power. By offering ferry services as well as rail services, TNL will have increased influence over ferry prices in addition to rail prices. This increase in power could be used to its advantage.
- Increase customer loyalty. Marketing promotions (eg frequent traveller schemes) could be shared across TNL and TT, reducing marketing costs and increasing customer loyalty and convenience by offering a 'one-stop' shop for both rail and ferry tickets.
- Increase market share through cross subsidies or a price war. TNL could offer rail link passengers reduced cost ferry tickets or cross subsidise the ferry business by reducing fares for the ferries (financed by higher priced rail link tickets) in order to build its market share of the ferry business. TNL could use a price war in the ferry business to build market share and destroy competition, funded by profits from the rail link business.
- Obtain tax relief. TNL may be able to make use of tax losses incurred by TT by offsetting losses against any profits in TNL.
- TNL may consider that it has the expertise required to be able to add value to TT and help it return to being a profitable business.
- TNL and TT are both in the transport business but there is still some diversification benefit that would reduce the risk of the combined group.

(a) (ii)

Competition authorities intervene where it is considered that the bid would have a serious effect on competition in the market by giving significant market power to a particular market participant or where the bid is contrary to public interest. Country T's competition authorities may be less concerned as the move would give Country T a competitive advantage over Country V.

The competition authorities of the Trade Group would be particularly interested due to the reduction in competition that would arise in a key communication link between two countries in the Union.

In this case, there is a high risk to TNL that the competition authorities find grounds to investigate the proposed acquisition further. If TNL were to own all ferry and rail links from Country T, it could be in a position to control prices and affect competition   It already has a monopoly position in respect of the rail link and it may not be considered in the public interest to also allow TNL to acquire significant control over the ferry operation.   For example, it could raise prices for rail link passengers and cross-subsidise the ferry business in an attempt to put VV out of business.

Whatever the final result, referring the bid to the regulatory authorities can be expected to significantly delay the bid and create uncertainty and costs for TNL at this key time when it needs to renegotiate bank borrowings. If they decide to intervene, the regulatory authorities would have the power to either prevent the acquisition going ahead or impose certain conditions on TNL. Such conditions might include, for example, price constraints or a requirement to operate the ferries from a port that is not so close to the rail link tunnel.

(b) (i)

Issues that the banks are likely to consider:

- How will TNL pay back the original borrowings if the banks do not agree to renew the loans?
- To what extent would the referral to the competition authorities affect TNL – for example, what price controls might be imposed and how would that affect TNL's profitability?
- What is the likely impact on TNL's future results of acquiring TT? Would it be likely, in practice, to realise synergistic benefits from the acquisition?
- Can TNL afford to buy TT; how would it be financed? Given that it is likely to be a hostile bid then TNL will need to pay a significant premium for TT.
- TNL's latest long term cash forecast and the sensitivity of cash flow to other possible government intervention (eg green taxes) or market prices (eg fuel and exchange rates)..
- How do the credit ratings agencies view TNL? Have they put TNL on 'Negative outlook' to indicate the possibility of a downgrade in the next few months. How should this impact on the banks' willingness to lend and on the interest rate offered?
- Deterioration in gearing levels – and hence risk.
  Gearing on 1 June 2004: 34% (= 190/(190 + 370))
  Current gearing: 39% (= 190/(295 + 190))
- Management reputation –What is the background and reputation of the current team?
- Impact of government assistance. If the tunnel is seen as strategically important for the Country might the Government step in and provide support to TNL. This would reduce the banks' risk.

(b) (ii)

Debt financing

Other forms of debt financing could also be considered such as a bond issue by issue to the public or private placement. However, TNL would need to have a sufficiently high rating to be successful in issuing a bond. A convertible bond might be more attractive and would typically have a lower interest rate, although the long term impact on equity has to be considered.

TNL may need to consider other alternatives such as issuing shares or seeking government support if the banks are unwilling to renew borrowings and a bond issue is not feasible.

Rights issue

A rights issue could be undertaken, however, shareholders may not wish to subscribe new capital at this point, especially given the recent fall in TNL's share price, leading to a loss in the value of their current investment.

In any case, the size of the rights issue could present a problem – at a 20% discount shares would be issued at T$ 2.36 per share before taking issue costs into account. This equates to 80.5 million shares which is an 80.5% increase in the number of shares currently in issue. Shareholders would be required to increase their investment in TNL by more than 50% and may not have the available funds or the inclination to increase their investment in TNL to that extent.

It should also be noted that equity is more costly to service than debt and could lead to a reduction in the value of the company due to the loss of the tax benefit on debt interest.

Private Equity/Venture Capital

These organisations more typically provide funds for new companies but private equity consortia do occasionally fund established companies to assist with growth that might be riskier than would be acceptable to banks or shareholders. The drawback is that they would probably want a substantial equity stake and would expect high returns and board presence.

Government funding

If no private investors are willing to invest in TNL, the company may need to approach the government for assistance. It is likely that the tunnel link is considered to be key to Country T's trade position, and so the government may be prepared to step in and offer funding as a last resort rather than see the company fail and the rail link cease to operate. However, government funding may have conditions attached which might restrict TNL's future development plans.